W9-DAM-920

THE MACARTHUR NEW TESTAMENT COMMENTARY

MATTHEW 24-28

John MacArthur, Jr.

MOODY PRESS/CHICAGO

© 1989 by
THE MOODY BIBLE INSTITUTE
OF CHICAGO

All rights reserved. No part of this book may be reproduced in any form without permission in writing from the publisher, exept in the case of brief quotations embodied in critical articles or reviews.

Unless noted otherwise, all Scripture quotations in this book are from *The New American Standard Bible,* © 1960, 1962, 1963, 1968, 1971, 1972, 1973, 1975, and 1977 by The Lockman Foundation, and are used by permission.

Library of Congress Cataloging in Publication Data
MacArthur, John, 1939-
    Matthew 24-28 / John MacArthur, Jr.
        p.   cm. — (The MacArthur New Testament commentary)
    ISBN 0-8024-0765-X
    1. Bible. N.T. Matthew XXIV-XXVIII — Commentaries.   I. Title.
II. Series: MacArthur, John, 1939-   MacArthur New Testament
commentary.
BS2575.3.M245   1989
226.2'077 — dc20   89-37678
                                                                                CIP

9 10 8

Printed in the United States of America

To Bob Provost, whose passion for world
evangelization has been a living illustration to me
of the spirit of our Lord's great commission

Contents

Preface

    It continues to be a rewarding divine communion for me to preach expositionally through the New Testament. My goal is always to have deep fellowship with the Lord in the understanding of His Word, and out of that experience to explain to His people what a passage means. In the words of Nehemiah 8:8, I strive "to give the sense" of it so they may truly hear God speak and, in so doing, may respond to Him.

    Obviously, God's people need to understand Him, which demands knowing His Word of truth (2 Tim. 2:15) and allowing that Word to dwell in us richly (Col. 3:16). The dominant thrust of my ministry, therefore, is to help make God's living Word alive to His people. It is a refreshing adventure.

    This New Testament commentary series reflects this objective of explaining and applying Scripture. Some commentaries are primarily linguistic, others are mostly theological, and some are mainly homiletical. This one is basically explanatory, or expository. It is not linguistically technical, but deals with linguistics when that seems helpful to proper interpretation. It is not theologically expansive, but focuses on the major doctrines in each test and on how they relate to the whole of Scripture. It is not primarily homiletical, although each unit of thought is generally treated as one chapter, with a clear outline and logical flow of thought.

Most truths are illustrated and applied with other Scripture. After establishing the context of a passage, I have tried to follow closely the writer's development and reasoning.

My prayer is that each reader will fully understand what the Holy Spirit is saying through this part of His Word, so that His revelation may lodge in the minds of believers and bring greater obedience and faithfulness—to the glory of our great God.

The Signs of Christ's Coming—part 1 The Background

(24:1-3)

And Jesus came out from the temple and was going away when His disciples came up to point out the temple buildings to Him. And He answered and said to them, "Do you not see all these things? Truly I say to you, not one stone here shall be left upon another, which will not be torn down."

And as He was sitting on the Mount of Olives, the disciples came to Him privately, saying, "Tell us, when will these things be, and what will be the sign of Your coming, and of the end of the age?" (24:1-3)

Jesus' message in Matthew 24-25 is commonly known as the Olivet discourse, so named because it was delivered to the disciples on the Mount of Olives. The theme of the discourse is Christ's second coming at the end of the present age to establish His millennial kingdom on earth.

The message was prompted by the disciples' question in 24:3, "Tell us, when will these things be, and what will be the sign of Your coming, and of the end of the age?" The answer Jesus gave is the longest answer given to any question asked in the New Testament, and its truths are absolutely essential for understanding His return and the amazing events associated with it. It is the revelation of our Lord, directly from His own lips, about His return to earth in glory and power.

The teaching of the Olivet discourse is much debated and frequently misunderstood, largely because it is viewed through the lens of a particular theological system or interpretive scheme that makes the message appear complex and enigmatic. But the disciples were not learned men, and Jesus' purpose was to give them clarity and encouragement, not complexity and anxiety. The intricate interpretations that are some-times proposed for this passage would have left the disciples utterly dumbfounded. It is preferable to take Jesus' words as simply and as straightforwardly as possible.

PROPHETIC EXPECTATIONS IN JUDAISM

In order to understand better the disciples' question on this occasion it is necessary to know something of the basic hopes and aspirations of the Judaism of that day. As always, the historical setting is an important key to the context. Throughout history people have had a strong desire to know the future, and few societies have been without their seers, mediums, fortune-tellers, and other prognosticators. By various means, all of them deceitful and many of them demonic, such futurists have offered gullible inquirers purported revelations of what lies ahead. Although the Mosaic law strictly forbade consulting mediums and soothsayers (Deut. 18:9-14), Israelites had frequently fallen prey to them, the most prominent instance being that of King Saul's consulting the medium of Endor (1 Sam. 28:3-25; see also 2 Kings 21:6).

There is no evidence that many Jews of Jesus' day were guilty of Saul's offense, but they did have an intense interest in the future. They were tired of being under the domination of pagan oppressors and were eager for the divinely-promised deliverance of their Messiah. The Jews were a noble, highly intelligent, and highly gifted people who, humanly speaking, were entirely capable of competent self-rule. Yet for many centuries they had been subdued by one foreign tyrant after another. The northern ten tribes had been conquered by Assyria in 722 B.C., and the southern two tribes fell to Babylon in 586 B.C. Following that were conquests by the Medo-Persians, the Greeks, and finally the Romans.

In their own minds, however, the Jews had always been their own people and had never truly been subjugated to any foreign ruler. It was that abiding and sometimes arrogant spirit of independence even in the midst of oppression that induced some of the Jews to declare before Jesus in the Temple, "We are Abraham's offspring, and have never yet been enslaved to anyone" (John 8:33). They knew all too well, of course, that outwardly they were indeed enslaved, and freedom from that enslavement was the overriding passion of most Jews. Although the majority of them were not associated with the militant Zealots, they all yearned for Rome to be overthrown and for Israel to become a free nation once again.

The Jews knew intimately the many Old Testament promises of future blessing, deliverance, and prosperity. They knew God had promised to vanquish all the enemies of His chosen people and to establish His eternal kingdom of righteousness and justice on earth. They knew that the Lord's Anointed One—His Messiah, or Christ—would come and establish the rule and reign of David again on earth, a reign of peace, prosperity, and safety that would never end. Their great longing was to see that day when God restored the kingdom as He had promised.

The Jews therefore had great hope for the future. They exulted as they read, "For a child will be born to us, a son will be given to us; and the government will rest on His shoulders; and His name will be called Wonderful Counselor, Mighty God, Eternal Father, Prince of Peace. There will be no end to the increase of His government or of peace, on the throne of David and over his kingdom, to establish it and to uphold it with justice and righteousness from then on and forevermore. The zeal of the Lord of hosts will accomplish this" (Isa. 9:6-7). They thrilled at the promise that "a shoot will spring from the stem of Jesse, and a branch from his roots will bear fruit. And the Spirit of the Lord will rest on Him, the spirit of wisdom and understanding, the spirit of counsel and strength, the spirit of knowledge and the fear of the Lord" (Isa. 11:1-2).

Israel took immense encouragement from the words of Jeremiah: " 'Behold, the days are coming,' declares the Lord, 'when I shall raise up for David a righteous Branch; and He will reign as king and act wisely and do justice and righteousness in the land. In His days Judah will be saved, and Israel will dwell securely; and this is His name by which He will be called, "The Lord our righteousness" ' " (Jer. 23:5-6; cf. 30:9-10). They longed for the day when the spoil taken from them would be divided among them (Zech. 14:1), when "living waters [would] flow out of Jerusalem" (v. 8), and "there [would] be no more curse, for Jerusalem [would] dwell in security" (v. 11). They rejoiced that "the God of heaven will set up a kingdom which will never be destroyed, and that kingdom will not be left for another people . . . but it will itself endure forever" (Dan. 2:44).

By the time of Jesus, the Jews had formed in their minds a very clear scenario of how they believed those predicted events would unfold. To understand what the Jewish expectations were, it is helpful to read their literature from that time. In his *A History of the Jewish People in the Time of Jesus Christ* ([Edinburgh: T & T Clark, 1893], pp. 154-87), Emil Schuer gives excerpts from numerous extrabiblical Jewish writings of that era which reveal those expectations.

First, consistent with the teaching of Zechariah 14 and other Old Testament prophecies, they believed that the coming of the Messiah would be preceded by a time of terrible tribulation. Just as a woman experiences intense pain shortly before the delivery of a child, so Israel would experience great torment shortly before the Messiah arrived.

2 Baruch 27 reported,

> And honour shall be turned into shame,
> And strength humiliated into contempt,
> And probity destroyed,
> And beauty shall become ugliness . . .
> And envy shall rise in those who had not thought aught
>   of themselves,
> And passion shall seize him that is peaceful,
> And many shall be stirred up in anger to injure many,
> And they shall rouse up armies in order to shed blood,
> And in the end they shall perish together with them.

According to another source, there would be "quakings of places, tumult of peoples, schemings of nations, confusion of leaders, disquietude of princes" (2 Esdras [4 Ezra] 9:3).

The Jewish *Sibylline Oracles* declared,

> From heaven shall fall fiery swords down to the earth. Lights shall come, bright and great, flashing into the midst of men; and earth, the universal mother, shall shake in these days at the hand of the Eternal. And the fishes of the sea and the beasts of the earth and the countless tribes of flying things and all the souls of men and every sea shall shudder at the presence of the Eternal and there shall be panic. And the towering mountain peaks and the hills of the giants he shall rend, and the murky abyss shall be visible to all. And the high ravines in the lofty mountains shall be full of dead bodies and rocks shall flow with blood and each torrent shall flood the plain. . . . And God shall judge all with war and sword, and there shall be brimstone from heaven, yea stones and rain and hail incessant and grievous. And death shall be upon the four-footed beasts. . . . Yea the land itself shall drink of the blood of the perishing and beasts shall eat their fill of flesh. (3:363ff.)

The Mishna anticipated that just before the coming of Messiah,

> arrogance increases, ambition shoots up, . . . the vine yields fruit yet wine is dear. The government turns to heresy. There is no instruction. The synagogue is devoted to lewdness. Galilee is destroyed, Gablan laid waste. The inhabitants of a district go from city to city without finding compassion. The wisdom of the learned is hated, the godly despised, truth is absent.

> Boys insult old men, old men stand in the presence of children. The son depreciates the father, the daughter rebels against the mother, the daughter-in-law against the mother-in-law. A man's enemies are his house-fellows.

Second, the popular eschatology of Jesus' day held that in the midst of that turmoil would appear an Elijah-like forerunner heralding the Messiah's coming. It was for that reason that so many Jews were drawn to John the Baptist. Jewish oral tradition maintained that the ownership of any disputed money or property would have to wait "till Elijah comes" before being finally settled.

The third event of that eschatology was the Messiah's appearance, at which time He would establish His kingdom age of glory and would vindicate His people.

The fourth event would be the alliance of the nations to fight against the Messiah. The *Sibylline Oracles* declared,

> The kings of the nations shall throw themselves against this land bringing retribution on themselves. They shall seek to ravage the shrine of the mighty God and of the noblest men whensoever they come to the land. In a ring round the city the accursed kings shall place each one his throne with the infidel people by him. And then with a mighty voice God shall speak unto all the undisciplined, empty-minded people and judgment shall come upon them from the mighty God, and all shall perish at the hand of the Eternal. (3:363-72)

In 2 Esdras [4 Ezra] is the prediction, "It shall be that when all the nations hear his (the Messiah's) voice, every man shall leave his own land and the warfare they have one against the other, and the innumerable multitude shall be gathered together desiring to fight against him" (13:33-35). In other words, unbelieving mankind will interrupt all its other warfare in order to unite against the Messiah.

The fifth eschatological event would be the destruction of those opposing nations. Philo wrote that the Messiah would "take the field and make war and destroy great and populous nations." The writer of 2 Esdras declared that the Messiah "shall reprove them for their ungodliness, rebuke them for their unrighteousness, reproach them to their faces with their treacheries—and when he has rebuked them he shall destroy them" (12:32-33). The book of Enoch reported that "it shall come to pass in those days that none shall be saved, either by gold or by silver, and none shall be able to escape. And there shall be no iron for war, nor shall one clothe oneself with a breastplate. Bronze shall be of no service, and tin shall not be esteemed, and lead shall not be desired. And all things shall be destroyed from the surface of the earth" (52:7-9). All the vast armaments and defenses of the nations will be useless against the Messiah.

Sixth would be the restoration of Jerusalem, either by renovation of the existing city or by the coming down of a completely new Jerusalem from heaven. In either case, the city of the great King would henceforth be pure, holy, and incorruptible. In the book of Enoch, Jerusalem was envisioned as having "all the pillars . . . new and the ornaments larger than those of the first" (Enoch 90:28-29).

Seventh, the Jews scattered throughout the world would be gathered back to Israel. Many Jews today still utter the ancient prayer "Lift up a banner to gather our dispersed and assemble us from the four ends of the earth." The eleventh chapter of the Psalms of Solomon gives a graphic picture of that regathering:

> Blow ye in Zion on the trumpet to summon the saints,
>> Cause ye to be heard in Jerusalem the voice of him
>>> that bringeth good tidings;
>> For God hath had pity on Israel in visiting them.
> Stand on the height, O Jerusalem, and behold thy children,
>> From the East and the West, gathered together by the Lord;
> From the North they come in the gladness of their God,
>> From the isles afar off God hath gathered them.
> High mountains hath he abased into a plain for them;
>> The hills fled at their entrance.
> The woods gave them shelter as they passed by;
>> Every sweet-smelling tree God caused to spring up for them,
>> That Israel might pass by in the visitation of the glory of
>>> their God.
>
> Put on, O Jerusalem, thy glorious garments;
>> Make ready thy holy robe;
>> For God hath spoken good for Israel forever and ever,
> Let the Lord do what he hath spoken concerning
>> Israel and Jerusalem;
>> Let the Lord raise up Israel by his glorious name.
> The mercy of the Lord be upon Israel forever and ever.

In the eighth event of the Messiah's coming Palestine would become the center of the world, and all nations would be subjugated to the Lord. "And all the isles and the cities shall say, How doth the Eternal love those men! For all things work in sympathy with them and help them. . . . Come let us all fall upon the earth and supplicate the eternal King, the mighty, everlasting God. Let us make procession to His Temple, for He is the sole Potentate" (*Sibylline Oracles* 3:690ff.).

Ninth and finally, the Jews of Jesus' day believed that with the establishment of the Messiah's kingdom would come a new and eternal age of peace, righteousness, and divine glory.

Those ancient views of the coming of Christ were extrapolated largely from Old Testament teachings, and they closely correspond to New Testament premillennial doctrine about His second coming. The major difference is that those Jews had no knowledge of His coming twice, the first time to offer Himself as a sacrifice for the world's sin and the second to establish His millennial kingdom on earth. The Jewish people were not looking for inward deliverance from sin but for outward deliverance from political oppression.

In the minds of the Jews of Jesus' day, the time was ripe for the Messiah's coming. They had suffered persecution and subjugation for many centuries and were at that time under the relentless power of Rome. When John the Baptist appeared on the scene, reminiscent of the preaching and life-style of Elijah, the people's interest was intensely piqued. And when Jesus began His ministry of preaching, with unheard of authority and of healing every sort of disease, many Jews were convinced that He was indeed the Messiah. When He rode into Jerusalem on the colt, the crowds were beside themselves with anticipation, and they openly hailed Him as the Messiah, the long-awaited Son of David (Matt. 21:9).

At that point, however, Jesus' ministry rapidly and radically departed from their expectations. According to their thinking, the next steps would be the gathering of the nations against the Messiah and His dramatic and effortless victory over them.

That idea apparently was also still in the minds of the Twelve. Jesus' many predictions that He must suffer, die, and be resurrected had simply not registered with them. In some way or another they either had discounted those teachings or had rationalized and spiritualized them into being something other than literal, physical, and historical realities.

PROPHETIC DISCUSSIONS WITH JESUS

In fairness to the disciples, the Old Testament prophets also saw the Messiah's coming and establishing His kingdom as a single event. The church age was a mystery to them, a mystery, as Paul explained, "which has been kept secret for long ages past, but now is manifested" (Rom. 16:25-26). Because Israel had obviously experienced tremendous tribulation, because Jesus declared Himself to be the Messiah and identified John the Baptist as His forerunner, and because He had accepted the Messianic acclaim of the people a few days earlier, the disciples understandably thought that the sequence of events would continue as they expected. They were now certain that Jesus' next move would be to demonstrate His inexorable power over the nations that would soon rise up against Him.

It was doubtlessly such thoughts that had kept Judas superficially committed to stay with Jesus. He expected to be in the Messiah's inner circle when the kingdom was inaugurated and to be given power, wealth, and prestige commensurate with that position.

NEAR THE TEMPLE

And Jesus came out from the temple and was going away when His disciples came up to point out the temple buildings to Him. And He answered and said to them, "Do you not see all these things? Truly I say to you, not one stone here shall be left upon another, which will not be torn down." (24:1-2)

Jesus had spent all day Wednesday of Passover week in **the temple,** giving His last public teaching and pronouncing His final and most intense judgment on the false religious leaders and on the nation of Israel. Now He **was going away** to the Mount of Olives to be alone with **His disciples.**

As they were leaving Jerusalem, the **disciples came up to point out the temple buildings** to Jesus. The other two synoptic gospels report that they were pointing to **the temple** in admiration, saying, "Teacher, behold what wonderful stones and what wonderful buildings!" (Mark 13:1; cf. Luke 21:5).

The temple and its adjunct **buildings** stood on the top of a mount. A massive retaining wall on the south and west sides helped support the mount itself as well as the Temple. The Temple was awe-inspiring by any standards, but to a group of common men from rural Galilee it must have been a breathtaking marvel. They could not conceive how such an enormous structure could have been built or decorated so magnificently. The Roman historian Tacitus reported that it was a place of immense wealth, and the Babylonian Talmud said, "He that never saw the temple of Herod never saw a fine building." Some of the stones measured 40 feet by 12 by 12 and weighed up to a hundred tons, quarried as a single piece and transported many miles to the building site.

The disciples were perhaps wondering how such an amazing edifice, especially one dedicated to the glory of God, could be left desolate, as Jesus had just predicted. They should have remembered Ezekiel's vision of God's glory departing from the Temple and going "up from the midst of the city" (Ezek. 11:23). The holy sanctuary that had once been God's house was His no longer. It is now "your house" Jesus had said to the unbelieving Jews before He left **the temple,** and it "is being left to you desolate" (Matt. 23:38), because the glory of the Lord would soon depart from it. The beautiful **buildings** that had been devoted to God's glory and that should have honored Jesus would henceforth be devoted to desolation and destruction.

Jesus therefore responded to the disciples' admiring comments by saying, **Do you not see all these things? Truly I say to you, not one stone here shall be left upon another, which will not be torn down.** The disciples' jaws must have dropped when they heard those incredible words. They could not imagine how the Temple could be destroyed or why God would allow such a thing to happen.

Yet that is exactly what God allowed less than forty years later. When the Romans sacked Jerusalem in A.D. 70 and massacred most of its citizens, they also set fire to the Temple and razed it, just as Jesus predicted. The only stones left intact were the huge foundation stones, which were not part of the Temple edifice proper. Josephus commented that a person visiting the site after the destruction could not believe that anyone had ever inhabited the place, much less that one of the most magnificent structures of the ancient world had stood there only a short while before.

Shocked as they were to realize that the Temple would be destroyed, the disciples were no doubt heartened as well, thinking that that event would be related to the Messiah's expected purification of Jerusalem, which would occur immediately after He destroyed the nations.

ON THE MOUNT

And as He was sitting on the Mount of Olives, the disciples came to Him privately, saying, "Tell us, when will these things be, and what will be the sign of Your coming, and of the end of the age?" (24:3)

Upon leaving the Temple, Jesus and the Twelve left Jerusalem through the eastern gate, crossed the Kidron Valley, and ascended the Mount of Olives. As they traveled that short distance, the disciples were probably discussing the question that Peter, James, John, and Andrew would ask Jesus on their behalf (Mark 13:3). As the sun was setting over Jerusalem and the Temple was silhouetted by the last rays of sunlight, they asked the Lord, **"Tell us, when will these things be, and what will be the sign of Your coming, and of the end of the age?"**

For some time the disciples had been convinced "that the kingdom of God was going to appear immediately" (Luke 19:11). Therefore, in the context of the situation and of the disciples' probable frame of mind, the word **when** seems to imply immediacy, suggesting the time might be tomorrow, the day after, or no later than the end of Passover.

These things referred to what Jesus had just been talking about, namely, the former house of God that would soon be left desolate (23:38) and destroyed (24:2). The disciples were expecting the final stages of the Messiah's work to unfold in rather quick succession. The nations surely would rise up against Him, He would defeat them swiftly, purify Jerusalem, regather the Jews from around the world, and establish His glorious kingdom.

"What will be the sign of Your coming?" they now wanted to know. "What would the first indicator be? How will we know when those remaining events will transpire?" They still understood the Messiah's **coming** as a single continuum of events, having no comprehension of the church age that would intervene between His two comings. And they probably thought that **the sign of** Christ's **coming** would be something appropriately spectacular, such as a great darkness at midday, a brilliant light at night, the appearance of an angelic host, or a great blare of heavenly trumpets.

This was possibly the most exciting part of the disciples' experience with Christ, as they contemplated the imminence of His millennial kingdom. Based on what Jesus had just said, the disciples believed that the next time the unbelieving Jews whom Jesus had just confronted in the Temple would see Him would be when He came in His glory and they would be constrained to declare, "Blessed is He who comes in the name of the Lord!" (23:39). More than ever, they were persuaded that that day could not be far off.

Even after the resurrection, the disciples still held to the same expectation. The last question they asked Jesus before His ascension was, "Lord, is it at this time You are restoring the kingdom to Israel?" (Acts 1:6). Jesus' death and resurrection had not lessened their anticipation but immensely heightened it. Surely now that He had proved death had no hold over Him it was time to proclaim Himself King, destroy His enemies, and inaugurate His kingdom.

The **coming** that the disciples had in mind was not a second coming. They saw His **coming** just as the Old Testament prophets had seen and predicted it, compressed into an unbroken series of events that would occur over a relatively short period of time.

Coming translates *parousia,* which has the basic meaning of presence and secondarily carries the idea of arrival. The disciples' question might therefore be paraphrased, "What will be the sign of Your manifesting Yourself in Your full, permanent presence as Messiah and King?" They did not use *parousia* in the specific and more technical sense that Jesus used it later in this chapter (vv. 27, 37, 39) and as it is often used elsewhere in the New Testament in referring to His second coming (see, e.g., 1 Thess. 3:13; 2 Thess. 2:8; 1 John 2:28). They were not thinking of Jesus' returning, because they had no idea of His leaving, but were thinking rather of His perfected Messianic presence, which they expected Him to manifest presently.

End translates *sunteleia,* a compound word that refers to completion, as in the final culmination of a planned series of events. In the disciples' minds **the end of the age** would accompany Jesus' full manifestation of His messianic power and glory, bringing to a close the era of man's sin and rebellion against God and ushering in the divine kingdom of righteousness and justice.

Jesus used the phrase **the end of the age** in the parable of the wheat and tares and the parable of the dragnet, where in both cases it represented the gathering of the wicked by God's angels in preparation for judgment (Matt. 13:39, 49). He also used the phrase at the conclusion of the Great Commission, assuring the disciples, "Lo, I am with you always, even to the end of the age" (Matt. 28:20).

The disciples' question was about the ultimate **end of the age**, not simply the end of an era or epoch of history, but the final end to the present world system of darkness and sin—an end they expected soon. It was also, of course, a question about the beginning of a new and eternal age of light, righteousness, truth, and justice. The ungodly would be forever damned, and the godly would be forever blessed. When would that transpire, they wanted to know, and what sign would herald its arrival?

The Signs of Christ's Coming—part 2 The Birth Pains

(24:4-14)

And Jesus answered and said to them, "See to it that no one misleads you. For many will come in My name, saying, 'I am the Christ,'" and will mislead many. And you will be hearing of wars and rumors of wars; see that you are not frightened, for those things must take place, but that is not yet the end. For nation will rise against nation, and kingdom against kingdom, and in various places there will be famines and earthquakes. But all these things are merely the beginning of birth pangs. Then they will deliver you to tribulation, and will kill you, and you will be hated by all nations on account of My name. And at that time many will fall away and will deliver up one another and hate one another. And many false prophets will arise, and will mislead many. And because lawlessness is increased, most people's love will grow cold. But the one who endures to the end, he shall be saved. And this gospel of the kingdom shall be preached in the whole world for a witness to all the nations, and then the end shall come. (24:4-14)

Verse 4 begins the Olivet discourse proper, which Jesus gave in response to the disciples' question, "Tell us, when will these things be, and what will be the sign of Your coming, and of the end of the age?"

(v. 3). As discussed in the last chapter, the Twelve "supposed that the kingdom of God was going to appear immediately" (Luke 19:11), and the events of the past few days had confirmed that idea even more firmly in their minds. They had long believed that Jesus was the Messiah and that John the Baptist was His prophesied forerunner. The acclaim of the crowds at Jesus' triumphal entry, at His cleansing the Temple, at His rebuking the religious leaders, as well as at His predicting the destruction of the Temple all combined to make them think He would soon manifest His messianic glory, subdue the nations that would rise up against Him, and establish His eternal kingdom. They had been unable to accept His numerous predictions that He would first have to suffer, die, and be raised up.

The disciples thought that Jesus' preaching, healing, comforting, rendering judgment, and restoring Israel would occur at the same general time in history. Like the Old Testament prophets who spoke of the Messiah, they saw only a single coming, comprised of a sequence of events (see, e.g, Isa. 61:1-11).

It was when Jesus read from that passage in Isaiah during the synagogue service in Nazareth that He gave perhaps the first clue that His coming would be in two parts. He stopped reading in the middle of verse 2, omitting the phrase "and the day of vengeance of our God." He then explained, "Today this Scripture has been fulfilled in your hearing" (Luke 4:18-21). He was emphasizing that He had not come at that time to render judgment but only to preach the gospel and heal diseases.

But because they had missed that clue, as well as the many more specific teachings about His coming to die for man's sin, the disciples were expecting Jesus to complete His messianic mission at any moment, perhaps in the next few days or weeks. They were on their tiptoes, as it were, waiting for something dramatic to happen. They sensed that the son of Isaiah 9:6 was ready to take on His shoulders the government of the kingdom of God, that the stone cut out without hands of Daniel 2:34 was ready to crush the power of evil men. The Messiah, the Prince, was ready to make an end of sins, make reconciliation for iniquity, bring in everlasting righteousness, and be anointed the most holy King. They sensed that the Son of Man would very soon be given dominion and glory in an eternal kingdom. They were convinced that very soon Israel would turn back to the Lord and call on His name and that He "will say, 'They are My people,' and they will say, 'The Lord is my God'" (Zech. 13:9).

But in the Olivet discourse, Jesus makes clear that that fulfillment was in the future. The message of Matthew 24-25 is a prophetic sermon that sweeps the Twelve into a time not yet come, a time they themselves would never experience.

There are at least seven indicators in the message itself that it refers to the distant future and could not apply either to the events related to the destruction of Jerusalem in A.D. 70, as many interpreters have suggested, or to the church age, as others propose.

The first indicator will be like birth pains, of which the false Christs (Matt. 24:5), international warfare (vv. 6*7a*), and famines and earthquakes (v. 7*b*) are "merely the beginning" (v. 8). The figure of birth pains was commonly used by ancient Jewish writers, especially in regard to the end times. The great modern Jewish scholar Alfred Edersheim wrote, "Jewish writings speak very frequently of the labor pains of Messiah."

Labor pains do not occur at conception or throughout pregnancy but just before birth. The figure of birth pains therefore would not have been appropriate to represent either the destruction of Jerusalem, which occurred very near the beginning of the church age, or the church age as a whole.

Paul reminded the Thessalonians that the return of Christ would come as a thief in the night—unexpectedly, quietly, and suddenly. Using the same figure Jesus used in the Olivet discourse, the apostle said that "while they are saying, 'Peace and safety!' then destruction will come upon them suddenly like birth pangs upon a woman with child; and they shall not escape" (1 Thess. 5:1-3).

Labor pains do not begin until shortly before delivery time, and they occur with increasing frequency until the baby is born. In the same way, the events connected with the Lord's return will not begin until just before His return, and they will occur with increasing rapidity, building up to an explosion of catastrophic events. The same epoch is pictured in the book of Revelation, as the seal judgments unfold over a period of perhaps years (see 6:1–8:1-6), the trumpet judgments over a much shorter period of time, perhaps weeks (see 8:7–9:21; 11:15-19), and the bowl judgments over the period of perhaps a few days or even hours (see 16:1-21).

The second indicator that those events are future is found in Matthew 24:13-14, in which Jesus speaks of believers who will endure the birth pains to the end. Since the disciples obviously did not live to the end of the age, the events of chapters 24-25 could not apply to them or to any other believers up to and including the present time. Because all believers living then will be raptured just before the Tribulation (1 Thess. 4:17), the events could not apply to any Christian living before that time. They can apply only to those who come to belief in Christ during the Tribulation, those whose genuine faith is proved by their endurance to the end (Matt. 24:13).

A third indicator is the worldwide proclamation of the gospel (Matt. 24:14). That event absolutely rules out any time during the apostolic age, when even the Roman empire was only partially evangelized. It could not even apply to modern times, when, despite the spread of the gospel through modern mass media to most parts of the world, there are still billions of people who have never heard the gospel. As implied in Matthew 24:14 and made clear in Revelation 14:6-7, the future worldwide declaration of which Jesus spoke will be miraculous and instantaneous.

A fourth indicator is "the abomination of desolation which was spoken of through Daniel the prophet" (Matt. 24:15). Daniel predicted that just before the Messiah sets up His kingdom and judges the world, the Antichrist "will put a stop to sacrifice and grain offering; and on the wing of abominations will come one who makes desolate, even until a complete destruction, one that is decreed, is poured out on the one who makes desolate" (Dan. 9:27). That is yet to occur.

A fifth indicator that Jesus is speaking of a future time is the "great tribulation, such as has not occurred since the beginning of the world until now, nor ever shall" (Matt. 24:21). The terrible events Jesus describes in this message will be the worst of all human history and will occur at the very end of the present age, when God's full and final judgment is meted out on ungodly men. Jesus is referring to the time predicted by Daniel when "there will be a time of distress such as never occurred since there was a nation until that time" and which will be accompanied by the resurrection of the righteous to everlasting life and of the wicked to everlasting condemnation (Dan. 12:1-2).

A sixth indicator is that "immediately after the tribulation of those days the sun will be darkened, and the moon will not give its light, and the stars will fall from the sky, and the powers of the heavens will be shaken, and then the sign of the Son of Man will appear in the sky" (Matt. 24:29-30). Those supernatural events obviously have not yet transpired.

The seventh and last indicator that Jesus was speaking of the distant future is the figure of the fig tree (Matt. 24:32-35). Just as the budding leaves of a fig tree signal that summer is near, so the occurring of the events Jesus mentions here will signal His imminent return. "This generation," that is, the generation living during the time of those end-time events, "will not pass away until all these things take place" (v. 34). The signs of Matthew 24-25 will all be fully experienced within one generation, a generation that could be no other than the generation living when Christ returns.

The whole fulfillment of the Olivet discourse, therefore, is future. It is not that most of the circumstances and conditions mentioned here have not been experienced before. There have been wars and rumors of wars virtually since the Fall, and there have been famines and earthquakes since the beginning of recorded history. But the events of Matthew 24-25 will be unique to the end times in detail, in sequence, in scale, and in extent. Some of the events, such as the disruption of the physical universe (24:29), will be completely unique.

The fact that Jesus spoke in the second person, especially in chapter 24, does not prove He was speaking to the disciples about their own generation. The Old Testament prophets frequently addressed messages to people yet unborn, some of whom would live hundreds of years in the future. God picked up the prophet, as it were, and transported him to the time of which he was to prophesy, and he spoke as if he were standing directly before those future generations (see, e.g., Isa. 33:17-24; 66:10-14; Zech. 9:9). Jesus was saying, in effect, "You who are alive at that time, . . ."

Beginning in Matthew 24:4, Jesus answers the disciples' questions, "When will these things be, and what will be the sign of Your coming, and of the end of the age?" (v. 3). He responds to the two parts of the question in reverse order. He does not deal with the "when" until 24:36, saying, "But of that day and hour no one knows, not even the angels of heaven, nor the Son, but the Father alone." In 24:4-14, He begins to answer the second part of the question by describing the initial group of six signs, the "birth pains" that will occur just before His coming: deception by false Christs (vv. 4-5), dissension among the nations of the world (vv. 6-7*a*), worldwide devastation (vv. 7*b*-8), deliverance of believers to tribulation (v. 9), defection of false believers (vv. 10-13), and the declaration of the gospel to the whole world (v. 14).

DECEPTION BY FALSE CHRISTS

And Jesus answered and said to them, "See to it that no one misleads you. For many will come in My name, saying, 'I am the Christ,'" and will mislead many. (24:4-5)

The first birth pain to signal Christ's return will be widespread deception by a proliferation of false Christs. There were false Christs, or Messiahs, before Jesus' time, and there have been others at various times since, including many in our own day. But in the end times their number and influence will vastly increase.

Jesus is warning those who will be living during the end times, which will not include believers of the church age (who will either have died or been raptured before the Tribulation). The deception of those days will be intensified and escalated as never before, as the Holy Spirit withdraws His restraining power and lets all hell break loose. The evils, deceptions, sorrows, tragedies, conflicts, and animosities of those days will exceed all others the world has ever known.

Because deception will be at its apex, Jesus warns, **See to it that no one misleads you.** *Blepō* (**see to it**) literally means simply "to see," but was often used, as here, in the sense of "keep your eyes open," or "beware." In his parallel account Luke reports Jesus as saying, "See to it that you be not misled; for many will come in My name, saying, 'I am

He,' and 'The time is at hand'; do not go after them" (21:8). Later in the discourse Jesus repeats the warning: "Then if anyone says to you, 'Behold, here is the Christ,' or 'There He is,' do not believe him. For false Christs and false prophets will arise and will show great signs and wonders, so as to mislead, if possible, even the elect" (Matt. 24:23-24). Empowered by demons, the end-time false Christs will manifest supernatural powers that previous ones have not possessed.

As the number of deceivers grows, so will the number of vulnerable people who desperately look for answers to the overwhelming calamities that torment them (see 2 Pet. 2:1-3; 2 Tim. 3:13). The world will begin to disintegrate, suffering will become unbearable, and sin will reach its maximum potential. The moral and spiritual influence of the church will be gone, and even more significantly, the restraining power of the Holy Spirit will be removed (see 2 Thess. 2:7). The world's systems and institutions will start to self-destruct from unbridled wickedness.

To take advantage of that desperate situation, an abundance of false and cleverly deceptive messiahs will arise, each claiming, **I am the Christ.** Their spurious gospels **will mislead many,** as they promise to deliver men from their problems and troubles. The epitome of that false group will be the Antichrist, the ultimate false messiah and deceiver. As Jesus Christ was righteousness incarnate, the Antichrist will be evil incarnate. In the book of Daniel he is called an insolent king, skilled in intrigue (8:23), a self-willed tyrant who magnifies himself above every god and speaks monstrous evil against the God of gods (11:36). Paul calls him the man of lawlessness and the son of destruction (2 Thess. 2:3), and in the book of Revelation he is called the beast (11:7; 13:1-10).

DISPUTES AND WARFARE AMONG THE NATIONS

And you will be hearing of wars and rumors of wars; see that you are not frightened, for those things must take place, but that is not yet the end. For nation will rise against nation, and kingdom against kingdom, (24:6-7a)

The second birth pain will involve intensified and unparalleled disputes and warfare among the nations and kingdoms of the world.

You will be hearing translates a form of the future tense of *mellō* that carries the idea of continual hearing. There will be constant talk of actual **wars** and of **rumors of wars,** to a degree the world has never known before. There doubtless will be both hot wars of physical combat and cold wars of economic and political conflict. Following the analogy of labor pains, the implication is that the conflicts will increase both in number and intensity as the return of Christ approaches, until they explode into a grand holocaust of bloodshed and carnage.

But believers during that time should not be **frightened,** Jesus says, because **those things** are certain evidence that God's plan is unfolding according to His will. Those events, ghastly and destructive as they will be, **must take place,** Jesus said. They are harbingers of the end, but they are **not yet the end**.

There seems to be no distinction between **nation** and **kingdom,** unless the former represents countries with a form of democracy and the latter those under a form of autocracy, or dictatorship. The point is that no group of people will be exempt from war or the threat of war. The conflicts will undoubtedly include racial, ethnic, and cultural as well as national confrontations, much as we see in the world today, except on a vaster and more intense scale. Confrontations of every sort will accelerate throughout the world. The books of Daniel in the Old Testament and Revelation in the New give many details regarding the coming conflict.

From Daniel we learn that "at the end time the king of the South will collide with [the Antichrist], and the king of the North will storm against him with chariots, with horsemen, and with many ships; and he will enter countries, overflow them, and pass through" (Dan. 11:40). The kingdom of the Antichrist will basically comprise the territory once held by the ancient Roman empire, in particular a western confederacy made up of a unified Europe. Daniel mentions that it will be a ten-nation empire (7:24), which cannot help bringing to mind the present European Common Market.

Daniel earlier spoke of Israel's making a covenant with the Antichrist in order to protect herself from her neighbors (Dan. 9:27). The Antichrist's confederacy will completely dominate that part of the world and exert an inordinate power over the rest of the world. The king of the South will come from some part of Africa, and the king of the North will likely be Russia, who will enlist the support of Middle East allies. Those vast military forces will converge on the Holy Land, called "the Beautiful Land" (Dan. 11:41). "Many countries will fall," Daniel goes on to explain, "but these will be rescued out of his [Antichrist's] hand: Edom, Moab and the foremost of the sons of Ammon. Then he will stretch out his hand against other countries, and the land of Egypt will not escape. But he will gain control over the hidden treasures of gold and silver, and over all the precious things of Egypt; and Libyans and Ethiopians will follow at his heels" (vv. 41-43).

The Antichrist apparently defeats the other great powers, at least temporarily. "But rumors from the East and from the North will disturb him, and he will go forth with great wrath to destroy and annihilate many. And he will pitch the tents of his royal pavilion between the seas and the beautiful Holy Mountain; yet he will come to his end, and no one will help him" (vv. 44-45). The northern and eastern forces regroup, and when the Antichrist goes to meet them he is utterly defeated and destroyed, with no one to help him. Revelation speaks of a great cavalry force of 200 million that will come from the East and destroy a third of mankind (Rev. 9:14-16). It is interesting that the mainland Chinese army passed that number some years ago.

That clash will be a war of mind-boggling magnitude. All the forces of a confederated Europe to the west, Russia to the north, Africa to the south, and Asia to the east will converge on Israel for an immense battle.

Consistent with Daniel's description, Zechariah prophesied that the Lord "will gather all the nations against Jerusalem to battle, and the city will be captured, the houses plundered, the women ravished, and half of the city exiled, but the rest of the people will not be cut off from the city. Then the Lord will go forth and fight against those nations, as when He fights on a day of battle" (Zech. 14:2-3).

Through Haggai the Lord said, " 'I will overthrow the thrones of kingdoms and destroy the power of the kingdoms of the nations; and I will overthrow the chariots and their riders, and the horses and their riders will go down, everyone by the sword of another. On that day,' declares the Lord of hosts, 'I will take you, Zerubbabel, son of Shealtiel, my servant,' declares the Lord, 'and I will make you like a signet ring, for I have chosen you,' declares the Lord of hosts" (Hag. 2:22-23). It is as if Zerubbabel, the governor of Judah during Haggai's time and a descendant of David, is pictured as the Messiah, David's greater Son, who will send His own army to destroy the armies of the world and will then ascend His rightful throne on earth.

It is not difficult in our day to see how such a worldwide conflagration could develop. For many decades the world has lived under the threat of nuclear warfare and the anxiety of increasing strife within and among virtually all nations.

The book of Revelation gives parallel and additional details of the wars and rumors of wars in which the nations and kingdoms of the world will be engaged during the end times. Christ, the Lamb, is portrayed with a scroll in His hand, representing, as it were, the Father's will and testament bequeathing the world to the Son (Rev. 6:1). As He opens each of the seven seals, the number required under ancient Roman law to keep a will inviolate, Christ sets in motion one of the God-ordained stages of His taking the world back for Himself.

Opening the first seal unleashes the Antichrist, the rider on a white horse who will go out to deceive with the intent to conquer (v. 2). There will not be open warfare at that time, but a false sense of peace and security. Just as Jesus predicted in the Olivet discourse, the first stage of Satan's final attack will be one of deception and subterfuge. When the second seal is opened, however, the rider on a red horse will be allowed to take that false peace from the world, "that men should slay one another; and a great sword was given to him" (v. 4).

John also saw tremendous conflict generated by three unclean spirits, high-ranking demons of Satan, who will perform great miracles and gather the leaders and armies of the world "together for the war of the great day of God the Almighty. . . . And they gathered them together to the place which in Hebrew is called Har-Magedon [Armageddon]" (Rev. 16:13-14, 16). Those demon-led forces will converge on Israel and on Jerusalem in particular in an intense but futile effort to prevent Christ, the King of kings, from reclaiming His earthly throne. As they fight each other, Christ will come and destroy them all (19:11-20).

But before the Lord comes to accomplish that final conquest, the Antichrist and the forces of the north, south, and east will engage in ruthless combat and succeed in slaughtering a third of the world's population. In the face of that unparalleled carnage man's last vestige of hope will vanish and stark terror will rule the day. Only believers who hold fast to the Lord will have the divinely-given strength and courage to avoid being petrified with fear.

DEVASTATION THROUGHOUT THE WORLD

and in various places there will be famines and earthquakes. But all these things are merely the beginning of birth pangs. (24:7b-8)

The next birth pain of the end time will be worldwide devastation. In addition to the deception of false Christs and warring dissension among the nations there will be **famines and earthquakes,** natural disasters of staggering proportions that will ensue as the cursed earth begins to disintegrate. Luke adds that there will also be plagues and terrors and great signs from heaven (21:11).

Earthquakes, epidemics of deadly disease, dreadful happenings of various sorts, and awesome changes in the sky will torment men. They will see the world begin to disintegrate before their eyes from the unbridled, destructive forces of evil that will ravage it during those indescribable days. The world has witnessed many earthquakes, famines, plagues, and even some heavenly signs, but those will be nothing compared to the calamities of the end times. They will occur **in various places** and apparently simultaneously. As some parts of the earth starve from **famines,** others will be shattered by **earthquakes,** others decimated by plagues, others paralyzed by unspecified terrors, and still others unnerved by changes in the heavens.

John foresaw that when Christ broke the fourth seal of the scroll, authority was given to death and hades "to kill with sword and with famine and with pestilence and by the wild beasts of the earth" (Rev. 6:8). When He broke the sixth seal, "there was a great earthquake; and the sun became black as sackcloth made of hair, and the whole moon became like blood; and the stars of the sky fell to the earth, as a fig tree casts its unripe figs when shaken by a great wind. And the sky was split apart like a scroll when it is rolled up; and every mountain and island were moved out of their places" (vv. 12-14).

When the Lamb broke the seventh seal, seven angels were revealed standing before God, and they were each given a trumpet of judgment. As the first trumpet was blown,

> there came hail and fire, mixed with blood, and they were thrown to the earth; and a third of the earth was burned up, and a third of the trees were burned up, and all the green grass was burned up.
>
> And the second angel sounded, and something like a great mountain burning with fire was thrown into the sea; and a third of the sea became blood; and a third of the creatures, which were in the sea and had life, died; and a third of the ships were destroyed.
>
> And the third angel sounded, and a great star fell from heaven, burning like a torch, and it fell on a third of the rivers and on the springs of waters; and the name of the star is called Wormwood; and a third of the waters became wormwood; and many men died from the waters, because they were made bitter.
>
> And a fourth angel sounded, and a third of the sun and a third of the moon and a third of the stars were smitten, so that a third of them might be darkened and the day might not shine for a third of it, and the night in the same way. (Rev. 8:7-12; cf. 16:1-11; Joel 2:10; Acts 2:19-20)

Crops and other vegetation will be devastated throughout the world, those who depend upon the sea for food will suffer famine, a third of the world's shipping will be destroyed, countless people will be poisoned from contaminated water supplies, and calendars, seasons, and tides will be thrown out of kilter. The physical and emotional agony will be so excruciating that men will gnaw "their tongues because of pain" (Rev. 16:10). "Their torment [will be] like the torment of a scorpion when it stings a man," and "men will seek death and will not find it; and they will long to die and death flees from them" (9:5-6).

Some time later, when the seventh angel poured out his bowl into the air,

> there were flashes of lightning and sounds and peals of thunder; and there was a great earthquake, such as there had not been since man came to be upon earth, so great an earthquake was it, and so mighty. And the great city was split into three parts, and the cities of the nations fell. . . . And every island fled away, and the mountains were not found. And huge hailstones, about one hundred pounds each, came down from heaven upon men; and men blasphemed God because of the plague of the hail, because its plague was extremely severe. (Rev. 16:17-21; cf. 11:13)

But all these things are merely the beginning of birth pangs.
There is much more to come.

DELIVERANCE OF BELIEVERS TO TRIBULATION

Then they will deliver you to tribulation, and will kill you, and you will be hated by all nations on account of My name. (24:9)

The fourth labor pain of the end times will be severe persecution of believers by the evil, ungodly world. More than ever before in history, the holy people of God will be treated in an unholy way, and in that sense they will be desecrated.

Paradidōmi (**will deliver**) has the basic meaning of giving over and was often used in a technical sense for arrest by the police or military (see Matt. 4:12). After being taken into custody, believers will suffer extreme **tribulation.** Many will be murdered, and all **will be hated by all nations on account of My name.** In his parallel passage, Mark reports that Jesus said, "They will deliver you to the courts, and you will be flogged in the synagogues, and you will stand before governors and kings for My sake, as a testimony to them" (13:9). The courts probably represent Gentile authority, and the synagogues obviously represent Jewish authority, indicating that persecution will come from both groups. Being identified with Christ's **name** will cost believers their freedom, their rights, their respect, and often their lives.

As already noted, those will be people who are saved after the rapture of the church, having been converted to Christ during the Tribulation. Many will be saved through the preaching of the two witnesses the Lord will send to minister for a period of three and a half years (Rev. 11:3). During that time the witnesses will be supernaturally protected (v. 4), but "when they have finished their testimony, the beast that comes up out of the abyss will make war with them, and overcome them and kill them" (v. 7). After three and a half days, they will be resurrected and taken up into heaven, and that miracle itself will cause additional people to be saved and to give "glory to the God of heaven" (vv. 11-13).

The persecution will not be directed so much against believers themselves as against God, whom they serve and represent. The unbelieving world will intensify its hatred of God, and because it cannot attack Him directly it will fiercely attack His people. When Paul said he bore in his body "the brand-marks of Jesus" (Gal. 6:17), he was affirming that he had received wounds that were really directed at Christ. Because people could not get to Christ, they abused the one who represented Him.

When the Holy Spirit withdraws His restraint and Satan is allowed greater freedom, the saints will suffer as they never have before. For those who openly profess Christ there will be no place to hide and no way of

23

escape. They will not be persecuted and martyred for what they do but for who they are. They will suffer **on account of** Christ's **name**, that is, because they are identified with Him.

When Christ broke the fifth seal of the scroll, John saw those martyred saints under the altar,

> the souls of those who had been slain because of the word of God, and because of the testimony which they had maintained; and they cried out with a loud voice, saying, "How long, O Lord, holy and true, wilt Thou refrain from judging and avenging our blood on those who dwell on the earth?" And there was given to each of them a white robe; and they were told that they should rest for a little while longer, until the number of their fellow servants and their brethren who were to be killed even as they had been, should be completed also. (Rev. 6:9-11)

Later John saw a "great multitude, which no one could count, from every nation and all tribes and peoples and tongues, standing before the throne and before the Lamb, clothed in white robes, and palm branches were in their hands; and they cry out with a loud voice, saying, 'Salvation to our God who sits on the throne, and to the Lamb'" (Rev. 7:9-10). One of the elders explained to the apostle that "these are the ones who come out of the great tribulation, and they have washed their robes and made them white in the blood of the Lamb" (v. 14).

The murders of which unbelieving mankind will not repent (Rev. 9:21) will include the killing of other unbelievers, but as with the Antichrist (13:7) and the great harlot (17:6), the most vicious assaults will be on the saints.

DEFECTION OF FALSE BELIEVERS

And at that time many will fall away and will deliver up one another and hate one another. And many false prophets will arise, and will mislead many. And because lawlessness is increased, most people's love will grow cold. But the one who endures to the end, he shall be saved. (24:10-13)

The fifth birth pain is a consequence of the fourth. As persecution intensifies in the end times and believers begin to be arrested, hated, and martyred for Christ's sake, many supposed Christians will defect. Although they will have had an outward identification with Christ, they will prove by their desertion that they never belonged to Him. When the persecution becomes too severe, they will forsake Christ and join fellow unbelievers in assailing God's people.

Jesus mentions three reasons for their defection: the price will be too high, the deception of false teachers will be too convincing, and sin will be too attractive.

THE COST WILL BE TOO HIGH

And at that time many will fall away and will deliver up one another and hate one another. (24:10)

Every noble cause has hangers-on who love to be associated with it while it is popular but who fall away as soon as criticism or conflicts arise. Christ's church is no exception. Throughout its history it has had adherents who like to bear the name Christian when it is acceptable and respected in society but who quickly lose their devotion when that name is maligned and those who bear it are persecuted (see Matt. 13:20-21).

The sham Christians who **will fall away** during the Tribulation will not be true believers who are simply weak and cowardly but unbelievers who reveal their true character when they openly reject Christ and viciously betray His people. They will not be like Peter, who in a moment of fear and weakness denied knowing Christ, but like Judas, who because of His inner hatred of Christ betrayed Him to His enemies.

John declares that such pretenders leave Christian fellowship because they were never truly a part of it. "They went out from us," he says, because "they were not really of us; for if they had been of us, they would have remained with us; but they went out, in order that it might be shown that they all are not of us" (1 John 2:19). Such people abandon Christ's visible church because they were never a part of His invisible church. They forsake God's earthly family because they were never born into His heavenly family. "If you abide in My word," Jesus said, "then you are truly disciples of Mine" (John 8:31); and on the day of judgment He will declare to false believers, "I never knew you; depart from Me, you who practice lawlessness" (Matt. 7:23).

"A disciple is not above his teacher, nor a slave above his master," Jesus said. "It is enough for the disciple that he become as his teacher, and the slave as his master. If they have called the head of the house Beelzebul, how much more the members of his household!" (Matt. 10:24-25). The true disciple of Christ is willing to suffer as Christ suffered, and no amount of affliction will cause Him to renounce his Lord and Savior. "Everyone therefore who shall confess Me before men, I will also confess him before My Father who is in heaven. But whoever shall deny Me before men, I will also deny him before My Father who is in heaven. . . . And he who does not take his cross and follow after Me is not worthy of Me" (vv. 32-33, 38; cf. 2 Tim. 2:12).

A professed Christian who turns His back on Jesus Christ and refuses to suffer for His sake was not a true believer in the first place. A person who genuinely belongs to Christ may sometimes falter and be disobedient, but he will never reject His Lord. The person who belongs to Christ continues to confess Him, to serve Him, and to suffer for Him when that is necessary. He does not endure because of his own strength and fortitude but because he is indwelt by Christ's own Spirit, who never fails to give sustaining grace to God's children.

The writer of Hebrews sounded the warning to those in the early church: "Take care, brethren, lest there should be in any one of you an evil, unbelieving heart, in falling away from the living God" (Heb. 3:12). Paul declared to Timothy, "It is a trustworthy statement: For if we died with Him, we shall also live with Him; if we endure, we shall also reign with Him; if we deny Him, He also will deny us" (2 Tim. 2:11-12).

This text leads us to believe that, just as during the present age, professing Christians living during the Tribulation will not all be authentic. Many will be counterfeit, and when the cost of discipleship becomes too demanding they will abandon Christ and His church. They will be like those would-be disciples who said to Jesus, "I will follow You wherever You go" and "Permit me first to go and bury my father" and "I will follow You, Lord; but first permit me to say good-bye to those at home." They will put their hand to the plow of discipleship, but they will not forsake the old life, demonstrating that they have never received the new. They are therefore not "fit for the kingdom of God," Jesus said, because their hearts have never been with Him (Luke 9:57-62).

The defecting false believers in the end time will not be satisfied simply with leaving the church but will join in its persecution. **They will deliver up one another and hate one another.** God's people will be betrayed by those who once were a part of their fellowship but who become offended at Christ when the cost rises too high. Both to save their own skins as well as to vent the hatred for the things of God they have always had in their hearts, they will turn informer and persecutor. At that time, Jesus said, "brother will deliver brother to death, and a father his child; and children will rise up against parents and have them put to death" (Mark 13:12; cf. Luke 21:16). Not only within the assembly at large but within individual families, those who do not truly belong to Christ will turn against those who do, even to the point of betraying their own children and parents into martyrdom.

THE DECEPTION WILL BE TOO CONVINCING

And many false prophets will arise, and will mislead many. (24:11)

Just as some false believers will defect because the cost is too high, others will defect because they are deceived about the gospel.

During the Tribulation **false prophets** will join the false christs (v. 5) in seeking to deceive people about God. They will persuasively teach doctrines that seem true and godly but are, in fact, false and satanic. The end time will be filled not only with overt evil such as the world has never seen before but also with false religion as never seen before. Until the very end, Satan will continue to use the guise of an angel of light (2 Cor. 11:14).

From Revelation 17 it becomes clear that false religions, here symbolized by the great harlot of Babylon, will flourish. The figure of a prostitute is used no doubt because the world religious system will prostitute itself, seeking by counterfeit gospels and other means to keep people from the true gospel and salvation. Despite their outward differences, the religions of that day will have one trait in common: hatred for the people of God, the true and purified brothers and sisters of Christ.

It is interesting that a characteristic of end-time false religion will be "sorceries" (Rev. 9:21), which translates *pharmakia,* from which we get the word *pharmacy.* Both the ancient Greek and the modern English terms relate to the ingestion of drugs. The use of mind-altering drugs was common in many ancient pagan religions, and in light of the modern epidemic of drug abuse and addiction, it would be surprising if the sorceries of the end time did not include the use of narcotics and hallucinogens.

SIN WILL BE TOO ATTRACTIVE

And because lawlessness is increased, most people's love will grow cold. But the one who endures to the end, he shall be saved. (24:12-13)

A third cause of defection will be the love of **lawlessness**, which, as it **is increased**, will cause **most people's love** for righteousness, truth, and the things of God to **grow cold**.

Although end-time **lawlessness** will certainly include disregard for human laws, it will be manifested most vehemently in **increased** disregard for God's law. Evil will multiply so rapidly and unashamedly that many people who are initially drawn to the gospel will turn away from it because of the multiplied enticements of sin.

The **lawlessness** will be diabolically aggressive and unabashed. Rather than trying to hide their sins, people will flaunt them, and such gross evil will draw many people, including some professed believers, away from whatever interest in the things of God they may once have had.

Describing the same period Jesus is talking about here, Paul warned,

> But realize this, that in the last days difficult times will come. For men will be lovers of self, lovers of money, boastful, arrogant, revilers, disobedient to parents, ungrateful, unholy, unloving, irreconcilable, malicious gossips, without self-control, brutal, haters of good, treacherous, reckless, conceited, lovers of pleasure rather than lovers of God; holding to a form of godliness, although they have denied its power; and avoid such men as these. (2 Tim. 3:1-5)

Global violence, immorality, lewdness, selfish desire, and every other moral vice will run rampant as unbridled sin expresses itself. Men will be engulfed in a tidal wave of corruption and they will glory in it.

But the one who endures to the end, he shall be saved, Jesus said. It is not that a person's endurance will produce salvation but that his endurance will be a Spirit-empowered product and proof of the reality that he *is* **saved.** Neither the high cost of discipleship nor the deception of false prophets nor the enticement of sin will cause true believers to renounce Christ, because He Himself will protect them from defection.

Endurance is always a mark of salvation. "You will be hated by all on account of My name," Jesus said, "but it is the one who has endured to the end who will be saved" (Matt. 10:22; cf. Luke 21:19). The person who endures in faith whatever hardship or persecution may come to him because of his relationship to Christ demonstrates that He belongs to Christ, and Christ assures that person that **he shall be saved.** He will eventually be delivered out of the present evil system of lawlessness and ungodliness into God's eternal kingdom of righteousness.

The perseverance of the saints in faith is a very basic element of salvation teaching in the New Testament. It states that people who are genuinely saved do not depart from the faith (see John 8:31; 1 Cor. 15:1-2; Col. 1:21-23; Heb. 2:1-3; 3:14; 4:14; 6:11-12; 10:39; 12:14; James 1:2-4).

Reference to salvation in the future tense in such passages as the ones just cited does not indicate its beginning but its completion. Endurance cannot initiate salvation any more than can any other human effort. But it does give evidence of the spiritual life that resides in the believer and is also a reminder to him that "He who began a good work in [him] will perfect it until the day of Christ Jesus" (Phil. 1:6; cf. John 10:27-29; Rom. 5:8-10; 2 Tim. 1:12; Heb. 7:25; 1 Pet. 1:5; Jude 24).

The one who endures to the end is the overcomer, the beloved child of God who does not fear suffering or death and who will be given the crown of life and will "not be hurt by the second death" (Rev. 2:10-11). Faith that perseveres is faith endowed and sustained by the indwelling Holy Spirit of Christ.

The enduring saints of the end times will be

the ones who come out of the great tribulation, and they have washed their robes and made them white in the blood of the Lamb. For this reason, they are before the throne of God; and they serve Him day and night in His temple; and He who sits on the throne shall spread His tabernacle over them. They shall hunger no more, neither thirst anymore; neither shall the sun beat down on them, nor any heat; for the Lamb in the center of the throne shall be their shepherd, and shall guide them to springs of the water of life; and God shall wipe every tear from their eyes. (Rev. 7:14-17)

DECLARATION OF THE GOSPEL TO THE WHOLE WORLD

And this gospel of the kingdom shall be preached in the whole world for a witness to all the nations, and then the end shall come. (24:14)

The sixth and last birth pain to indicate that the end time is near will be the worldwide declaration of the gospel to a degree never yet seen. Before the Lord Himself appears, **this gospel of the kingdom shall be preached in the whole world for a witness to all the nations**.

Despite the deception of false christs and false teachers, the unparalleled warfare and pestilence and disaster, the fierce persecution of the saints, and the defection of false believers, the **gospel of** Christ's **kingdom** will continue to be proclaimed. Despite the Antichrist's tyrannical rule and hell's belching out its demons to wreak havoc on earth, the Lord Jesus Christ will not be without witness.

Just before the bowl judgments are poured out and the final great holocaust begins, and just before the increasingly rapid birth pains issue in the kingdom, God will supernaturally present the gospel to every person on earth. He will send an angel with "an eternal gospel to preach to those who live on the earth, and to every nation and tribe and tongue and people," saying, "Fear God, and give Him glory, because the hour of His judgment has come; and worship Him who made the heaven and the earth and sea and springs of waters" (Rev. 14:6-7).

That will be the final and total evangelization of the world, miraculously proclaimed from heaven. After that proclamation man's day will be finished, his rebellion will be over, and his opportunity for salvation will be over, because **then the end shall come.**

The Signs of Christ's Coming—part 3 The Abomination of Desolation

(24:15)

3

Therefore when you see the abomination of desolation which was spoken of through Daniel the prophet, standing in the holy place (let the reader understand), (24:15)

People have a natural longing for a better day, a time of peace and harmony among nations, of greater economic stability, and of decreased crime, disease, and discord. But Scripture is clear that, despite temporary times of improvement, things are destined to become much worse before they permanently become better. Human society faces a time that is going to be more calamitous than any ever experienced before. "Then there will be a great tribulation," Jesus said, "such as has not occurred since the beginning of the world until now, nor ever shall" (Matt. 24:21). The Tribulation will encompass the entire world but will focus on the nation and people of Israel. It will mark the end of man's day and the coming of God's.

The prediction of the time of trouble did not originate in the Olivet discourse or in Jesus' previous teaching but in the prophetic teachings of the Old Testament. As Isaiah looked forward to that day, the day of the Lord, the day of great judgment, and the day of Messiah's establishing His kingdom on earth, he wrote: "Now it will come about in that day that the remnant of Israel, and those of the house of Jacob who have escaped, will never again rely on the one who struck them, but will truly rely on the Lord, the Holy One of Israel" (Isa. 10:20).

A time is coming when most of the people of Israel will be massacred by an enemy they thought was their friend, and only a remnant will elude the slaughter. At the time of the very end, just before the time of judgment, Israel will suffer vicious betrayal by one they trusted and they will be subjected to a holocaust from which few will escape. Those who are spared will turn back to the Lord and be saved. They will no longer trust in themselves or in any human ally but will henceforth trust only in the Lord. "A remnant will return," the prophet says, "the remnant of Jacob, to the mighty God. For though your people, O Israel, may be like the sand of the sea, only a remnant within them will return; a destruction is determined, overflowing with righteousness" (Isa. 10:21-22).

Jeremiah envisioned the same terrible time and presents additional dimensions:

> For thus says the Lord, "I have heard a sound of terror, of dread, and there is no peace. Ask now, and see, if a male can give birth. Why do I see every man with his hands on his loins, as a woman in childbirth? And why have all faces turned pale? Alas! for that day is great, there is none like it; and it is the time of Jacob's distress, but he will be saved from it. And it shall come about on that day," declares the Lord of hosts, "that I will break his yoke from off their neck, and will tear off their bonds; and strangers shall no longer make them their slaves. But they shall serve the Lord their God, and David their king, whom I will raise up for them." (Jer. 30:5-9)

Excruciating pain, like that of childbirth without anesthetic, will be experienced by all of mankind. Even men will be on their knees as if in labor, holding themselves as they writhe in agony. Yet out of that suffering will come the deliverance, repentance, and salvation of Israel.

Daniel foresaw that the archangel "Michael, the great prince who stands guard over the sons of your people, will arise. And there will be a time of distress such as never occurred since there was a nation until that time; and at that time your people, everyone who is found written in the book, will be rescued" (Dan. 12:1).

Zechariah wrote,

> "And it will come about in all the land," declares the Lord, "that two parts in it will be cut off and perish; but the third will be left in it. And I will bring the third part through the fire, refine them as silver is refined, and test them as gold is tested. They will call on My name, and I will answer

them; I will say, 'They are My people,' and they will say, 'The Lord is my God.'" Behold, a day is coming for the Lord when the spoil taken from you will be divided among you. For I will gather all the nations against Jerusalem to battle, and the city will be captured, the houses plundered, the women ravished, and half of the city exiled, but the rest of the people will not be cut off from the city. (Zech. 13:8-14:2)

In Matthew 24-25 Jesus was speaking of that coming time of indescribable horror in the world that will focus on the nation of Israel, a time of which Isaiah, Jeremiah, Daniel, and Zechariah had already spoken in considerable detail. Although Israel as a nation and the Jewish people in general have endured many periods of great suffering throughout history, including the destruction of Jerusalem and the Temple by the Romans in A.D. 70 and the extermination of many millions of them by Nazi Germany and communist Russia in modern times, the holocaust of the end time will vastly exceed those.

In 24:4-14 Jesus foretold six signs of His coming again that would be like birth pains, which come at the very end of a pregnancy and with increasing rapidity and severity until the child is born. Now He predicts the sign that will trigger those birth pains.

As explained in the previous chapter, Jesus' use of **you** in the Olivet discourse does not refer to the disciples or to anyone else living at that time but rather refers prophetically to those who will be living in the end time, just before He returns.

The event that activates the birth pain signs will be **the abomination of desolation** and will be like the abomination **spoken of through Daniel the prophet.** In his parallel passage, Luke adds that Jesus said, "But when you see Jerusalem surrounded by armies, then recognize that her desolation is at hand" (21:20). In other words, it is while Jerusalem is encompassed by enemy nations who threaten to destroy her that this sign will occur.

For several decades, the modern nation of Israel has increasingly become a major focal point of world events, events that involve not only the Middle East but also the great powers of the United States, Russia, China, and many nations of Europe. Naval fleets from the United States and Russia continue to grow in strength and readiness in the Mediterranean Sea, the Arabian Sea, the Persian Gulf, and the other great bodies of water in that part of the world.

During the end times, the Antichrist will head a confederacy of ten European nations that will generally correspond to the territory of the ancient Roman empire (see Dan. 7:24; cf. 2:40-43), and he will at first pretend to be Israel's deliverer from her enemies, and she will make an alliance with him (9:27). But after he is victorious over the nations from the south, north, and east who have come against Israel, he will reveal

33

his true evil character and his hatred for Israel and for God (Dan. 11:40-45). It is while occupying Israel under the guise of being her protector that the Antichrist will commit **the abomination of desolation**.

Bdelugma (**abomination**) denotes an object of disgust, repulsion, and abhorrence. In Scripture it is used primarily to denote things associated with idolatry and gross ungodliness. The Hebrew equivalent was often used of rites and paraphernalia associated with the wicked conduct of pagan religions. In the book of Revelation it is used to represent the immoralities and spiritual uncleanness of the false religious system known as "Babylon the great, the mother of harlots" (17:45). In the new heaven and new earth there will be "nothing unclean and no one who practices abominations and lying" (21:27).

The abomination of desolation may be translated, "the abomination which makes desolate, or lays waste." In other words, **the abomination** *causes* the **desolation**.

The prophet Daniel referred to the abomination of desolation three times (9:27; 11:31; 12:11). Virtually every Bible scholar, no matter what his views on eschatology, identifies that abomination as the sacrilege committed by Antiochus IV, the Syrian king who ruled Palestine from 175-165 B.C. as a surrogate of the Greek empire. He took to himself the title Theos Epiphanes, which means "manifest god," but his enemies nicknamed him Epimanes, which means "madman" or "the insane one." Ironically, when he died in 163, he was totally insane, outraged to the point of madness because of his military defeats by the Jewish rebel Judas Maccabaeus. The text of Daniel 11:21-35 perfectly describes the rule of Antiochus, who gained his throne "by intrigue" (v. 21), made numerous excursions into Egypt (vv. 24-27), broke his covenant with Israel (v. 28), and desecrated the Temple in Jerusalem (v. 31).

The apocryphal books of 1 and 2 Maccabees vividly portray the time of Antiochus and the Jews' zealous resistance to his brutal and sacrilegious tyranny. He slaughtered countless thousands of Jewish men, sold many of their wives and children into slavery, and tried to completely obliterate the Jewish religion. He desecrated the Temple by sacrificing a pig, the most ceremonially unclean of all animals, on the altar and forcing the priests to eat its flesh. He then set up in the Temple an idol of Zeus, the pagan deity he fancied himself as manifesting. That horrible defilement by Antiochus was a preview of the even greater **abomination of desolation** to be committed by the Antichrist in the end time.

Daniel had predicted: "Seventy weeks have been decreed for your people and your holy city, to finish the transgressions, to make an end of sin, to make atonement for iniquity, to bring in everlasting righteousness, to seal up vision and prophecy, and to anoint the most holy place" (9:24). "Seventy weeks" is literally "seventy sevens" and refers to years (cf. 9:2). In other words, 490 years would transpire before the Messiah would return to establish His eternal kingdom of righteousness. As Daniel explained in the following verse, that measurement would begin at "the issuing of a decree to restore and rebuild Jerusalem," the decree issued by King Artaxerxes in 445 B.C. (see Neh. 2:5-6). The prophet also explained that "seven weeks and sixty-two weeks" (69 weeks, or 483 years) would pass "until Messiah the Prince" (Dan. 9:25). It has been calculated that exactly 483 years elapsed from that decree of Artaxerxes until Jesus' triumphal entry into Jerusalem, when He was acclaimed Messiah and King by the multitude (for detailed explanations of those dates, see Sir Robert Anderson's *The Coming Prince* [Grand Rapids: Kregel, 1954] and Harold Hoehner's *Chronological Aspects of the Life of Christ* [Grand Rapids: Zondervan, 1977]).

After that time and before the seventieth and final week of years, "the Messiah will be cut off and have nothing, and the people of the prince who is to come will destroy the city and the sanctuary" (Dan. 9:26). That is a picture of Jesus' crucifixion and of the destruction of Jerusalem and the Temple in A.D. 70.

Then the deceitful prince "will make a firm covenant with the many for one week, but in the middle of the week he will put a stop to sacrifice and grain offering; and on the wing of abominations will come one who makes desolate, even until a complete destruction, one that is decreed, is poured out on the one who makes desolate" (v. 27). That last week, or seven-year period, of the seventy weeks will begin when Israel makes a covenant with the Antichrist, thinking he will be her great deliverer.

In modern Israel, fear of the Arabs and the Russians runs very deep. Not only do those combined enemies outnumber Israel in manpower and weaponry by several hundred times but their hatred for Jews is intense. Ezekiel prophesied that Magog (identified by Josephus as the land of what is now Russia), Meshech and Tubal (Asia Minor, or modern Turkey), Persia (modern Iran and Afghanistan), Ethiopia (including modern Sudan), Put (Libya), and other nations will unite against Israel (Ezek. 38:26).

I have heard Israeli soldiers say that if Arabs believe Allah tells them to kill Jews, that is what they will do, and any treaties or peace pacts that forbid such action will mean nothing.

As the modern Satan-inspired alliance of Russia and many Arab nations continues to grow, it becomes evident that the prophetic picture of the end time is unfolding. When that threat to her becomes extreme, Israel will seek security and protection from a powerful ally by making a pact with the European confederacy to the west, which will also be satanically energized.

Halfway through the final week of years, at the end of the first three and a half years, the deceptive leader of the western confederacy

(Antichrist) will violently turn against Israel, set himself up as God, and commit the abomination of desolation that activates the Great Tribulation, which brings about intense persecution of Jews.

Interpreters have proposed numerous identities for **the holy place,** some suggesting it is the city of Jerusalem and others that it is the holy of holies, the inner sanctum of the Temple. In the only other passage where the phrase is used in the New Testament, it plainly refers to the Temple itself (Acts 21:28), and that seems to be the only reasonable meaning to take for it in Matthew 24:15. David also referred to the Temple as the Lord's holy place (see Ps. 24:3).

"And from the time that the regular sacrifice is abolished, and the abomination of desolation is set up, there will be 1,290 days" (Dan. 12:11). The desecration of the Temple will not be momentary but continuous, described by Jesus as **standing in the holy place.** From the time the daily sacrifice is canceled and the abomination of desolation begins, 1290 days will pass until the end, 30 more days than three and one half years. Yet according to Revelation 12:6, the Great Tribulation will last 1260 days. It seems that the best explanation for those additional days is that they will cover the time when the Messiah descends to the Mount of Olives, creates the great valley in which the nations of the world will be judged, and executes that judgment (see Zech. 14:4-5; Matt. 25:31-46).

Daniel continues by saying, "How blessed is he who keeps waiting and attains to the 1,335 days!" (12:12), which adds an additional 45 days. That additional time would seem to be a transition period during which the Lord establishes His throne in Jerusalem and sets up places of leadership throughout the earth that will be governed in His behalf by His appointed representatives. So there are the 1260 days of trouble, followed by 30 days to break down man's kingdom and 45 days to set up the Lord's.

Further details of **the abomination of desolation** are given in the book of Revelation. Pictured as the beast coming up out of the sea, the Antichrist will be given "a mouth speaking arrogant words and blasphemies; and authority to act for forty-two months was given to him" (Rev. 13:1, 5). Forty-two months translates into three and a half years, or 1,260 days, which will be the Great Tribulation, the second half of the last week of years. As the Antichrist continues his blasphemies against God's name, tabernacle, and heavenly citizens, "it was given to him to make war with the saints and to overcome them; and authority over every tribe and people and tongue and nation was given to him. And all who dwell on the earth will worship him, everyone whose name has not been written from the foundation of the world in the book of life of the Lamb who has been slain" (vv. 7-8). His cohort, the false prophet, will then join him and perform great signs and wonders in order to promote the worship of the Antichrist and will even enable an image of the beast to talk and cause the deaths of those who refuse to worship (vv. 11-15).

Antiochus Epiphanes set up an idol in the Temple to be worshiped by the Jews, but the Antichrist will set himself up as God and demand worship from all mankind. He will end all sacrifice in the Temple and commit the abomination that makes **the holy place** desecrated and desolate, a place utterly detestable to Jews.

Then the Antichrist, the man of lawlessness, "the son of destruction, who opposes and exalts himself above every so-called god or object of worship, . . . takes his seat in the temple of God, displaying himself as being God" (2 Thess. 2:3-4). He is "the one whose coming is in accord with the activity of Satan, with all power and signs and false wonders, and with all the deception of wickedness for those who perish, because they did not receive the love of the truth so as to be saved" (vv. 9-10). That is the abomination of desolation.

The exhortation **let the reader understand** reinforces the fact that Jesus was not giving the warnings in the Olivet discourse to the disciples themselves or to their generation but to believers in the end time, who will read those truths in Scripture and thereby be enabled to **understand** the trials they are enduring.

The Signs of Christ's Coming—part 4
Perils to Come
(24:16-28)

Then let those who are in Judea flee to the mountains; let him who is on the housetop not go down to get the things out that are in his house; and let him who is in the field not turn back to get his cloak. But woe to those who are with child and to those who nurse babes in those days! But pray that your flight may not be in the winter, or on a Sabbath; for then there will be a great tribulation, such as has not occurred since the beginning of the world until now, nor ever shall. And unless those days had been cut short, no life would have been saved; but for the sake of the elect those days shall be cut short. Then if anyone says to you, "Behold, here is the Christ," or "There He is," do not believe him. For false Christs and false prophets will arise and will show great signs and wonders, so as to mislead, if possible, even the elect. Behold, I have told you in advance. If therefore they say to you, "Behold, He is in the wilderness," do not go forth, or, "Behold, He is in the inner rooms," do not believe them. For just as the lightning comes from the east, and flashes even to the west, so shall the coming of the Son of Man be. Wherever the corpse is, there the vultures will gather. (24:16-28)

Perhaps no subject in Scripture is more intriguing than the second coming of Jesus Christ, and none should be more motivating to the believer and the unbeliever alike. "Therefore knowing the fear of the Lord," Paul declared, "we persuade men" (2 Cor. 5:11). Realizing that Christ will one day come in terrible judgment, the sensible unbeliever should be motivated to repent and receive Him as Lord and Savior. The obedient Christian will be motivated to faithfully present the gospel to unbelievers in order that they might have the opportunity to be saved. The faithful Christian is also motivated by the reward he will receive when His Lord returns, and with Paul he has the "ambition, whether at home or absent, to be pleasing to Him" (v. 9).

In Matthew 24:16-28 Jesus continues to describe some of the perils that will accompany His return to establish His earthly millennial reign. But before giving those additional signs of His coming, He tells all Jews and all believing Gentiles who are living in Judea during the Tribulation what their response to the abomination of desolation should be.

THE RESPONSE

Then let those who are in Judea flee to the mountains; let him who is on the housetop not go down to get the things out that are in his house; and let him who is in the field not turn back to get his cloak. But woe to those who are with child and to those who nurse babes in those days! But pray that your flight may not be in the winter, or on a Sabbath; (24:16-20)

As mentioned previously, the abomination of desolation (see v. 15) will precipitate the first series of dangers and catastrophes that Jesus compared to birth pains (vv. 4-14). When the Antichrist desecrates the restored Jerusalem Temple and demands that all the world worship him as God, the second three and a half years of the Tribulation, called the Great Tribulation (see v. 21), will begin. **Then,** Jesus said, **let those who are in Judea flee to the mountains.** That statement is a warning of the severity of the holocaust to come and an exhortation to **flee** from it.

Because of their proximity to the profaned Temple headquarters of the Antichrist in Jerusalem, **those who are in Judea** will be in the greatest and most immediate danger from that extremely powerful and malevolent agent of Satan. Although everyone on earth will be subject to his tyranny, the Antichrist's supreme fury will be vented against Jews, regardless of their religious persuasion or lack of it, and also against all Christians. Jewish Christians will be in the greatest jeopardy of all, being doubly despised by Satan's forces.

Since God first called and made His eternal covenant with Abraham, Satan has sought to destroy God's chosen people, the Jews, and their God-ordained nation of Israel. To have destroyed the Jews would have been to destroy God's redemptive plan for mankind, because "salvation is from the Jews" (John 4:22). To have eliminated the Jews before Jesus was born would have broken the line of promise and thwarted the birth and therefore the redemptive ministry of the Messiah, who had to be a descendant of Abraham and of David. Having failed at that, however, Satan still seeks to destroy individual Jews in order to prevent Christ's ultimate redemption of them and to destroy Israel as a nation in order to prevent its restoration under His divine rule. It must be added that God has allowed Satan some success in his attacks on Jews. Because of their covenant violation, unbelief, and apostasy, Satan has sometimes actually acted as God's executioner to punish them.

Because they will refuse to worship him and especially because they belong to God, the Antichrist will also unleash exceptional fury against those who come to believe in Jesus during the last days. As already noted, those nearest Jerusalem will be in the severest and most immediate danger.

Phuegō (**flee**) is related to the English term *fugitive,* a person who takes flight in order to escape danger. The only hope will be to run for safety, symbolized in the exhortation to flee **Judea** as quickly as possible and take refuge in **the mountains**.

From Zechariah we learn that not every Jew will be successful in the attempt to escape. "'And it will come about in all the land,' declares the Lord, 'that two parts in it will be cut off and perish; but the third will be left in it. And I will bring the third part through the fire, refine them as silver is refined, and test them as gold is tested'" (Zech. 13:8-9a). When the Antichrist moves against the Jews of **Judea** and other parts of Palestine, he will slaughter millions of them, apparently in a short period of time. That slaughter will also be a divine purging of the rebel Jews and the third that are left are the saved, of whom the Lord says, "They will call on My name, and I will answer them; I will say, 'They are My people,' and they will say, 'The Lord is my God'" (v. 9b). The holocaust of that day will surpass every other catastrophe that has "occurred since the beginning of the world until now, nor ever shall" (Matt. 24:21). As noted in the previous chapter, the massacres of Jews by the Romans in A.D. 70 and by the Nazis during the World War II will pale by comparison. Two out of every three Jews in the Holy Land will die under the fury of Satan as he enacts the judgment of God on the rebels of the Jewish nation.

Many Christians will also be slaughtered, not as an act of God's judgment but in acts of ungodly persecution. When the fifth seal of judgment was broken, John "saw underneath the altar the souls of those who had been slain because of the word of God, and because of the testimony which they had maintained; and they cried out with a loud voice, saying, 'How long, O Lord, holy and true, wilt Thou refrain from judging and avenging our blood on those who dwell on the earth?'" (Rev. 6:9-10). Those martyred saints will wonder when the carnage of their brothers and sisters will stop and God will judge and punish their murderers. In response to their cry, "there was given to each of them a white robe; and they were told that they should rest for a little while longer, until the number of their fellow servants and their brethren who were to be killed even as they had been, should be completed also" (v. 11). Through the Antichrist and his other agents, both human and demon, Satan will make all-out war on the saints, butchering all he can find (Rev. 13:7) until his evil hosts are "drunk with the blood of the saints, and with the blood of the witnesses of Jesus" (17:6).

For the saved Jews there will be divine help in fleeing and hiding. John saw Israel, the woman who "gave birth to a son, a male child, who is to rule all the nations with a rod of iron," flee "into the wilderness where she had a place prepared by God, so that there she might be nourished for one thousand two hundred and sixty days." The apostle then saw the archangel "Michael and his angels waging war with the dragon. And the dragon and his angels waged war, and they were not strong enough, and there was no longer a place found for them in heaven. And the great dragon was thrown down, the serpent of old who is called the devil and Satan, who deceives the whole world; he was thrown down to the earth, and his angels were thrown down with him" (Rev. 12:5-9). The 1,260 days is equivalent to three and a half years, the second half of the seven-year Tribulation. During that Great Tribulation, God will provide a place of refuge for those of His people who escape the Antichrist's onslaught.

They will succeed in their flight to **the mountains,** probably to the east and south of Jerusalem, perhaps to the cliff caves around the Dead Sea and in the hills of Moab and Edom. John reports that "the two wings of the great eagle were given to the woman, in order that she might fly into the wilderness to her place, where she was nourished for a time and times and half a time, from the presence of the serpent" (Rev. 12:14). Some modern commentators have suggested that "the great eagle" represents El Al, the official Israeli airline. But it seems more likely that the eagle represents Michael himself, by whose power God's people will be transported to safety.

Our Lord continues the call for urgency, stressing the need for immediate flight by insisting that, for example, a person **who is on the housetop** should **not** even **go down to get the things out that are in his house.** Most Palestinian houses of Jesus' day had outside stairways leading to **the housetop,** where the family often went in the evening to relax and cool off from the work and heat of the day. The person who happens to be on his roof when he hears of the abomination of desolation should not waste even the few minutes required to go back into the

house to retrieve a few precious **things** to take with him into the mountains. No material possession will be worth the risk of the slightest delay. Nor should a person **turn back to get his cloak**. If he is working on the far side of a field and has left **his cloak** in the house or on a fence some distance away, he should leave it there and run.

That will not be the time even for taking a stand for Christ but only for fleeing into His arms, as it were. The time for testimony will be past and, by the word of the Lord Himself, believers' only sensible option will be flight.

It will be an especially tragic and burdensome time for pregnant women, **those who are with child**, and nursing mothers with small **babes**. Women in such conditions will not be able to move fast and will therefore be at greater risk of being captured and killed. An even more horrible prospect, however, will be that of having their unborn **child** slashed in the womb and of their tiny **babes** dashed to pieces before their eyes. Both of those heinous practices were common among the ancient Babylonians and Assyrians and are precisely the judgment that rebellious Israel was promised through Hosea (13:16).

It was by the massacre of hundreds of male Hebrew babies that Satan convinced Pharaoh he could destroy the Israelites in Egypt and by which he convinced Herod he could destroy the Christ child. The Antichrist apparently will employ the same hellish activities during the Great Tribulation. With the Holy Spirit removed and the church raptured, the malevolence of Satan will be unrestrained and untempered.

Although Palestinian winters are mild compared to those in many parts of the world, even slightly inclement weather could be a hindrance when the Antichrist begins his final aggression against God's people. Therefore Jesus said, **Pray that your flight may not be in the winter**.

Those seeking to escape should also pray that they will not have to flee **on the Sabbath,** when legalistic Jews who are not fleeing might try to stone or otherwise impede those whom they believe to be profaning **the Sabbath**—just as their forefathers had sought to stone Jesus for breaking their Sabbath traditions.

Jesus' point was that no possession would be worth the risk of retrieving and no hindrance could be considered small. Because of the imminent unmatched terror, single-minded, undeterred flight will be the only order of the day.

THE PERILS

for then there will be a great tribulation, such as has not occurred since the beginning of the world until now, nor ever shall. And unless those days had been cut short, no life would have been saved; but for the sake of the elect those days shall be cut short.

Then if anyone says to you, "Behold, here is the Christ," or "There He is," do not believe him. For false Christs and false prophets will arise and will show great signs and wonders, so as to mislead, if possible, even the elect. Behold, I have told you in advance. If therefore they say to you, "Behold, He is in the wilderness," do not go forth, or, "Behold, He is in the inner rooms," do not believe them. For just as the lightning comes from the east, and flashes even to the west, so shall the coming of the Son of Man be. Wherever the corpse is, there the vultures will gather. (24:21-28)

Jesus here identifies three more signs of His return, signs that will occur immediately after the abomination of desolation and that will warrant fast flight into the mountains. Those signs will be: severe calamity (vv. 16-22), subtle confusion (vv. 23-27), and sinful corruption (v. 28).

SEVERE CALAMITY

for then there will be a great tribulation, such as has not occurred since the beginning of the world until now, nor ever shall. And unless those days had been cut short, no life would have been saved; but for the sake of the elect those days shall be cut short. (24:21-22)

The abomination of desolation will mark the beginning of the **great tribulation,** the last three and one half years before Christ appears to rule the world from His throne in Jerusalem. That **great tribulation** will be **such as has not occurred since the beginning of the world until now, nor ever shall.** No time or event in the history of Israel fits the description of the holocaust Jesus is here speaking of. The horrifying time is further described in some detail in Revelation 6-16, where the seal, trumpet, and bowl judgments exhibit the escalating intensity of God's wrath upon sinful, rebellious mankind. Both the books of Revelation and of Daniel make clear that the Antichrist will tyrannize the world for "a time, times, and half a time" (Dan. 7:25; 12:7; Rev. 12:14), that is, a year, two years, and a half year, or three and one half years (Rev. 11:2; 13:5). Clearly, the events described by our Lord, by Daniel, and by John must refer to the same great holocaust at the end time, just before the millennial kingdom is established on earth.

God's message for Israel is that things are going to get immeasurably worse before they become better. That nation and its people will suffer treachery, desecration of the rebuilt Temple, indescribable persecution, and brutal slaughter that will be totally unparalleled in history.

And unless those days had been cut short, Jesus went on to say, **no life would have been saved; but for the sake of the elect**

those days shall be cut short. *Koloboō* (**cut short**) can carry the idea of stopping instantly, and that could be the meaning in this context. Since the length of the Great Tribulation is repeatedly stated as being divinely ordained at three and one half years, its length could not be reduced without God's contradicting His own Word. The idea would therefore be that God has predetermined that **those days** of calamity will stop **short** of total destruction.

But since Jesus spoke of **those days** rather than the more general eschatological phrase "that day," it seems that His reference was probably to twenty-four-hour **days.** In that case, God will supernaturally shorten the daylight hours in order to give His fleeing people the added protection of more darkness.

When the sixth judgment seal is broken, there will be "a great earthquake; and the sun [will become] black as sackcloth made of hair, and the whole moon [will become] like blood; and the stars of the sky [will fall] to the earth, as a fig tree casts its unripe figs when shaken by a great wind. And the sky [will be] split apart like a scroll when it is rolled up" (Rev. 6:12-14). During the fourth trumpet judgment "a third of the sun and a third of the moon and a third of the stars [will be] smitten, so that a third of them might be darkened and the day might not shine for a third of it, and the night in the same way" (8:12). During the fifth bowl judgment the kingdom of the beast will be darkened by God's angel (16:10). At least three times during the Great Tribulation the heavenly bodies that give light to the earth will be radically altered in ways that will progressively reduce the daylight until the Antichrist's forces are compelled to operate in total darkness. God will use that darkness **for the sake of the elect,** using it to hide them from their would-be destroyers.

The elect could represent the nation of Israel, which is often referred to in the Old Testament as God's elect, or chosen, people (see, e.g., Isa. 45:4). It could also include those who become Christians during the Tribulation (see Rev. 17:14). Both applications seem appropriate, because God will preserve a redeemed remnant of the nation of Israel as well as some redeemed Gentiles. He will shorten the daylight hours so that the Antichrist cannot complete his massacre of Jews and saints.

It should be noted that this is the first use of the term **elect** in the New Testament, and through it Jesus introduced a new concept concerning those who belong to Him. They have been divinely chosen and called out as His own people and indeed His very own children. And when God chooses people for Himself, He will restructure the entire universe if that becomes necessary to protect them and to fulfill His promises concerning them. (For further discussion of election, see the author's commentary on Ephesians, pp. 10-13.)

Obviously total darkness could not last very long. Not only would nothing grow but little work could be done, and temperatures all across the earth would rapidly drop to unendurable levels. But in that brief time, the anguish from darkness—added to the famine, pestilence, warfare, and other catastrophes—will become so acute that men will gnaw "their tongues because of pain" (Rev. 16:10).

SUBTLE CONFUSION

Then if anyone says to you, "Behold, here is the Christ," or "There He is," do not believe him. For false Christs and false prophets will arise and will show great signs and wonders, so as to mislead, if possible, even the elect. Behold, I have told you in advance. If therefore they say to you, "Behold, He is in the wilderness," do not go forth, or, "Behold, He is in the inner rooms," do not believe them. For just as the lightning comes from the east, and flashes even to the west, so shall the coming of the Son of Man be. (24:23-27)

Those who heed Jesus' advice to flee into the mountains and are protected by God from harm will also be especially vulnerable to false teaching and promises. Having left their homes with only the clothes on their backs, they will not have the least security of material possessions. Many of them will have left families and friends behind and will be strangers to each other.

It seems evident from Jesus' warning here that false teachers will infiltrate the company of those who flee. Those false teachers will be Satan's emissaries who hope to entice Jews and believers away from their refuge and into the hands of Antichrist. They will share his satanic desire to annihilate all Jews and all Christians.

Satan is the father of lies (John 8:44), and since he first tempted Eve, one of his primary weapons has been deceit. As he has done many times in the past and will have already done many times during the Tribulation (see Matt. 24:5), Satan will inspire the appearance of false Christs. The refugees will hear such claims as, **"Behold, here is the Christ," or "There He is."** Some of the false teachers will claim Christ is in their own midst, and others will perhaps claim He is back in Jerusalem or elsewhere in Judea.

Those spurious religious leaders, the **false Christs and false prophets,** will even perform **great signs and wonders,** giving supernatural evidence to support their claims. They will mimic their leader, the Antichrist, who will demonstrate "all power and signs and false wonders" (2 Thess. 2:9). Those **great signs and wonders** will be so awesome and convincing that they would **mislead, if possible, even the elect**.

It is obvious from Jesus' saying, **if possible,** that the Antichrist and his false Christs and prophets will not be able to deceive **the elect.** Satan has never been able to deceive Christians about the identity of their Lord. "My sheep hear My voice," Jesus said, "and I know them, and they follow Me; and I give eternal life to them, and they shall never perish; and no one shall snatch them out of My hand" (John 10:27-28). Once a person comes to know the true Christ through saving faith in Him, he can never be duped by anyone, including Satan himself, into acknowledging a counterfeit Christ.

The **elect** in that day will not be destroyed because God will sovereignly protect them by reordering the entire universe, and they will not be deceived because they will have the Spirit-inspired knowledge of the true Christ within them.

But those protected ones will nevertheless be under verbal assault. Satan will vigorously try to use the turmoil of the times to undermine the confidence of the refugees and to persuade them to follow a false Messiah, who would immediately betray them to the Antichrist once they were outside God's sanctuary. With the world falling apart, the stars falling, the sun and moon being radically reduced in light, millions dying from disease and starvation, and thousands of their fellow countrymen having been mercilessly slaughtered, the refugees will be emotionally drained and utterly vulnerable to the subterfuge of the false Christ's and prophets, were it not for God's gracious provision.

The fugitives will have access to Jesus' words recorded here. **Behold, I have told you in advance,** He said, speaking to them prophetically across the intervening centuries. **If therefore they say to you, "Behold, He is in the wilderness," do not go forth, or, "Behold, He is in the inner rooms," do not believe them.** "Beware of all claims about My identity or whereabouts," He was saying. "Pay attention only to what I am teaching you now, not to anything else you will hear or see in that day, no matter how authentic and compelling the message and accompanying signs may seem to be."

How, then, will those protected ones know when the true Lord really does appear to establish His kingdom? How will they distinguish His true coming from the many counterfeits? **For just as the lightning comes from the east, and flashes even to the west, so shall the coming of the Son of Man be,** Jesus assures them. His coming will not be stretched over a long period of time but will be quick, sudden, public, visible, universal, and unimaginably glorious. As the astonished disciples stood staring up into the sky after Jesus had ascended into the clouds, the two angels said to them, "This Jesus, who has been taken up from you into heaven, will come in just the same way as you have watched Him go into heaven" (Acts 1:11). An angel said to John in his vision on Patmos, "Behold, He is coming with the clouds, and every eye will see

Him, even those who pierced Him" (Rev. 1:7). Christ's appearance not only will be unmistakable to those in hiding on that day but to every human being on earth, including His most implacable enemies.

For those who belong to Him, Christ's coming will be marvelous deliverance, but for those who have resisted and opposed Him it will be the ultimate day of tragedy. "The kings of the earth and the great men and the commanders and the rich and the strong and every slave and free man, [will hide] themselves in the caves and among the rocks of the mountains; and they [will say] to the mountains and to the rocks, 'Fall on us and hide us from the presence of Him who sits on the throne, and from the wrath of the Lamb'" (Rev. 6:15-16).

Until the Lord appears in that predicted and unquestionable way, those who are hiding should remain where they are. After the true Christ appears, however, His people and His enemies will exchange places, as it were. Those who had been hiding in the mountains and caves will be released to freedom and blessing, and their would-be captors and murderers will themselves seek refuge, as the righteous wrath of God replaces and punishes the evil wrath of man and of Satan.

SINFUL CORRUPTION

Wherever the corpse is, there the vultures will gather. (24:28)

That statement was possibly a common proverb in Palestine, as it could be in many parts of the world. Even in highly civilized modern societies, **vultures** circling over the carcass of a dead animal are not an uncommon sight in the countryside, especially in remote areas.

By the end of the Great Tribulation, the world will have filled up its full measure of sin and will have spiritually decayed into a wretched and virtually lifeless carcass. As it lies like a dead animal in the wilderness, Christ will appear to make final disposition of that **corpse** through His righteous and terrible judgment.

The Signs of Christ's Coming—part 5 The Sign of the Son of Man

(24:29-31)

But immediately after the tribulation of those days the sun will be darkened, and the moon will not give its light, and the stars will fall from the sky, and the powers of the heavens will be shaken, and then the sign of the Son of Man will appear in the sky, and then all the tribes of the earth will mourn, and they will see the Son of Man coming on the clouds of the sky with power and great glory. And He will send forth His angels with a great trumpet and they will gather together His elect from the four winds, from one end of the sky to the other. (24:29-31)

In clear, concise, straightforward terms the Lord Himself describes what will be the most momentous event of all time, His return to earth in divine glory. Throughout the history of the church, believers have looked forward with earnest anticipation to the coming again of their Lord Jesus Christ. "For the grace of God has appeared, bringing salvation to all men," Paul wrote to Titus, "instructing us to deny ungodliness and worldly desires and to live sensibly, righteously and godly in the present age, looking for the blessed hope and the appearing of the glory of our great God and Savior, Christ Jesus" (Titus 2:11-13). Believers are continually to live righteous lives, motivated in great part by their continual expectation of the Lord's return.

Much of the world is familiar with the circumstances and features of Christ's first coming, such as His birth in Bethlehem, the magi guided by the star and bringing Him gifts, and the shepherds in the fields hearing the angel choir. Many people have heard something about His teachings and miracles and His crucifixion and resurrection. But even many professed Christians are little acquainted with what Scripture teaches about His second coming.

In Matthew 24:29-31, Jesus gives a vivid picture of the moment of His appearing, the sign of all signs of His coming again and of the end of the age, about which the disciples had just inquired (v. 3). Within these three verses Jesus presents five key truths about this supreme sign of His appearance: the sequence of events (v. 29a), the scene in the heavens (v. 29b), the sign in the sky (v. 30a), the strength and glory of the Lord (v. 30b), and the selection by the angels (v. 31).

THE SEQUENCE OF EVENTS

But immediately after the tribulation of those days (24:29a)

Jesus states unequivocally that the central sign of His return will occur **immediately after the tribulation of those days,** that is, at the end of the Great Tribulation (v. 21), the second three and a half years of the seven-year Tribulation period.

The context makes clear that **those days** refer to the preceding days of **tribulation** that Jesus has just been describing (vv. 4-28). They are the final days of unsurpassed tragedy (v. 21) that will mark the end of the present world age, days during which sin will be unrestrained on the earth, the church will have been raptured, and Satan will have been allowed almost unrestricted freedom in his final but futile attempt to usurp rule of the earth for himself. With the abomination of desolation (v. 15) Satan will inaugurate the Great Tribulation, desecrating the restored Temple and slaughtering every Jew and Christian he can lay hands on. The Lord's coming to reign will take place at the conclusion of this time of **tribulation**.

As was noted in the last chapter, during **those days,** two out of three Jews in Palestine will be slaughtered, only a third being preserved (Zech. 13:8-9). One hundred forty-four thousand of them will be saved to evangelize the world, 12,000 from each of the twelve tribes of Israel (Rev. 7:4; cf. 14:1-5). Those Jews will be supernaturally sealed and protected by God, and no effort by the Antichrist or his collaborators will be able to destroy them.

THE SCENE IN THE HEAVENS

the sun will be darkened, and the moon will not give its light, and

the stars will fall from the sky, and the powers of the heavens will be shaken, (24:29b)

Jesus here describes the heavenly setting of His appearance. The whole universe will begin to disintegrate, apparently with great rapidity. The **sun . . . and the moon** will cease to give **light,** and **the stars will** even **fall from the sky.** From Luke's parallel account we learn that there will be "dismay among nations, in perplexity at the roaring of the sea and the waves, men fainting from fear and the expectation of the things which are coming upon the world; for the power of the heavens will be shaken" (Luke 21:25-26).

The events will be so calamitous that men will faint from absolute terror. The Greek term behind "faint" means to expire or stop breathing, indicating that people will literally die of fright. No hurricane, tornado, tidal wave, earthquake, volcanic eruption, or combination of those natural disasters in history will have approached the extreme disruption of those end-time days.

During that time **the powers of the heavens will be shaken** by Jesus Christ, the One who "upholds all things by the word of His power" (Heb. 1:3). Just as He created everything, He also sustains everything, and without His full sustaining power, gravity will weaken and the orbits of the stars and planets will fluctuate. Astronomers can predict coming stellar events centuries in advance only because of the absolute consistency of the divinely ordered and uniform laws that control the operation of the stars and planets. But when the Lord withdraws the least of His power from the universe, nothing in it will function normally, and every aspect of the physical world will be disrupted beyond imagination. All the forces of energy, here called **powers of the heavens,** which hold everything in space constant, will be in dysfunction. The heavenly bodies will career helter-skelter through space, and all navigation, whether stellar, solar, magnetic, or gyroscopic, will be futile because all stable reference points and uniform natural forces will have ceased to exist or else become unreliable.

The earth is held together by the power of God, and when that power is diminished, the resulting chaos will be inconceivable. Speculations such as the one just cited, no matter how scientifically derived, can only remotely approximate what the actual situation will be like.

But just as the withdrawal of a small part of God's sustaining power will cause such pervasive chaos and destruction, so will His supernatural control of that disintegration prevent the total destruction of the earth. His sovereign power will preserve and restore it and its people for the establishing of His millennial kingdom.

Some seven centuries before Christ, Isaiah had predicted the end-time devastation:

Wail, for the day of the Lord is near! It will come as destruction from the Almighty. Therefore all hands will fall limp, and every man's heart will melt. And they will be terrified, pains and anguish will take hold of them; they will writhe like a woman in labor, they will look at one another in astonishment, their faces aflame. Behold, the day of the Lord is coming, cruel, with fury and burning anger, to make the land a desolation; and He will exterminate its sinners from it. For the stars of heaven and their constellations will not flash forth their light; the sun will be dark when it rises, and the moon will not shed its light. Thus I will punish the world for its evil, and the wicked for their iniquity; I will also put an end to the arrogance of the proud, and abase the haughtiness of the ruthless. I will make mortal man scarcer than pure gold, and mankind than the gold of Ophir. (Isa. 13:6-12)

Although that prophecy applied immediately to the destruction of Babylon (v. 1; cf. Dan. 5:30-31), which occurred in 539 B.C., those events described by Isaiah are obviously far too universal and catastrophic to have related entirely to Babylon. The devastation of ancient Babylon was but a microcosm of what will happen to the whole universe in the end time.

Isaiah continues to depict events that could in no way describe the relatively mild and confined judgment on Babylon by the Medo-Persians (v. 17).

Therefore I shall make the heavens tremble, and the earth will be shaken from its place at the fury of the Lord of hosts in the day of His burning anger. And it will be that like a hunted gazelle, or like sheep with none to gather them, they will each turn to his own people, and each one flee to his own land. Anyone who is found will be thrust through, and anyone who is captured will fall by the sword. Their little ones also will be dashed to pieces before their eyes; their houses will be plundered and their wives ravished. (vv. 13-16)

That series of catastrophes is clearly worldwide, affecting all nations and all people.

Isaiah later presents still further details of end-time destruction:

Draw near, O nations, to hear; and listen, O peoples! Let the earth and all it contains hear, and the world and all that springs from it. For the Lord's indignation is against all the nations, and His wrath against all their armies; He has utterly destroyed them, He has given them over to slaughter. So their slain will be thrown out, and their corpses will give off their stench, and the mountains will be drenched with their blood. And all the host of heaven will wear away, and the sky will be rolled up like a scroll; all their hosts will also wither away as a leaf withers from the vine, or as one withers from the fig tree. For My sword is satiated in heaven, behold it shall descend for judgment upon Edom, and upon the people whom I have devoted to destruction. (34:1-5)

It is from those passages in Isaiah that Jesus' teaching and John's vision were drawn. Edom is the southernmost region to which the great battle of Armageddon will extend. The total area involved will be two hundred miles long (Rev. 14:20), stretching from Bozrah, the capital of Edom, in the south (see Isa. 34:6) to the hills of Lebanon, just north of the Valley of Armageddon.

About a hundred years before Isaiah, the prophet Joel wrote of a vast, incredibly devastating locust plague that foreshadowed the disasters of the end time, the coming "day of the Lord" (Joel 2:1). The locusts marched across the land like a destroying army. "Before them the earth quakes, the heavens tremble, the sun and the moon grow dark, and the stars lose their brightness. And the Lord utters His voice before His army; surely His camp is very great, for strong is He who carries out His word. The day of the Lord is indeed great and very awesome, and who can endure it?" (vv. 10-11; cf. vv. 4-5). The blotting out of natural light by those billions of insects illustrates the vastly greater darkening of the heavens by the direct intervention of God in the end time. "And I will display wonders in the sky and on the earth," the Lord continued to declare through Joel; "blood, fire, and columns of smoke. The sun will be turned into darkness, and the moon into blood, before the great and awesome day of the Lord comes" (vv. 30-31; cf. Rev. 6:12-13).

The prophet Haggai wrote, "For thus says the Lord of hosts, 'Once more in a little while, I am going to shake the heavens and the earth, the sea also and the dry land. And I will shake all the nations; and they will come with the wealth of all nations; and I will fill this house with glory,'" (Hag. 2:6-7). That is the time, Paul says, that the cursed universe is anxiously awaiting. "For the creation was subjected to futility, not of its own will, but because of Him who subjected it, in hope that the creation itself also will be set free from its slavery to corruption into the freedom of the glory of the children of God. For we know that the whole creation groans and suffers the pains of childbirth together until now" (Rom. 8:19-22).

THE SIGN IN THE SKY

and then the sign of the Son of Man will appear in the sky, and then all the tribes of the earth will mourn, and they will see the Son of Man coming on the clouds of the sky (24:30a)

Next Jesus describes the supreme **sign** of His "coming, and of the end of the age," about which the disciples had asked a few moments earlier (v. 3). He had already mentioned a number of lesser, though astounding, signs that would precede His coming, including the sign of the abomination of desolation that would precipitate them (vv. 4-15). But the sign of signs will be **the Son of Man** Himself, who **will appear in the sky**.

Many of the early church Fathers, such as Chrysostom, Cyril of Jerusalem, and Origen, imagined that this sign would be an enormous blazing cross, visible to the entire world, that would pierce the total darkness then shrouding the world. Other interpreters have suggested it will be the Shekinah glory of the Lord's presence returning to earth. It is likely that the Shekinah glory will be involved, as the unveiled Christ Jesus makes His appearance. But the sign is not just His glory; it is Christ Himself, **the Son of Man**, who **will appear in the sky**.

The sign of should be translated as a Greek subjective genitive, indicating that **the sign** will not simply relate to or point to **the Son of Man** (as with an objective genitive) but will indeed *be* **the Son of Man**. In other words, Jesus Himself will be the supreme and final sign of His coming. In the midst of the world's unrelieved blackness—physical, emotional, and spiritual—Jesus Christ will manifest Himself in His infinite and undiminished glory and righteousness. Just as the destructive catastrophes of the Great Tribulation will be utterly unparalleled (v. 21), so will be this manifestation of the glory and power of Christ.

The sight of Him in blazing glory will be so unbearably fearful that rebellious mankind will cry out for the mountains and rocks to fall on them to hide them "from the presence of Him who sits on the throne" (Rev. 6:16). But instead of being driven to the Lord in reverent repentance, they will flee from Him in continued rejection, cursing and blaspheming His name (16:9).

Some people, however, will be brought to their knees in brokenness, acknowledging their need of God's forgiveness and redemption. When they see **the Son of Man** in His glory and righteousness, they will finally confess their own wickedness and unrighteousness. There will be some from **all the tribes of the earth** who **will mourn** over their rebellion against God and their rejection of His Son. Having heard the gospel proclaimed (v. 14; Rev. 14:6), those people will turn from and **mourn** over their sin and receive Christ as Lord and Savior.

Among the repentant will be many Jews. Through Zechariah the Lord promised His people: "And I will pour out on the house of David and on the inhabitants of Jerusalem, the Spirit of grace and of supplication, so that they will look on Me whom they have pierced; and they will mourn for Him, as one mourns for an only son, and they will weep bitterly over Him, like the bitter weeping over a first-born. In that day there will be great mourning in Jerusalem" (Zech. 12:10-11). Having realized that they have rejected their Messiah, they will turn to Him in faith, casting themselves on His mercy. At that time the "fulness of the Gentiles [will have] come in; and thus all Israel will be saved; just as it is written, 'The Deliverer will come from Zion, He will remove ungodliness from Jacob'" (Rom. 11:25-26; cf. Isa. 59:20).

Just as Jesus ascended to heaven in the clouds, He will also return "in just the same way" (Acts 1:11). When He appears at His second coming, **the Son of Man** will come **on the clouds of the sky** (cf. Matt. 26:64; Mark 13:26; Luke 21:27). In his night visions Daniel beheld "with the clouds of heaven One like a Son of Man . . . coming, and He came up to the Ancient of Days and was presented before Him. And to Him was given dominion, glory and a kingdom, that all the peoples, nations, and men of every language might serve Him" (Dan. 7:13-14). In his vision on Patmos, John also saw Jesus "coming with the clouds." Then, he said, "every eye will see Him, even those who pierced Him; and all the tribes of the earth will mourn over Him" (Rev. 1:7).

The **clouds** into which Jesus ascended and on which He will return seem to be distinctive. The psalmist wrote of God's using clouds as His chariot (Ps. 104:3), and Isaiah pictures "the Lord . . . riding on a swift cloud" (Isa. 19:1). But whether **the clouds of the sky** on which Jesus appears are natural or supernatural, His use of them at that time will be extraordinary and unique. In the midst of black chaos, He will use those **clouds** to manifest Himself in His complete divine majesty.

Speaking of the end time, Zechariah wrote, "And it will come about in that day that there will be no light; the luminaries will dwindle. For it will be a unique day which is known to the Lord, neither day nor night, but it will come about that at evening time there will be light" (Zech. 14:6-7; cf. Jer. 30:7). At the end of that insufferable period of darkness and anguish, the light will come, not by the reillumination of the sun, moon, and stars but by the brilliance of Christ's own divine glory, which will later light the eternal new heaven and new earth. In that day there will be "no need of the sun or of the moon to shine upon [the new Jerusalem], for the glory of God [will] illumine it, and its lamp [will be] the Lamb" (Rev. 21:23), "and there shall no longer be any night; and they shall not have need of the light of a lamp nor the light of the sun, because the Lord God shall illumine them" (22:5).

Although all believers before the Tribulation will have died or been raptured (1 Thess. 1:10; Rev. 3:10), they will witness Christ's glorious appearance on earth. They will, in fact, "be revealed with Him in glory" (Col. 3:4), having already been wondrously and appropriately clothed as the bride of Christ for the marriage supper of the Lamb "in fine linen, bright and clean," which is "the righteous acts of the saints" (Rev. 19:8). When the church is taken into the presence of the Lord just before the

Tribulation, she will fellowship with Him at that supper during the seven-year cataclysm on earth. Also present will be the Old Testament saints, "those who are invited to the marriage supper of the Lamb" (v. 9). As Christ's bride, the church will not need an invitation to the wedding feast; but everyone who believed in God before Christ's incarnation will be graciously invited to participate.

It seems that the church, and perhaps the Old Testament believers as well, will probably be included in "the armies which are in heaven, clothed in fine linen, white and clean," which follow Christ "on white horses" (Rev. 19:14). Instead of looking up to the sky as Christ appears, as everyone on earth will be doing, the saints of all ages will be looking down from the sky as they return to earth with Him.

While unbelievers on earth are dying from fright, disease, or from the Antichrist's carnage, those who are coming to salvation and who escape being killed during the Tribulation will have great reason to rejoice at Christ's appearing. In his account of the Olivet discourse Luke reports that Jesus says to those surviving saints: "When these things begin to take place, straighten up and lift up your heads, because your redemption is drawing near" (Luke 21:28).

THE STRENGTH AND GLORY OF THE LORD

with power and great glory. (24:30b)

As already seen in the cataclysmic events that will shake the heavens and earth at the end time, Christ's return will be accompanied by incredible demonstrations of His divine **power** over the universe, including Satan and his demons. He will demonstrate His power to protect His chosen people, His power to redeem the elect, His power to restore the devastated earth, and His power to establish His rule on earth.

In His great **power** the Lord will conquer and destroy all His enemies, including ungodly men who followed and worshiped the beast, by casting them into the lake of fire (Rev. 19:20). He will also "make an end of sin, to make atonement for iniquity, to bring in everlasting righteousness" (Dan. 9:24). In the restored and purified earth the destructive nature and instincts of wild animals will be radically reversed to make them docile and harmless. No animal will attack or molest another animal or any human being, and the carnivorous will become vegetarian.

> The wolf will dwell with the lamb, and the leopard will lie down with the kid, and the calf and the young lion and the fatling together; and a little boy will lead them. Also the cow and the bear will graze; their young will lie down together; and the lion will eat straw like the ox. And the nursing

child will play by the hole of the cobra, and the weaned child will put his hand on the viper's den. They will not hurt or destroy in all My holy mountain, for the earth will be full of the knowledge of the Lord as the waters cover the sea. (Isa. 11:6-9)

By His **power** Christ will eliminate drought, floods, crop failures, and starvation. "And it will come about in that day," declared Zechariah, "that living waters will flow out of Jerusalem, half of them toward the eastern sea and the other half toward the western sea; it will be in summer as well as in winter" (Zech. 14:8).

Along with those overwhelming demonstrations of Christ's divine power will be equally spectacular manifestations of His **great glory.** "When the Son of Man comes in His glory, and all the angels with Him, then He will sit on His glorious throne" (Matt. 25:31).

Adam and Eve had a glimpse of God's glory as they walked and talked with Him in the Garden of Eden. The children of Israel had glimpses of it in the pillar of fire that led them through the wilderness, and Isaiah had a glimpse of it in his heavenly vision. Peter, James, and John had a glimpse of Christ's glory on the mount of transfiguration, when "His face shone like the sun, and His garments became as white as light" (Matt. 17:2). Many years later, Peter was still awed by that experience, declaring, "We were eyewitnesses of His majesty. For when He received honor and glory from God the Father, such an utterance as this was made to Him by the Majestic Glory, 'This is My beloved Son with whom I am well-pleased'—and we ourselves heard this utterance made from heaven when we were with Him on the holy mountain" (2 Pet. 1:16-18).

But no human being has yet seen the full unveiled glory of God in Christ, and no one will ever see it until Jesus appears at His second coming and all mankind sees Him at once. At that time no one will have to ask who He is, for He will be perfectly recognized by every human being on earth. There will be no mistaking His identity then as there was when He came in His incarnation. All mankind will see the Son of Man in His full **glory** and immediately recognize Him as God—though all will not honor Him as God.

THE SELECTION BY THE ANGELS

And He will send forth His angels with a great trumpet and they will gather together His elect from the four winds, from one end of the sky to the other. (24:31)

After the unrepentant ungodly have been judged and destroyed, and the repentant mourners have trusted in Christ and been saved, **He will send forth His angels with a great trumpet and they will**

57

gather together His elect. Among their other responsibilities, **angels** are God's gatherers. In that day they will be used to gather unbelievers for judgment and punishment (Matt. 13:41, 49) and believers for reward and glory.

In ancient Israel, as in many ancient lands, the trumpet was used to announce important convocations, and the sound of the angel's **great trumpet** will signal the assembling all of God's saints on earth, from wherever they might be, **from the four winds, from one end of the sky to the other.** Many of them will doubtless still be hiding in caves, fearful for their lives. The gathered ones will include the 144,000 Jewish witnesses, their converts, and the converts of the angelic preachers. They will include the Old Testament saints, gathered out of their graves and joined with their redeemed spirits. Those will all be assembled together before Christ and ushered into the glory of His eternal kingdom.

The Signs of Christ's Coming—part 6 The Final Generation (24:32-35)

Now learn the parable from the fig tree: when its branch has already become tender, and puts forth its leaves, you know that summer is near; even so you too, when you see all these things, recognize that He is near, right at the door. Truly I say to you, this generation will not pass away until all these things take place. Heaven and earth will pass away, but My words shall not pass away. (24:32-35)

The blessed hope of every Christian is the return of his Lord and Savior, Jesus Christ. "In the future there is laid up for me the crown of righteousness," Paul wrote, "which the Lord, the righteous Judge, will award to me on that day; and not only to me, but also to all who have loved His appearing" (2 Tim. 4:8). God's Word instructs believers not only "to deny ungodliness and worldly desires and to live sensibly, righteously and godly in the present age," but also to be "looking for the blessed hope and the appearing of the glory of our great God and Savior, Christ Jesus" (Titus 2:12-13). Nothing in this world, Paul says, can compare "with the glory that is to be revealed to us" (Rom. 8:18), "the freedom of the glory of the children of God" (v. 21), "the redemption of our body" (v. 23), and "the revelation of our Lord Jesus Christ" (1 Cor. 1:7).

Believers anticipate the day when they will "all be changed, in a moment, in the twinkling of an eye" and their perishable and mortal bodies put on the imperishable and immortal (1 Cor. 15:51-53), when "death is swallowed up in victory" (v. 54), and when "the saints will judge the world" (6:2). They look forward to the day when they will be "absent from the body and . . . at home with the Lord" (2 Cor. 5:8) and when the church will be presented to Christ as His pure virgin bride (11:2). They look forward to the day when they will see Him just as He is and become like Him (1 John 3:2).

The theme of Christ's second coming permeates the New Testament and is the great anticipatory reality of Christian living. The Lord's return will be as real and as historical an event as His first coming. Believers look *back* to the moment of saving faith in Christ, when their souls were redeemed. They look *forward* to the return of Christ, when their bodies will be redeemed and they will enter into the promised fullness of salvation. In that day Satan will be defeated, the curse lifted, Christ worshiped, the creation liberated and restored, sin and death conquered, and the saints glorified.

Among the many passages in Scripture that describe the Lord's coming again, Matthew 24-25 is unequaled because it is the message from Jesus' own lips about His return. After He told them of the series of signs that will precede His coming, including the supreme sign of His personal appearance, the disciples no doubt were still wondering about the time when those dramatic signs would begin, about what their duration would be, and about how long it would be from the sign in heaven of His appearing to His establishing the kingdom.

In Matthew 24:32-35 Jesus gives another parable about a fig tree. The parable summarizes and illustrates what He had just said and acts as a transition to His answer to the disciples' question about when His coming would be (see v. 3). In this parable and its explanation, four elements can be discerned: an uncomplicated analogy (v. 32), an un-mistakable application (vv. 33-34), an unprecedented alteration (v. 35a), and an unchanging authority (v. 35b).

AN UNCOMPLICATED ANALOGY

Now learn the parable from the fig tree: when its branch has already become tender, and puts forth its leaves, you know that summer is near; (24:32)

Parables had a two-fold purpose in Jesus' ministry. When unexplained, they concealed truth; when explained, they revealed truth. When Jesus gave a parable to the multitudes or to the unbelieving religious leaders without also giving an explanation, it was a riddle to them. When He gave a parable to His disciples and explained it, it was a vivid illustration that made a truth clear and understandable.

When the disciples asked Jesus, "Why do You speak to them [the multitudes] in parables?" He replied, "To you it has been granted to know the mysteries of the kingdom of heaven, but to them it has not been granted. . . . Therefore I speak to them in parables; because while seeing they do not see, and while hearing they do not hear, nor do they understand" (Matt. 13:10-11,13). Then He said to the disciples, "But blessed are your eyes, because they see; and your ears, because they hear," and He proceeded to tell them the meaning of the parable of the sower (vv. 16-23).

In light of the fact that Jesus' parables were given for the sake of helping the disciples understand His teaching, it is evident that He told **the parable from the fig tree** to give them further light about His second coming.

Unfortunately, this parable, like many others, has often been made confusing and misleading by those who view it as a complicated allegory rather than a simple analogy. Some interpreters, for instance, contend that the fig tree represents Israel. A popular version of that view is that the budding of the fig tree refers to Israel's becoming a political state in 1948. Because Jesus does not identify the fig tree as Israel, that meaning would have been totally obscured to the disciples and to every other believer who lived before the twentieth century. In that view, Jesus would not have been employing the parable to clarify His meaning but to conceal it. Some who hold to that interpretation suggest that the budding of leaves on the fig tree represents a spiritual revival in the new state of Israel. But modern Israel, though very much alive physically, is one of the most secular nations on earth. As a state, it is very resistant, if not hostile, to the gospel.

This parable is simple and uncomplicated, and in the context of what the Lord had just been saying, its meaning should not be hard to discern. Palestine had an abundance of fig trees, which were not only grown commercially but were also found in many family yards, for the sake of the delicious fruit as well as for the shade they provided during the hot summer months.

Jews were used to the fig tree's functioning as an illustration. Jotham used it in his story shouted to the inhabitants of Shechem from the top of Mount Gerizim (Judg. 9:10-11); Jeremiah saw two baskets of figs in his vision after Nebuchadnezzar took captives from Judah to Babylon (Jer. 24:1-10); Hosea used it as a figure in his prophecy about Israel (Hos. 9:10); and Joel used a splintered fig tree to illustrate the devastation of Judah by a plague of locusts (Joel 1:4-7).

Few figures would have been better known to the disciples than that of **the fig tree,** which Jesus Himself had used on numerous other occasions as a teaching aid (see Matt. 7:16; 21:19; Luke 13:6-9).

Manthanō (**learn**) means to genuinely understand and accept a teaching, to accept it as true and to apply it in one's life. It was sometimes used of acquiring a life-long habit. Paul declared that he had "learned [*manthanō*] to be content in whatever circumstances" he was in (Phil. 4:11). That sort of learning is much more than mere head knowledge; it involves genuine acceptance of a truth and determination to live a life consistent with it. Jesus wanted the disciples to **learn** in their inmost beings what He was teaching, to understand and receive it with regard to its great importance.

He reminded them of a commonly known fact about a fig tree: **when its branch has already become tender, and puts forth its leaves, you know that summer is near.** In other words, when the sap begins to flow into the branches, making them **tender,** and new **leaves** appear on the tree, **you know that summer is near.** Even children knew that a budding fig tree meant it was spring and that **summer** would soon follow, when the ripened figs would be harvested.

Throughout the gospel of Matthew, the figure of harvest represents judgment, the time of separating unbelievers from believers and of condemning the unbelievers to judgment. John the Baptist spoke of the Lord's coming with "His winnowing fork . . . in His hand [to] thoroughly clear His threshing floor; and He will gather His wheat into the barn, but He will burn up the chaff with unquenchable fire" (Matt. 3:12; cf. v. 10). As He looked out over the multitudes in Galilee who came out to see Him, Jesus said to the disciples, "The harvest is plentiful, but the workers are few. Therefore beseech the Lord of the harvest to send out workers into His harvest" (Matt. 9:37-38). Without saving faith in Him, those thousands of people, and millions of others like them, were destined to judgment. That field of people was ripening for God's judgment just as a field of wheat or a budding fig tree ripens for the harvesters. In the parable of the wheat and tares Jesus spoke of the farmer's allowing the good wheat and the bad tares to grow together until harvest time, when the tares could be accurately identified and destroyed (Matt. 13:30).

In all of those instances, the harvest symbolizes a time of rewarding the righteous and punishing the wicked. In this present parable of the fig tree Jesus was simply illustrating to the disciples that, when the signs He had just been describing begin to transpire, the time of His return will be very near.

AN UNMISTAKABLE APPLICATION

even so you too, when you see all these things, recognize that He is near, right at the door. Truly I say to you, this generation will not pass away until all these things take place. (24:33-34)

When the context is studied carefully, Jesus' application of the parable is as unmistakable as its analogy is uncomplicated. **All these things** can only refer to what He has been talking about—the birth pains (vv. 4-14), the abomination of desolation (v. 15), the need to flee because of the impending perils (vv. 16-28), and the catastrophic upheaval of the universe (v. 29). Those **things** will indicate that **He is near**, just as the budding fig tree indicates that summer, the harvest time, is near.

In the NASB text, **He** translates the Greek verb *estin*, which literally means "it is," as the term is most commonly rendered. In Luke's account Jesus says, "the kingdom of God is near" (21:31), which is consistent with the reading of "it" (KJV) in Matthew 24:33. The supreme event of the last day, and the event about which the disciples had queried Jesus (v. 3), was the Lord's personal coming to establish His kingdom. The basic idea is therefore the same, whether the pronoun is **He** or "it" or whether the antecedent is the appearance of Christ, Christ Himself, or Christ's kingdom. When Christ's appearing **is near**, He Himself will be near and His kingdom will be **near**. When those signs occur, the divine King will be **right at the door**, knocking and ready to come in.

Giving further application, Jesus said, **Truly I say to you, this generation will not pass away until all these things take place.** As explained in chapter 2 of this volume, **this generation** refers to the generation living during the end time. The signs of Matthew 24-25 will be experienced within one **generation**, the generation living when Christ returns.

This generation cannot refer to the disciples' generation, as many interpreters have maintained. Some who hold that view believe Jesus simply made a human guess and was mistaken. "After all," they argue, "didn't Jesus say that 'of that hour no one knows, not even the angels in heaven, nor the Son, but the Father alone'?" (Mark 13:32). But that is a spurious argument. Jesus does not here specify the historical time of His coming but rather the events that will identify it. And it is one thing to recognize that it was in God's sovereign plan for the Son not to have certain knowledge during His incarnation, so that He did not know the exact timetable and knew He did not know it. It is quite another thing to contend that He was capable of bad guesses and liable to propagating an idea He had no idea was wrong or questionable. If Jesus was wrong about the time of His coming, He could have been wrong about any or every other thing He taught. His temporary, divinely-imposed limitations during His time of humiliation in no way imply that what He taught may have been less than perfectly truthful or authoritative.

Some of those who believe Jesus was speaking of the disciples' generation claim the terrible events He mentions here refer to the destruction of Jerusalem by the Romans in A.D. 70. But as we have noted before, the events of Matthew 24 are much too universal and cataclysmic to represent the dreadful but geographically limited devastation of

Jerusalem. That did not involve "famines and earthquakes" (Matt. 24:7), believers' being "hated by all nations" (v. 9), false Christs and false prophets (vv. 5, 11), the preaching of the gospel to the whole world (v. 14), or the abomination of desolation (v. 15). Nor were the sun darkened, the moon extinguished, or the stars dislodged from their places (v. 29). Most important of all, Jesus certainly did not appear then. It is strange logic to argue that Jesus could accurately foretell the destruction of Jerusalem some forty years hence but be mistaken about His returning at that time. Or if, as some suggest, the teaching here was merely symbolic and allegorical, with the limited destruction of Jerusalem representing the vastly greater destruction of the end time, what event in A.D. 70 could possibly have symbolized Jesus' return, which is the main subject of the discourse?

Those who hold that the fig tree is Israel usually affirm that **this generation** refers to the Jewish people, indicating they would **not pass away** as a race **until these things take place.** That idea is true, and the perpetuity of the Jews is clearly taught elsewhere in Scripture, but it does not seem to fit this context. All Jews firmly believed in God's promise of an everlasting kingdom of David, and for Jesus to have meant that the Jews would survive until the Messiah ushered in His kingdom would have been superfluous and pointless. And if Jesus had intended that meaning, He could easily have referred to the Jews as "My people," "God's people," or the like. To allude to them as **this generation** would seem obtuse and confusing.

Another interpretation is that **this generation** refers to the Christ-rejecting people of Jesus' day. In that case Jesus would have been saying that ungodly, rebellious mankind would survive until the Messiah's coming. *Genea* (**generation**) was sometimes used to represent a particular kind of people. In the Septuagint (Greek Old Testament) the term is used to refer to a righteous people as well as an unrighteous people. But again, although that interpretation is linguistically possible, it does not fit the context and also would have been superfluous and pointless, because no Jew doubted that many unbelieving, ungodly people would be alive to be judged when the Messiah came. In the minds of most Jews, the essential work of the Messiah would be to deliver Israel from its ungodly oppressors. He could hardly judge the nations and put His enemies under His feet if they had already been eradicated.

We are left then with the simple and most reasonable interpretation that the leaves of the fig tree represent the birth pains and the other signs of His coming Jesus has mentioned in this chapter and that **this generation** refers to the people living at the end time who will view those signs. In partial answer to the disciples' question concerning the *when* of His coming, Jesus said that it will occur very soon after those signs are witnessed, before the **generation** who sees them has time to **pass away.** He is speaking to the same prophetically distant "you" He has been addressing throughout the chapter (see vv. 4, 6, 9, 15, 25). As mentioned previously, Jesus was speaking as some of the Old Testament prophets often spoke, as if they were standing directly before future generations (see, e.g., Isa. 33:17-24; 66:10-14; Zech. 9:9).

Matthew 24:34 is an explanation of the parable of the fig tree. The idea is that, just as the budding of fig leaves means it is not long until summer, so the **generation** alive when the signs occur will not have long to wait for Christ's appearance. Those who witness the birth pains will witness the birth. As the books of Daniel and Revelation make clear, the total time of the Tribulation will be but seven years, and the period of the Great Tribulation, in which the signs will appear, will only be three and a half years (cf. Dan. 12:7; Rev. 11:2-3; 12:6).

Among those who believe that **this generation** refers to those who will be alive during the end time, there are two basic views as to the makeup of that future people. Posttribulationists, who hold that the rapture will take place *after* the Tribulation, believe that **this generation** could include the redeemed presently living if the Tribulation were to occur during their lifetimes. In other words, any believer alive at the beginning of the Tribulation would be subject to its calamities, including possible martyrdom. Only those believers who survive that great holocaust would therefore be raptured, after enduring seven years of hell on earth. Then they would almost immediately come back to earth with the Lord when He appears with His saints to establish the millennial kingdom.

Pretribulationists, on the other hand, maintain that the church, defined as believers of this present age, will be raptured just before the Tribulation. **This generation** could not, in this view, include any of the redeemed alive now. For many reasons, the pretribulation view seems most faithful to New Testament teaching.

First of all, chapters 2-3 of Revelation speak of the church on earth, and chapters 4-5 speak of the church in heaven. But beginning with chapter 6, which introduces the Tribulation, there is no further mention of the church until chapter 18.

Second, there is the total absence of New Testament instruction to the church as to how it should endure and conduct itself during the Tribulation.

Third, if it is to occur at the end of the Tribulation, the rapture would seem to be pointless. The church not only would not be spared the torments of the Tribulation but would almost immediately turn around, as it were, and come back to earth with Christ. Otherwise, who would be left on earth during the Millennium? The unredeemed will have been destroyed, and the returning saints from heaven will have spiritual bodies and will not be married or have families (Matt. 22:30). Yet human life will carry on during the Millennium, with children being born just as before.

Fourth, Jesus' promise to the church at Philadelphia is more than a promise to that local body of believers and more than a promise to keep them from ordinary testing. That "hour of testing" will "come upon the whole world," and it will test all those "who dwell upon the earth." The Lord promises that the whole church, those who "have kept the word of My perseverance," will be kept from the perils and agonies of the Tribulation (Rev. 3:10).

Fifth, Jesus promised those who believe in Him that He was going to prepare places for all of them in His Father's house and that He would come again and receive them to Himself. According to the posttribulation view, He would not be taking believers back to heaven to dwell with Him but simply meeting them quickly in the air and returning with them immediately to earth. Yet He said He was preparing a place for His people to dwell, not just to visit briefly.

Sixth, The first 69 weeks of the 70-week period of Daniel's prophecy lasted from "the issuing of a decree to restore and rebuild Jerusalem," the decree issued by King Artaxerxes in 445 B.C. (see Neh. 2:5-6), "until Messiah the Prince" (Dan. 9:25), that is, the time of Christ. As mentioned in chapter 3 of this volume, it has been calculated that exactly 483 years (69 weeks of years) elapsed from that decree of Artaxerxes until Jesus' entry into Jerusalem on Palm Sunday, when He was acclaimed Messiah and King by the multitude. That prophecy of Daniel was given to and about Israel, and it seems inappropriate to involve the church in the last week (the seven-year Tribulation) when it clearly was not involved in the first 69.

Finally, if the rapture will not occur until after the Tribulation, Paul's words of assurance to the Thessalonian church beg for relevance. Some of the Thessalonian Christians thought their believing loved ones who had died would miss the rapture. Paul therefore encouraged them with the words:

> We do not want you to be uninformed, brethren, about those who are asleep, that you may not grieve, as do the rest who have no hope. For if we believe that Jesus died and rose again, even so God will bring with Him those who have fallen asleep in Jesus. For this we say to you by the word of the Lord, that we who are alive, and remain until the coming of the Lord, shall not precede those who have fallen asleep. For the Lord Himself will descend from heaven with a shout, with the voice of the archangel, and with the trumpet of God; and the dead in Christ shall rise first. Then we who are alive and remain shall be caught up together with them in the

clouds to meet the Lord in the air, and thus we shall always be with the Lord. (1 Thess. 4:13-17)

Had the early church been expecting to endure the Tribulation rather than enjoy the rapture, they would have rejoiced that their loved ones had already died and thereby escaped that horrible trial. But they were obviously looking forward to something joyous, which they thought their departed loved ones and friends would not experience. They were not looking forward to the Antichrist but to Christ. They were not looking for the ordeal of the Tribulation but for the glory of the rapture. They were not looking for the terror of the Antichrist's appearing but for the blessed hope of Christ's appearing.

This generation will therefore be composed of Jews and Gentiles who are alive at the rapture but are not taken up because they do not know the Lord Jesus Christ. Among that **generation,** however, will be many who will later come to salvation during the Tribulation through the witness of the divinely called and protected 144,000 Jewish believers (Rev. 7:38) and the supernatural preaching of the angelic messenger (14:6-7).

AN UNPRECEDENTED ALTERATION

Heaven and earth will pass away, (24:35a)

Jesus says explicitly that both **heaven and earth will pass away.** That expression first appears in 5:18, where it is not primarily used as a prophecy but as an analogy to express the enduring quality of the Word of God. It is used similarly in this text. The universe will fail, but what Jesus has just said will not fail to come to complete fulfillment. That analogical use of this phrase does not, however, preclude a directly prophetic intent. It is clearly predicted in the Old and New Testaments that the universe will be dramatically affected in the divine judgment of God. But that event will occur a thousand years after the return of Christ, when **heaven and earth** as we now know them will cease to exist (cf. 2 Pet. 3:10; Rev. 21:1).

AN UNCHANGING AUTHORITY

but My words shall not pass away. (24:35b)

Finally, Jesus declared, although the heaven and the earth will pass away, **My words shall** never **pass away.** On another occasion He said, "It is easier for heaven and earth to pass away than for one stroke of a letter of the Law," that is, His Word, "to fail" (Luke 16:17). It is not possible for the Word of God to be broken (John 10:35), including what Jesus says here about the end time. The psalmist established the same great truth when he wrote that Scripture is "clean, enduring forever" (Ps. 19:9). Whatever is touched by sin must pass away. The Word is untouched! It is like silver refined seven times in a furnace of fire—utterly pure (Ps. 12:6).

The Signs of Christ's Coming—part 7 Ready or Not

(24:36-51)

But of that day and hour no one knows, not even the angels of heaven, nor the Son, but the Father alone. For the coming of the Son of Man will be just like the days of Noah. For as in those days which were before the flood they were eating and drinking, they were marrying and giving in marriage, until the day that Noah entered the ark, and they did not understand until the flood came and took them all away, so shall the coming of the Son of Man be. Then there shall be two men in the field; one will be taken, and one will be left. Two women will be grinding at the mill; one will be taken, and one will be left. Therefore be on the alert, for you do not know which day your Lord is coming. But be sure of this, that if the head of the house had known at what time of the night the thief was coming, he would have been on the alert and would not have allowed his house to be broken into. For this reason you be ready too; for the Son of Man is coming at an hour when you do not think He will.

Who then is the faithful and sensible slave whom his master put in charge of his household to give them their food at the proper time? Blessed is that slave whom his master finds so doing when he comes. Truly I say to you, that he will put him in charge of all his possessions. But if that evil slave says in his heart, "My

master in not coming for a long time," and shall begin to beat his fellow slaves and eat and drink with drunkards; the master of that slave will come on a day when he does not expect him and at an hour which he does not know, and shall cut him in pieces and assign him a place with the hypocrites; weeping shall be there and the gnashing of teeth. (24:36-51)

The familiar expression "Here I come, ready or not" could well be applied to Jesus' second coming, because He is coming according to the sovereign plan of God, with no regard for worldwide or individual readiness. Jesus is coming when He is coming, because the when and how of His return have long since been predetermined in the sovereign wisdom of God.

In response to the disciples' question, "Tell us, when will these things be, and what will be the sign of Your coming, and of the end of the age?" (24:3), Jesus told them of the birth pains that would immediately precede His coming (vv. 4-28), of the abomination of desolation (v. 15), which would precipitate those signs, and of the supreme sign of His own appearing on the clouds of heaven (v. 30). Now He gives them a partial answer to the "when" part of the question.

Although there will be observable, worldwide, and unmistakable indications of His coming just before it occurs, the exact time will not be revealed in advance. **Of that day and hour no one knows,** Jesus declared categorically. The signs He had just been describing will be conclusive proof that His arrival is very near. Once they have begun, the *general* time period of His return will be known, because one of the key purposes of the signs will be to make it known. But even during those sign-days the precise **day and hour** of Jesus' appearing will not be known, a truth He reiterates several times in this Olivet discourse (see 24:42, 44, 50; 25:13).

As has been noted, the books of Daniel and Revelation both make clear that the full Tribulation will last seven years and that the second part of it, the Great Tribulation, will last three and a half years (Dan. 7:25; 9:27; 12:7; Rev. 11:2-3; 12:14; 13:5). Then, "immediately after the tribulation of those days," Jesus said, "the Son of Man [will come] on the clouds of the sky with power and great glory" (Matt. 24:29-30). Precisely *how* is not immediately said.

Daniel and Revelation also speak of an expanded period of 1,290 days (Dan. 12:11; Rev. 12:6), 30 days more than the basic 1,260 of the Great Tribulation. Daniel also mentions a 1,335-day period (Dan. 12:12), adding another 45 days to make a total addition of 75. As suggested in chapter 3 of this volume, it seems that the best explanation for those additional days is that they will cover the time when the Messiah descends to the Mount of Olives, creates the great valley in which the nations of the world will be judged, and executes that judgment (see Zech. 14:45; Matt. 25:31-46).

Nevertheless, even with all those indisputable signs and precisely designated periods, the exact **day and hour** will not be known by any human beings, not even Tribulation believers, in advance. Although the Lord gives no reason for their not knowing, it is not difficult to imagine some of the problems that such knowledge would cause. For one thing, if unbelievers knew the precise time of Christ's arrival, they would be tempted to put off receiving Him as Lord and Savior until the last moment, thinking they could make the decision any time they wanted before He actually is scheduled to appear.

But even if they planned to wait until the precise date and hour of Christ's appearing, they would not know if they would live until that time. Like the rich farmer (Luke 12:16-20), they will have no guarantee of the length of their lives and therefore have no guarantee they will still be alive when Christ appears. Although the *generation* living when the signs begin will not pass away until Christ returns (Matt. 24:34), many individual members of that generation will pass away, some by natural causes and a large percentage at the hand of the Antichrist.

Even if they knew the precise time of Christ's appearing and were certain they would live until then, they would be fooling themselves to think they could simply receive Him before that time. The fact that they will have put off trusting in Christ for as long as they have will be certain evidence they have no sincere desire to follow Him as Lord and Savior. If the indescribable perils of the Tribulation will not persuade them to turn to the Lord, the knowledge of His exact arrival time certainly would not.

As far as believers are concerned, knowledge of that specific time might also make them careless, causing them to withdraw and become spiritually sedentary, thinking it would be pointless to make plans for serving the Lord or to make further effort to win the lost. No one, believer or unbeliever, could think or function normally knowing the exact **day and hour** of Christ's coming.

Neither will the supernatural world know the precise time, not **even the angels of heaven.** Although the righteous angels enjoy intimacy with God, hovering around His throne to do His bidding (Isa. 6:2-7) and continually beholding His face (Matt. 18:10), they are not privy to this secret. The angels will be directly and actively involved in the end time as God's agents to separate the saved from the unsaved (see Matt. 13:41, 49), but for His own reasons God the Father will not reveal in advance exactly when He will call them into that service.

Still more amazingly, not even **the Son** knew at the time He spoke these words or at any other time during His incarnation. Although He was fully God as well as fully man (John 1:1, 14), Christ voluntarily restricted His use of certain divine attributes when He became flesh.

"Although He existed in the form of God, [He] did not regard equality with God a thing to be grasped," that is, to be held onto during His humanness (Phil. 2:6). It was not that He lost any divine attributes but that He voluntarily laid aside the use of some of them and would not manifest those attributes except as directed by His Father (John 4:34; 5:30; 6:38).

Jesus demonstrated His divine omniscience on many occasions. "He did not need anyone to bear witness concerning man for He Himself knew what was in man" (John 2:25). When, for example, Nicodemus came to Him at night, Jesus already knew what he was thinking and answered his question before it was asked (John 3:13).

But there were certain self-imposed restrictions in His human knowledge. He told the disciples, "All things that I have heard from My Father I have made known to you" (John 15:15). Jesus obediently restricted His knowledge to those things that the Father wanted Him to know during His earthly days of humanity. The Father revealed certain things to the Son as He reveals them to all men—through the Scripture, through the Father's working in and through His life, and through the physical manifestations of God's power and glory (see Rom. 1:19-20). Jesus learned much of His earthly knowledge just as every human being learns, and it is for that reason that He was able to keep "increasing in wisdom" (Luke 2:52). In addition to those ways, some truths were revealed to the Son directly by the Father. But in every case Jesus' human knowledge was limited to what His heavenly Father provided.

Therefore, even on this last day before His arrest, **the Son** did not know the precise day and hour He would return to earth at His second coming. During Christ's incarnation, **the Father alone** exercised unrestricted divine omniscience.

It seems probable that Christ regained full divine knowledge after the resurrection, as implied in His introduction to the Great Commission: "All authority has been given to Me in heaven and on earth" (Matt. 28:18). Just prior to His ascension, He told the disciples, "It is not for you to know times or epochs which the Father has fixed by His own authority" (Acts 1:7). He repeats the truth that the disciples would not be told the time of His appearing, but He did not exclude His own knowledge, as He did in the Olivet discourse.

The three attitudes Jesus mentions in Matthew 24:37-51 are specifically addressed to the generation (Matt. 24:34) that will be alive during the Tribulation and that will witness the signs described in verses 4-29. Those attitudes are: alertness (vv. 37-42), readiness (vv. 43-44), and faithfulness (vv. 45-51).

ALERTNESS

For the coming of the Son of Man will be just like the days of

Noah. For as in those days which were before the flood they were eating and drinking, they were marrying and giving in marriage, until the day that Noah entered the ark, and they did not understand until the flood came and took them all away, so shall the coming of the Son of Man be. Then there shall be two men in the field; one will be taken, and one will be left. Two women will be grinding at the mill; one will be taken, and one will be left. Therefore be on the alert, for you do not know which day your Lord is coming. (24:37-42)

Jesus used the Flood to illustrate the point He was making about **the coming of the Son of Man,** namely, that the attitude that prevailed during **the days of Noah . . . before the flood** will also characterize most people living during the end time just before Christ returns. They will not be expecting His coming and will not care about it. Despite the perilous signs and wonders, they will simply be unconcerned about the things of the Lord, especially the prospect of His imminent return to judge them.

Many people doubtless will try to explain the extraordinary end-time phenomena on a scientific and rational basis, expecting to discover a natural cause for the cataclysms. Like their counterparts today, they will look everywhere for answers except to the Word of God.

At Jesus' first coming, most men refused to recognize Him for who He was. He healed every sort of disease, cast out demons, made water into wine, stilled a raging storm, and raised the dead, but even most of His own people refused to believe in Him. In fact the Jewish religious leaders were so determined to discredit Jesus that they accused Him of casting out demons in the power of Satan (Matt. 12:24).

Sinful, materialistic, hypocritical, godless mankind is willfully blind to God's truth, no matter how compelling that truth may be. And when God's truth exposes their wickedness, they make every effort to oppose and condemn it.

On one occasion "the Pharisees and Sadducees came up" to Jesus, "and testing Him asked Him to show them a sign from heaven. But He answered and said to them, 'When it is evening, you say, "It will be fair weather, for the sky is red." And in the morning, "There will be a storm today, for the sky is red and threatening." Do you know how to discern the appearance of the sky, but cannot discern the signs of the times?' " (Matt. 16:1-3). By that time in His ministry the Lord had performed hundreds, perhaps thousands, of miracles, all of which testified to His divinity and His messiahship, yet those religious leaders refused to acknowledge Him. Because their hearts were determinedly set against Jesus, no sign could have brought them to belief. He therefore said to them, "An evil and adulterous generation seeks after a sign; and a sign will not be given it, except the sign of Jonah" (v. 4). As Jesus explained on an earlier occasion, the sign of Jonah was His resurrection from the dead (12:39-40). That sign did not convince unbelievers, either. Just as most of their forefathers had done, they shut their minds to God's Word and God's messengers, even ignoring the teaching and miracles of the very Son of God. Worse even than ignore Him, they put Him to death.

During the time of the Tribulation, mankind will be hardened to sin and ungodliness as never before in history. As evil men get worse and worse (2 Tim. 3:13), the world then becomes spiritually darker and even physically darker. Unbelieving people will more intensely indulge their sins and more vehemently oppose God's truth and God's people. During the Tribulation the Holy Spirit will be removed from the earth, and evil and Satan will be unrestrained (2 Thess. 2:6-7). During the fifth trumpet judgment, demons bound in the bottomless pit will be unleashed on the earth to wreak unprecedented torment on unbelieving mankind, being forbidden to harm God's people (Rev. 9:1-5).

As people run amok in sin and every form of debauchery and ungodliness, they will become more and more impervious to God's truth and resentful of His standards of righteousness. They will be so vile, wretched, and preoccupied with sex, drugs, alcohol, materialism, and pleasure seeking that they will believe every explanation for the end-time signs except the one given in Scripture. Rather than turning to God in repentance, they will curse Him (Rev. 9:21).

In the days of Noah before the Flood, **they were eating and drinking, they were marrying and giving in marriage.** While Noah built the ark, he also preached (2 Pet. 2:5), but the people were just as unconcerned about his preaching as about the ark he was building, thinking both were meaningless and absurd. They laughed when he spoke of the coming flood. They had never seen rain, much less a flood, because until that time the earth was apparently covered by a vapor canopy that provided all the moisture necessary for life to flourish. Because they had never seen such a calamity, they discounted the idea that it could happen. They therefore went about their daily routines of **eating and drinking** and of **marrying and giving in marriage.** It was business as usual until the day **Noah entered the ark** and it started to rain.

Even when his prediction began to be fulfilled before their eyes, they did not take his warning to heart. Noah had built and preached for 120 years, yet without having the slightest impact on anyone outside his immediate family. The people were so untouched by God's truth that **they did not understand** their perilous situation **until the flood came and took them all away** into a godless eternity. **Flood** translates *kataklusmos,* which means deluge or washing away, and is the term from which the English *cataclysm* is derived. Only after it was too late did the people of that generation **understand** their tragic destiny.

That is precisely the attitude and response that will prevail before **the coming of the Son of man.** The perilous signs, the abomination of desolation, the disruption of the heavenly bodies, and the preaching of God's witnesses during the Tribulation will have no effect on the majority of men. They will see God's signs but attribute them to natural causes or to supernatural causes apart from God. They will hear His Word, in one instance supernaturally preached worldwide by an angel (Rev. 15:6-7), but they will respond with disdain or indifference. They will heed neither warnings nor appeals from God up until the very moment **the Son of Man** appears to confront them in righteous judgment.

During the Tribulation there will be multitudes won to Christ (Rev. 7:9-14), including the 144,000 Jewish witnesses who will preach His gospel (Rev. 7:1-8), and there will be marvelous revival in the nation of Israel (Rom. 11:26). But that time will be dominated not by belief but by unbelief, not by holiness but by wickedness, not by godliness but by ungodliness. It will be epitomized by secularism and false religion, even as most of the world is today, but to an immeasurably worse degree.

Like the people of Noah's day, the generation of the Tribulation will be warned and warned and warned again. Some of them will have been warned many times before the Tribulation, while the church is still on earth proclaiming the gospel.

When the Son of Man finally appears in His second-coming judgment, **then there shall be two men in the field; one will be taken, and one will be left. Two women will be grinding at the mill; one will be taken, and one will be left.** Jesus is giving a figure parallel to the unbelievers of Noah's day being **taken** away by the judgment through the Flood. When He returns, **one will be taken** to judgment and the other **will be left** to enter the kingdom. This is the same separation described in the next chapter by the figures of sheep and goats (25:32-46). The ones **left** will be Christ's sheep, His redeemed people whom He will preserve to reign with Him during the Millennium.

But even until the very end, as Peter declared in his sermon at Pentecost, just "before the great and glorious day of the Lord shall come . . . it shall be that everyone who calls on the name of the Lord shall be saved" (Acts 2:20-21). In that final moment when the King comes to establish His kingdom, some people will turn to Christ in sincere faith and be redeemed. They will be set apart as the Lord's sheep by the angels and will inherit the kingdom prepared for them.

Therefore be on the alert, Jesus said, **for you do not know which day your Lord is coming.** The phrase **be on the alert** translates a present imperative, indicating a call for continual expectancy.

When the Lord comes, the ungodly will be swept away, having forever lost their opportunity for salvation. Just as believers today do not know at what time the Lord is coming to take them to Himself in the rapture, the generation alive during the Tribulation will not know the exact time of His appearing to judge the ungodly and to establish His kingdom.

Malachi envisioned believers in the last day apparently discussing among themselves the possibility that they would inadvertently and mistakenly be separated out with the wicked and be condemned. But "the Lord gave attention and heard it, and a book of remembrance was written before Him for those who fear the Lord and who esteem His name. 'And they will be Mine,' says the Lord of hosts, 'on the day that I prepare My own possession, and I will spare them as a man spares his own son who serves him.' So you will again distinguish between the righteous and the wicked, between one who serves God and one who does not serve Him" (Mal. 3:16-18).

Peter declared,

> For if God did not spare angels when they sinned, but cast them into hell and committed them to pits of darkness, reserved for judgment; and did not spare the ancient world, but preserved Noah, a preacher of righteousness, with seven others, when He brought a flood upon the world of the ungodly; and if He condemned the cities of Sodom and Gomorrah to destruction by reducing them to ashes, having made them an example to those who would live ungodly thereafter; and if He rescued righteous Lot, oppressed by the sensual conduct of unprincipled men (for by what he saw and heard that righteous man, while living among them, felt his righteous soul tormented day after day with their lawless deeds), then the Lord knows how to rescue the godly from temptation [or trial], and to keep the unrighteous under punishment for the day of judgment. (2 Pet. 2:4-9)

Christians at that time must be alert, even though they will be secure and have no cause for dread.

READINESS

But be sure of this, that if the head of the house had known at what time of the night the thief was coming, he would have been on the alert and would not have allowed his house to be broken into. For this reason you be ready too; for the Son of Man is coming at an hour when you do not think He will. (24:43-44)

Be sure of this translates what could be either a Greek imperative or an indicative. As an imperative it would be a form of command, but that idea seems inappropriate here, because Jesus was simply stating the obvious, a truism. As an indicative it would be a statement of fact as a reminder. "As everyone knows," He was saying, **"if the head of the**

house had known at what time of the night the thief was coming, he would have been on the alert and would not have allowed his house to be broken into." No sane thief would announce his intention of robbing a house, and no sane **head of the house** who knew in advance **at what time of the night the thief was coming** would fail to be **on the alert** in order to prevent **his house** from being **broken into**.

The generation living during the Tribulation is specifically told they will not know the exact time of Jesus' appearing, but they are informed in detail as to what the signs immediately preceding it will be. In other words, to carry out the figure Jesus uses here, they will know with absolute certainty that **the thief** will be breaking into **the house** sometime very soon and that they should be prepared accordingly.

It goes without saying that Jesus was not comparing Himself in character to a thief but was comparing His coming to the stealth and unexpectedness of a thief's coming. The New Testament frequently compares the second coming to a thief's coming (Luke 12:35-40; 1 Thess. 5:2; 2 Pet. 3:10; Rev. 3:3; 16:15), for the obvious reason that, as Jesus here points out, a thief never tries to rob a place where he knows he is expected, and certainly not at the exact time he is expected.

In one sense, however, Jesus will come in the role as well as with the unexpectedness of a thief. As far as the ungodly are concerned, He will come and take away everything they have, all the things they have cherished and trusted in instead of Him.

As already noted, it seems impossible that most people in that day will not be expecting Jesus' coming. In light of the absolute destructiveness and horror of the signs of the end time they will witness, how could they not turn to God for help and mercy? How could they possibly attribute those things simply to natural causes? Yet most of them will be so overwhelmingly blinded by sin and self-will that no amount of evidence will cause them to seek God. Instead, hostility toward God will reach a fever pitch never known before on earth, not even during the times of Noah. **For this reason, you be ready too,** Jesus said, just as Noah and his family were ready.

In this context, being **ready** seems to refer primarily to being saved, of being spiritually prepared to meet Christ as Lord and King rather than as Judge. As Jesus had already warned (Matt. 24:37-42), everyone in the end time should be expectantly alert for His appearing, and as He mentions in verses 45-51, faithfulness to Him by those who are already saved is commanded. But the indispensable preparation for His coming, apart from which expectancy will be pointless and faithfulness will be impossible, is the preparation of salvation, of being redeemed through the blood of Christ. Otherwise a person will be ready only for judgment and damnation.

The Lord reemphasizes the fact that no one on earth will know exactly when He is coming, not even by an accidental right guess. He proclaims categorically: **The Son of Man is coming at an hour when you do not think He will.** In divine fury and glory, **the Son of Man** will come in total surprise to every human being. Even believers who are expectantly and faithfully ready for His coming will nevertheless be astonished when He actually arrives. Their readiness will enable them to meet the Lord with gladness and without shame, but it will not provide advance knowledge of His precise arrival time.

Luke reports a similar warning Jesus gave on another occasion. "Be dressed in readiness, and keep your lamps alight," He said. "And be like men who are waiting for their master when he returns from the wedding feast, so that they may immediately open the door to him when he comes and knocks. Blessed are those slaves whom the master shall find on the alert when he comes; truly I say to you, that he will gird himself to serve, and have them recline at the table, and will come up and wait on them" (Luke 12:35-37). When the Lord returns, those who are ready not only will find themselves in their Lord's gracious presence but will be served personally by His own divine hand.

FAITHFULNESS

Who then is the faithful and sensible slave whom his master put in charge of his household to give them their food at the proper time? Blessed is that slave whom his master finds so doing when he comes. Truly I say to you, that he will put him in charge of all his possessions. But if that evil slave says in his heart, "My master in not coming for a long time," and shall begin to beat his fellow slaves and eat and drink with drunkards; the master of that slave will come on a day when he does not expect him and at an hour which he does not know, and shall cut him in pieces and assign him a place with the hypocrites; weeping shall be there and the gnashing of teeth. (24:45-51)

Jesus now presents another analogy to reinforce His point, using the familiar imagery of a trusted **slave whom his master put in charge of** feeding the entire **household.** The particular responsibility of the **slave** is incidental to Jesus' point, which is that every believer is a **slave** of Jesus Christ and therefore obligated to serve Him in every way. Every believer has been given a divine stewardship and responsibility in the work of Christ on earth, and in that stewardship he is to be **faithful and sensible.** His life, breath, energy, talents, spiritual gifts, and every other good thing he has are trusts from God to be used in His service and to His glory.

Blessed is that slave, Jesus said, **whom his master finds so**

doing when he comes. Truly I say to you, that he will put him in charge of all his possessions. Here Jesus is obviously addressing believers, those who have submitted to Him as Savior and Lord, as divine **master.** The believer who is found faithful to the Lord in what he has been given will be given **charge of all** of the Lord's **possessions,** having inherited the absolute fullness of the kingdom of God as a fellow heir of Jesus Christ (Rom. 8:17). Not only that, but "He who overcomes," Jesus said, "I will grant to him to sit down with Me on My throne, as I also overcame and sat down with My Father on His throne" (Rev. 3:21).

Unbelievers, represented by the **evil slave,** will also be held responsible for what they do with their stewardship from God. During the end time, some unbelievers will remain openly sinful and rebellious against God, caring nothing for His truth or His mercy. Others will be aware of their lost condition and of their need of a Savior but will put off believing, thinking they will have time after fulfilling their own selfish interests but before He comes in judgment. They will say by their lives if not by their words, **My master is not coming for a long time.**

Jesus is teaching that every person in the world holds his life, possessions, and abilities in trust from God, whether or not he acknowledges that trust or even acknowledges God. He will therefore be held accountable by his Creator for how he uses what he has been given. That truth is seen in the parable of the king recorded in Matthew 18:23-34. Even the prodigal son of Luke 15 demonstrates that an unbeliever is squandering God-given stewardship.

The evil activities Jesus then mentions, the beating of **fellow slaves** and eating and drinking **with drunkards,** are not meant to characterize every unbeliever during the Tribulation. But those activities reflect the attitude many of them will have. Because they think the Lord will not come **for a long time,** they will feel free to indulge themselves in whatever sins and pleasures they desire.

But **the master of that slave will come on a day when he does not expect him and at an hour which he does not know.** In this case the **master** will not come as Savior and King to bless and to reward but will come as Judge and Executioner to condemn and to destroy. He will **cut** the unbelieving slave **in pieces and assign him a place with the hypocrites** in eternal fire.

The phrase **cut . . . in pieces** is from *dichotomeō* and literally means to cut into two parts. It is used in that strict sense in the Greek translation of the Old Testament in regard to the preparation of an animal sacrifice (Ex. 29:17). To Jews it would therefore carry the unmistakable idea of destruction and death.

The fact that such persons will be assigned along **with the hypocrites** suggests that they were not hypocrites. Just as today, many people in the end time will be open and honest about their unbelief, even wearing such honesty as a badge of intellectual and moral integrity. But honest unbelievers are just as lost as **hypocrites** who pretend to have faith. They will go to the same place as the religious phonies they feel superior to and despise.

When He appears, the same resplendent glory and power (see Matt. 24:30) that will draw His own people to Him in loving gratitude will repel most unbelievers in hateful indignation. For the former it will be the time of final reception and redemption; for the latter it will be the time of final rejection and judgment.

All unbelievers—those who completely reject the Lord and those who think one day they will trust in Him, those who are honest in their unbelief and those who are hypocritical in their faith—will suffer the same destiny of hell. In that place there will be **weeping . . . and the gnashing of teeth,** figures representing inconsolable grief and unremitting torment.

The thrust of Jesus' warning is not simply to inform unbelievers about the horror of facing an eternal hell but to use that dreadful prospect as a motive for believing in Him in order to escape it. His appeal is to believe while there is opportunity, rather than foolishly wait for a supposedly more propitious time that might never come and might not be taken advantage of if it did come.

In his commentary on this passage, William Barclay relates the following story to illustrate the danger of spiritual procrastination:

> There is a fable which tells of three apprentice devils who were coming to this earth to finish their apprenticeship. They were talking to Satan, the chief of the devils, about their plans to tempt and to ruin men. The first said, "I will tell them that there is no God." Satan said, "That will not delude many, for they know that there is a God." The second said, "I will tell men that there is no hell." Satan answered, "You will deceive no one that way; men know even now that there is a hell for sin." The third said, "I will tell men that there is no hurry." "Go," said Satan, "and you will ruin men by the thousand." The most dangerous of all delusions is that there is plenty of time. (*The Gospel of Matthew,* vol. 2 [Philadelphia: Westminster, 1975], p. 317)

Why, one wonders, is Christ waiting so long to come again? First of all, He is waiting for evil to run its course. In his vision on Patmos, John saw an angel come "out of the temple, crying out with a loud voice to Him who sat on the cloud, 'Put in your sickle and reap, because the hour to reap has come, because the harvest of the earth is ripe.' And He who sat on the cloud swung His sickle over the earth; and the earth was reaped" (Rev. 14:15-16). The imagery depicts a field whose crop is completely ready for harvesting, here indicating the harvest of final judgment on unbelieving mankind. Not until the angel notifies Him that the harvest is ripe, will Christ come to earth and execute judgment. God's sovereign purpose is to allow sin to reach its full evil limits, to run its complete destructive course.

Second, the Lord is waiting for all those whose names are written in the Lamb's book of life to be saved. There must be the coming in of "the fulness of the Gentiles" (Rom. 11:25), the gathering in of Gentile saints into the church during the present age. It is also necessary for "all Israel [to] be saved" (v. 26), for all the believing sons of Abraham to be brought into the kingdom by faith in their Messiah and King.

Peter declares, "Do not let this one fact escape your notice, beloved, that with the Lord one day is as a thousand years, and a thousand years as one day. The Lord is not slow about His promise, as some count slowness, but is patient toward you, not wishing for any to perish but for all to come to repentance" (2 Pet. 3:8-9). What seems to human beings to be a long period of time is but a moment to God, and they should not rely on their own finite perceptions of time to judge the delay in fulfilling His promises. It is not that God could not act in judgment at any time He chose, but that in His sovereign patience and love He is allowing the fullest time possible for men to repent and come to Him in faith.

But because He has chosen to delay judgment for what has already been thousands of years, some people in the last days will mockingly declare, "Where is the promise of His coming? For ever since the fathers fell asleep, all continues just as it was from the beginning of creation" (2 Pet. 3:3-4). Like scientific uniformitarians, who believe that natural laws have always and will always operate in exactly the same way they operate now, latter-day religious scoffers will assume that because God has not yet judged the world He never will. "It escapes their notice," however, Peter goes on to say, "that by the word of God the heavens existed long ago and the earth was formed out of water and by water, through which the world at that time was destroyed, being flooded with water" (vv. 5-6). The mockers will foolishly ignore the most catastrophic upheaval the world has yet experienced, in which every human being on earth was killed except for Noah and his family.

In Matthew 24-25 Jesus addresses those who will be alive during the generation of the Tribulation (Matthew 24:34). But believers today should be prepared for the Lord's coming in the rapture of the church, in which the Lord takes them to heaven, just as believers in the end time should be prepared for His appearing in power and glory to establish the millennial kingdom.

To the church at Rome Paul wrote these sobering words:

> [You know] the time, that it is already the hour for you to awaken from sleep; for now salvation is nearer to us than when we believed. The night is

almost gone, and the day is at hand. Let us therefore lay aside the deeds of darkness and put on the armor of light. Let us behave properly as in the day, not in carousing and drunkenness, not in sexual promiscuity and sensuality, not in strife and jealousy. But put on the Lord Jesus Christ, and make no provision for the flesh in regard to its lusts. (Rom. 13:11-14)

Paul commended the first generation church in Corinth for "awaiting eagerly the revelation of our Lord Jesus Christ" (1 Cor. 1:7), and he reminded the Philippian believers that "our citizenship is in heaven, from which also we eagerly wait for a Savior, the Lord Jesus Christ" (Phil. 3:20). The writer of Hebrews admonished believers, "Let us consider how to stimulate one another to love and good deeds, not forsaking our own assembling together, as is the habit of some, but encouraging one another; and all the more, as you see the day drawing near" (Heb. 10:24-25).

James's counsel is, "Be patient; strengthen your hearts, for the coming of the Lord is at hand" (James 5:8). Peter wrote, "The end of all things is at hand; therefore, be of sound judgment and sober spirit for the purpose of prayer" (1 Pet. 4:7), and John declared, "Children, it is the last hour; and just as you heard that antichrist is coming, even now many antichrists have arisen; from this we know that it is the last hour" (1 John 2:18). And the last words spoken directly by Jesus in Scripture are, "Yes, I am coming quickly" (Rev. 22:20).

The Signs of Christ's Coming—part 8 The Fate of the Unprepared (Waiting for Christ's Return)

(25:1-13)

Then the kingdom of heaven will be comparable to ten virgins, who took their lamps, and went out to meet the bridegroom. And five of them were foolish, and five were prudent. For when the foolish took their lamps, they took no oil with them, but the prudent took oil in flasks along with their lamps. Now while the bridegroom was delaying, they all got drowsy and began to sleep. But at midnight there was a shout, "Behold, the bridegroom! Come out to meet him." Then all those virgins rose, and trimmed their lamps. And the foolish said to the prudent, "Give us some of your oil, for our lamps are going out." But the prudent answered, saying, "No, there will not be enough for us and you too; go instead to the dealers and buy some for yourselves." And while they were going away to make the purchase, the bridegroom came, and those who were ready went in with him to the wedding feast; and the door was shut. And later the other virgins also came, saying, "Lord, lord, open up for us." But he answered and said, "Truly I say to you, I do not know you." Be on the alert then, for you do not know the day nor the hour. (25:1-13)

Here Jesus gives another of the several warning parables in the

Olivet discourse (see 24:43, 45-51) that illustrate His repeated and specific declarations that the exact time of His second coming will not be known in advance. It will be at a time when it is least expected (24:36, 42, 44, 50; 25:13). As discussed earlier, the general time will be known by those who heed the birth pain signs He has given (24:4-29), because that is the purpose of those signs (v. 33). But the precise time of His personal appearing in power and great glory (24:30) will not be known in advance even by the heavenly angels. It was not known by Jesus Himself during His incarnation (v. 36).

The parable of the ten virgins is given to accentuate the incalculable importance of being spiritually prepared to meet Christ when He returns to earth, because after He appears, unbelievers who are then alive will have no further chance for salvation.

The setting for this parable was a typical Jewish wedding ceremony. In Israel, as well as in most other parts of the ancient Near East, a wedding was the most celebrated social event. Virtually everyone in a village or in a neighborhood community of a large city would be involved as a participant or as a guest. It was a time of great happiness and festivity.

A Jewish marriage consisted of three parts, the first of which was the engagement. Most often arranged by the fathers of the bride and groom, the engagement amounted to a contract of marriage in which the couple had little, if any, direct involvement. The second stage was the betrothal, the marriage ceremony at which the bride and groom exchanged vows in the presence of family and friends. At that point the couple was considered married, and their relationship could be broken only by formal divorce, just as if they had been married for many years. If the husband happened to die during the betrothal, the bride was considered a widow, although the marriage had not been physically consummated and the two had never lived together. The betrothal could last for many months, sometimes a year, during which time the groom would establish himself in a business, trade, or farming and would make provision for a place for the couple to live.

At the end of the betrothal period the wedding feast would be held, and it was in the feast and its related celebrations that the entire community became involved. This festivity, which could last a week, began with the groom's coming with his groomsmen to the bride's house, where her bridesmaids were waiting with her. Together the bride and groom and their attendants would then parade through the streets proclaiming that the wedding feast was about to begin. The procession was generally begun at night, and lamps or torches were used by the wedding party to illumine their way and to attract attention.

At the end of the feast period, a close friend of the groom, who acted much like a best man, would take the hand of the bride and place it in the hand of the groom, and the couple would for the first time be left alone together. The marriage would be consummated and the couple would henceforth live together in their new home. It was that third part of the marriage rite that Jesus used as the framework for this parable.

As the parable unfolds, Jesus focuses first on the bridesmaids, then on the bridegroom, and finally on the warning that the parable is given to reinforce.

THE BRIDESMAIDS

Then the kingdom of heaven will be comparable to ten virgins, who took their lamps, and went out to meet the bridegroom. And five of them were foolish, and five were prudent. For when the foolish took their lamps, they took no oil with them, but the prudent took oil in flasks along with their lamps. Now while the bridegroom was delaying, they all got drowsy and began to sleep. (25:1-5)

The world was not ready to accept Christ when He came to earth the first time, although His coming had been clearly and repeatedly predicted by the Old Testament prophets. The Messiah was to have a forerunner who would be a voice crying in the wilderness, and John the Baptist was that forerunner. He was to be born in Bethlehem, the son of a virgin, and in the line of David. Jesus uniquely and exclusively met those qualifications. He was to minister in Galilee of the Gentiles and exhibit great miraculous power, and He did those things. Nevertheless, when "He came to His own, . . . those who were His own did not receive Him" (John 1:11).

Preparation for His second coming will be more decisive and consequential than preparation for His first, because those who rejected Him during His incarnation had continued opportunity to be saved as long as they were alive. Doubtlessly many of those who cried out for Jesus' crucifixion in place of Barabbas or who voted against Him in the Sanhedrin were later convicted to turn to Him as Lord and Savior. But there will be no such continued opportunity when Jesus comes again. When He appears **then,** the opportunity for salvation and citizenship in **the kingdom of heaven** will be past.

Then refers to the time of Christ's unexpected appearing in power and glory, about which He was speaking. At that time, He said, spiritual preparedness for entrance into **the kingdom of heaven will be comparable** to the preparedness of a certain **ten virgins** who served as bridesmaids at a wedding.

As with all of Jesus' parables, the message of this one is simple. It is meant to illustrate truths He has just been teaching: that He is coming again, that He will then judge sinners and reward the righteous, that people must be ready, and that His coming will be unexpected. The central truth is that once He has arrived, there will be no second chance and the opportunity for salvation will be gone forever.

The parable is not an allegory, as many interpreters have claimed. Every small facet of the story does not carry a mystical meaning that is subject to speculation and imagination. Nor does every part of the parable have application to Christian living, as devotionalists frequently maintain. Still less is the parable a confused and clumsy teaching effort on Jesus' part, as some liberal interpreters suggest. The fact that details such as the bride's identity and the place where the virgins slept are not mentioned has no bearing on the point Jesus was making. For His purpose, the story was clear and complete.

There may be significance in the fact that there were **ten virgins,** because Jews considered **ten** to be a number representing completion. According to Josephus, a minimum of ten men was required to celebrate the Passover. The same number was required to establish a synagogue and to give an official wedding blessing. The attendants were **virgins** because it was the custom of that day that bridesmaids be chaste young women who had never been married.

Although the English **lamps** is derived from *lampas,* in New Testament times that Greek term was used primarily of torches, as it is translated in John 18:3, where it denotes the torches carried by the soldiers who arrested Jesus. Another word, *luchnos,* was generally used for a lamp. The torches used by wedding attendants consisted of tightly wrapped cloths attached to long poles. In addition to lighting the way for the procession, the **lamps,** or torches, served to identify members of the wedding party, marking them off as special participants. It was therefore important that each of the bridesmaids have a torch.

To meet translates *hupantēsis,* a noun that literally means "a meeting" and was often used of the official welcoming of a dignitary. In the context of Jesus' teaching about His return and of the parable's illustrating the coming of His kingdom, **the bridegroom** is obviously Christ Himself. The **ten virgins** are professed believers in Him, and the **lamps,** or torches, symbolize their outward identity with His church. The torches also represent expectation of His imminent return, the preparation and readiness of the bridesmaids **to meet the** divine **bridegroom** when He comes to gather them for His wedding feast, **the kingdom of heaven.**

The ten bridesmaids represent professed disciples of Christ who claim to love the prospect of His appearing and who demonstrate outward readiness for entrance into His kingdom. In appearance the ten were indistinguishable. They were all dressed appropriately in wedding garments and all had the required torch to carry in the wedding procession. But they were not truly alike, which is the point of the parable, because they were not all prepared—**five of them were foolish, and five were prudent.**

The evidence that some of the bridesmaids were unprepared despite their outward appearance was the fact that **they took no oil with them.** They carried torches that looked exactly like those of the others, but they had nothing to burn in them, nothing that would give light and significance. A torch without fuel is obviously worthless, and a profession of faith in Jesus Christ without a saving relationship to Him is infinitely more worthless, because one is left in spiritual darkness.

The prudent bridesmaids, however, **took oil in flasks along with their lamps.** Their outward profession was substantiated by inward possession. They had the **oil** of preparedness, namely, the reality of the light of the saving grace of God within them. The **oil** is similar to the wedding garments in Jesus' parable of the wedding feast that a king gave for his son. The man without the proper wedding clothes who attempted to crash the celebration was thrown out into the darkness (Matt. 22:11-13). The king had invited everyone in his realm to the feast, regardless of social standing, wealth, or character. He made every effort to see that no one was excluded, sending his servants into every obscure part of the country (vv. 9-10). The only condition for attending the feast was the wearing of the wedding clothes provided by the king, symbolizing the divinely bestowed grace apart from which no person can come to God. Because that presumptuous, self-satisfied man would not allow himself to be attired in the king's clothing, he was rejected.

Like that man without proper wedding clothes, five of the bridesmaids were without proper torches. They had a form of godliness but had no spiritual life or power because they did not belong to God (cf. 2 Tim. 3:5). They were committed to Jesus Christ religiously, intellectually, socially, and no doubt emotionally. But they were not committed to Him in their hearts because their hearts had not been regenerated by His saving grace. They had the appearance of faith, but it was dead (cf. James 2:17). They were in darkness, not light.

The warning Jesus gave in this parable is repeated over and over in the gospels, a continually recurring theme of His teaching. He warns that professed believers are like wheat and tares; some are genuine and some are false. They are compared to various kinds of soils, some of which give initial evidence of productivity but only one of which genuinely receives the seed of the gospel and allows it to take root and grow. It was not a popular message in Jesus' day and is not a popular message today, even in many evangelical churches.

No conclusion regarding the number who will be saved can be drawn from the fact that the bridesmaids were divided evenly between the foolish and the prudent. But the proportion suggests, however, that a large part of the professing church does not belong to God. And the situation is obviously pervasive or Jesus would not have spent so much time warning about it. It existed during Jesus' earthly ministry, in apostolic times, and throughout the church until the present. And it is evident from this parable that it will also exist at the end of the Tribulation.

The statement that **the bridegroom was delaying** reinforces Jesus' teaching that His second coming will be unexpected. It will not be delayed from the divine perspective but from the human. Because so much time will have elapsed since His first coming, most people, including many professed Christians, will be carrying on business as usual when He appears (see Matt. 24:38, 43). Jesus may also have been giving the disciples a hint that He would not be returning as soon as they anticipated (see Luke 19:11). But the main thrust of the parable, like the main thrust of the entire discourse, is directed to the generation who will be living during the latter part of the Great Tribulation (Matt. 24:34). Even the short period of time that will elapse between the signs of His coming and His actual appearance will cause some people to think the Lord is **delaying** His return.

That idea is supported by the bridesmaids' becoming **drowsy** and falling **to sleep.** They were expecting the bridegroom's coming and were gathered together awaiting Him, all in seeming preparedness. There is no indication in this context that **sleep** represents laziness or faithlessness. Even the prudent bridesmaids fell asleep, illustrating still again that no one, not even faithful saints, will know exactly when Christ will appear. The **sleep** of the foolish bridesmaids might suggest their false confidence, whereas the **sleep** of the prudent ones could suggest their genuine security and rest in the Lord.

In one sense, life should go on much as usual for the believer who eagerly anticipates the Lord's return. Readiness for His coming is not evidenced by going apart somewhere to wait idly for Him but by being about His business with enthusiastic dedication. Even the most ardent service of the Lord does not exclude such normal activities as eating, drinking, laboring, and sleeping. Therefore, when Christ comes, "there shall be two men in the field; one will be taken, and one will be left. Two women will be grinding at the mill; one will be taken, and one will be left" (Matt. 24:40-41).

It will not be their common participation in the normal activities of human life that will distinguish the prepared from the unprepared when the Lord returns, but the supernatural, internal participation in the life of God that only believers will possess.

The nineteenth-century Bible commentator William Arnot observed: "There is not a more grand or a more beautiful spectacle on earth than a great assembly reverently worshipping God together. No line visible to human eye divides into two parts the goodly company; yet the goodly company is divided into two parts. The Lord reads our character and marks our place. The Lord knows them that are his, and them that are not his, in every assembly of worshippers" (*The Parables of Our Lord* [London: Nelson, 1869], p. 290).

The Lord can look down on every group of bridesmaids, as it were, and accurately judge between those who are unbelieving and deceived about their readiness, and therefore foolish, and those who genuinely believe and are therefore wise. But when He appears in power and glory at His second coming, the difference will be apparent for all to see. The torches of believers will shine brightly, but those of unbelievers will not even burn.

THE BRIDEGROOM

But at midnight there was a shout, "Behold, the bridegroom! Come out to meet him." Then all those virgins rose, and trimmed their lamps. And the foolish said to the prudent, "Give us some of your oil, for our lamps are going out." But the prudent answered, saying, "No, there will not be enough for us and you too; go instead to the dealers and buy some for yourselves." And while they were going away to make the purchase, the bridegroom came, and those who were ready went in with him to the wedding feast; and the door was shut. And later the other virgins also came, saying, "Lord, lord, open up for us." But he answered and said, "Truly I say to you, I do not know you." (25:6-12)

At **midnight** most people are typically deep in sleep, just as the bridesmaids were, and the bridegroom's arrival at that time underscores still again the unexpectedness of Christ's return. The children of Israel began their journey out of Egypt at midnight (Ex. 12:29), and rabbinical tradition held that the Messiah would come to earth at that hour.

All of the bridesmaids knew the groom would be coming soon and they were gathered at the bride's house waiting for Him. They were well aware that the engagement and betrothal periods were over and that the final festivities were about to begin. But they did not know precisely when He would arrive until they were awakened with the **shout, "Behold, the bridegroom! Come out to meet him."**

In the same way, people living during the end of the Tribulation will have seen all the signs of His coming and will know that His appearing is imminent. But they will not know the moment of His arrival until they see Him "coming on the clouds of the sky" (Matt. 24:30).

As soon as the bridegroom's presence was announced, **all those virgins rose, and trimmed their lamps.** Trimming the **lamps,** or torches, probably amounted to cutting off any ragged edges of the cloth and then saturating it with oil to make it ready for lighting. At that moment **the foolish** bridesmaids realized their predicament: they had no oil. It was not that they had been unaware of their lack of oil but that they were not concerned enough about it to acquire it before the bridegroom's arrival. Perhaps they thought they could quickly run down to the oil shop anytime they wanted and secure what they needed in plenty of time. Or perhaps they thought they could borrow oil if the shop were closed, the recourse they now tried to take. No reason is given for their negligence, no doubt because the reason is irrelevant. Because they had ample warning that the bridegroom was coming and had ample opportunity to be totally prepared for His arrival, nothing could excuse their failure.

When the Lord appears at the end of the Tribulation, many professed Christians will frantically realize their lack of spiritual life. They will not have heeded Paul's advice to the Corinthian church: "Test yourselves to see if you are in the faith; examine yourselves! Or do you not recognize this about yourselves, that Jesus Christ is in you—unless indeed you fail the test?" (2 Cor. 13:5). They will be self-deceived, perhaps believing that mere association with the things and the people of Christ has made them a part of Christ's true church. Some may think that being born into a Christian family will make them a member of God's family. We know with certainty that many will be trusting in their good works, saying to Christ, "on that day, 'Lord, Lord, did we not prophesy in Your name, and in Your name cast out demons, and in Your name perform many miracles?' And then [He] will declare to them, 'I never knew you; depart from Me, you who practice lawlessness'" (Matt. 7:22-23).

When **the foolish said to the prudent, "Give us some of your oil, for our lamps are going out,"** . . . **the prudent answered, saying, "No, there will not be enough for us and you too; go instead to the dealers and buy some for yourselves."** When **the foolish** bridesmaids apparently tried to light their dry torches, the cloth would only smolder and keep **going out.** And by then it was too late for help.

The point of the **prudent** bridesmaids' response was not that they were selfish and calloused but that they were helpless to provide oil for their foolish friends. Their own oil was **not** . . . **enough** to share with anyone else; it was necessary that each **buy** her own.

Just as one person cannot transfer part of his physical life to another person, neither can he share spiritual life, which is indivisible and unique to each person who has it. Like physical life, spiritual life is a direct, individual gift from God and is nontransferable. The saved cannot themselves become saviors. Those who receive grace cannot impart it. When the call to the judgment seat of God comes to an unbeliever, whether at death or at the Lord's coming, the intercession of all the saints in heaven and on earth could do him absolutely no good. After that time there is no second chance, no purgatory, no hope.

Salvation cannot be bought, and the buying of oil from **the dealers** refers simply to securing salvation from its only source, God. It is bought in the sense that Isaiah used the term when he wrote, "Ho! Every one who thirsts, come to the waters; and you who have no money come, buy and eat. Come, buy wine and milk without money and without cost" (Isa. 55:1). The same idea is used by Jesus in His parables of the treasure found in a field and of the pearl of great price (Matt. 13:44-46). In both cases, the discoverer sold everything he possessed in order to obtain that which was valued about all else. In that sense, the price for salvation is the entire relinquishment of one's own merit, which has no value in itself but must be surrendered because it is an absolute barrier to God's grace.

Paul declared with the deepest conviction and sincerity, "I could wish that I myself were accursed, separated from Christ for the sake of my brethren, my kinsmen according to the flesh, who are Israelites" (Rom. 9:3-4). He was willing to give up his own salvation and become forever separated from Christ if that could somehow save his fellow Jews. But he knew such a thing was impossible. They could not come to God apart from their own acceptance of His Son as Lord and Savior. The apostle could proclaim the gospel fully and faithfully, as he always did (see Acts 20:27), but he could not dispense the grace he had received.

Stressing the necessity for individual appropriation of the gospel, Jesus said,

> Everyone who comes to Me, and hears My words, and acts upon them, I will show you whom he is like: he is like a man building a house, who dug deep and laid a foundation upon the rock; and when a flood rose, the torrent burst against that house and could not shake it, because it had been well built. But the one who has heard, and has not acted accordingly, is like a man who built a house upon the ground without any foundation; and the torrent burst against it and immediately it collapsed, and the ruin of that house was great. (Luke 6:47-49)

People who build their lives on any other foundation than Jesus Christ are doomed to destruction. They do not have the necessary grace, imputed righteousness, resident holiness of God, or transformed character to counter the destructiveness of sin, whose ultimate consequence is death. In short, they have no spiritual life and therefore no eternal hope. They may feel happy about Jesus, admire His teachings, and enjoy the fellowship of His people. They may look as prepared for His coming as do true believers, having torches like the rest, but they have no oil with which to light them.

While they were going away to make the purchase, the bridegroom came, and those who were ready went in with him to

the wedding feast; and the door was shut. The tragedy, of course, was that there was then no more opportunity **to make the purchase,** and the search for the oil merchant was in vain, because all the shops were closed.

In another of His many illustrations about lost opportunity for salvation, Jesus said,

> Once the head of the house gets up and shuts the door, and you begin to stand outside and knock on the door, saying, "Lord, open up to us!" then He will answer and say to you, "I do not know where you are from." Then you will begin to say, "We ate and drank in Your presence, and You taught in our streets"; and He will say, "I tell you, I do not know where you are from; depart from Me, all you evildoers." There will be weeping and gnashing of teeth there when you see Abraham and Isaac and Jacob and all the prophets in the kingdom of God, but yourselves being cast out. (Luke 13:25-28)

Therefore when the foolish virgins returned from their unsuccessful search for oil and **came saying, "Lord, lord, open up for us,"** the bridegroom **answered** from within the house, **"Truly I say to you, I do not know you."** Those five were sham attendants who had never belonged to the wedding party but had managed to dress and act like true bridesmaids. Now the pretense was over, and their sinful, foolish character was exposed.

It will be a moment of sheer terror when unbelievers face a holy God and realize with absolute certainty that they are eternally lost. That must have been the feeling of the people of Noah's day when they saw the flood waters rise above their heads and knew the door to the ark was unalterably shut.

Although the parable of the ten virgins illustrates the time of Christ's second coming, its truths apply to an unbeliever's facing God at death in any age. At that moment the opportunity for salvation will be past and all hope gone forever.

THE WARNING

Be on the alert then, for you do not know the day nor the hour. (25:13)

For the fifth time in the discourse (see 24:36, 42, 44, 50) Jesus called on those who will be alive during the last days of the Tribulation to be **alert,** because they will **not know the day nor the hour** of His appearing. They would know its nearness by the catastrophic signs, but the exact **day** and the exact **hour** they would not know.

"Be on guard," Jesus had said in the Temple on the previous day, "that your hearts may not be weighed down with dissipation and drunkenness and the worries of life, and that day come on you suddenly like a trap; for it will come upon all those who dwell on the face of all the earth. But keep on the alert at all times, praying in order that you may have strength to escape all these things that are about to take place, and to stand before the Son of Man" (Luke 21:34-36).

In his epic poem *Idylls of the King*, Alfred Lord Tennyson used figures from the parable of the ten virgins in a song directed to the wicked Queen Guinevere, who learned too late the cost of sin:

> Late, late, so late, and dark the night and chill!
> Late, late, so late, but we can enter still.
> Too late, too late, ye cannot enter now.
>
> No light had we, for that we do repent;
> And, learning this, the Bridegroom will relent.
> Too late, too late, ye cannot enter now.
>
> No light, so late, and dark and chill the night!
> O let us in, that we may find the light.
> Too late, too late, ye cannot enter now.
>
> Have we not heard the Bridegroom is so sweet?
> O let us in, tho' late, to kiss His feet!
> No, no, too late! Ye cannot enter now.

The Signs of Christ's Coming—part 9
The Tragedy of Wasted Opportunity (Working Until Christ's Return)
(25:14-30)

9

For it is just like a man about to go on a journey, who called his own slaves, and entrusted his possessions to them. And to one he gave five talents, to another, two, and to another, one, each according to his own ability; and he went on his journey. Immediately the one who had received the five talents went and traded with them, and gained five more talents. In the same manner the one who had received the two talents gained two more. But he who received the one talent went away and dug in the ground, and hid his master's money. Now after a long time the master of those slaves came and settled accounts with them. And the one who had received the five talents came up and brought five more talents, saying, "Master, you entrusted five talents to me; see, I have gained five more talents." His master said to him, "Well done, good and faithful slave; you were faithful with a few things, I will put you in charge of many things, enter into the joy of your master." The one also who had received the two talents came up and said, "Master, you entrusted to me two talents; see, I have gained two more talents." His master said to him, "Well done, good and faithful slave; you were faithful with a few things, I will put you in charge of many things; enter into the joy of your master." And the one also who had received the one talent came up and said, "Master, I knew you to be a hard man, reaping where you did not sow, and gathering where you scattered no seed. And I was afraid, and went away and hid your talent in the ground; see, you have what is yours." But his master answered and said to him, "You wicked, lazy slave, you knew that I reap where I did not sow, and gather where I scattered no seed. Then you ought to have put my money in the bank, and on my arrival I would have received my money back with interest. Therefore take away the talent from him, and give it to the one who has the ten talents." For to everyone who has shall more be given, and he shall have an abundance; but from the one who does not have, even what he does have shall be taken away. And cast out the worthless slave into the outer darkness; in that place there shall be weeping and gnashing of teeth. (25:14-30)

In his poem *Maud Muller*, John Greenleaf Whittier wrote the well-known lines, "For all sad words of tongue or pen, the saddest are these: 'It might have been!'"

Scripture is replete with admonitions to take advantage of opportunity while it is available. Solomon wrote, "Cast your bread on the surface of the waters, for you will find it after many days," and, "Sow your seed in the morning and do not be idle in the evening, for you do not know whether morning or evening sowing will succeed, or whether both of them alike will be good" (Eccles. 11:1, 6). That same man of wisdom wrote, "He who gathers in summer is a son who acts wisely, but he who sleeps in harvest is a son who acts shamefully" (Prov. 10:5). His father, David, had written, "As for me, my prayer is to Thee, O Lord, at an acceptable time" (Ps. 69:13). Another psalmist wrote, "Come, let us worship and bow down; let us kneel before the Lord our Maker. For He is our God, and we are the people of His pasture, and the sheep of His hand. Today, if you would hear His voice, do not harden your hearts" (Ps. 95:6-8).

Isaiah exhorted, "Seek the Lord while He may be found; call upon Him while He is near" (Isa. 55:6). Jeremiah reminded his readers that "even the stork in the sky knows her seasons; and the turtledove and the swift and the thrush observe the time of their migration; but My people do not know the ordinance of the Lord" (Jer. 8:7; cf. Heb. 3:7-8). Paraphrasing his preceding quotation from Isaiah, Paul admonished the Corinthian believers, "Behold, now is 'the acceptable time,' behold, now is 'the day of salvation'" (2 Cor. 6:2; cf. Isa. 49:8).

Jesus repeatedly called on men to make the most of spiritual opportunities. "For a little while longer the light is among you. Walk while you have the light, that darkness may not overtake you; he who walks in the darkness does not know where he goes. While you have the light, believe in the light, in order that you may become sons of light" (John 12:35-36).

The tragedy of wasted opportunity is the theme of Jesus' parable of the talents, the second of two parables relating to the kingdom of heaven and, in particular, to men's readiness for Jesus' coming to establish the kingdom at His second coming (see Matt. 25:1). The parable of the virgins (vv. 1-13) focuses on readiness manifested in waiting, whereas the parable of the talents focuses on readiness manifested in working. The five virgins who had oil for their lamps represent believers who possess saving grace; the two faithful servants who invested their talents represent believers who exhibit the serving life. Together the two parables depict the balance of believers' looking forward to His coming with anticipation while living in preparedness for His coming through faithful service.

Frequently, one or the other of those precepts either is lost or overemphasized. Although believers are to rejoice continually in the prospect of their Lord's coming again, they are not to sit back in idleness and do nothing. Saving faith is serving faith. On the other hand, they are not to become so caught up in serving the Lord that they forget to contemplate and rejoice in His return. It was perhaps because they thought the Lord was coming momentarily that some of the believers at Thessalonica fell into undisciplined, careless living and decided to do no work at all. Consequently they became busybodies who did nothing productive and even disrupted the church. Paul rebuked them severely and commanded them "to work in quiet fashion and eat their own bread." He then admonished the whole church not to "grow weary of doing good" (2 Thess. 3:10-13).

Peter challenged mockers who had the opposite problem. They were so convinced that the Lord would *not* come soon that they abandoned all moral restraint and lived in selfish profligacy (2 Pet. 3:3-4). Peter reminded them that the people of Noah's day responded in the same way to Noah's prediction of the Flood, which came upon them suddenly and at a time they did not expect. In the same way, the apostle declared, Christ will appear suddenly in the end time, bringing the "judgment and destruction of ungodly men" (vv. 5-7).

It should be noted that, despite some resemblances, the parable of the talents and the parable of the minas (Luke 19:11-27) are not variations of the same story. The mina parable was given several days earlier, and the two accounts have as many differences as similarities.

Though the parable of the talents has relevance to every generation, the Lord was still speaking directly about the generation that will be living just before His return in glory (24:34), the exact time of which will not be known in advance but the imminence of which will be manifested by spectacular and unmistakable signs (24:3-29).

The parable of the talents illustrates four basic aspects of spiritual opportunity: the responsibility we receive, the reaction we have, the reckoning we face, and the reward we gain.

The Responsibility We Receive

For it is just like a man about to go on a journey, who called his own slaves, and entrusted his possessions to them. And to one he gave five talents, to another, two, and to another, one, each according to his own ability; and he went on his journey. (25:14-15)

The antecedent of **it** is the kingdom of heaven (see v. 1), of which this parable is another illustration. Some translations add "the kingdom of heaven" to verse 14 in italics to make the connection clear. Even the phrase **it is** appears in italics in the NASB, being added because there is no main subject or verb in the Greek text of this verse. Both subject and verb are understood to continue over from verse 1, namely, "the kingdom of heaven will be comparable to," making it obvious that Jesus is continuing to teach about the kingdom.

As frequently mentioned in this commentary series, it is important to understand that in the New Testament the kingdom of heaven and its synonymous phrase, the kingdom of God, refer to the sphere of God's dominion in Christ. But while maintaining that basic meaning, the expression is used in two distinct ways. Sometimes it designates the invisible body of all redeemed people. The Lord used it in that sense when He declared, "Truly I say to you, unless you are converted and become like children, you shall not enter the kingdom of heaven" (Matt. 18:3; cf. 25:34). That is the kingdom in its pure, exclusive sense.

But sometimes the kingdom of heaven refers to the visible, outward body of those who profess to know and serve Christ. Jesus made clear that in that outward manifestation of the kingdom both the true and the false will be found, the genuine Christian and the imitation (see section on Matt. 13).

It is in this visible, outward sense that Jesus refers to the kingdom both in the parable of the virgins and in the parable of the talents. The foolish virgins and the faithless slave do not represent professed pagans, atheists, agnostics, or reprobates but those who profess to belong to Christ. In each account, both genuine and counterfeit believers are depicted.

The **man** who was **about to go on a journey** obviously was planning to be gone for a long time, perhaps for many months or even a year or more. In order for his estate to be well managed in his absence, he **called his own slaves, and entrusted his possessions to them.**

The fact that these were **his own slaves** reinforces the idea that Jesus was illustrating the outward, organizational church, composed of those who allege to belong to Him, and not to mankind in general. Many people in the gospels are referred to as Christ's disciples although some of them proved to be false. Such were the disciples who were offended at His teaching about eating His flesh and drinking His blood (see John 6:52-66). The traitor Judas not only is called a disciple but an apostle (Luke 6:13-16). Even those false followers, by virtue of being attached outwardly to the church, have been entrusted with certain of the Lord's **possessions.**

Doulos, the singular of **slaves,** was a general term that referred to any kind and level of bondservant. It was used of common laborers and menial household servants as well as of skilled craftsmen and artists and highly-trained professionals. Their commonness was in being the personal property of their owners, who often had the power of life and death over them.

A wealthy person would often have special **slaves** who functioned as overseers of his household and managers of his business. In many cases some of a man's slaves were much better educated and skilled than he was. Highly trusted slaves sometimes had a virtual free hand within proscribed areas of responsibility even when the owner was at home. When he left town for any length of time, they acted almost in his full authority, having the equivalent of what we now refer to as power of attorney. They were responsible for handling all the assets and business operations of their owner for his benefit and profit.

The man in Jesus' parable had three such trusted slaves to whom he **entrusted** certain of **his possessions** while he was away. **To one he gave five talents, to another, two, and to another, one, each according to his own ability.** Satisfied that his money was in capable hands, **he** then **went on his journey.**

The numbers of **talents** given to the slaves have no significance in themselves but simply illustrate a wide range of responsibilities, from the very high and demanding to the relatively low and easy. It *is* significant, however, that the responsibilities were given to **each according to his own ability.** The owner knew his slaves intimately, and he entrusted each one only with the responsibility he reasonably could be expected to handle.

Used in a context such as this, **talents** always referred to money, but the word itself simply represented a measure of weight. The value of a specific coin depended on its weight and its composition. A talent of gold, for example, was extremely valuable, a talent of silver less valuable, and a talent of copper or bronze much less valuable still. But as with the number of talents given to each man, the metal content of the coins, and therefore their actual worth, is irrelevant to Jesus' point. He was emphasizing common accountability for differing levels of responsibility based on individual **ability.**

Because the parable illustrates the kingdom of heaven, the **man** in the story obviously represents Christ Himself, and the going on a **journey** represents the time He is away from earth between His first and His second advents. The **slaves** depict professed believers, members of the Lord's visible church whom He has entrusted with various resources to use in His behalf until He returns.

Jesus mentions only three levels of responsibility, but those are suggestive of the extremely wide range of individual abilities among people, who vary greatly in natural talent, intellect, and other capabilities. They also vary greatly in opportunity and privilege. Some church members have heard the gospel and studied Scripture since early childhood, whereas others know only the rudiments of the faith and have had little opportunity to learn more. Those who are true believers are also given spiritual gifts that vary widely from person to person (see Rom. 12:4-8; 1 Cor. 12:4-11). Some Christians are privileged to live and work closely with others of like faith and are continually encouraged and corrected by fellow believers. Other Christians, however, are the only believers in their families or even in their community or town. God knows intimately the abilities, gifts, opportunities, and circumstances of every person, and He graciously assigns responsibilities accordingly.

Even among the Twelve there were different levels of responsibility. Peter, James, and John were clearly the inner circle, and of that group Peter was the most prominent. From among the many devoted believers in the church at Jerusalem, James soon became the acknowledged leader, with commensurate responsibilities and obligations. The implication of the parable of the talents is that, even in the millennial kingdom and throughout eternity, the redeemed will continue to have different levels of responsibility.

The issue of the parable pertains to what each slave does with the fairly assessed responsibility he has been given. The noblest motive in the heart of a faithful servant would be to accomplish as much as possible for the sake of his master during the master's absence. That was also the master's desire: not equal return from each of his slaves but relatively equal effort according to ability.

It is significant that, although the slaves with the five and the two talents did not produce equal profits, they produced equal percentages of profit, doubling what they had been given. In the same way, Christians with different capabilities and opportunities may produce differing results while working with equal faithfulness and devotion. The Lord therefore assures His servants that "each will receive his own reward according to his own labor" (1 Cor. 3:8).

THE REACTION WE HAVE

Immediately the one who had received the five talents went and traded with them, and gained five more talents. In the same manner the one who had received the two talents gained two more. But he who received the one talent went away and dug in the ground, and hid his master's money. (25:16-18)

The slave **who had received the five talents** was eager to serve his master, and he therefore **immediately . . . went and traded with them, and gained five more talents.** This man represents the genuine believer whose supreme desire is to serve God, fulfilling what Jesus declared to be the first and greatest commandment, to "love the Lord your God with all your heart and with all your soul and with all your might" (Deut. 6:5; cf. Matt. 22:37).

In this context, **traded** carries the broad connotation of doing business over a period of time. The slave did not simply make one good investment and then sit back, but rather **traded** and retraded as long as his master was away. He may have been involved in a number of commercial ventures, some of them simultaneously. The point, however, is not in the particular type of work he did but in the fact that he used to full advantage all the resources his master had given him. His industry **gained five more talents** for his master, doubling the amount with which he had started.

In the same manner the one who had received the two talents gained two more. Although the second slave was given less than half as much to work with, he performed just as faithfully and industriously as the first. Like his fellow slave, he doubled his master's money. Both men demonstrated supreme commitment to their master by making the most of what they had, by maximizing their opportunities.

The behavior of the third slave, however, was radically different. **He who received the one talent went away and dug in the ground, and hid his master's money.** Hiding valuables in the ground was a common practice in the ancient world, where there were no bank vaults or safe deposit boxes. It was a simple and sensible way to protect such things as jewels and coins (see Matt. 13:44).

But hiding working resources in the ground was hardly a sensible way to carry on a business and earn a profit. The slave had not **received**

the one talent to protect it but to use it wisely for his master's profit. Although he had been given fewer resources than the other two slaves, he had the same obligation to use what he had to his maximum ability.

THE RECKONING WE FACE

Now after a long time the master of those slaves came and settled accounts with them. And the one who had received the five talents came up and brought five more talents, saying, "Master, you entrusted five talents to me; see, I have gained five more talents." His master said to him, "Well done, good and faithful slave; you were faithful with a few things, I will put you in charge of many things, enter into the joy of your master." The one also who had received the two talents came up and said, "Master, you entrusted to me two talents; see, I have gained two more talents." His master said to him, "Well done, good and faithful slave; you were faithful with a few things, I will put you in charge of many things; enter into the joy of your master." And the one also who had received the one talent came up and said, "Master, I knew you to be a hard man, reaping where you did not sow, and gathering where you scattered no seed. And I was afraid, and went away and hid your talent in the ground; see, you have what is yours." But his master answered and said to him, "You wicked, lazy slave, you knew that I reap where I did not sow, and gather where I scattered no seed. Then you ought to have put my money in the bank, and on my arrival I would have received my money back with interest. (25:19-27)

The exact length of time the owner was gone is not mentioned and is irrelevant, except that it was **a long time.** In the context of the Olivet discourse, in which Jesus repeatedly states that His second coming will be at a time when He is not expected (see 24:36, 42, 44, 50; 25:13), the implication is that **the master of those slaves came** back unexpectedly.

The first order of business upon his return was to determine what the slaves had done with his assets, and he therefore sat down and **settled accounts with them.**

In this discourse Jesus was addressing those who would be alive at the time of His return (24:34), and the statement in the parable that the **master** was gone **a long time** (cf. 25:5) suggests that He was indirectly telling the Twelve that His coming back would not be as soon as they anticipated (see Luke 19:11). He did not tell them that it would not be in their lifetimes, because that would have tended to decrease their motivation for diligence. The idea was that, whether He would be gone for a seemingly long or seemingly short time by their human reckoning, they would have opportunity to serve Him and were obligated to be about His work.

Some years ago, certain segments of evangelicalism became preoccupied with Christ's return, and some church members quit their jobs or sold their businesses and began watching for His appearance. One man I knew sold everything he had for about half a million dollars, some of which he used to buy thousands of New Testaments and distribute them around the world. He also bought and distributed various religious ornaments and trinkets he thought would arouse people's interest in Christ. But soon he was bankrupt as well as frustrated and disheartened that his confidence in the Lord's immediate return proved unfounded.

When the master called his servants together to settle the accounts, the first one reported, **Master, you entrusted five talents to me; see, I have gained five more talents.** The man was not boasting but simply relating the truth of the matter. There is no hint of pride or self-congratulation. He knew that everything he started with had been **entrusted** to him by his **master**, and that he had only done what he should have done. He exhibited the attitude Jesus said every obedient disciple should have: "When you do all the things which are commanded you, say, 'We are unworthy slaves; we have done only that which we ought to have done'" (Luke 17:10).

Near the end of his life, Paul wrote Timothy, "I am already being poured out as a drink offering, and the time of my departure has come. I have fought the good fight, I have finished the course, I have kept the faith; in the future there is laid up for me the crown of righteousness, which the Lord, the righteous Judge, will award to me on that day" (2 Tim. 4:6-8). He was not boasting but simply expressing a deep sense of fulfillment and rejoicing. He was confident the Lord knew the integrity of his heart and would be faithful to reward Him according to His gracious promises.

When the **master said to him, "Well done, good and faithful slave,"** he was commending the slave's attitude more than just his accomplishment. He first of all commended the man's excellent character, which expressed itself in excellent service.

Because the **master** represents the Lord Himself when He returns in glory and power to establish His kingdom, it is remarkable to contemplate that the holy, just, perfect Lord of the universe will deign to praise His true disciples for their faithfulness, imperfect as it will have been. Yet that is the glorious prospect of every child of God who, like Paul, loves Christ's appearing (2 Tim. 4:8).

The **master** not only highly praised his servant but highly rewarded him, declaring, **"You were faithful with a few things, I will put you in charge of many things."**

Not only will the Lord entrust greater earthly tasks to those who prove themselves faithful, but their heavenly reward will be opportunity for greater service to Him throughout eternity. Christ's faithful servants living on earth when He returns will enter into the millennial kingdom in their same earthly bodies and will be given responsibilities commensurate with their previous faithfulness. Believers who have died or been raptured will come to earth with the Lord in their glorified bodies, and they, too, will be given rulership in proportion to their faithfulness to God while they lived on earth. Both in the millennial and the eternal manifestations of the kingdom, those who have been faithful on earth will be **put . . . in charge of many things** much greater in significance than the **few things** over which they previously were faithful stewards.

Of the many things heaven will be, it will not be boring. Our heavenly perfection, for example, will not be a matter simply of never making a mistake. Nor will it be always making a hole in one or a home run, as it were. Rather it will be a time of ever-expanding and increasingly joyous service, and the saints who then will serve the most and rejoice the most will be those who have served the Lord most steadfastly while on earth. Every soul in heaven will equally possess eternal life and will be equally righteous, equally Christlike, and equally glorious. Everyone will be equally perfect, because perfection has no degrees. The difference will be in opportunities and levels of service. Just as the angels serve God in ranks, so will redeemed men and women, and the degree of their heavenly service will have been determined by the devotedness of their earthly service.

Heaven will not involve differing qualities of service, because everything heavenly is perfect. Everything done for the Lord will be perfectly right and perfectly satisfying. There will be no distinctions of superiority or inferiority, and there will be no envy, jealousy, or any other remnant of sinful human nature. Whatever one's rank or responsibility or opportunity, those will be God's perfect will for that individual and therefore will be perfectly enjoyed. In a way that is beyond our present comprehension, believers will be both equal and unequal in the Millennium and in the eternal state.

In the parable of the pounds, the nobleman who was going into a far country to receive a kingdom gave ten of his servants one mina each to do business with until he returned. When the nobleman came back, the servant who had multiplied his mina tenfold was rewarded with authority over ten cities and the one who had multiplied his mina fivefold was given authority over five cities (Luke 19:12-19). In that parable it is even more explicit that Jesus was speaking of millennial and eternal rewards, because they are specifically bestowed after the nobleman's kingdom was established. And as in the parable of the talents, the kingdom rewards are given in proportion to earthly faithfulness.

Jesus also mentions a second reward the master gives to the faithful slave: **enter into the joy of your master.** Not only will believers be rewarded in heaven with still greater opportunity for service, but they will even share the divine **joy of** their **master.** In addition to sharing the Lord's divine sinlessness and holiness they will also share His divine **joy.**

Imagine the consummate ecstasy believers will have when they fully comprehend the significance of having their sins forever abolished and their righteousness forever established! It was the joyful prospect of providing that gracious redemption that motivated Christ to endure the cross and despise its shame (Heb. 12:2).

The second slave made the same report as the first, the only difference being that he had doubled **two talents** instead of five, and therefore **gained two talents more.** The master's response to the second slave was also identical: **"Well done, good and faithful slave; you were faithful with a few things, I will put you in charge of many things; enter into the joy of your master."**

The third slave, however, did not present the master with earnings but with an accusatory and self-serving excuse. Having done nothing with what he had been given, he said, **"Master, I knew you to be a hard man, reaping where you did not sow, and gathering where you scattered no seed. And I was afraid, and went away and hid your talent in the ground; see, you have what is yours."**

Like the other two, that slave was identified as belonging to the master (see v. 14), representative of his belonging to Christ's church before the second coming. But in two distinct ways he proved that his identification with Christ was superficial and did not involve genuine faith or regeneration.

First of all, he produced absolutely nothing with the talent he had been given and did not even make an attempt to use it for his master's benefit and profit.

As already mentioned, this slave does not represent an atheist or even an agnostic, because he recognized the master as his legitimate owner and no doubt made a pretense of honoring the master while he was away. He did not misuse his talent on immoral and selfish pursuits like the prodigal son or embezzle it like the unmerciful servant of Matthew 18. He simply disregarded the stewardship he had been given.

In much the same way, unbelieving church members live in the environment of God's redeemed community and enjoy exposure to the teaching of His word and the fellowship of His people. But in spite of their spiritual privilege, they make no positive response to the gospel and therefore can render no fruitful service.

Second, this slave demonstrated his counterfeit allegiance by deprecating his master's character, accusing him of being **a hard man, reaping where** he **did not sow, and gathering where** he had **scattered no seed.** He charged his owner with being unmerciful and dishonest.

That slave represents the professing Christian whose limited knowledge of God leads him to conclude that He is distant, uncaring, unjust, and undependable. Instead of judging themselves in light of God's inerrant Word, such people judge God in the light of their own perverted perceptions. They not only justify themselves but do so at God's expense.

His erroneous estimation of his master's character was sufficient proof that this slave had no intimate or reliable knowledge of him. That slave portrays the unregenerate church member who has no spiritual fruit in his life and no spiritual worship in his heart. He is blind to the Lord's kindness, grace, compassion, mercy, honor, majesty, and glory because he has never surrendered himself to the Lord's sovereignty and grace.

Everything about that man contradicted his professed commitment to his master. In a certain way he **was afraid** of his master, but it was not the fear of reverential awe but of irreverent contempt. As his own words testified, he resented and despised the master and had no love or respect for him at all. His relationship to the master was one of enmity rather than peace, of hatred rather than love, of rejection rather than faith.

This slave represents a professed Christian whose view of God is corrupt because his unredeemed heart is still corrupt. He views God through the lens of his own depraved convictions.

In response to the unfaithful slave's rationalization, the master said, **"You wicked, lazy slave, you knew that I reap where I did not sow, and gather where I scattered no seed. Then you ought to have put my money in the bank, and on my arrival I would have received my money back with interest."**

The **slave** was **wicked** in that he unjustly besmirched the character of his master, and he was **lazy** in that he did nothing with the talent entrusted to him. By repeating the slave's charge against him, the master did not acknowledge its truthfulness. He rather said, in effect: "You think I am a hard man, do you, harvesting crops that do not belong to me? If you really thought that, why did you not take the talent and put it in the bank, where it could at least draw interest?"

The ancient Roman Empire had a banking system that was in many respects like those of modern times. The maximum loan rate was 12 percent simple interest, and the interest earned on deposits was probably about half that rate. The slave with the one talent therefore could have reaped at least a 6 percent return by making virtually no effort at all. The fact that he did not attempt even to earn simple **interest** on the money confirmed his total irresponsibility and his indifference to the master.

Even if the slave's accusation against his owner had been valid, it would not have excused his indolence. If anything, it would have made it more foolhardy. "If you thought I demand a return even on that which does not belong to me," the master countered, in effect, "did you think I would not require a return on that which *does* belong to me?" The slave was verbally hanged with his own rope.

The truth of the matter was that the slave had no real concern for his master one way or the other, and his excuse seems to have been more spur of the moment than planned. He did not expect the master's return and did not expect to be held accountable, and when he was caught by surprise he simply threw out an outrageous charge that made no sense.

The distinguishing mark of the first two servants was that they used their opportunity to serve the Lord before His return, which they eagerly awaited, and thereby proved the genuineness of their salvation. They were willing to invest everything they had in the service of their Master. The third servant, on the other hand, put aside what God had given him and went about his own selfish business. He called himself a servant of God but demonstrated conclusively he was not.

The master was angry with the third slave not simply because he lost a profit but because the slave wasted his opportunity. Jesus' point was that having little to work with is no excuse for not using it at all. Even a person with limited exposure to Scripture and who possesses few talents and has few opportunities for service is fully obligated to use those blessings in God's service.

In T. S. Eliot's play *Murder in the Cathedral,* the chorus chants, "Yet we have gone on living, living and partly living." Those words are reminiscent of the three slaves in this parable. Two of them were truly alive, whereas the other had only the appearance of life. Two of them built their houses on a foundation of rock, the other built his on sand. Two of them were wheat, the other was a tare.

The profit earned by the first two servants represents the accomplishment and satisfaction of a life that belongs to the Lord and is faithfully dedicated to His service. The failure of the third servant to use that with which he had been entrusted by his master represents the emptiness, uselessness, and worthlessness of a life in which profession of faith in Christ is proved false and meaningless by the careless waste of privilege and opportunity.

THE REWARD WE GAIN

Therefore take away the talent from him, and give it to the one who has the ten talents. "For to everyone who has shall more be given, and he shall have an abundance; but from the one who does not have, even what he does have shall be taken away. And cast out the worthless slave into the outer darkness; in that place there shall be weeping and gnashing of teeth. (25:28-30)

Jesus made clear that the visible church will always include both genuine and spurious Christians. Every church has tares that, except to God, are indistinguishable from the wheat. Their true character cannot be determined by what they do outwardly, because unbelievers can be quite active in the church and seemingly interested in its work. As far as the Lord is concerned, however, the work they do is not in His service or for the benefit of His kingdom. Whatever such a person may do with the abilities he has from the Lord, they are spiritually unproductive and might as well be hidden away. In the kingdom of God, the realm of His sovereign rule—whether in the visible earthly church or in the millennial kingdom—there will be no acceptable service offered to Him except that offered by true believers.

Therefore when Christ returns, He will figuratively **take away the talent from him, and give it to the one who has the ten talents.** As He had declared on at least one previous occasion (see Matt. 13:12), Jesus now said again: **"To everyone who has shall more be given, and he shall have an abundance; but the one who does not have, even what he does have shall be taken away."**

Those who demonstrate by their spiritual fruitfulness that they belong to God will be given even greater opportunity to bear fruit for Him. But those who demonstrate by their unproductiveness that they do not belong to God will lose even the benefits the ꜋ once had. Such a person **does not have** any true blessings from God because he has made them worthless through disuse. But the reality of what those blessings could have been will be given to someone who has proved his genuineness. The divine principle is that those who trust in Christ will gain everything, and those who do not trust in Him will lose everything.

The third slave was not simply unfaithful but faithless. A true Christian who wastes his abilities, spiritual gifts, and opportunities will have his work "burned up, [and] he shall suffer loss; but he himself shall be saved, yet so as through fire" (1 Cor. 3:15). The person represented by this slave, however, has no faith at all and therefore no saving relationship to God. No matter how much he may appear to have been blessed by God and to have served Him, one day he will hear from the Lord's own lips the devastating words, "I never knew you; depart from Me, you who practice lawlessness" (Matt. 7:23).

The third slave was utterly **worthless,** and his fate was to be **cast out . . . into the outer darkness; in that place there shall be weeping and gnashing of teeth.** Just like the man who tried to crash the king's wedding feast without the proper garment (Matt. 22:11-13), this unproductive, counterfeit servant was destined for destruction.

Outer darkness is a common New Testament description of hell. "God is light," John declared, "and in Him there is no darkness at all" (1 John 1:5). Light signifies God's presence, and **darkness** signifies his absence. Hell not only is eternal darkness but eternal torment. **In that place there shall be weeping and gnashing of teeth,** signifying the unrelieved agony of being separated from God's presence and goodness.

Judgment of the Nations
(25:31-46)

10

But when the Son of Man comes in His glory, and all the angels with Him, then He will sit on His glorious throne. And all the nations will be gathered before Him; and He will separate them from one another, as the shepherd separates the sheep from the goats; and He will put the sheep on His right, and the goats on the left. Then the King will say to those on His right, "Come, you who are blessed of My Father, inherit the kingdom prepared for you from the foundation of the world. For I was hungry, and you gave Me something to eat; I was thirsty, and you gave Me drink; I was a stranger, and you invited Me in; naked, and you clothed Me; I was sick, and you visited Me; I was in prison, and you came to Me." Then the righteous will answer Him, saying, "Lord, when did we see You hungry, and feed You, or thirsty, and give You drink? And when did we see You a stranger, and invite You in, or naked, and clothe You? And when did we see You sick, or in prison, and come to You?" And the King will answer and say to them, "Truly I say to you, to the extent that you did it to one of these brothers of Mine, even the least of them, you did it to Me." Then He will also say to those on His left, "Depart from Me, accursed ones, into the eternal fire which has been prepared for

the devil and his angels; for I was hungry, and you gave Me nothing to eat; I was thirsty, and you gave Me nothing to drink; I was a stranger, and you did not invite Me in; naked, and you did not clothe Me; sick, and in prison, and you did not visit Me." Then they themselves also will answer, saying, "Lord, when did we see You hungry, or thirsty, or a stranger, or naked, or sick, or in prison, and did not take care of You?" Then He will answer them, saying, "Truly I say to you, to the extent that you did not do it to one of the least of these, you did not do it to Me." And these will go away into eternal punishment, but the righteous into eternal life. (25:31-46)

The Bible makes clear that all sin is known to God and that all sin must be punished. Moses declared, "Be sure your sin will find you out" (Num. 32:23), and the writer of Proverbs testified that "adversity pursues sinners" (Prov. 13:21). Moses also wrote, "Thou hast placed our iniquities before Thee, our secret sins in the light of Thy presence" (Ps. 90:8). In other words, what may appear to us to be secret is actually in the full, clear view of God. No sin escapes God's notice or God's judgment. The consequence of sin is like a shadow that cannot be shaken, and what the wicked "deserves will be done to him" (Isa. 3:11). Judgment for sin is inevitable.

Paul sums up that basic truth in his letter to the Romans: "The wrath of God is revealed from heaven against *all* ungodliness and unrighteousness of men" (1:18, emphasis added). Later in that same letter the apostle wrote, "There will be tribulation and distress for *every* soul of man who does evil" (2:9, emphasis added). No sin and no sinner is exempted from God's judgment and punishment.

Not even the sins of Christians are exempt. The marvelous and gracious privilege granted to Christians, however, is to have had the judgment and punishment for all their sins placed upon the Lord Jesus Christ, who died as the substitute for sinners. By God's divine grace working through their obedient trust in His Son, believers have the guilt and penalty for their sins nailed to the cross with Christ, who made atonement sufficient even for the sins of the whole world.

But those who do not receive Jesus Christ as Lord and Savior must bear the penalty for their own sins, which is spiritual death and eternal damnation. The warning to unbelievers is stated over and over again in Scripture by word and demonstrated by direct acts of divine judgment. When Adam committed the first sin, there was judgment of massive proportions, confirming for all time the seriousness with which God views evil. That sin committed by one man not only devastated the human race but the entire created universe with it. During the time of Noah, iniquity had become so widespread and vile that God destroyed all mankind except for the eight righteous souls in Noah's immediate family. Sodom and Gomorrah became so utterly wicked that God destroyed those cities simultaneously with fire and brimstone (Gen. 19:24-25). Throughout history God has chosen sovereignly to judge certain nations, cities (see Matt. 11:21-24), and individuals, and those judgments stand as divine signposts to mankind, warning that no person or group of people, no matter how powerful by human standards, can sin with impunity (cf. 1 Cor. 10:6-12).

God's judgment is a repeated theme both in the Old and New Testaments. The judgment emphasized in the Old Testament is primarily temporal, whereas that in the New Testament is primarily eternal. With significant exceptions, the Old focuses on punishment suffered in this world and the New on punishment suffered in the next. The Old more often speaks about God's physically destroying nations, punishing cities, or afflicting individuals because of their wickedness. The New, on the other hand, more often speaks of judgment that lasts through all eternity.

No one in Scripture spoke more of judgment than Jesus. He spoke of sin that could not be forgiven, of the danger of losing one's soul forever, of spending eternity in the torments of hell, of existing forever in outer darkness, where there will be perpetual weeping and gnashing of teeth. No pictures of judgment are more intense and sobering than those Jesus portrayed.

Yet nothing Jesus said or did was inconsistent with His gracious love. He wept at the impending punishment coming on Jerusalem's people (Luke 19:41-44). His warnings of judgment and punishment were acts of love, divine appeals for men to turn from their sin in order to escape the condemnation that would otherwise be inevitable. One of love's supreme desires is to protect those it loves from harm, and Jesus therefore spoke so much of judgment because, in His infinite love and grace, it was not His wish nor the Father's "for any to perish but for all to come to repentance" (2 Pet. 3:9). What more important and loving warning could there be than warning about the eternal damnation every human being faces apart from Jesus Christ? Jesus sought to draw men to Himself not only through the attractiveness of salvation but through the horrors of its only alternative.

Jesus' closing words in the Olivet discourse—a sermon on His second coming given privately to the disciples after His last public teaching in the Temple—were one of the most severe and sobering warnings of judgment in all of Scripture. Pictured as the divine separation of the righteous sheep from the unrighteous goats, that judgment will occur just before Christ establishes His millennial kingdom on earth. Not only will it determine the ultimate, eternal destinies of everyone living at the end of the Tribulation but will also determine who will and will not enter the kingdom. Only those who belong to the King, believers who have been born into God's spiritual family and been made citizens of His spiritual kingdom, will enter His glorious kingdom.

The judgment of the sheep and goats is not mentioned in any of the other gospels, no doubt because they do not focus on Christ's kingship, as does Matthew. For that same reason Matthew places much greater emphasis on all aspects of the Lord's second coming than do the other gospels, because it is at His return that He will manifest Himself as King of kings and Lord of lords in consummate regal glory and power (Rev. 19:11-16).

THE SETTING OF JUDGMENT

But when the Son of Man comes in His glory, and all the angels with Him, then He will sit on His glorious throne. And all the nations will be gathered before Him; (25:31-32a)

THE JUDGE

But when the Son of Man (25:31a)

The sovereign Judge over the separation of the sheep and goats will be Christ Himself, **the Son of Man.** Jesus had earlier declared that "not even the Father judges anyone, but He has given all judgment to the Son, in order that all may honor the Son, even as they honor the Father" (John 5:22). God the Father has delegated all judgment authority to the Son, the Lord Jesus Christ.

The most common title Jesus used of Himself was **the Son of Man.** That title affirmed His incarnation, His identity with mankind, His time of humiliation and sacrifice. It reflected His condescension, His submissiveness, His humility, His meekness, and His gracious love for fallen humanity.

That title also tended to be less offensive than "Son of God." To have referred regularly to Himself as the Son of God would have aroused additional and needless hostility from the Jewish religious leaders, and they would have given even less heed to His teaching than they did.

In a similar way, to have referred regularly to Himself as King would have aroused the hostility and opposition of the Roman authorities, who were quick to suppress any hint of insurrection.

In addition to those reasons, for Jesus regularly to have used any such exalted title of Himself would have tempted His followers to be presumptuous and arrogant, missing His message of spiritual salvation. It would have greatly increased their already staunch conviction that, as Messiah, He would soon overthrow the Roman yoke and establish His earthly kingdom on the throne of David.

In addition to those reasons, His referring to Himself as **Son of Man** provided a profound contrast with the titles and roles He will have when He comes in glory. It suggested a clear distinction between His two comings.

On the other hand, His referring to Himself both as **Son of Man** and as heavenly King (vv. 34, 40) reinforced the truth that He is indeed both. The condescending, humble, and humiliated **Son of Man** will return one day as the glorious, sovereign, reigning, and judging King of kings and Lord of lords.

Until this point in His ministry Jesus had never directly referred to Himself as King. He had told a parable about a king who represented God the Father (Matt. 22:1-14); but not until now, talking privately to the Twelve (24:3), did He speak of *Himself* as King. Even when Pilate asked, "Are You the King of the Jews?" Jesus replied simply, "It is as you say" (Matt. 27:11). But Pilate did not take that claim seriously, at least not in a political sense, as evidenced by the fact that he offered the Jews an opportunity to secure Jesus' release, knowing "that because of envy they had delivered Him up" (vv. 17-18).

For a long while the Jewish people, and certainly their religious leaders, knew that Jesus claimed to be a kind of king, because He claimed to be Messiah (see Luke 23:2). It was because they hoped that, as Messiah, He would conquer Rome and reign over a delivered Israel that they had acclaimed Him during the triumphal entry. There was no misunderstanding among Jews that Jesus claimed to be Messiah, the coming great King. Nor could there be any misunderstanding that He claimed to be God's own Son. But publicly, Jesus nevertheless was always judicious in the way He made such claims. He did not want to needlessly incite the ire of His enemies.

Now, however, in privacy with His disciples on the Mount of Olives, He unambiguously declared that He, **the Son of Man,** would one day take His rightful place as the great King and Judge. The point of this account is that, sitting "on His glorious throne" (v. 31), He will reign over the earth and that His first act as sovereign Lord will be to decide who enters His millennial, earthly kingdom and who does not. And because His kingdom will encompass the entire earth, it is obvious that those who are not allowed to enter will not remain on earth. As Jesus explicitly states, "these will go away into eternal punishment" (v. 46).

The certainty of God's ultimate judgment of the wicked was prophesied even by "Enoch, in the seventh generation from Adam." Through divine revelation, that ancient man of God declared, "Behold, the Lord came with many thousands of His holy ones, to execute judgment upon all, and to convict all the ungodly of all their ungodly deeds which they have done in an ungodly way, and of all the harsh things which ungodly sinners have spoken against Him" (Jude 14-15).

In light of the utter and perfect holiness of the Almighty and the persistent sinfulness and ungodliness of man that Enoch pointed out, it is not the Lord's coming in wrath to render judgment that is amazing but rather His first coming in grace to offer salvation. The wonder is not that Jesus will some day come in glory to judge the world but that He first came in humility to save sinners. The marvel is not that God promises to condemn sinners for their sin but that He first offers them deliverance from it. In coming to save those who trust in Him, the Lord Jesus Christ demonstrated His great love for the unlovely by bearing the penalty of their sin, dying the death they deserve. What is remarkable is that He came to redeem sinners who are worthy only of His judgment.

THE TIME

comes in His glory, and all the angels with Him, (25:31b)

The time of judgment will be Christ's return, when He **comes in His glory.** Although we do not know at what precise time in history that event will occur (Matt. 24:36, 42, 44, 50), we know that He will appear "immediately after the tribulation" (24:29).

Apparently His judgment will be instantaneous, at the moment He appears, and when that occurs the opportunity for faith in Him will be past. As pictured in the parable of the virgins, when the Bridegroom comes the door will be shut (Matt. 25:10). When the Lord comes to earth in glory with His angels and saints, there will be no opportunity for unbelievers then living to receive Him as Messiah.

The full Tribulation will last seven years, and the second half of it, the Great Tribulation, will last three and a half years, or 1260 days (Dan. 7:25; 9:27; 12:7; Rev. 11:2-3; 12:14; 13:5). Daniel also spoke of an expanded period of 1290 days (Dan. 12:11), 30 days more than the basic 1260 of the Great Tribulation, and then of a 1335-day period (Dan. 12:12), adding another 45 days to make a total addition of 75. As suggested in chapter 3 of this volume, it seems that the best explanation for those additional days is that they will cover the time when the Messiah descends to the Mount of Olives, creates the great valley in which the nations of the world will be judged, and then executes that judgment (see Zech. 14:4-5). But whatever transpires during those additional days, there will be no further opportunity for people to receive and confess Jesus Christ as their Lord.

Accompanying and assisting the Lord at His appearing in glory and judgment will be the magnificent host of all His heavenly **angels.** At that time, Paul says, "the Lord Jesus shall be revealed from heaven with His mighty angels in flaming fire, dealing out retribution to those who do not know God and to those who do not obey the gospel of our Lord Jesus" (2 Thess. 1:7-8).

When He appears, "immediately after the tribulation of those days the sun will be darkened, and the moon will not give its light, and the stars will fall from the sky, and the powers of the heavens will be shaken, and then the sign of the Son of Man will appear in the sky, and then all the tribes of the earth will mourn, and they will see the Son of Man coming on the clouds of the sky with power and great glory. And He will send forth His angels" (Matt. 24:29-31).

The Lord will come not only with His angels but with His saints. "When Christ, who is our life, is revealed," Paul assured the Colossian believers, "then you also will be revealed with Him in glory" (Col. 3:4). The Old Testament saints, the saints of the church who will have died, the saints who will have been raptured, and the saints who will have been martyred during the Tribulation will all accompany Christ and join the saints still living on earth when He descends to earth to establish His millennial kingdom.

THE PLACE

then He will sit on His glorious throne. (25:31c)

The place of Christ's judgment will be the earth, where **He will sit on His glorious throne.** Then "there will be no end to the increase of His government or of peace, on the throne of David and over his kingdom, to establish it and to uphold it with justice and righteousness from then on and forevermore" (Isa. 9:7). Christ will first reign over the restored earth for a thousand years and then over the newly created heavens and earth throughout all eternity.

While Mary was still only betrothed to Joseph, the angel told her, "Behold, you will conceive in your womb, and bear a son, and you shall name Him Jesus. He will be great, and will be called the Son of the Most High; and the Lord God will give Him the throne of His father David; and He will reign over the house of Jacob forever; and His kingdom will have no end" (Luke 1:31-33).

David's throne was in Jerusalem, and that is therefore where Christ's throne will be. When Jesus returns, "His feet will stand on the Mount of Olives, which is in front of Jerusalem on the east; and the Mount of Olives will be split in its middle from east to west by a very large valley, so that half of the mountain will move toward the north and the other half toward the south" (Zech. 14:4). From that passage it becomes obvious that the Jerusalem then in existence will be cataclysmically transformed to be made suitable as the place of Christ's divine, **glorious throne.**

When the Lord returns, "the nations [will] be aroused and come up to the valley of Jehoshaphat," where He will declare, "Put in the sickle, for the harvest is ripe. Come, tread, for the wine press is full; the vats overflow, for their wickedness is great. Multitudes, multitudes in the valley of decision! For the day of the Lord is near in the valley of decision" (Joel 3:12-14). But the decisions in that day will not be made by men but by God. The time for deciding to receive Christ will be past, and the decisions people already will have made regarding Him will determine His decision regarding them. Those for whom He is Lord and Savior will enter the kingdom, and those who have rejected Him will be forever excluded. At that time the Lord will roar "from Zion and [will utter] His voice from Jerusalem, and the heavens and the earth [will] tremble. But the Lord is a refuge for His people and a stronghold to the sons of Israel. Then you will know that I am the Lord your God, dwelling in Zion My holy mountain. So Jerusalem will be holy, and strangers will pass through it no more" (Joel 3:16-17).

At the ascension, an angel made clear that Jesus' return would be bodily and historical, not figurative or merely spiritual. He told the astonished disciples, "This Jesus, who has been taken up from you into heaven, will come in just the same way as you have watched Him go into heaven" (Acts 1:11). When He returns to earth He will reign personally on a literal **throne**, in a literal Jerusalem, and over a literal people.

THE SUBJECTS

And all the nations will be gathered before Him; (25:32a)

The subjects of Christ's judgment will be **all the nations.** *Ethna* (**nations**) has the basic meaning of peoples and here refers to every person alive on earth when the Lord returns. Although He will have taken all believers into heaven at the Rapture, during the following seven years of the Tribulation many other people will come to believe in Him. During that dreadful time, multitudes of Gentiles (see Rev. 7:9, 14), as well as all surviving Jews (Rom. 11:26), will be brought to faith in Christ.

As Jesus makes clear later in this passage, those who are alive on earth when He returns will include both saved and unsaved, represented by the sheep and the goats, respectively. And those two separate peoples will have two separate destinies. The believers will be ushered into the kingdom and the unbelievers into eternal punishment (Matt. 25:46).

Just as death immediately crystallizes eternity for unbelievers when they die, so will the second coming of Christ crystallize eternity for unbelievers who are then alive. They will be destroyed on the spot and ushered instantaneously into judgment and eternal punishment.

But believers who are alive at the Lord's coming in glory will go directly into the earthly kingdom in their earthly bodies. There is no indication in Scripture that those saints will experience any sort of transformation at that time. But mingling with them and ruling over them will be the glorified saints of all ages who will then be reigning with Christ (Rev. 20:4). Although their bodies will be of vastly different orders, those two groups of saints will be able to communicate and interact with each other just as Jesus communicated and interacted with the disciples in His glorified body after the resurrection.

Amillennialists do not believe Christ will reign in a literal, thousand-year kingdom on earth. They consider the Millennium to be a figurative, spiritualized picture of Christ's reigning on earth through the hearts of His redeemed people. But what would be the purpose of God's giving His saints glorified bodies capable of living on the physical earth if they would never have opportunity to live there? The resurrected Christ was the perfect illustration of millennial kingdom living by glorified saints, because before His ascension He demonstrated His ability to live on this earth in the same glorified body in which He would forever occupy heaven.

There will be reproduction during the kingdom, but apparently all the children born to the redeemed people who enter it will not become redeemed themselves—any more than children born to redeemed parents in any age necessarily become redeemed themselves. At the end of the millennial kingdom there appear to be many unbelievers, who will participate in Satan's final rebellion against God (Rev. 20:7-9). Obviously, those rebels will be descendants of the saints who went directly into the kingdom at Christ's return. We should not be surprised that there are those who will not believe in Christ even though He will be in their presence. Most of His hearers did not believe the first time He came, either.

That final rebellion against the glorified Christ and His kingdom of perfect love, wisdom, justice, and righteousness gives final and irrefutable testimony to man's natural depravity. Although their environment will be perfect in every respect and Satan will be bound and unable to tempt or in any other way influence men, some people will nevertheless reject Christ even during the Millennium. The only possible source of their sin and rebellion will be their own corrupt hearts (cf. Jer. 17:9).

Contrary to what some Bible teachers and theologians claim, the idea of a literal, physical, earthly Millennium did not originate in modern times. As the astute German theologian Erich Sauer has well documented, belief in such a literal thousand-year, earthly kingdom was the common and orthodox view of the early church, from New Testament times through the middle of the third century (see his *The Triumph of the Crucified* [Grand Rapids: Eerdmans, 1951]). Early church Fathers such as Papias, Justin, Tertullian, and Hippolytus all affirmed a literal and earthly future kingdom ruled directly by Christ. It was only later, as allegorical hermeneutics became fashionable, that literal millennialism was rejected in favor of a spiritualized interpretation (p. 144).

Those who reject a literal Millennium must do one or more of three things. The first is to confuse Israel and the church, taking the church to be a spiritualized form of the ancient nation of Israel. In that case, the Old Testament curses were for literal Israel, being already fulfilled, and the promises of blessing to Israel would be fulfilled in the church, but in a spiritual, not literal, way. That kind of divided, inconsistent hermeneutics in unacceptable. The second is to make present or past what is clearly future, assuming that all the promises to the literal nation and people of Israel have already been fulfilled, making the earthly kingdom unnecessary. The third is to arbitrarily spiritualize certain Old Testament prophecies, taking predicted places, events, or persons as being merely symbols of spiritual ideas or truths instead of physical and historical realities.

In the book just mentioned above (pp. 144-53), Erich Sauer suggests five compelling arguments for a literal and historical future kingdom. First of all, such a kingdom would be the only adequate confirmation of the truthfulness and reliability of God's promises. Isaiah predicted that the Messiah would establish an everlasting kingdom on the throne of David (Isa. 9:6-7). Paul declared that "the gifts and the calling of God are irrevocable," referring specifically to His promises to ancient Israel (Rom. 11:29). But if those promises were merely figurative, their fulfillments could never be verified and would be meaningless. In particular, the prophecies about the Messiah would have no clear meaning and could never be verified. But Isaiah himself declared that the Lord's promises are more unshakable than the mountains (Isa. 54:10) and Israel's endurance as a nation will be as permanent as the new heavens and the new earth that the Lord will one day create (66:22). Jeremiah affirmed that God's covenant promises are more secure than the pattern of night following day (Jer. 33:20) and more stable than the courses of the sun, moon, and stars (31:35-36).

Second, an earthly millennial kingdom is the only explanation of the end times that corresponds to Jesus' teaching in the gospels. For example, His promise to the apostles that one day they would "sit upon twelve thrones, judging the twelve tribes of Israel" (Matt. 19:28) would be meaningless apart from a literal, historical restoration of Israel.

Third, an earthly millennial kingdom is the only consistent interpretation of Messianic prophecy. It is obvious from the gospel records that a great many of those prophecies were literally fulfilled during Jesus' lifetime. He was born in Bethlehem, just as Micah predicted (5:2). He rode into Jerusalem on a donkey, was betrayed for thirty pieces of silver, and was pierced in the side, just as Zechariah predicted (9:9; 11:12; 12:10). His hands and feet were literally pierced, precisely as the psalmist predicted (22:16; cf. 16:10), and He literally died, was buried, and was resurrected, just as Isaiah predicted (53:8-12).

Those fulfillments were so obviously literal that no one suggests the predictions of them were merely symbolic of spiritual truths. Yet many other equally specific and detailed predictions about the Messiah, such as His establishing an eternal throne over the kingdom of David, were just as obviously *not* fulfilled during Jesus' earthly ministry. Therefore, to reject the idea of a literal Millennium is to maintain that some of the Old Testament prophecies were literal and some were not. And to take that position is to assume arbitrarily that all prophecies not literally fulfilled by New Testament times are to be spiritualized.

At the time they were written, *all* Old Testament predictions obviously pertained to the future. By what logic or authority, then, does one take some of their fulfillments to be literal and others to be only figurative?

Fourth, an earthly, visible kingdom is the best possible way for Jesus Christ to demonstrate that He is the supreme ruler over His creation. How else could He prove Himself to be King of kings and Lord of lords? How could He verify that His rulership is superior to that of all other monarchs if He had no opportunity to rule an earthly kingdom? How better could He prove Himself to be the supremely just King than by personally meting out justice to His subjects? How better could He prove Himself to be the infinitely merciful Lord than by personally showing mercy on His subjects? To do those things He would have to have an earthly kingdom, because in heaven there is no need either for justice or for mercy.

Could it be that, besides the brief time between the creation of Adam and the Fall, the world will know no dominion but Satan's? Could it be that God will literally destroy but not literally restore this vast creation, all of which longs to "be set free from its slavery to corruption into the freedom of the glory of the children of God" and in that longing "groans and suffers the pains of childbirth" (Rom. 8:21-22)?

The perfect millennial kingdom will testify through all eternity that Jesus Christ is the supreme sovereign, who alone can bring absolute harmony and peace to a world even while it is still infected by sin.

Fifth, an earthly millennial kingdom is the only and necessary bridge from human history to eternal glory. Paul declares that in the end Christ will deliver "up the kingdom to the God and Father, when He has abolished all rule and all authority and power" and that "He *must* reign until He has put all His enemies under His feet" (1 Cor. 15:24-25, emphasis added). What other kingdom could Christ deliver to His Father but an earthly kingdom? The Father already possesses the kingdom of heaven. The Millennium could not refer to the church as a spiritualized form of the kingdom, because the kingdom that Christ will deliver to the Father will include His subjected enemies, of which there are none in the redeemed church. And it will be a kingdom over which Christ exercises total authority, which could not apply to any kingdom the world has known thus far, including the ancient theocracy of Israel during its most faithful days.

The thousand-year reign of Christ can only refer to a literal, earthly kingdom that Jesus Christ could present to the Father in the way Paul describes in 1 Corinthians 15. It is the kingdom of a literal earth, which Christ will literally and personally judge, restore, rejuvenate, and rule in righteousness for a literal one thousand years. And at the end of that time, after Satan is released for a brief period and then permanently defeated and cast into the lake of fire, Christ will present that earthly kingdom to His heavenly Father.

THE PROCESS OF JUDGMENT

and He will separate them from one another, as the shepherd separates the sheep from the goats; and He will put the sheep on His right, and the goats on the left. Then the King will say to those on His right, "Come, you who are blessed of My Father, inherit the kingdom prepared for you from the foundation of the world. For I was hungry, and you gave Me something to eat; I was thirsty, and you gave Me drink; I was a stranger, and you invited Me in; naked, and you clothed Me; I was sick, and you visited Me; I was in prison, and you came to Me." Then the righteous will answer Him, saying, "Lord, when did we see You hungry, and feed You, or thirsty, and give You drink? And when did we see You a stranger, and invite You in, or naked, and clothe You? And when did we see You sick, or in prison, and come to You?" And the King will answer and say to them, "Truly I say to you, to the extent that you did it to one of these brothers of Mine, even the least of them, you did it to Me." Then He will also say to those on His left, "Depart from Me, accursed ones, into the eternal fire which has been prepared for the devil and his angels; for I was hungry, and you gave Me nothing to eat; I was thirsty, and you gave Me nothing to drink; I was a stranger, and you did not invite Me in; naked, and you did not clothe Me; sick, and in prison, and you did not visit Me." Then they themselves also will answer, saying, "Lord, when did we see You hungry, or thirsty, or a stranger, or naked, or sick, or in prison, and did not take care of You?" Then He will answer them, saying, "Truly I say to you, to the extent that you did not do it to one of the least of these, you did not do it to Me." And these will go away into eternal punishment, but the righteous into eternal life. (25:32b-46)

The process of Christ's judgment will include the absolute and unerring separation of the saved from the unsaved. When all the nations and peoples of the earth will have been gathered before Him at His return, the Lord Jesus Christ **will separate them from one another, as the shepherd separates the sheep from the goats.**

In the ancient Near East, as in much of that land still today, **sheep** and **goats** are frequently herded together. But sheep are docile, gentle creatures, whereas goats are unruly and rambunctious and can easily upset the sheep. Because they do not feed or rest well together, the shepherd often separates them for grazing and for sleeping at night.

In a similar way the Lord Jesus Christ will separate believers from unbelievers when He returns to establish His millennial kingdom. **He will put the** believing **sheep on His right,** the place of favor and blessing. But the unbelieving **goats** He will put **on the left,** the place of disfavor and rejection.

In ancient biblical times, a father's blessing was extremely important, because it determined who would receive the major part of the inheritance. When Jacob was about to bless his two grandsons, Ephraim and Manasseh, he was careful to place his right hand on the one who would receive the inheritance. Because the major blessing normally went to the eldest son, Manasseh was placed on Jacob's right and Ephraim on his left. But when the time for blessing came, Jacob crossed his hands so that his right hand was on Ephraim's head rather than Manasseh's. Against Joseph's objection, Jacob insisted on giving the major blessing to Ephraim, because God had chosen him over his brother (Gen. 48:8-20).

THE INHERITANCE OF THE SAVED

Then the King will say to those on His right, "Come, you who are blessed of My Father, inherit the kingdom prepared for you from the foundation of the world. For I was hungry, and you gave Me something to eat; I was thirsty, and you gave Me drink; I was a stranger, and you invited Me in; naked, and you clothed Me; I was sick, and you visited Me; I was in prison, and you came to Me." Then the righteous will answer Him, saying, "Lord, when did we see You hungry, and feed You, or thirsty, and give You drink? And when did we see You a stranger, and invite You in, or naked, and clothe You? And when did we see You sick, or in prison, and come to You?" And the King will answer and say to them, "Truly I say to you, to the extent that you did it to one of these brothers of Mine, even the least of them, you did it to Me." (25:34-40)

Jesus here reveals unequivocally that the Son of Man who sits on the glorious throne (v. 31) is also the Son of God, the divine **King.** After his subjects are separated, **the King will say to those on His right,**

"Come, you who are blessed of My Father, inherit the kingdom prepared for you from the foundation of the world." Those will be the believers who have survived the holocaust of the Tribulation, and they will be ushered alive into the millennial kingdom, which has been prepared for them from the foundation of the world.

Doubtlessly anticipating the salvation-by-works interpretations that would be made of verses 35-45, the Lord made clear that believers will not inherit the kingdom based on good deeds they will have or will not have performed on earth. Their inheritance was determined countless ages ago, even from the foundation of the world. Those who enter the kingdom will not do so on the basis of the service they have performed for Christ but on the basis of their being blessed by the Father because of their trust in His Son. They will in no way earn a place in the kingdom. A child does not earn an inheritance but receives it on the basis of his being in the family. In exactly the same way, a believer does not earn his way into the kingdom of God but receives it as his rightful inheritance as a child of God and a fellow heir with Jesus Christ (Rom. 8:16-17).

Prepared for you accentuates the selectivity of salvation. From before the time the world was created, God sovereignly chose those who will belong to Him. And "whom He foreknew, He also predestined to become conformed to the image of His Son, that He might be the first-born among many brethren" (Rom. 8:29). The source of salvation is the Father's blessing, the reception of salvation is through faith, and the selectivity of salvation is in the advance preparation of the Father made in ages past. Stressing the same truth, Peter declared, "Blessed be the God and Father of our Lord Jesus Christ, who according to His great mercy has caused us to be born again to a living hope through the resurrection of Jesus Christ from the dead, to obtain an inheritance which is imperishable and undefiled and will not fade away, reserved in heaven for you, who are protected by the power of God through faith for a salvation ready to be revealed in the last time" (1 Pet. 1:3-5).

The good deeds commended in Matthew 25:35-36 are the fruit, not the root, of salvation. It cannot be emphasized too strongly that they are not the basis of entrance into the kingdom. Christ will judge according to works only insofar as those works are or are not a manifestation of redemption, which the heavenly Father has foreordained. If a person has not trusted in Jesus Christ as Lord and Savior, no amount of seemingly good works done in His name will avail to any spiritual benefit. To such people the Lord will say, "I never knew you; depart from Me, you who practice lawlessness" (Matt. 7:23).

Nevertheless, the genuinely righteous deeds Jesus mentions in verses 35-36 are measurable evidence of salvation, and He therefore highly commends those who have performed them. He is saying, in effect,

"Come into My kingdom, because you are the chosen children of My Father, and your relationship to Him is made evident by the service you have rendered to Me by ministering to your fellow believers, who, like you, are My brothers" (v. 40).

The Lord then lists six representative areas of need: being **hungry, thirsty, a stranger, naked, sick,** and **in prison.** The kingdom is for those who have ministered to such needs in the lives of God's people, because those good deeds evidence true, living faith. They are characteristic of God's children and kingdom citizens. "If a brother or sister is without clothing and in need of daily food," James warns, "and one of you says to them, 'Go in peace, be warmed and be filled,' and yet you do not give them what is necessary for their body, what use is that? Even so faith, if it has no works, is dead, being by itself" (James 2:15-17). John proclaims the same truth in similar words: "Whoever has the world's goods, and beholds his brother in need and closes his heart against him, how does the love of God abide in Him? Little children, let us not love with word or with tongue, but in deed and truth" (1 John 3:17-18). Scripture is very clear in teaching that the evidence for assurance of true salvation is not found in a past moment of decision but in a continuous pattern of righteous behavior.

The response by those whom the King commends is remarkable and is another proof of their salvation. Because they have ministered in a spirit of humility and selflessness and not to be seen and honored by men (see Matt. 6:2, 5, 16), they have seemingly forgotten about the many things they have done and are surprised that these are worthy of such mention by the Lord.

The King addresses them as **the righteous,** not simply because they have been declared righteous in Christ but because they have been made righteous by Christ. Their works of service to fellow believers give evidence that they are themselves the product of divine "workmanship, created in Christ Jesus for good works, which God prepared beforehand, that we should walk in them" (Eph. 2:10).

The good deeds mentioned in these verses all deal with common, everyday needs. There is no mention of monumental undertakings or of spectacular accomplishments (cf. Matt. 7:21-23, where the claim to the spectacular is useless) but only of routine, day-to-day kindnesses that help meet the needs of fellow believers. Nothing more evidences conversion than a life marked by the compassion of God and the meekness and love of Christ. When the disciples of John the Baptist wanted evidence that Jesus was the Messiah, He replied by telling them not just about His spectacular healings but also about how He treated those in need (Matt. 11:4-6). When He announced His messianic credentials to the people of Nazareth, He again reflected not on the amazing but on the way He treated the poor, the prisoners, the blind, and the downtrodden (Luke

4:18-19). The person who belongs to Christ will demonstrate such compassion and be humble about it.

When the King's self-effacing servants ask, "**Lord, when did we** do all those things for You?" **the King will answer and say to them, "Truly I say to you, to the extent that you did it to one of these brothers of Mine, even the least of them, you did it to Me."**

The King's addressing these people as **brothers of Mine** gives still further evidence that they are already children of God and do not become so because of their good works. The writer of Hebrews declared, "For both He who sanctifies and those who are sanctified are all from one Father; for which reason He is not ashamed to call them brethren" (Heb. 2:11). "The one who joins himself to the Lord is one spirit with Him," Paul says (1 Cor. 6:17), and because of that union a believer can say, "It is no longer I who live, but Christ lives in me; and the life which I now live in the flesh I live by faith in the Son of God, who loved me, and delivered Himself up for me" (Gal. 2:20).

When the disciples were arguing about which one of them was the greatest in the kingdom of heaven, Jesus set a small child in front of them and said, "Truly I say to you, unless you are converted and become like children, you shall not enter the kingdom of heaven" (Matt. 18:3). A person who does not come to Christ in the humble trustfulness that is characteristic of small children will have no part in His kingdom at all, much less be considered great in it. Jesus continued, "Whoever then humbles himself as this child, he is the greatest in the kingdom of heaven. And whoever receives one such child in My name receives Me" (vv. 4-5). The physical child standing before them represented the spiritual child of God, the person who is converted (v. 3) by believing in Christ (v. 6). The person who lovingly serves the children of God proves himself to be a child of God.

"He who receives you receives Me," Jesus told the disciples on another occasion, "and he who receives Me receives Him who sent Me" (Matt. 10:40). Whatever believers do for each other they also do for their Lord Jesus Christ, and the person who genuinely receives and serves Christians in Christ's name proves he himself is a Christian. The self-giving service of Christians to each other in Christ's name is a key external mark that identifies them as God's people. Jesus said, "By this all men will know that you are My disciples, if you have love for one another" (John 13:35).

It is to the practical manifestations of such love that Christ the King will call attention as he ushers the Tribulation saints into His millennial kingdom. Believers during those seven years, especially during the devastating last three and one-half years, will have great need for the basics Jesus has just mentioned. Because of their identity with Christ, they will often be hungry, thirsty, without decent shelter or clothing, sick, imprisoned, and alienated from the mainstream of society.

Those who will have met the needs of fellow believers will themselves have suffered great need. Few, if any, believers during the frightful days of the Tribulation will be able to give out of abundance. Most of them will have resources hardly sufficient to meet their own needs. Their divinely inspired generosity to each other will have set them apart as the Lord's people even before, as returning King, He publicly declares them to be His own.

THE CONDEMNATION OF THE UNSAVED

Then He will also say to those on His left, "Depart from Me, accursed ones, into the eternal fire which has been prepared for the devil and his angels; for I was hungry, and you gave Me nothing to eat; I was thirsty, and you gave Me nothing to drink; I was a stranger, and you did not invite Me in; naked, and you did not clothe Me; sick, and in prison, and you did not visit Me." Then they themselves also will answer, saying, "Lord, when did we see You hungry, or thirsty, or a stranger, or naked, or sick, or in prison, and did not take care of You?" Then He will answer them, saying, "Truly I say to you, to the extent that you did not do it to one of the least of these, you did not do it to Me." And these will go away into eternal punishment, but the righteous into eternal life. (25:41-46)

To the lost who will be gathered **on His left** the King will say, **"Depart from Me, accursed ones, into the eternal fire which has been prepared for the devil and his angels."** Joining the unredeemable **devil and his angels** in the **eternal fire** of hell will be those human beings who refused to believe.

It is just as obvious that Christ does not condemn these people because they failed to serve Him (vv. 42-43) as it is that He does not save the others because they did serve Him (vv. 34-35). These are **accursed** because they rejected Christ, just as those who enter the kingdom are righteous (v. 37) because they accepted Him. Their rejection of Christ left them in a state where they were not able to do righteous deeds.

Jesus is speaking of eternal *separation* from God and from His goodness, righteousness, truth, joy, peace, and every other good thing. He is speaking of eternal *association* with **the devil and his angels** in the place of torment God **prepared** for them. He is speaking of eternal *isolation*, where there will be no fellowship, no consolation, and no encouragement. He is speaking of eternal *duration* and of eternal *affliction*, from which there will be no relief or respite.

The evidence that those rejected people never belonged to Christ will be that they did not love and serve His people. Their response to believers' needs will have been just the opposite of those who enter the kingdom. When, vicariously through the needs of His people, Christ was **hungry** or **thirsty** or **a stranger** or **naked** or **sick** or **in prison,** those unbelievers refused to minister to Him. And in so doing they proved they did not belong to Him.

Like the righteous who are received into the kingdom, the accursed who are rejected will also be amazed at the Lord's words to them. But they will ask, **"Lord, when did we** *not* **minister to you in those ways?"** He will reply, **"Truly I say to you, to the extent that you did not do it to one of the least of these, you did not do it to Me."** To fail to serve Christ's people is to fail to serve Him, and to fail to serve Him is to prove one does not belong to Him.

It is significant that the marks of lostness Jesus mentions here are not gross sins committed but rather simple acts of kindness *not* committed. The five foolish virgins who had no oil for their lamps were not shut out of the wedding feast because they were morally wicked but because they were unprepared for the bridegroom (see Matt. 25:1-13). In the same way, the slave with one talent was not cast into outer darkness because he embezzled the master's money but because he failed to invest it (vv. 14-30). Also in the same way, a person who is shut out of the kingdom of God is not condemned because of the greatness of his sin but because of the absence of his faith. It is not that those who are damned to hell are equally wretched and vile; their common reason for damnation is lack of faith.

Jesus uses the same word (*aiōnios,* **eternal**) to describe salvation and condemnation. If believers will be in heaven with God forever, the lost will be in hell with the devil forever.

Since the millennial kingdom will be worldwide, there will be no place on earth for the accursed to go. They will be slain on the spot and go immediately into the **eternal punishment** of hell, suffering permanent, everlasting crystallization of their state of spiritual death. At the end of the thousand years their bodies will be raised (cf. John 5:2829), and they will again stand before God for final sentencing and final condemnation in bodies suited for hell's torments.

But **the righteous** will go away **into eternal life,** to spend all eternity glorified with their Lord and Savior. In marvelous contrast to the prospect of the accursed, at the end of the thousand-year earthly kingdom the righteous will discover that their eternal blessedness will only have begun.

Preparing for Christ's Death

(26:1-16)

11

And it came about that when Jesus had finished all these words, He said to His disciples, "You know that after two days the Passover is coming, and the Son of Man is to be delivered up for crucifixion." Then the chief priests and the elders of the people were gathered together in the court of the high priest, named Caiaphas; and they plotted together to seize Jesus by stealth, and kill Him. But they were saying, "Not during the festival, lest a riot occur among the people."

Now when Jesus was in Bethany, at the home of Simon the leper, a woman came to Him with an alabaster vial of very costly perfume, and she poured it upon His head as He reclined at the table. But the disciples were indignant when they saw this, and said, "Why this waste? For this perfume might have been sold for a high price and the money given to the poor." But Jesus, aware of this, said to them, "Why do you bother the woman? For she has done a good deed to Me. For the poor you have with you always; but you do not always have Me. For when she poured this perfume upon My body, she did it to prepare Me for burial. Truly I say to you, wherever this gospel is preached in the whole world, what this woman has done shall also be spoken of in memory of her."

> **Then one of the twelve, named Judas Iscariot, went to the chief priests, and said, "What are you willing to give me to deliver Him up to you?" And they weighed out to him thirty pieces of silver. And from then on he began looking for a good opportunity to betray Him.** (26:1-16)

Chapter 26 begins the last and most pivotal section of Matthew's presentation of the gospel. Everything else has been a prologue, an introduction to the great conclusion, which focuses on the cross of Jesus Christ—the culmination of the gospel and the culmination of redemptive history, the only eternal hope of fallen mankind.

The hymn writer John Bowring exulted,

> In the cross of Christ I glory,
>   Tow'ring o'er the wrecks of time.
> All the light of sacred story
>   Gathers round its head sublime.

Everything in the sacred story of God's redemptive plan does indeed center on the cross, apart from which no other revelation or work of God would have any ultimate value for sinful man. It is through the cross of Christ alone that the Lord has provided the way for sinners to be saved and united with Him, the holy God. There is no salvation, no gospel, no biblical Christianity apart from the cross of Christ. It is because he unequivocally believed that central biblical truth Paul could tell the Corinthians, "I determined to know nothing among you except Jesus Christ, and Him crucified" (1 Cor. 2:2).

The cross is the essence of redemptive truth—foreshadowed in the acceptable sacrifice of Abel, in the ark that saved Noah and his family, in the substitute ram provided to Abraham on Mount Moriah as the substitute for Isaac, in the deliverance of Israel from Egypt, in the struck rock that brought forth water in the wilderness, in the Levitical sacrifices, in the serpent lifted up in the wilderness for healing, in Boaz as Ruth's kinsman redeemer, and in countless other Old Testament persons and events. In the deepest sense, all Old Testament truth and history point unerringly to the cross of Jesus Christ. John the Baptist, the last prophet of the Old Covenant, testified of Jesus, "Behold, the Lamb of God who takes away the sin of the world!" (John 1:29). Above all else, the Christian gospel is the message of the death and resurrection of Jesus Christ, and that is the dominant and supreme focus of both testaments, the Old as well as the New.

Matthew deals with the cross in a concise and straightforward way. His gospel could well be called an expanded narrative of the cross, and in the last three chapters he focuses on this central theme in several culminating elements. In chapter 26 he details the preparation for the cross and the arrest of Jesus. In chapter 27, he presents Jesus' trials, execution, and burial. And in chapter 28 he narrates the Lord's resurrection victory over death and His final instructions to the disciples.

Chapter 26 picks up the narrative at the end of the Olivet discourse, which **Jesus had** just **finished.** It was still Wednesday, an unusually eventful day that had included Jesus' teaching the multitudes in the Temple and His excoriating the Jewish religious leaders for their hypocritical ungodliness. Upon leaving the Temple, He went with His disciples to the Mount of Olives, where He privately taught them about His second coming (Matt. 24:3–25:46).

Then the Lord abruptly brought them back to the central reality of His first coming. For the fourth and last time (see Matt. 16:21; 17:22-23; 20:18-19) He told them of His inevitable death, which would occur only two days hence (26:2). The crucifixion itself was the next major event in Messiah's mission. Before He should return in glory and power He must die in willing and humble submission to His Father's plan.

In 26:1-16, Matthew presents four incidents that give distinct perspectives on the preparations for Jesus' imminent death: the preparation of sovereign grace (v. 2), the preparation of hateful rejection (vv. 3-5), the preparation of loving worship (vv. 6-13), and the preparation of betraying hypocrisy (vv. 14-16). Each of those events was in the eternal plan of God for the redemption of the world, and each one transpired precisely according to that divine master plan.

THE PREPARATION OF SOVEREIGN GRACE

You know that after two days the Passover is coming, and the Son of Man is to be delivered up for crucifixion. (26:2)

In His incarnation, Jesus voluntarily limited the use of His omniscience, His glory, and certain other attributes of His deity (cf. Phil. 2:7-8). In His humility and self-imposed limitations as a man, Jesus taught only the divine truth that His heavenly Father revealed to Him. "The Father Himself who sent Me," Jesus said, "has given Me commandment, what to say, and what to speak" (John 12:49; cf. Matt. 24:36).

Now Jesus knew it was the Father's time for Him to die, and He not only declared again that He must suffer and be crucified but specified that His death was only **two days** away, at the beginning of **the Passover.** At that divinely appointed time **the Son of Man** would **be delivered up for crucifixion.**

Unbelieving skeptics have long tried to explain Jesus' death as a quirk of fate, the unintended termination of a well-meaning revolution that was discovered and crushed or the sad end to the delusions of a madman. Others picture Jesus as a visionary whose dreams were ahead of the age in which He lived, or as a prophet who overstated His claims and thereby roused the ire of the religious establishment. But such assertions do not square with the gospel accounts and are blasphemous.

As already noted, Jesus had predicted at least three times previously that He would suffer to the death but would rise again. He had even indicated that His death would be in Jerusalem and that He would rise on the third day. He was on a divine timetable, and no human plans or power could cause that timetable to vary in a single detail. "No one has taken [My life] away from Me," He declared, "but I lay it down on my own initiative. I have authority to lay it down, and I have authority to take it up again" (John 10:18). When Pilate said to Jesus, "'Do You not know that I have authority to release You, and I have authority to crucify You?' Jesus answered, 'You would have no authority over Me, unless it had been given you from above'" (John 19:10-11).

There were many times when people sought to kill Jesus but were unable to do so. The Jewish religious leaders began plotting His death soon after He began His public ministry (John 5:18), but they were not able to fulfill that intention until it fit into God's timetable.

The first attempt on Jesus' life was made shortly after He was born, when Herod massacred all the male infants in the vicinity of Bethlehem. God sent an angel to warn Joseph to take Jesus and His mother to Egypt until the danger was over. On one occasion when He was ministering in a synagogue in His home town of Nazareth, the people became incensed by His claim to be fulfilling Isaiah's prophecy and by His reminding them of several instances when God chose to bless certain Gentiles rather than Jews. They succeeded in leading Him to the edge of a high cliff on the outskirts of the city, but before they could throw Him to His death, He miraculously passed through their midst and went His way (Luke 4:16-30).

After Jesus healed the crippled man at the pool of Bethesda, the Jewish leaders began "seeking all the more to kill Him, because He not only was breaking the Sabbath, but also was calling God His own Father, making Himself equal with God" (John 5:18). To some people Jesus became known as "the man whom they are seeking to kill" (John 7:25). But when the Temple police were sent to arrest Him for healing a man on the Sabbath, they returned empty-handed. When the chief priests and Pharisees asked the officers why they did not bring Jesus back with them, they replied, "Never did a man speak the way this man speaks" (John 7:44-46).

All of those attempts to kill Jesus, and perhaps others that are not recorded, failed because it was not God's time or God's way for the Son to die. Only the sovereign grace of God could have brought Jesus to the cross. No human power could have accomplished it apart from God's will, and no human power could now prevent it, because it was now God's plan. As Jesus declared at the Last Supper, "the Son of Man is going as it has been determined" (Luke 22:22). And as Peter declared at Pentecost, Jesus was "delivered up by the predetermined plan and foreknowledge of God" (Acts 2:23).

The appropriate time for Jesus to die was at **Passover**, when the sacrificial lambs were slain, because that celebration pointed to "the Lamb of God who takes away the sin of the world!" (John 1:29). The sacrifices of all the other lambs were but faint symbols of what the true Lamb was soon to accomplish in reality.

As Philip explained to the Ethiopian, Jesus was the Lamb predicted by Isaiah, led to slaughter but not opening His mouth (Acts 8:32-34). As Paul declared to the Corinthian believers, Jesus was "Christ our Passover [who] also has been sacrificed" (1 Cor. 5:7). As Peter proclaimed to the scattered and persecuted saints of the first-century church, Jesus was the unblemished Lamb "foreknown before the foundation of the world, but [who] has appeared in these last times for the sake of you" (1 Pet. 1:19-20). As John saw on Patmos, Jesus was "the Lamb that was slain to receive power and riches and wisdom and might and honor and glory and blessing" (Rev. 5:12).

THE PREPARATION OF HATEFUL REJECTION

Then the chief priests and the elders of the people were gathered together in the court of the high priest, named Caiaphas; and they plotted together to seize Jesus by stealth, and kill Him. But they were saying, "Not during the festival, lest a riot occur among the people." (26:3-5)

As Jesus was speaking to His disciples that Wednesday evening on the Mount of Olives, the Sanhedrin, composed primarily of **the chief priests and the elders of the people**, was **gathered together in the court** of the palace **of the high priest, named Caiaphas**. The **chief priests** represented the wealthy and influential religious nobility and **the elders** represented the wealthy and influential lay nobility. Scribes were present when Jesus was taken to Caiaphas's house after He was arrested (Matt. 26:57), and it is likely that some of them were also there at this time.

According to the famous Jewish historian Josephus, the full name of the **high priest** was Joseph **Caiaphas**. He was a conniving, treacherous, and deceitful man depicted in Scripture in the one-dimensional role of

Jesus' antagonist. In every passage where he is mentioned, he is seen pursuing the destruction of Jesus. Like Herod, his hatred and fear of Jesus was not theological but political. Caiaphas wanted to destroy Jesus because he feared that He posed a serious threat to his position and power over the Jewish people. Driven purely by greed and selfish, jealous ambition, he had no sense of justice, righteousness, or propriety. He had no regard for his country, his people, or his religion, except as those could be used to personal advantage. His basic operating principle was expediency, epitomized for all time in his infamous declaration: "It is expedient for you that one man should die for the people, and that the whole nation should not perish" (John 11:50).

The high priesthood traditionally was passed on through the Levitical line, but during the Roman occupation the position generally was sold or bestowed as a political favor. Because the Jewish people would not have tolerated a high priest without some Levitical heritage, **Caiaphas** married the daughter of Annas, his predecessor in the high priesthood. The two men even served jointly for a period of time (see Luke 3:2). Caiaphas served as high priest from A.D. 15 to 37, an unparalleled tenure. To hold the office for that long required a close relationship with Rome, and over the period of some hundred years, 28 different men served as high priest. Caiaphas's successor lasted only 50 days in office.

Caiaphas was the epitome of the decadent religious system that now dominated Israel. Wicked as he was, he alone could enter the Holy of Holies on the Day of Atonement and offer the sacrifice. He supervised all the priestly functions in the Temple and profited from the merchandising there that had so incensed Jesus that He twice drove out the money changers and sellers of sacrificial animals (John 2:14-16; Matt. 21:12-13).

The Sanhedrin had assembled in Caiaphas's house for one purpose: to plot how they could **seize Jesus.** They wanted to do it **by stealth** in order not to antagonize the masses in the city where Jesus was popular; and once they had Him firmly in their grasp they would then **kill Him** when it seemed propitious. They had endured more of Him than they could tolerate and were determined to put an end to His exposure of their hypocrisy and ungodliness and His threat to their power and wealth. Apparently they planned to arrest Him as soon as possible, before He had opportunity to escape or amass further support among the people. He would then be held in custody until the Passover crowds had left Jerusalem, making it safer to put Him to death, perhaps also in secret. Therefore **they were saying, "Not during the festival."**

Jerusalem was swollen to near bursting with pilgrims from all parts of the world who had come to worship at the Passover **festival.** According to Josephus, some 256,500 sacrificial lambs were slain during a typical Passover. And because tradition required that no fewer than ten people were to eat of one lamb, the number of celebrants could have exceeded two million. Many of the worshipers would have been from Galilee and other places where Jesus had ministered and gained great popularity for His powerful preaching and miracle working. And a large number of those admirers doubtlessly were among the multitudes who, only a few days earlier, had strewn garments and palm branches on the road before Jesus and acclaimed Him with shouts of "Hosanna to the Son of David; blessed is He who comes in the name of the Lord" (Matt. 21:9).

From the standpoint of the Jewish leaders, therefore, Passover was the worst possible time for them to take direct action against Jesus, especially to put Him to death. They feared it would surely cause **a riot . . . among the people.** But Passover was the time God had chosen, and those hateful rejecters would crucify Jesus according to God's plan rather than their own. During the many times when they wanted to kill Jesus immediately, they could not. Now, when they wanted to postpone putting Him to death, they could not. God's time was not eight days hence but two, not after the Passover but at its commencement. When, by God's sovereign allowance, Jesus' enemies finally succeeded in putting Him to death, it was at the very time they most wanted to avoid.

THE PREPARATION OF LOVING WORSHIP

Now when Jesus was in Bethany, at the home of Simon the leper, a woman came to Him with an alabaster vial of very costly perfume, and she poured it upon His head as He reclined at the table. But the disciples were indignant when they saw this, and said, "Why this waste? For this perfume might have been sold for a high price and the money given to the poor." But Jesus, aware of this, said to them, "Why do you bother the woman? For she has done a good deed to Me. For the poor you have with you always; but you do not always have Me. For when she poured this perfume upon My body, she did it to prepare Me for burial. Truly I say to you, wherever this gospel is preached in the whole world, what this woman has done shall also be spoken of in memory of her." (26:6-13)

Matthew here presents a flashback to the previous Saturday, when Jesus came into the area of **Bethany** and Bethphage, just east of Jerusalem near the Mount of Olives (see Matt. 21:1; Mark 11:1). In this touching account, a third preparation for Jesus' crucifixion is portrayed. It is in stark contrast to that of the Sanhedrin, reflecting loving worship rather than hateful rejection.

While in **Bethany** Jesus and the disciples were invited to **the home of Simon the leper** for supper. From John's account we learn that Mary, Martha, and Lazarus were also present and that Martha served the meal, probably as a gesture of friendship to **Simon** as well as to the Lord (John 12:1-3).

Since a **leper** was not allowed to live in towns or cities or to associate with nonlepers, it is clear that **Simon** had been cleansed. And because that dread disease was incurable by medical means, he apparently had been healed miraculously by Jesus. In deep gratitude for that deliverance, he had asked Jesus and the others to his house for a meal.

During the supper **a woman,** whom Matthew does not identify but John tells us was Mary (12:3), **came to Him with an alabaster vial of very costly perfume, and she poured it upon His head as He reclined at the table.** From Mark we learn that the **very costly perfume** was worth "over three hundred denarii," a year's wages for a common laborer or soldier, and that the expensive **alabaster vial** was broken, making Mary's act even more costly (Mark 14:3-5).

Mary had always been specially attentive to the Lord's teaching (see Luke 10:39), and it seems that on this occasion she accepted the reality and understood the significance of Jesus' impending death better than the Twelve. She may have sensed that in His tragic death somehow lay her redemption. She understood what the disciples did not want to understand, that Jesus had to die in order to be raised again. Unlike them, she was not caught up in the carnal, selfish desire for Christ to establish His earthly kingdom immediately in order to share in the glory and privilege that event would bring.

In an act of unmeasured love, Mary **poured** the perfume **upon His head as He reclined at the table.** The perfume was a pound of pure nard, John tells us, which she also used to anoint Jesus' feet (John 12:3). In that adoring testimony of love and honor Mary poured out her soul in worship even as she poured out the perfume. Being absolutely controlled by adoration for her Lord, she lost all sense of restraint and economy.

Mary did not offer that valuable possession to support a program or a ministry but offered it to Christ Himself. She did not selfishly seek a visible and tangible result from her generosity but without hesitation offered her most expensive earthly possession to the Lord in an act of effusive, adoring worship.

Having no comprehension of what prompted Mary to do what she was doing, the insensitive **disciples were indignant when they saw this, and** piously asked, **"Why this waste?"** At the instigation of the traitorous Judas (see John 12:4-5) they suggested that the "**perfume might have been sold for a high price and the money given to the poor.**" Even had that pragmatic and seemingly altruistic notion been pursued, however, it would not likely have benefited many **poor** people. Because Judas was treasurer of the group and also a thief, he no doubt would have embezzled most of the money for himself (see John 12:6). Now that he was totally disillusioned with Jesus, he probably felt even more justified in stealing whatever he could before going his own way.

Although the disciples' indignation was not voiced openly but only among themselves (Mark 14:4) and to Mary, **Jesus** was **aware of this** and rebuked them for it. "**Why do you bother the woman?**" He asked, "**For she has done a good deed to Me. For the poor you have with you always; but you do not always have Me.**"

In the parable of the sheep and the goats the Lord had just graphically taught that meeting the physical needs of His people is of the utmost importance and is a mark of genuine salvation (Matt. 25:34-36). But He was very soon to end His earthly ministry and return to His Father in heaven. And before He returned He would suffer, die, and be raised up. This was therefore not the time for philanthropy but adoration, not the time for charity but for worship. Just as she had done on an earlier occasion, Mary now had "chosen the good part" (Luke 10:42) and was performing a beautiful **good deed** to her Lord.

Genuine worship is the supreme service a Christian can offer to Christ. There is a time for ministering to the poor, the sick, the naked, and the imprisoned. There is a time for witnessing to the lost and seeking to lead them to the Savior. There is a time for discipling new believers and helping them grow in the faith. There is a time for careful study and teaching of God's Word. But above all else that the Lord requires of His people is their true worship, without which everything else they may do in His name is empty and powerless.

The worshiper emulated by Mary does not ask, "How much is it going to cost?" or, "Do I have the time?" Like her, the true worshiper gives Jesus whatever he has, knowing it is trifling compared to what has been received from Him.

In this particular and unique act of worship, when Mary **poured this perfume upon** Jesus' **body,** without her even realizing it **she did it to prepare** Him **for burial.** It became a symbolic deed that anticipated His death and burial.

What Mary did was of such lasting significance that Jesus declared, "**Truly I say to you, wherever this gospel is preached in the whole world, what this woman has done shall also be spoken of in memory of her.**" Through the accounts of this story in three of the gospels, the Holy Spirit secured for posterity a memorial to her love and generous worship. In fulfillment of the Lord's prediction, for nearly two thousand years **what this woman** did has indeed been **spoken of in memory of her.** She is perpetually an example to all Christians of unselfish, sacrificial adoration.

THE PREPARATION OF BETRAYING HYPOCRISY

Then one of the twelve, named Judas Iscariot, went to the chief priests, and said, "What are you willing to give me to deliver Him up to you?" And they weighed out to him thirty pieces of silver. And from then on he began looking for a good opportunity to betray Him. (26:14-16)

In contrast to Mary, who gave an open testimony of loving worship, **Judas Iscariot** gave clandestine testimony of betraying hypocrisy.

Going **to the chief priests,** probably while they were still assembled in Caiaphas's house, Judas asked callously, **"What are you willing to give me to deliver Him up to you?"** No doubt pleasantly amazed that one of Jesus' own disciples would be the means of their destroying Him, the religious leaders eagerly **weighed out to** Judas **thirty pieces of silver.** For the price of a slave (see Ex. 21:32), Judas not only sold out his teacher and leader and friend but betrayed the very Son of God, who had come to be his Savior.

Having irrevocably committed himself to the treachery, **from then on,** Judas **began looking for a good opportunity to betray** the Lord. In the eyes of Jesus' enemies, the **good opportunity** would be when He was "apart from the multitude" (Luke 22:6), as He soon would be in the Garden of Gethsemane. In the greatest example of forsaken opportunity the world has ever known, Judas forever turned his back on the Lord and on his own salvation. And the Lord forever turned His back on Judas.

The Last Passover
(26:17-30)

12

Now on the first day of Unleavened Bread the disciples came to Jesus, saying, "Where do You want us to prepare for You to eat the Passover?" And He said, "Go into the city to a certain man, and say to him, 'The Teacher says, "My time is at hand; I am to keep the Passover at your house with My disciples."'" And the disciples did as Jesus had directed them; and they prepared the Passover.

Now when evening had come, He was reclining at the table with the twelve disciples. And as they were eating, He said, "Truly I say to you that one of you will betray Me." And being deeply grieved, they each one began to say to Him, "Surely not I, Lord?" And He answered and said, "He who dipped his hand with Me in the bowl is the one who will betray Me. The Son of Man is to go, just as it is written of Him; but woe to that man by whom the Son of Man is betrayed! It would have been good for that man if he had not been born." And Judas, who was betraying Him, answered and said, "Surely it is not I, Rabbi?" He said to him, "You have said it yourself."

And while they were eating, Jesus took some bread, and

after a blessing, He broke it and gave it to the disciples, and said, "Take, eat; this is My body." And when He had taken a cup and given thanks, He gave it to them, saying, "Drink from it, all of you; for this is My blood of the covenant, which is poured out for many for forgiveness of sins. But I say to you, I will not drink of this fruit of the vine from now on until that day when I drink it new with you in My Father's kingdom."

And after singing a hymn, they went out to the Mount of Olives. (26:17-30)

As noted throughout these volumes, Matthew presents Jesus as King, the sovereign Lord of the universe come to earth in human flesh. Even in the midst of Jesus' betrayal, mock trials, and execution, He is revealed in humble but regal dignity. Far from diminishing His majesty and glory, those events portray the powerful and culminating expression of His sovereign grace and power. Through man's ultimate act of sinful depravity, God accomplished His ultimate act of righteous redemption.

In the previous chapter, four initial elements of preparation for Jesus' death were unfolded. Each of those involved the plan and work of others than Christ Himself. Now, on Jesus' last day (Thursday) with the disciples until after His resurrection, Matthew presents four elements of Jesus' own preparation for His sacrificial death: experiencing the final Passover (26:17-25), establishing the Lord's Supper (vv. 26-30), helping the impotent disciples (vv. 31-35), and praying to the Father (36-39). The present chapter will discuss the first two of those elements.

EXPERIENCING THE FINAL PASSOVER

Now on the first day of Unleavened Bread the disciples came to Jesus, saying, "Where do You want us to prepare for You to eat the Passover?" And He said, "Go into the city to a certain man, and say to him, 'The Teacher says, "My time is at hand; I am to keep the Passover at your house with My disciples."'" And the disciples did as Jesus had directed them; and they prepared the Passover.

Now when evening had come, He was reclining at the table with the twelve disciples. And as they were eating, He said, "Truly I say to you that one of you will betray Me." And being deeply grieved, they each one began to say to Him, "Surely not I, Lord?" And He answered and said, "He who dipped his hand with Me in the bowl is the one who will betray Me. The Son of Man is to go, just as it is written of Him; but woe to that man by whom the Son of Man is betrayed! It would have been good for that man if he had not been born." And Judas, who was betraying Him, answered and said, "Surely it is not I, Rabbi?" He said to him, "You have said it yourself." (26:17-25)

Leading up to and including the beginning of the final Passover meal are four sub-elements of Jesus' own preparation for His sacrificial death: setting the time (vv. 17-19), sharing the table (v. 20-21a), shocking the Twelve (vv. 21b-24), and signifying the traitor (v. 25).

SETTING THE TIME

Now on the first day of Unleavened Bread the disciples came to Jesus, saying, "Where do You want us to prepare for You to eat the Passover?" And He said, "Go into the city to a certain man, and say to him, 'The Teacher says, "My time is at hand; I am to keep the Passover at your house with My disciples."'" And the disciples did as Jesus had directed them; and they prepared the Passover. (26:17-19)

The Jewish calendar was filled with religious celebrations, many of them involving feasts. The feast of Pentecost, or of Weeks, commemorated God's provision at harvest time (see Ex. 23:16). It was that feast which the Jews were celebrating in Jerusalem when the Holy Spirit came upon believers and Peter delivered his first sermon (Acts 2). The feast of Tabernacles, or Booths, commemorated Israel's wandering in the wilderness for forty years, when they lived in temporary dwellings and were dependent on God's direct provision for food and water (see Lev. 23:33-43). The Day of Atonement was the highest holy day of the year, culminating in the once-a-year sacrifice offered for sins in the Holy of Holies by the high priest. The blood of the sacrifice was then sprinkled on the altar, symbolizing God's provision of atonement for the sins of His people (Lev. 23:27-32). The feast of Purim celebrated the protection from slaughter of the Jewish exiles in Persia through the intervention of Queen Esther (Esther 9:16-19). The feast of Dedication, or Hanukkah, commemorated the victory of Judas Maccabeus over the Syrian despot Antiochus Epiphanes and the restoration of Temple worship in 164 B.C. (see 1 Macc. 4:36-61).

But in many ways the feast of Passover, closely associated with the feast of Unleavened Bread, was the central feast of the Jewish year. These two feasts combined to make an eight-day celebration that began with the Passover. As reflected in Matthew 26:17, the two were so closely connected in the minds of Jews that the feast of **Unleavened Bread** was used as a comprehensive designation that included **the Passover**. The two names were, in fact, used interchangeably to designate the entire eight day celebration. Technically, however, the **Passover** was celebrated only on **the first day**, the fourteenth of Nisan, and the feast of the **Unleavened Bread** followed from the fifteenth through the twenty-first of Nisan.

Both feasts commemorated the deliverance of Israel from Egyptian bondage. The feast of **Unleavened Bread** was named after the type of bread the Israelites were to take with them as they left Egypt in haste. Ordinary bread of that day, as in our own, used leaven, or yeast, to make it rise and become soft. Before a batch of bread was baked, a piece was pulled off and saved as a starter for the next batch. When it was later placed in fresh dough it would cause it to ferment and rise, and in every household that process was continually repeated.

Throughout Scripture leaven is used to represent influence, usually evil influence. Therefore, as a symbol of leaving behind all evil influence of their cruel and pagan captors, the Israelites were not to take with them any remnants of leavened bread they had prepared in Egypt. As part of the memorial they were henceforth to celebrate each year, they were to remove all leaven from their houses and eat only unleavened bread for seven days (Ex. 12:14-15).

As already noted, the **Passover** celebration began the day before the feast of Unleavened Bread, although traditionally it was considered to be the first day of the combined festival. The Mosaic law required that sacrificial lambs for Passover be selected on the tenth day of the first month (originally called Abib and later Nisan) and that the lamb be kept in the household until it was sacrificed on the fourteenth (Ex. 12:2-6). In the year Jesus was crucified (whether taken as A.D. 30 or 33), the tenth of Nisan was the Monday of Passover week. Therefore, although the incident is not mentioned in the gospels, the disciples would have selected a lamb on the day of Jesus' triumphal entry into Jerusalem, perhaps keeping it at the home of Mary, Martha, and Lazarus in Bethany, where they were staying.

As mentioned in the preceding chapter, over 250,000 sacrificial lambs were slain during a typical Passover in Jesus' day. And because tradition required that no fewer than ten people or more than twenty were to eat of one lamb, the number of celebrants easily would have exceeded two million. Because the lambs had to be slaughtered within a two-hour period, an enormous amount of blood poured from the altar site in a very short period of time. Eventually it drained into the Kidron Valley, just east of the Temple, and for several days after Passover made that brook run bright crimson. The Brook Kidron thereby became still another symbol to Jews, reminding them of the necessity of the sacrificial shedding of blood for the atoning of sin.

Yet the blood of all those lambs together could not cleanse a single sin, just as it was "impossible for the blood of bulls and goats to take away sins" (Heb. 10:4). Those thousands of lambs were but pictures of the one perfect sacrifice that the Son of God Himself was about to make on Calvary, as the sinless, unblemished Lamb of God, offering "one sacrifice for sins for all time" (Heb. 10:12).

It was probably early on that Thursday morning that **the disciples came to Jesus, saying, "Where do You want us to prepare for You to eat the Passover?"** As mentioned above, they already would have selected a lamb several days earlier, but they had numerous other preparations to make. They would have to have the lamb slaughtered by a priest at the Temple, which, as explained below, could be done only between the hours of three and five in the afternoon. If they had not already done so, they would have to buy unleavened bread, wine, bitter herbs, and the dip for the Passover meal.

Each part of the meal was symbolic of some aspect of the deliverance from Egypt. Just as lambs had been slaughtered that long-ago night in Egypt and their blood sprinkled on the door posts to protect the firstborn from the death angel, so lambs were now slaughtered and their blood sprinkled on the altar. Likewise, the lamb was cooked and fully eaten the same evening, just as in Egypt. The four cups of wine served during the meal symbolized God's four promises to His ancient people just before their deliverance from Egypt: "I will bring you out from under the burdens of the Egyptians, and I will deliver you from their bondage. I will also redeem you with an outstretched arm and with great judgments. Then I will take you for My people, and I will be your God" (Ex. 6:6-7).

The bowl into which the unleavened bread, the bitter herbs, and sometimes the bare hands were dipped (see Matt. 26:23) contained a paste called *charoseth*, composed of finely ground apples, dates, pomegranates, and nuts. That thick,brownish mixture was perhaps symbolic of the mud and clay used in the making of bricks for the Egyptians. Sticks of cinnamon, representing the straw used for the brick making, were also sometimes added to the *charoseth*. Into this mixture the bitter herbs would be dipped and eaten, as reminiscent of the bitterness of bondage coupled with the sweetness of deliverance.

The Passover lamb was to be slain at "twilight" (Ex. 12:6), which translates a Hebrew term literally meaning "between the two evenings." Josephus explains that time as being between the ninth and eleventh hours of the Jewish day, which would be between three and five o'clock in the afternoon. After being slaughtered by the priest in the Temple court and having had some of its blood sprinkled on the altar, the lamb would then be taken home, roasted whole, and eaten in the special evening meal with the unleavened bread, bitter herbs, *charoseth*, and wine. Any of it that was not eaten before morning was to be burned (Ex. 12:8-10).

It is likely that by this time, that is, Thursday morning, the disciples would have bought the herbs, fruit, nuts, unleavened bread, and wine. But they did not as yet have a place to eat the meal, which had to be done within the city limits of Jerusalem. For obvious reasons, rooms suitable for eating a Passover meal were at a premium. Perhaps thinking that Jesus already had arranged for a room, the disciples asked Him, **"Where do You want us to prepare for You to eat the Passover?"**

Jesus' answer no doubt was more than a little perplexing to the two disciples, identified by Luke as Peter and John (Luke 22:8; cf. Mark 14:13), who were sent to take care of the matter.

First of all they were to **go into the city** and find **a certain man,** obviously someone they did not know. From the other two synoptic gospels we learn that the man would be carrying a pitcher of water (Mark 14:13; Luke 22:10). That would have set him apart noticeably for identification, because it was highly unusual for a man to carry such a domestic article.

When the man was found, the disciples were to **say to him, "The Teacher says, 'My time is at hand; I am to keep the Passover at your house with My disciples.'"** The man carrying the water pitcher was probably a servant in the **house** where the meal was to be eaten. Therefore when Peter and John followed the servant home, they repeated Jesus' words to the owner, who then showed them "a large upper room furnished and ready" (Mark 14:14-15).

That clandestine approach to securing a meeting place was necessary to prevent Jesus' premature betrayal. Had the Lord announced the place earlier, Judas would surely have told the chief priests and elders (see Matt. 26:14-16), who would have arrested Jesus secretly there after dark and before the meal and the vital instruction He planned as part of it. Even when the instructions were given to Peter and John, Judas had no way of knowing the location. He and the other nine would not find out until they arrived that evening.

In God's redemptive plan it was necessary for Jesus **to keep the Passover . . . with** His **disciples.** It would be His last opportunity to teach them (see John 13–17) and to have intimate fellowship with them. But more importantly even than that, it would be the time of His transforming the Passover supper of the Old Covenant, marked by the shedding of lambs' blood, into the Lord's Supper of the New Covenant, which would be marked by the shedding of His own blood (Luke 22:20). He therefore eliminated any possibility of His arrest before that crucial task could be accomplished.

Because Jesus told Peter and John to identify Him as **the Teacher,** it seems probable that the servant carrying the water pitcher, and certainly the owner of the house, were believers in the Lord. Likely Jesus secretly had prearranged for the room with the owner, who is nowhere identified by name. In any case, the Lord knew in advance that the accommodations would be large, located on an upper level, and be fully furnished for the meal (Mark 14:15).

Jesus' statement, **"My time is at hand,"** was perhaps more for the sake of the disciples than the two men whom Peter and John would encounter. **Time** does not translate *chronos,* which refers to a general space or succession of time, but rather to *kairos,* a specific and often predetermined period or moment of time. Jesus' **time** was also, of course, the Father's time, the divinely appointed time when the Son would offer Himself as the sacrifice for the sins of the world (cf. 1 John 2:2). Until now, that monumental time had not come and could not have come (see John 7:6), but at this particular Passover it could not fail to come, because it was divinely ordained and fixed. That last Passover supper would set in motion the final, irreversible countdown, as it were, for the crucifixion.

I am to keep the Passover translates what is sometimes called a prophetic present tense, because it uses the normal form of the Greek present tense to state the future as if it had already arrived. Understanding the statement in that way is fitting, because our Lord was on a divine mission set in a divine timetable, both of which were unalterable. He not only was ordained to celebrate that last **Passover** Himself but to celebrate it **with** His **disciples.**

The profundity of Jesus' declaration is not apparent on the surface. As the events surrounding this occasion are carefully studied, however, it becomes clear that this seemingly rather ordinary statement was of momentous significance.

First of all, our Lord declared His commitment to keeping the Passover. He observed the Passover for the same reason He had been baptized, "to fulfill all righteousness" (Matt. 3:15). Not only as a Jew but also as God's own Son it was incumbent upon Him to obey every divine commandment of the Old Testament law. "Do not think that I came to abolish the Law or the Prophets," He declared at the beginning of His ministry; "I did not come to abolish, but to fulfill" (Matt. 5:17).

Observing this particular feast was especially important to Jesus. As recorded in Luke's account, He told the disciples, "I have earnestly desired to eat this Passover with you before I suffer" (Luke 22:15). It was by divine imperative that Jesus not only observe this last Passover of His earthly ministry but that He observe it with the Twelve.

It was without hesitation that **the disciples,** Peter and John, **did as Jesus had directed them; and they prepared the Passover.** Peter and John would then have had to get the lamb, probably at Bethany, and take it to the Temple for sacrifice. They were doubtlessly charged with this important task because they were the most intimate with Jesus of the

Twelve. In any case, the tradition required that only two men could carry a given lamb into the Temple. Otherwise the court of sacrifice would have been hopelessly crowded, with thousands of animals to be slain and only two hours in which to do it.

It is clear from this passage in Matthew, as well from many others in all four gospel records, that Jesus and the disciples ate the Passover meal on Thursday evening. Certain other passages, however, such as the one cited below from John's gospel, indicate that some Jews celebrated the Passover on Friday, which seems to create a contradiction and has given some scholars what they think is proof of scriptural error.

The apostle John notes that after the Passover meal Jesus took His disciples out of the city to the Garden of Gethsemane, which was on the western slope of the Mount of Olives. He was arrested there and taken first to the high priest Annas (John 18:13) and then to the house of his father-in-law, Caiaphas, who also still held the title of high priest (v. 24). A few hours later, while it was still early on Friday morning, Jesus was taken to Pilate. But the Jewish leaders would "not enter into the Praetorium in order that they might not be defiled, but might eat the Passover" (v. 28). Unlike Jesus and the disciples, those Jews obviously had not yet eaten the Passover.

Some interpreters suggest that because those religious leaders would surely have celebrated the Passover at the proper time, Jesus must have moved His observance up a day. But Jesus was meticulous in His observance of the Mosaic law and would not have desecrated such an important feast by observing it at the wrong time. Even had He wanted to do such a thing, however, He could not have, because the lamb eaten at the Passover meal first had to be slaughtered by a priest in the Temple and have its blood sprinkled on the altar. No priest would have performed that ritual a day earlier, or even an hour earlier, than the law prescribed.

Other scholars suggest that the chief priests and elders involved in Jesus' arrest were a day late in their observance. But in spite of their control of the Temple, even those ungodly men would not have dared make an exception for themselves for this most celebrated of all feasts. Not only that, but John recognized Friday as the legitimate Passover day, reporting that when Pilate finally agreed to Jesus' crucifixion "it was the day of preparation for the Passover" (John 19:14). In the same verse he states that "it was about the sixth hour," that is, noon on Friday.

Some three hours later, "about the ninth hour," Jesus cried out from the cross, "My God, My God, why hast Thou forsaken Me?" (Matt. 27:46). Shortly after that, "Jesus cried out again with a loud voice, and yielded up His spirit" (v. 50). John therefore specifically recounts that our Lord died within the prescribed time of sacrifice for the Passover lambs, from three to five o'clock in the afternoon of Passover day. At the very time those lambs were being sacrificed in the Temple, "Christ our Passover also [was] sacrificed" on Calvary (1 Cor. 5:7).

In addition to that evidence for a Friday Passover and crucifixion is the fact that, just as the tenth of Nisan was on a Monday the year Jesus was crucified, the fourteenth (the day of Passover, Ex. 12:6) was on the following Friday. Still further evidence is Joseph of Arimathea's taking Jesus' body down from the cross on "the preparation day, that is, the day before the Sabbath" (Mark 15:42; cf. John 19:42). That day of preparation referred to the weekly preparation for the Sabbath, not preparation for the Passover, as in John 19:14. Unless it was qualified (such as being for the Passover), the day of preparation always referred to preparation for the Sabbath and was commonly used to designate Friday, the day before the Sabbath (Saturday).

Why, then, did Jesus observe the Passover on the previous evening? The answer lies in a difference among the Jews in the way they reckoned the beginning and ending of days. From Josephus, the Mishna, and other ancient Jewish sources we learn that the Jews in northern Palestine calculated days from sunrise to sunrise. That area included the region of Galilee, where Jesus and all the disciples except Judas had grown up. Apparently most, if not all, of the Pharisees used that system of reckoning. But Jews in the southern part, which centered in Jerusalem, calculated days from sunset to sunset. Because all the priests necessarily lived in or near Jerusalem, as did most of the Sadducees, those groups followed the southern scheme.

That variation doubtlessly caused confusion at times, but it also had some practical benefits. During Passover time, for instance, it allowed for the feast to be celebrated legitimately on two adjoining days, thereby permitting the Temple sacrifices to be made over a total period of four hours rather than two. That separation of days may also have had the effect of reducing both regional and religious clashes between the two groups.

On that basis the seeming contradictions in the gospel accounts are easily explained. Being Galileans, Jesus and the disciples considered Passover day to have started at sunrise on Thursday and to end at sunrise on Friday. The Jewish leaders who arrested and tried Jesus, being mostly priests and Sadducees, considered Passover day to begin at sunset on Thursday and end at sunset on Friday. By that variation, predetermined by God's sovereign provision, Jesus could thereby legitimately celebrate the last Passover meal with His disciples and yet still be sacrificed on Passover day.

Once again we see how God sovereignly and marvelously provides for the precise fulfillment of His redemptive plan. Jesus was anything but a victim of men's wicked schemes, much less of blind circumstance. Every word He spoke and every action He took were divinely directed and secured. Even the words and actions by others against Him were divinely controlled (see, e.g., John 11:49-52; 19:11).

SHARING THE TABLE

Now when evening had come, He was reclining at the table with the twelve disciples. And as they were eating, (26:20-21a)

It was now sometime after six o'clock on Thursday **evening.** Although the original Passover meal in Egypt was eaten in haste while standing, with loins girded, sandals on the feet, and staff in hand (Ex. 12:11), the ceremony had changed through the years and had become more leisurely. Therefore, rather than standing, Jesus was **reclining at the table with the twelve disciples . . . as they were eating.**

The **eating** of the Passover meal involved a strictly defined sequence. First, the initial cup of red wine mixed with water was served. Wine was always mixed with water before drinking, but during Passover it was diluted with a double amount of water, lest anyone should desecrate the most sacred occasion by becoming drunk. Partaking of the first cup was preceded by the giving of thanks to God (see Luke 22:17).

Second, the ceremonial washing of hands preceded the main part of the meal, signifying the need for moral and spiritual cleansing and holiness of heart. Because they were celebrating God's deliverance from spiritual bondage to sin as they remembered His deliverance from physical bondage to Egypt, it was important that celebrants come to the table cleansed.

It is significant that shortly after that the disciples started another "dispute among them as to which one of them was regarded to be greatest" (Luke 22:24). After having cleansed their hands, it was obvious that their hearts were still as proud, self-serving, and ambitious as ever (cf. Mark 9:34). It may have been at this time that Jesus "rose from supper, and laid aside His garments; and taking a towel, . . . began to wash the disciples' feet" (John 13:4-5). The Lord specifically explained to the disciples that He had washed their feet "as an example that you also should do as I did to you" (v. 15). Washing another person's feet was normally done by a servant and was considered by most Jews to be the most demeaning of tasks. Jesus' example of humble, selfless service was a stinging rebuke of the disciples' pride and a profound lesson in condescending love.

To that visualized rebuke the Lord added a verbal one, saying, "The kings of the Gentiles lord it over them; and those who have authority over them are called 'Benefactors.' But not so with you, but let him who is the greatest among you become as the youngest, and the leader as the servant" (Luke 22:25-26).

The third part of the Passover meal was the eating of bitter herbs, symbolic of the bitter bondage their forefathers had endured in Egypt. As mentioned above, these herbs and pieces of unleavened bread were dipped in the *charoseth,* the thick mixture of ground fruit and nuts.

The fourth part was the taking of the second cup of wine. When the head of the household, the Lord in the present case, took that second cup, he would explain the meaning of the Passover.

Following that would be singing from the Hallel, which means "praise" and is the term from which *hallelujah* is derived. The Hallel consisted of Psalms 113–18, and at this point the first two were normally sung.

After the singing, the roasted lamb would be brought out. The head of the household would again wash his hands and then break pieces of the unleavened bread and hand them out to be eaten with the lamb.

SHOCKING THE TWELVE

He said, "Truly I say to you that one of you will betray Me." And being deeply grieved, they each one began to say to Him, "Surely not I, Lord?" And He answered and said, "He who dipped his hand with Me in the bowl is the one who will betray Me. The Son of Man is to go, just as it is written of Him; but woe to that man by whom the Son of Man is betrayed! It would have been good for that man if he had not been born." (26:21b-24)

Paradidōmi (**betray**) literally means to give over and was often used of delivering a prisoner over to prison or punishment. Jesus had mentioned His impending death to the disciples several times, but this was the first time He mentioned His betrayal. And it was especially painful for the disciples to hear Jesus say that the betrayer would be **"one of you."**

In the ancient Near East, the eating of a meal with someone was considered a mark of friendship, and therefore to eat with a person just before betraying him would be to compound the treachery. When David experienced the betrayal of a trusted friend, he lamented: "For it is not an enemy who reproaches me, then I could bear it; nor is it one who hates me who has exalted himself against me, then I could hide myself from him. But it is you, a man my equal, my companion and my familiar friend. We who had sweet fellowship together, walked in the house of God in the throng" (Ps. 55:12-14).

Being well aware of Jesus' many enemies, the disciples were hardly surprised that He would be betrayed. But it was unbelievable that the betrayer would be one of their own group. Understandably, they were **deeply grieved.** John reports that they were "at a loss to know of which one He was speaking" (John 13:22). Judas was perhaps among the least suspected, because his being the group's treasurer indicates his integrity was thought to be beyond reproach. In the midst of their agonizing and probable tears, the disciples "began to discuss among themselves which one of them it might be who was going to do this thing" (Luke 22:23). While discussing the matter among themselves, they may have pointed accusing fingers at one another, as Luke's account might suggest (cf. v. 24). But to their credit, the primary concern of each man was the possibility of his own culpability, and **they each one began to say to Jesus, "Surely not I, Lord?"**

It was doubtlessly because Jesus had just rebuked them for their self-serving egotism and fleshly ambition that they now showed signs of genuine humility and self-distrust. They were brought face to face with the sinfulness of their own hearts. Because their sins of pride had been so clearly exposed, they were open even to the possibility that somehow they had unwittingly said or done something that endangered their Lord.

Jesus' response did nothing to alleviate their anxiety. In fact, it emphasized again that the betrayer was one of them. He said cryptically, **"He who dipped his hand with Me in the bowl is the one who will betray Me."** Because each one of them had **dipped his hand . . . in the bowl,** the disciples had no better idea of the betrayer's identity than before. Jesus did, however, assure them that only one of them was guilty and that the others genuinely belonged to Him. "I do not speak of all of you," He said. "I know the ones I have chosen; but it is that the Scripture may be fulfilled, 'He who eats My bread has lifted up his heel against Me'" (John 13:18). Jesus' quotation from Psalm 41:9 referred to Ahithophel's betrayal of David by helping Absalom plot against his father (see 2 Sam. 16:15–17:3). Ahithophel was an Old Testament parallel to Judas, the ultimate betrayer.

But Jesus then put the betrayal in its divine perspective by assuring the disciples that the heinous act would work to the fulfillment of God's sovereign plan. **The Son of Man is to go, just as it is written of Him.** Jesus did not fall into Judas's trap but rather Judas, by his wicked rejection of Christ, became an instrument of God's plan. God would use even that vile scheme to work the righteousness of **the Son of Man.** The betrayal had been **written** ages beforehand in the pages of divine prophecy. Jesus Christ was "delivered up by the predetermined plan and foreknowledge of God" (Acts 2:23). Judas's malicious decision to reject and betray Christ was used by God in fulfilling Christ's gracious mission of redemption. An unholy man in the hands of a holy God was used to accomplish a holy purpose.

Contrary to the perverted reasoning of some interpreters, the fact that this sinful act was used by God to provide salvation from sin did not justify Judas by making evil good. God's sovereignly turning evil to His own righteous purposes does not make a sin any less sinful or the sinner any less guilty. God turned Judas's betrayal to His own divine purposes, but He did not thereby transform the son of perdition (John 17:12) into a son of righteousness. Judas was not an unwitting saint but a willing devil (John 6:70). The suggestion that he intentionally betrayed Jesus in order that the world might be redeemed through the crucifixion is as unscriptural as it is ludicrous. He had no interest in the salvation of the world or the coming of the kingdom. He was a consummate thief, a disillusioned, selfish mercenary who soon would sell out his teacher and friend for a mere thirty pieces of silver.

The Lord made clear that Judas's destiny was damnation. Despite the fact that God used the betrayal to fulfill prophecy, Jesus said, **"Woe to that man by whom the Son of Man is betrayed! It would have been good for that man if he had not been born."** Judas's future in hell was so terrifying that he would have been infinitely better off **if he had not been born.** He is the most graphic and tragic example of the people about whom the writer of Hebrews says that, because they "go on sinning willfully after receiving the knowledge of the truth, there no longer remains a sacrifice for sins, but a certain terrifying expectation of judgment, and the fury of a fire which will consume the adversaries. . . . How much severer punishment do you think he will deserve who has trampled under foot the Son of God, and has regarded as unclean the blood of the covenant by which he was sanctified, and has insulted the Spirit of grace?" (Heb. 10:26-27, 29).

Yet Jesus' fearsome warning of judgment seems also to have been a final gracious appeal for Judas to turn to Him for salvation before it would forever be too late. He refused.

SIGNIFYING THE TRAITOR

And Judas, who was betraying Him, answered and said, "Surely it is not I, Rabbi?" He said to him, "You have said it yourself." (26:25)

Had Judas not said to Jesus the same thing as the others, he would have become suspect. He therefore imitated their astonished disbelief and parroted their anxious queries to the Lord. He even called Jesus **Rabbi,** as if to reinforce his feigned loyalty.

Jesus did not respond with a direct accusation but said simply, **"You have said it yourself,"** affirming that Judas had condemned himself out of his own mouth.

It is obvious the other disciples did not overhear that brief exchange, because Peter privately asked John to question Jesus about the betrayer's identity, which he did. "Jesus therefore answered, 'That is the one for whom I shall dip the morsel and give it to him.' So when He had dipped the morsel, He took and gave it to Judas, the son of Simon

Iscariot" (John 13:24-26). John thereby learned the appalling truth about Judas, but he apparently did not tell Peter at that time.

As soon as Judas took the morsel he sealed his destiny for all eternity, because "Satan then entered into him" (John 13:27). The supreme adversary of God and the ruler of darkness came himself to reside in Judas, and he became hellish to the core of his being in a way that perhaps no other human being has exceeded. In betraying the Son of God, Judas became the archsinner of all human history.

Lest that devil incarnate participate further in the Passover meal with them or in any way interfere with Jesus' last precious moments with the true disciples, and to set him loose for the final scenes of his treachery, the Lord said to the betrayer, "What you do, do quickly" (v. 27b). Except for John, the others did not know why Jesus gave that instruction to Judas but supposed "because Judas had the money box, that Jesus was saying to him, 'Buy things we have need of for the feast'; or else, that he should give something to the poor" (vv. 28-29). Jesus knew who the betrayer was; John knew; and Judas himself knew. But the rest did not know.

ESTABLISHING THE FUTURE PROVISION

And while they were eating, Jesus took some bread, and after a blessing, He broke it and gave it to the disciples, and said, "Take, eat; this is My body." And when He had taken a cup and given thanks, He gave it to them, saying, "Drink from it, all of you; for this is My blood of the covenant, which is poured out for many for forgiveness of sins. But I say to you, I will not drink of this fruit of the vine from now on until that day when I drink it new with you in My Father's kingdom." (26:26-29)

After Judas left and Jesus was alone with the eleven faithful disciples, He transformed the Passover of the Old Covenant into the Lord's Supper of the New Covenant.

Passover was the oldest of Jewish festivals, older even than the covenant with Moses at Sinai. It was established before the priesthood, the Tabernacle, or the law. It was ordained by God while Israel was still enslaved in Egypt, and it had been celebrated by His people for some 1,500 years.

But the Passover Jesus was now concluding with the disciples was the last divinely sanctioned Passover ever to be observed. No Passover celebrated after that has been authorized or recognized by God. Significant as it was under the Old Covenant, it became a remnant of a bygone economy, an extinct dispensation, an expired covenant. Its observance since that time has been no more than a religious relic that serves no divinely acknowledged purpose and has no divinely blessed significance.

To celebrate the Passover is to celebrate the shadow, after the reality has already come. Celebrating deliverance from Egypt is a weak substitute for celebrating deliverance from sin.

In fact, Christ ended the Passover and instituted a new memorial to Himself. It would not look back to a lamb in Egypt as the symbol of God's redeeming love and power, but to the very Lamb of God, who, by the sacrificial shedding of His own blood, took away the sins of the whole world. In that one meal Jesus both terminated the old and inaugurated the new.

Jesus' institution of the new memorial consisted of three primary elements: the directive (vv. 26a, 27), the doctrine (vv. 26b, 28), and the duration (v. 29).

THE DIRECTIVE

And while they were eating, Jesus took some bread, and after a blessing, He broke it and gave it to the disciples, and said, "Take, eat; . . . " And when He had taken a cup and given thanks, He gave it to them, saying, "Drink from it, all of you; (26:26a, 27)

It is not certain as to what part of the meal **they were eating** at this time, but the supper was still in progress, and our Lord instituted the new memorial in the midst of the old.

First, **Jesus took some bread** and offered a **blessing** of thanks to His heavenly Father, as He always did before eating (see, e.g., Matt. 14:19; 15:36). The unleavened bread was baked in large, flat, crisp loaves, which Jesus **broke** into pieces before He **gave it to the disciples** with the instruction, **"Take, eat."** The fact that He **broke** the bread does not symbolize a broken body, because John makes clear that, in fulfillment of prophecy, "Not a bone of Him shall be broken" (John 19:36; cf. Ps. 34:20), just as no bones of the original Passover lambs in Egypt were broken (Ex. 12:46).

Shortly after that, **when He had taken a cup and given thanks** again, **He gave it to them saying, "Drink from it, all of you."** The verb behind **given thanks** is *eucharisteō,* and it is from that term that we get Eucharist, as the Lord's Supper is sometimes called.

As would be expected, all eleven disciples drank of it (Mark 14:23). It should be noted that the Roman Catholic practice of not allowing the entire congregation to partake of the cup is in direct contradiction of Jesus' explicit directive, of the disciples' obedient example, and of Paul's later teaching (see 1 Cor. 10:16, 21; 11:28).

Those two acts of Jesus were normal features of the Passover, in which unleavened bread was eaten and diluted wine was drunk at several points during the meal. This was probably the third **cup**, called the cup of blessing. Paul refers to it by that name in his first letter to the Corinthians: "Is not the cup of blessing which we bless a sharing in the blood of Christ?" (10:16). It is from the King James translation of that verse (". . . is it not the communion of the blood of Christ?") that Communion, another name for the Lord's Supper, is derived. A few verses later Paul refers to this cup as "the cup of the Lord" (v. 21).

THE DOCTRINE

"this is My body. . . . for this is My blood of the covenant, which is poured out for many for forgiveness of sins" (26:26b, 28)

Breaking the unleavened bread was a normal part of the traditional Passover ceremony. But Jesus now gave it an entirely new meaning, saying, **"This is My body."** The original unleavened bread symbolized severance from the old life in Egypt, carrying nothing of its pagan and oppressive "leaven" into the Promised Land. It represented a separation from worldliness and sin and the beginning of a new life of holiness and godliness.

By His divine authority, Jesus transformed that symbolism into another. From henceforth the bread would represent Christ's own **body**, sacrificed for the salvation of men. Luke reports that Jesus added, "given for you; do this in remembrance of Me" (22:19), indicating He was instituting a memorial of His sacrificial death for His followers to observe.

In saying the bread **is** His **body**, Jesus obviously was not speaking literally. A similarly foolish misunderstanding already had caused the Pharisees to ridicule Him and many superficial disciples to desert Him (see John 6:48-66). It is the same misunderstanding reflected in the Roman Catholic doctrine of transubstantiation. That literalistic notion is an absurd misinterpretation of Scripture.

Jesus' statement about eating His body was no more literal than His saying He is the Vine and His followers are the branches (John 15:5) or than John the Baptist's calling Him the Lamb of God (John 1:29).

As the disciples drank of the cup Jesus said, **"This is My blood of the covenant."** From Luke we learn that the Lord specified "new covenant" (22:20), clearly distinguishing it from all previous covenants, including the Mosaic.

When God made covenants with Noah and Abraham, those covenants were ratified with blood (Gen. 8:20; 15:9-10). When the covenant at Sinai was ratified, "Moses took the blood and sprinkled it on the people, and said, 'Behold the blood of the covenant, which the Lord has made with you in accordance with all these words'" (Ex. 24:8). When God brought reconciliation with Himself, the price was always blood, because "without shedding of blood there is no forgiveness" (Heb. 9:22;

cf. 1 Pet. 1:2). A sacrificial animal not only had to be killed but its blood had to be shed. "The life of all flesh is its blood" (Lev. 17:14), and therefore for a life truly to be sacrificed, its blood had to be shed.

Jesus therefore did not simply have to die but had to shed His own precious blood (1 Pet. 1:19). Although He did not bleed to death, Jesus bled both before He died and as He died—from the wounds of the crown of thorns, from the lacerations of the scourging, and from the nail holes in His hands and feet. After He was dead, a great volume of His blood poured out from the spear thrust in His side.

Obviously there was nothing in the chemistry of Christ's blood that saves. And although the shedding of His blood was required, it symbolized His atoning death, the giving of His unblemished, pure, and wholly righteous life for the corrupt, depraved, and wholly sinful lives of unregenerate men. Representative of the giving of that sinless life was the pouring out of that precious blood **for many for forgiveness of sins.** That blood made atonement for the sins of all mankind, Gentile as well as Jew, who place their trust in the Lord Jesus Christ. The **many** includes those who trusted in God before Christ died as well as those who have and will trust in Him after His death. Abel, Noah, Abraham, Moses, David, and every other true believer who lived before Christ, was saved by Christ's atoning death, as are believers of the New Covenant age. It was because of that truth that Jesus declared to the unbelieving Jewish leaders, "Your father Abraham rejoiced to see My day, and he saw it and was glad" (John 8:56).

THE DURATION

But I say to you, "I will not drink of this fruit of the vine from now on until that day when I drink it new with you in My Father's kingdom." (26:29)

As noted above, the divinely-ordained Passover remembrance ended when Jesus celebrated it that night with His disciples. Any observance of it since that time has been based solely on human tradition, the perpetuation of an outward form that has long since lost its spiritual significance. But for those who belong to Jesus Christ, that event in the upper room began a new remembrance of redemption that the Lord will honor until He returns in glory.

Fruit of the vine was a common Jewish colloquialism for wine, which Jesus told the disciples He would not **drink** with them again **until that day when** He would **drink it new with** them in His **Father's kingdom.** He had instructed them to remember Him in the eating of the unleavened bread, which represents His sacrificed body, and in the drinking of the cup, which represents His shed blood as a sacrifice for sin. "Do this," He said, "as often as you drink it, in remembrance of Me" (1 Cor. 11:25). That memorial was to continue **until that day** in His **Father's kingdom.**

The Lord's promise to drink with the disciples in that future kingdom was another assurance to them of His return, an assurance that would take on intensified meaning after His death, resurrection, and ascension. "When I return to establish My **kingdom**," He promised them, "you will all be there and you will all **drink** the cup **new with** Me." In other words, the Lord's Supper not only is a reminder of our Lord's sacrifice for our sins but also a reminder of His promise to return and share His kingdom blessings with us. From those words we learn that the end of this present age does not signal the end of this observance.

The supper concluded with the **singing** of **a hymn,** probably Psalm 118, the last psalm of the Hallel. Then **they went out to the Mount of Olives,** where Jesus would pray fervently to His Father, be betrayed by Judas, and be arrested by the officers of the chief priests and elders.

Helping the Impotent Disciples (26:31-35)

13

Then Jesus said to them, "You will all fall away because of Me this night, for it is written, 'I will strike down the shepherd, and the sheep of the flock shall be scattered.' But after I have been raised, I will go before you to Galilee." But Peter answered and said to Him, "Even though all may fall away because of You, I will never fall away." Jesus said to him, "Truly I say to you that this very night, before the cock crows, you shall deny Me three times." Peter said to Him, "Even if I have to die with You, I will not deny You." All the disciples said the same thing too. (26:31-35)

As much as Christians might like to think of themselves as being spiritually strong, those who are mature know from experience as well as from Scripture that in themselves they are weak. They would like to think they could never deny the Lord, contradict His Word, or be ashamed to be called by His name. But they know that every believer succumbs to those things from time to time. They find themselves in an environment of unrighteousness but do nothing to correct it. They have an opportunity to speak for Christ but say nothing. They need to be bold for the cause of Christ but instead are timid.

When I was young I often thought of what I might do if the Lord sent me to a place of difficult service where I faced the choice of being obedient to Him or risking death. I had read many stories of Christians who were martyred rather than renounce their Lord and I wanted to believe I would have such devotion. But I always had doubts, because I knew that in situations far less threatening than martyrdom I had failed to be as faithful as I should have been.

We look back to the apostles as model believers, as men of supreme faith who unflinchingly endured every hardship and persecution for their Lord. But it was not until after Pentecost that they did indeed become such men. On the last night of Jesus' earthly life, contrary to their self-confident assertions of loyalty and bravery, they demonstrated anything but faith and heroism. They discovered, along with everyone who reads the record of Scripture, that, in themselves, they were fearful, cowardly, and impotent.

As Jesus came to the Mount of Olives with the eleven remaining disciples after the Last Supper, He knew He soon would be betrayed and arrested, as He had told the disciples at least three times. He also knew that His disciples would desert Him and flee for their lives, which fact He now revealed to them for the first time; and they had as much difficulty believing the second prediction as the first. They still could hardly comprehend that it was possible for the Messiah to be put to death, much less that such a dreadful event would be the supreme act of God's redemptive plan. Nor could they believe that, regardless of what might happen to Jesus, they themselves could be anything less than steadfastly loyal.

The self-affirmations they expressed on this occasion were based on false feelings of personal strength and commitment. They thought their love and devotion to Christ were greater than they were and that their ability to handle temptation and intimidation was greater than it was.

Of all the things Jesus could have said to them, of all the things about which He could have warned them, He chose to tell them on this occasion of their imminent and certain desertion of their Master. Their failure to live up to their high estimation of themselves would prove to be a profound and unforgettable lesson, a lesson that, along with the reality of the resurrection and the coming of the Holy Spirit to indwell them, would change the course of their lives.

The incident recorded in 26:31-35 is integral to Matthew's presentation of Jesus' preparation for the cross. As He prepared to die for the sins of the world, Jesus needed to teach the disciples the need of continually dying to themselves (cf. 1 Cor. 15:3, 31; 2 Cor. 5:15) and of never trusting in themselves (cf. 2 Cor. 1:9).

Besides the certainty of Jesus' resurrection and the empowering of the Holy Spirit within them, perhaps the most important thing the disciples needed was an honest awareness of their own weakness. They desperately needed the poverty of spirit (see Matt. 5:3) without which no person can come to Christ and without which no believer can be effectively used by Christ. The first step to spiritual strength is the sincere, humble acknowledgment of one's own spiritual weakness (cf. 2 Cor. 12:9-10).

That is a lesson every child of God needs to learn and relearn. Because it is not difficult to stand firm in doctrine and moral standards when we are among fellow Christians, we are tempted to think we would never desert our Lord by compromising those truths and standards. But when we are out in the unbelieving world and are separated from the strength of Christian fellowship, we discover how unfounded such self-confidence is. Paul even had to remind the faithful Timothy that "God has not given us a spirit of timidity, but of power and love and discipline" (2 Tim. 1:7), because Timothy had evidenced some proneness to be ashamed of his Lord (v. 8).

There is no place in the life of a believer for shame of Christ or for defection and desertion. Shame of Christ is characteristic of unbelievers (see Mark 8:38) and should never be found in Christians. Because of his continual reliance on the Lord, Paul could truthfully affirm to Timothy, "I also suffer these things, but I am not ashamed; for I know whom I have believed and I am convinced that He is able to guard what I have entrusted to Him until that day" (2 Tim. 1:12). To the Roman church he declared with equal confidence, "I am not ashamed of the gospel, for it is the power of God for salvation to everyone who believes" (Rom. 1:16).

As the disciples soon learned that last night with their Lord, without His help faithfulness to Him is impossible. No believer is equipped in his own understanding or power to engage in spiritual warfare with the flesh, the world, and Satan. That important truth is beautifully expressed by nineteenth-century hymn writer John E. Bode in the hymn, "O Jesus, I Have Promised." In one stanza the affirmation "I shall not fear the battle" is qualified by "if Thou art by my side," and the affirmation "Nor wander from the pathway" is qualified by "if Thou wilt be my guide."

In predicting their desertion the Lord also taught the disciples another lesson about His divine omniscience. Precisely as He declared, all of them fled in fear when He was arrested a short while later that same evening (Matt. 26:56).

Although the disciples are essential participants in this account and are instructive examples for us, Matthew's central focus, as always, is on Christ as King. It seems the gospel writer's intent is to preserve the dignity and glory of the King of kings even in the midst of defection, betrayal, and supreme malevolence.

Skeptics are inclined to ask such questions as: "What kind of leader is this whose followers all leave Him in the time of His greatest need? What kind of leader is it who has so little control over those under Him that He cannot keep them from running away when the battle gets hot? Have not many men heroically stood their ground for lesser causes and in face of greater danger? How could one who made such great claims as Jesus have been such a poor judge and builder of men?"

But Matthew reveals how, in the purpose of God, the disciples' failure actually enhances and intensifies the grandeur of the Lord's achievement. By way of contrast, their impotence served to magnify His power, their unfaithfulness served to magnify His faithfulness, and their dishonor served to magnify His majesty.

In the Upper Room Jesus had given the first two elements of His own preparation for His sacrificial death: experiencing the final Passover (vv. 17-25) and establishing the Lord's Supper (vv. 26-30). After his account of Jesus' leaving Jerusalem and going to the Mount of Olives (v. 30) with the eleven disciples who remained (see John 13:26-30), Matthew presents this third element: helping the impotent disciples (vv. 31-35).

Christ shut down the Old Covenant of the Jewish economy with His celebration of the last Passover meal and ushered in the New Covenant in His own blood with the institution of the Lord's Supper. Then He taught this profound lesson to the men who, despite their imminent display of frailty, would become the principal human instruments in establishing His church.

From John's gospel we learn that after the Lord's Supper Jesus gave the eleven an extensive message that traditionally has been called the Upper Room discourse. In chapters 14-17 John records Jesus' teaching about believers' being with Him in heaven and serving Him on earth; the coming of the Holy Spirit; the meaning of true peace, faithfulness, joy, love, and fruitfulness; the opposition believers can expect in the world; and His second coming. He concluded by offering a beautiful and profound intercessory prayer on their behalf and in their presence.

But the synoptic writers (Matthew, Mark, and Luke) do not include that teaching. Instead they each move directly from the end of the Lord's Supper to the scene on the Mount of Olives (see Matt. 26:30; Mark 14:26; Luke 22:39).

As Jesus and the disciples left the upper room and proceeded to the eastern gate, they doubtlessly had to negotiate their way through teeming crowds of pilgrims who were preparing to celebrate Passover on the following day, according to the prevailing custom in Judah. For reasons explained in the previous chapter, the Judeans and Sadducees observed Passover a day later than the Galileans and Pharisees. Many of those preparing to celebrate on Friday probably had not yet secured rooms in which to eat the Passover meal and were making other last-minute preparations.

As Jesus and the disciples descended into the valley east of the city and crossed the brook Kidron, it was still flowing full from the late winter rains and was running bright red from the blood of the thousands of lambs slain that afternoon. The group headed up the western slope of the Mount of Olives toward the Garden of Gethsemane, a familiar place they had visited many times before. Gethsemane means "olive press," and that garden was one among numerous others on the Mount of Olives. Because there was little room for garden plots inside Jerusalem, many of its inhabitants cultivated small gardens just outside the city. It may have been that the Garden of Gethsemane belonged to one of Jesus' friends, who made it available to Him as a place of meditation and retreat. There would have been little hope for that in the crowded, noisy city.

Before they reached the garden, Jesus stopped and warned the disciples of their forthcoming desertion. The teaching of the Upper Room discourse had consisted largely of positive promises, but now it was time for a negative message, a warning that the self-assured disciples could not bring themselves to believe. We witness a vivid demonstration both of Jesus' omniscience and of the disciples' ignorance.

JESUS' OMNISCIENCE

Then Jesus said to them, "You will all fall away because of Me this night, for it is written, 'I will strike down the shepherd, and the sheep of the flock shall be scattered.' But after I have been raised, I will go before you to Galilee." (26:31-32)

As they were nearing the Garden of Gethsemane, **Jesus said to** the disciples, **"You will all fall away because of Me this night."** *Skandalizō* (**fall away**) is the term from which *scandal* is derived and has the literal meaning of setting a trap, snare, or stumbling block. In Jesus' day the word most often was used metaphorically, as it always is in the New Testament. Jesus predicted that the disciples would soon confront an obstacle that would make them stumble and **fall away** from their loyalty to Him.

He knew that **all** the disciples would desert Him and that they would be shocked and offended at His prediction of their abandonment. He knew they would fall away **because of** their fear of being associated with Him (**Me**) and that they would flee that very **night**, just as they did (v. 56).

While Jesus faced the cross with courage and valor that were distinctly divine, the disciples would be fleeing with typically human fear and cowardice. Even as He faced sin, death, and Satan for them, they would risk nothing for Him.

It was as if Jesus were seated at the control booth of a television studio monitoring prerecorded events on a large bank of screens before Him and determining which would be aired at a given time. Every event of that night, just as every event of His entire life, was under God's direct divine authority. No act was accidental and no word was incidental. He not only knew exactly what He Himself would do but what the disciples, the religious and political leaders, the soldiers, and the multitudes would do. He could see every movement as if it had already transpired and hear every word as if it had already been spoken.

In Matthew's portrayal Jesus loses nothing of His majesty and dignity even as, in the eyes of the world, He faced imminent defeat and ignominy. His own sovereign plan was unfolding, and the supposed victim was in reality the foreordained Victor.

Jesus' comment **for it is written** referred to Zechariah 13:7, which predicted the desertion He had just mentioned. He then quoted part of that verse: **"I will strike down the shepherd, and the sheep of the flock shall be scattered."** In quoting the Old Testament prophecy Jesus assured the disciples that their abandonment of Him, just as Judas's betrayal, was part of the eternal plan of God.

Without Jesus' explanation, the Zechariah passage would have been impossible for the disciples to have understood correctly. Zechariah's prediction was veiled, and its meaning could not have been discerned apart from the Lord's own interpretation. Zechariah was speaking about idolatrous false prophets whom the Lord would remove from among His people, but some of whom would renounce their deceitful practices (13:2-6). But in verse 7 the attention turns abruptly to a man the Lord calls "My Shepherd, . . . the man, My Associate." "The man, My Associate" could be rendered "the mighty man of My union" or "the mighty man equal to Me," clearly indicating that this person also was deity. It is against this divine Shepherd-Associate that God commanded the sword to be struck: "Strike the Shepherd that the sheep may be scattered."

In the broadest sense, the sheep that would be scattered represented Israel. Because Israel as a nation rejected and crucified her Messiah, Jerusalem and the Temple were destroyed. From that time (A.D. 70) the people of Israel were scattered throughout the world—where they have largely remained scattered for nearly 2,000 years. Even today, only a minority of them live in the state of Israel.

But **the sheep** of whom Jesus spoke that night on the Mount of Olives were the disciples, the first group, as it were, representative of and picturing all those who would **be scattered** when He, **the shepherd,** was struck.

But Jesus immediately encouraged the disciples with the assuring words **"But after I have been raised, I will go before you to Galilee."** Jesus faced death with supreme courage because He knew He had supreme power over death. But the disciples were still afraid of death, and even of imprisonment or humiliation. Jesus knew He would be raised from the dead by the power of His Father, just as He had predicted to the Twelve many times before (see Matt. 16:21; 17:9, 23; 20:18-19; cf. Rom. 6:4). Even more certain than the faith by which Abraham believed God could raise Isaac from the dead (Heb. 11:17-19) was the divine omniscience of Jesus. By that knowledge our Lord knew His heavenly Father would raise His only begotten Son from the dead on the third day.

The hard-headed and weak in faith disciples should have remembered and believed those predictions of their Lord. They should have remembered those whom Jesus Himself raised from the dead, especially Lazarus, at whose raising He declared, "I am the resurrection and the life; he who believes in Me shall live even if he dies" (John 11:25). But fear had eclipsed their memory and subdued their belief.

In His infinite patience Jesus told them again that He would be **raised** and that He would then **go before** them **to Galilee** and meet them there. That, of course, is exactly what He did. Outside the garden tomb, the angel told the two Marys, "Go quickly and tell His disciples that He has risen from the dead; and behold, He is going before you into Galilee, there you will see Him" (Matt. 28:7). When the resurrected Lord appeared to the two women a few moments later, He repeated the promise and the instruction (v. 10). Sometime later "the eleven disciples proceeded to Galilee, to the mountain which Jesus had designated. And when they saw Him, they worshiped Him" (vv. 16-17). Matthew's inspired record of the disciples' tragic weakness clearly affirms the omniscience of the Lord Jesus.

THE DISCIPLES' IGNORANCE

But Peter answered and said to Him, "Even though all may fall away because of You, I will never fall away." Jesus said to him, "Truly I say to you that this very night, before the cock crows, you shall deny Me three times." Peter said to Him, "Even if I have to die with You, I will not deny You." All the disciples said the same thing too. (26:33-35)

Peter either missed or disregarded what Jesus had just said about His being raised and appearing to them. He was so concerned about defending his loyal character that, in typical boldness, he blurted out, **"Even though all may fall away because of You, I will never fall away."** Proud, self-confident Peter, convinced of the strength of his love for Jesus, presumptuously proclaimed himself to be the truest of the true.

Like a self-willed child, Peter seemed to hear only what he wanted to hear and believe only what he wanted to believe. During the Last Supper, only an hour or so earlier, Jesus had given the disciples a similar warning. Speaking specifically to Peter, He said, "Simon, Simon, behold, Satan has demanded permission to sift you like wheat" (Luke 22:31). Though directed right at Peter, the "you" in this verse is plural (*humas*), indicating that the warning extended to the other disciples as well. They would all be so severely tested by Satan that it would seem as if they were being shaken violently like a tray of wheat in the harvester's hand. "But I have prayed for you [singular]," Jesus went on to say, "that your faith may not fail; and you, when once you have turned again, strengthen your brothers" (v. 32).

But Peter was oblivious to the Lord's words. Instead of acknowledging his need and expressing gratitude for the Lord's protection, Peter boasted, "Lord, with You I am ready to go both to prison and to death!" (v. 33). Unimpressed with that claim, Jesus responded, "I say to you, Peter, the cock will not crow today until you have denied three times that you know Me" (v. 34). With those compassionate but stinging words, Jesus singled out Peter as one who not only would desert Him but would even deny Him.

The Lord now repeated the prediction: **"Truly I say to you that this very night, before a cock crows, you shall deny Me three times."** Peter did not believe his Master this time any more than he had a few hours earlier. With amazing brashness and pride, he obviously thought that, wise as Jesus was, He was mistaken about the dependability and courage of his foremost disciple.

The Jews divided the night into four parts: evening, from six to nine; midnight, nine to twelve; cock crow, twelve to three; and morning, three to six. The third period gained its name from the fact that roosters began to crow about the end of that period and continued to crow periodically until after daybreak.

By the time Jesus and the disciples reached the Mount of Olives it was probably near midnight. Jesus was therefore predicting that, within a very few hours, Peter would deny the Lord **three times**—before three in the morning, when **a cock** would normally begin to crow. As Peter should have known, that is precisely what happened. No sooner had his third denial, augmented with a curse, come out of his mouth than "immediately a cock crowed" (v. 74).

But Peter's pride did not allow him to think such a thing was conceivable. His pride on this occasion was manifested in at least three ways. In the first place He contradicted the Lord, as he had done at other times. Shortly after Peter confessed that Jesus was "the Christ, the Son of the living God," he "took Him aside and began to rebuke Him" for predicting His suffering and death, "saying, 'God forbid it, Lord! This shall never happen to you'" (Matt. 16:16, 22).

Second, Peter's pride was manifested in his considering himself better than all the other disciples, claiming that, although they might desert Jesus, he would never do so. Third, he trusted in his own strength, foolishly declaring, **"I will never fall away"** and a few moments later adding, **"Even if I have to die with You, I will not deny You."** Sharing Peter's misguided self-confidence, though perhaps to less extreme degrees, **"All the disciples said the same thing too."**

The disciples were still ignorant about many things. They were ignorant of their own weakness and of Satan's strength. They were ignorant of the great power that fear would soon have over them. And they would not accept Jesus' interpretation of the Old Testament prophecy He had just quoted regarding the shepherd's being struck and the sheep being scattered. In other words they were wilfully ignorant, because they persisted in trusting their own understanding above the Lord's.

Like the disciples, believers only parade their ignorance when they claim to be wise, courageous, and self-sufficient. And often, as with the disciples, the Lord allows them to learn the hard way that they are really foolish, cowardly, and weak.

In humble, sinless grace Jesus was willing to go to the cross and shed His blood for the proud, foolish, and sinful disciples. Although He knew they soon would be ashamed of Him and even desert and deny Him, He was not ashamed of them. In spite of their pride, weakness, desertion, and denials, He would draw them again to Himself in perfect love. In a gracious act of divine mercy He would forgive and restore them.

Thankfully, our Lord is devoted to restoring disciples who have fallen and been unfaithful. In his first epistle John reminds his readers of that comforting truth. "If we confess our sins," he wrote, "He is faithful and righteous to forgive us our sins and to cleanse us from all unrighteousness" (1 John 1:9). Paul echoes that wonderful grace of recovery when he instructs spiritual believers to act as Christ's agents to restore in love fellow believers who have fallen into sin (see Gal. 6:1).

After Pentecost the eleven men who had deserted their Lord in fear and shame were hardly recognizable. When they were imprisoned by the high priest for preaching and healing and then were miraculously released by an angel, "they entered into the temple about daybreak, and began to teach" again. And when they were rearrested, flogged, and ordered by the entire Sanhedrin "to speak no more in the name of Jesus," they were "rejoicing that they had been considered worthy to suffer shame for His name. And every day, in the temple and from house to house, they kept right on teaching and preaching Jesus as the Christ" (see Acts 5:12-42).

The presence of the now-indwelling Holy Spirit within them doubtless was the source of power in the apostles' new-found courage and dedication. But even the power of the indwelling Spirit of Christ is no guarantee of faithfulness. Long after he had been indwelt by the Spirit, Peter discovered again how spiritually unreliable and impotent he was when he acted in the flesh rather than in the Spirit. Having been intimidated by the Judaizers, he refused for a while to have fellowship with Gentile believers and was severely rebuked face to face and publicly by Paul for his hypocrisy (Gal. 2:11-14).

It therefore seems certain that another factor besides the indwelling Spirit contributed to the apostles' later faithfulness—namely, the lesson they learned so bitterly at the end of the Lord's ministry about their own ignorance and foolish self-sufficiency and about Christ's divine omniscience and gracious sufficiency. They remembered His patient love and mercy in pulling them back to Himself, despite their cowardly and despicable defection. They had experienced His mercy so intimately and so profoundly that they were determined never to forsake Him again. But they knew that, in themselves, they were as weak as ever and that their only prospect for faithfulness was total obedience to and dependence on Him.

Could they have known it, the restored disciples would joyously have sung the beloved hymn "How Firm a Foundation," two of the stanzas of which are:

> Fear not, I am with thee; O be not dismayed,
>   For I am thy God, and will still give thee aid;
> I'll strengthen thee, help thee, and cause thee to stand,
>   Upheld by My righteous, omnipotent hand.
>
> The soul that on Jesus hath leaned for repose,
>   I will not, I will not desert to its foes;
> That soul, though all hell should endeavor to shake,
>   I'll never, no, never, no, never forsake!

The Son in Sorrow
(26:36-46)

14

Then Jesus came with them to a place called Gethsemane, and said to His disciples, "Sit here while I go over there and pray." And He took with Him Peter and the two sons of Zebedee, and began to be grieved and distressed. Then He said to them, "My soul is deeply grieved, to the point of death; remain here and keep watch with Me." And He went a little beyond them, and fell on His face and prayed, saying, "My Father, if it is possible, let this cup pass from Me; yet not as I will, but as Thou wilt." And He came to the disciples and found them sleeping, and said to Peter, "So, you men could not keep watch with Me for one hour? Keep watching and praying, that you may not enter into temptation; the spirit is willing, but the flesh is weak." He went away again a second time and prayed, saying, "My Father, if this cannot pass away unless I drink it, Thy will be done." And again He came and found them sleeping, for their eyes were heavy. And He left them again, and went away and prayed a third time, saying the same thing once more. Then He came to the disciples, and said to them, "Are you still sleeping and taking your rest? Behold, the hour is at hand and the Son of Man is being betrayed into the hands of sinners. Arise, let us be going; behold, the one who betrays Me is at hand!" (26:36-46)

In a sermon entitled "The Man Christ Jesus" preached on April 12, 1885, Charles Haddon Spurgeon commented, "It will not be enough for you to hear, or read [about Christ]; you must do your own thinking, and consider your Lord for yourselves. . . . The wine is not made by gathering the clusters, but by treading the grapes in the wine-vat: under pressure the red juice leaps forth. Not the truth as you read it, but the truth as you meditate upon it, will be a blessing to you. . . . Shut yourself up with Jesus, if you would know him." Just before that he had said, "[Yet] I am never more vexed with myself than when I have done my very best to extol his dear name. What is it but holding a candle to the sun?" Spurgeon concludes, "I cannot speak as I would of Him. The blaze of this Sun blinds me!" (*The Metropolitan Tabernacle,* vol. 31 [London: Passmore & Alabaster, n.d.], pp. 209, 213).

Even when one's best is done to study about and meditate on the Lord Jesus Christ, it becomes clear that the mystery is far too deep for human comprehension. We know and believe that He is fully God and also fully man, but to state and even sincerely believe such a paradox is not to understand it. It is far too profound even for Christian minds enlightened by the Holy Spirit to fathom. With humility, awe, and reverence we follow the Lord on His circuitous route to the cross.

By now it was probably near midnight on the Thursday of Passover week in A.D. 33 (or perhaps 30). Jesus' three years of ministry were completed. He had preached His last public sermon and performed His last miracle. He also had celebrated the last Passover with His disciples. But infinitely more important than that, He had come to *be* the last and ultimate Passover Lamb, the perfect and only sacrifice for the sins of the world.

As we look further into our Lord's last night before death, we grasp what we can of the sacredness of this powerful moment in His life and ministry. But we realize that no amount of study or insight can give more than a glimpse of the divine-human agony He experienced there.

One of Philip Bliss's beautiful hymns contains the words,

> Man of sorrows, what a name,
> For the Son of God who came,
> Ruined sinners to reclaim!
> Hallelujah, what a Savior!

The hymn writer borrowed his description of Christ from Isaiah, who predicted that the Messiah would be "a man of sorrows, and acquainted with grief" (Isa. 53:3).

There is no record in Scripture of Jesus' laughing, but there are numerous accounts of His grieving, His sadness, and even His weeping. He wept at the grave of Lazarus (John 11:35) and wept over Jerusalem at the time of His triumphal entry (Luke 19:41). Jesus knew sorrow upon sorrow and grief upon grief as no other man who has ever lived. But the sorrow He experienced in the Garden of Gethsemane on the last night before His crucifixion seemed to be the accumulation of all the sorrow He had ever known, which would accelerate to a climax the following day.

We cannot comprehend the depth of Jesus' agony, because, as sinless and holy God incarnate, He was able to perceive the horror of sin in a way we cannot. Therefore even to attempt to understand the suffering of Jesus that night on the Mount of Olives is to tread on holy ground. The mystery is too profound for human beings to comprehend and even for angels. We can only stand in awe of the God-Man.

Like every other aspect and detail of Jesus' life and ministry, His agony in the garden was integral to the foreordained, divine plan of redemption. It was part of Jesus' preparation for the cross, where the climactic event in the work of that redemption would transpire.

Ever and always the teacher, Jesus used even this struggle with the enemy in the garden the night before the cross to teach the disciples and every future believer another lesson in godliness, a lesson about facing temptation and severe trial. The Lord not only was preparing Himself for the cross but also, by His example, preparing His followers for the crosses He calls them to bear in His name (see Matt. 16:24).

Matthew 26:36-46 reveals three aspects of Jesus' striving in the garden: His sorrow, His supplication, and His strength. And in clear contrast to their Lord's unremitting struggle we see also the disciples' indifferent lethargy.

SORROW

Then Jesus came with them to a place called Gethsemane, and said to His disciples, "Sit here while I go over there and pray." And He took with Him Peter and the two sons of Zebedee, and began to be grieved and distressed. Then He said to them, "My soul is deeply grieved, to the point of death; remain here and keep watch with Me." (26:36-38)

After the eleven disciples echoed Peter's boast and insisted on their loyalty to Jesus even to the point of dying with Him if necessary (v. 35), they **then** moved with Him **to a place** on the Mount of Olives **called Gethsemane.** Although He had not announced in advance where He was going, "Jesus had often met there with His disciples," and it was that fact that enabled Judas to find Him so easily later that night (John 18:2).

The name **Gethsemane** means "olive press," and the garden probably belonged to a believer who allowed Jesus to use it as a place of retreat and prayer. As William Barclay points out, the owner of **Gethsem-ane,** like the owner of the donkey on which Jesus rode into Jerusalem and the owner of the upper room, was a nameless friend who ministered to the Lord during His final hours. "In a desert of hatred," Barclay observes, "there were still oases of love" (*The Gospel of Matthew,* vol. 2 [Westminster, 1958], p. 384).

It is likely that the garden was fenced or walled and had an entrance, perhaps even a gate. Jesus asked **His disciples** to **sit** at the entrance and keep Him from being disturbed while He went into the garden to **pray.** He did not use the normal word for praying (*euchomai*), which was often used of asking or petitioning other people, but the intensified *proseuchomai,* which was used only of praying to God.

Jesus had told the disciples two days earlier that "after two days the Passover is coming, and the Son of Man is to be delivered up for crucifixion" (26:2). And just a few moments earlier He had told them, "You will all fall away because of Me this night" (v. 31). They knew they were at a crisis point, and, like their Lord, they should have seen it as a time for deep concern and fervent prayer. Luke reports that Jesus told the disciples now that they should "pray that [they might] not enter into temptation" (Luke 22:40; cf. Matt. 6:13), a warning He later repeated (Matt. 26:41). But there is no indication that they uttered a single breath of prayer, no hint that they called on the Father to strengthen them. In smug self-confidence, they still thought of themselves as loyal, dependa-ble, and invincible. Like many believers throughout the history of the church, they foolishly mistook their good intentions for strength. The sinless Son of God felt a desperate need for communion with His heavenly Father, but His sinful, weak disciples, as so often they do today, felt no desperation about their weakness and vulnerability.

Leaving the other eight disciples at the entrance, Jesus **took with Him Peter and the two sons of Zebedee,** James and John. Through the years commentators have speculated as to why Jesus took only three disciples with Him and why He chose those particular men. As already mentioned, He probably left most of the disciples at the entrance to stand guard, lest He be interrupted before He finished praying. Some interpreters suggest that He chose Peter, James, and John because they were the weakest and needed most to be with Him. But the fact that they made more noticeable blunders than the others does not indicate they were the weakest but rather the most forward and presumptuous. They were, in fact, the obvious leaders among the Twelve and were the inner circle to whom Jesus gave special attention throughout His ministry.

It was surely for that reason that the Lord took those three with Him to pray. He wanted to teach them further about facing strong temptation with confidence in God rather than in themselves. In light of their self-declared dependability (v. 35), the disciples needed to learn the humility and poverty of spirit that is necessary before God can effectively use His people (see Matt. 5:3). He wanted Peter, James, and John to be convinced and convicted of their foolish smugness and feelings of invincibility. And He wanted them, in turn, to teach their fellow disciples that lesson.

Jesus did not take them along in order to have their companionship, sympathy, or help. He loved them deeply and doubtlessly enjoyed their company, but He knew them far too well to expect them to be of any assistance to Him in this crucial hour. He took them along for their benefit, not His.

His purpose also was to teach that, as important and helpful as the fellowship and support of other believers can be, there are times when one's only help is direct communion with God in prayer. He wanted to show them vividly that, in His humanness, even the divine Son of God needed the sustenance of His heavenly Father.

Fallen, sinful humanity refuses to acknowledge its weakness, but the unfallen, sinless Son of Man well knew His human weakness. When He became flesh and dwelt among men as a man, He accepted the weaknesses that are common to all humanity. He experienced the weaknesses of hunger, thirst, pain, and temptation. Now He was about to experience the supreme human weakness: death.

In acknowledging His human weakness and His consequent need for His heavenly Father's presence and strength, Jesus did what the disciples saw no need for doing. It was because He looked to His Father that He endured and passed every temptation, including sin-bearing and death—the severest test of all. Every moment of Jesus' life, from His first cry as an infant to His last cry from the cross, was lived in total submission to His heavenly Father. And through that sinless submission during His humanity He became a high priest who can fully "sympathize with our weaknesses, . . . one who has been tempted in all things as we are, yet without sin" (Heb. 4:15).

Every Christian at times faces temptations, trials, and heartaches that threaten to overwhelm him. In the depths of such testings, even our dearest and most spiritual friends are unable to provide the needed solace and strength. God expects believers to encourage and strengthen one another, and that is an essential means through which He builds up His children (see Luke 22:32; Acts 18:23; Heb. 10:25). But there are times when only direct, intimate communion with the Lord in intense prayer can provide the strength to meet their desperate need.

Jesus' ministry began and ended with relentless temptation directly by Satan. After He was baptized by John the Baptist, Jesus went into the wilderness of Judea and fasted for forty days and nights. At the end of that period the devil tempted Him three times, and each time Jesus responded with Scripture (Matt. 4:3-10). While Jesus agonized in the garden on the last night of His earthly life, the devil tempted Him again three times, and each time He responded by praying earnestly to His Father.

On both occasions, the temptations were private, personal solicitations directly by Satan to Jesus, and apart from His own revelation we would know nothing of them. The two weapons He used were Scripture and prayer, weapons the Lord provides each of His children (see Eph. 6:17-18).

As He went into the garden with the three disciples, Jesus **began to be grieved and distressed.** It was not that He had never experienced grief or distress over sin and death and over the isolation from His heavenly Father they would bring. He had always known that He had come to earth to suffer and die for the sins of the world. But the climax of His anguish now **began** to intensify as never before, as His becoming sin in our place and His consequent estrangement from God drew near. His very soul was repulsed by the encroachment of His sinbearing, not because of the physical pain He would endure but because of His taking upon Himself there the full magnitude and defilement of all man's iniquity. His agony over that prospect was beyond description or understanding.

When Jesus wept at the grave of Lazarus (John 11:35), it was not for Lazarus or for the grieving sisters, because He was about to restore His dear friend and their brother to life. He rather wept because of the power of sin and death over mankind, and possibly, even then, over the imminent prospect of His becoming sin.

But now a very deep and desolate kind of loneliness began to sweep over Him that caused Him to be severely **distressed.** In addition to the cross were personal disappointments that perhaps pressed Jesus into deeper depression. First was the treachery of Judas, an earthly lucifer who betrayed the loving and selfless Son of God, who graciously had taught and ministered to Judas for three years. Then there was the desertion of the eleven other disciples, made more tragic by the fact that, for them, He was Savior and Lord. He had been their teacher, healer, encourager, forgiver, supporter, and friend. Yet He would soon be forsaken by those He would never forsake. There would be outright denial by Peter, the one in whom Jesus had invested the most. In return, He would be the object of Peter's shame and the cause for Peter's cursing. Jesus would also be rejected by Israel, God's chosen and covenant people, through whom He came in the flesh and to whom He came as Messiah, Redeemer, and King.

In addition to the rejections were the blatant injustices He would face. The very Creator of justice would Himself be subjected to the ultimate injustice of mankind. He would be vilified and defrauded in the petty courts of sinful, spiteful, lying men—and that in the name of God. The One whom angels praise and with whom God the Father is well pleased would be cursed and mocked by the vile and wicked multitudes, many of whom had a few days earlier sung His praises and attempted to make Him their king.

Jesus confronted a loneliness that no other man could experience. The Son of God, who communed with the Father and the Holy Spirit and with all the holy angels of heaven, would find Himself forsaken by His Father as He became sin. He would be so identified with iniquity that the hosts of heaven would have to turn their backs on Him. And the same sin that repulsed them repulsed Him, the sinless, holy, pure, and undefiled Son of righteousness.

As the mortal Son of man, the undying Son of God had to take death upon Himself, and that, too, was grievous and depressing. As part of His divine mission of redemption, Christ came to earth to "taste death for everyone" (Heb. 2:9). As Alfred Edersheim wrote, "He disarmed Death by burying its shaft in His own heart," and death thereby had no more arrows (*The Life and Times of Jesus the Messiah* [Grand Rapids: Eerdmans, 1971], 2:539). But that last arrow of death caused the Lord inexpressible torment.

Although Satan's activity is not mentioned in this event by the gospel writers, his evil presence is fully evidenced by the fact that he entered Judas (John 13:27), who went out from the upper room to carry out the betrayal. His words and activity are not recorded, but we can be certain of his participation and of his intent. At the first great episode of temptations in the wilderness, Satan tempted Jesus to demand His rights, first for food, then for protection, and finally for sovereignty over the world. Now he tempted the Son of God again to demand His rights. Jesus did not deserve to suffer, much less to die. He deserved honor, glory, and reverence, not the cross. Why, the devil perhaps whispered in Jesus' ear, should the Author of justice be submitted to such gross injustice? Why should the Creator of life be submitted to the ignominy of death? He called Jesus to revolt against God and thus disqualify Himself from being the sacrifice for sin and the destroyer of Satan, death, and hell.

In all of those temptations—in the wilderness, in the garden, and throughout Jesus' earthly life—Satan sought to make Him disobey God and to rebel as he had done. He knew that in Christ's obedience to the Father was his (Satan's) own destruction. Therefore the intent of every temptation of Jesus was to lead Him away from the cross God had planned. It was when Peter brazenly declared that Jesus would never be crucified that the Lord said to him, "Get behind Me, Satan!" (Matt. 16:23). Although Peter's desire was to protect His Master, nothing he said could have been more contrary to His Master's will and work, or more supportive of Satan's effort.

After dismissing Satan-filled Judas from the upper room, Jesus said, "I will not speak much more with you, for the ruler of the world is coming, and he has nothing in Me" (John 14:30). Jesus was speaking about the intense conflict with Satan He would soon experience in the garden, where the ruler of the world would make his final onslaught. Just as in the wilderness, he would engulf Jesus in three great waves of temptation, each designed for the single purpose of causing Him to avoid the cross, in open revolt against God, thus preventing the work of salvation and leaving all men under the damnation of hell.

From the time of Jesus' arrest until His death, Satan seemed to have the upper hand in the events, but that was both temporary and by divine allowance. Jesus told the chief priests and the officers of the Temple when they came to arrest Him, "This hour and the power of darkness are yours" (Luke 22:53). That was Satan's hour, and by the Father's permission he attacked the Son with the full power of his malevolence. Satan's purpose was to induce Jesus to compromise His holiness and to relinquish submission to the Father and thereby deflect Him from the cross. God's purpose, on the other hand, was to prove the Son's righteousness and to demonstrate the Son's power over the severest temptations Satan could devise. Scripture nowhere teaches that Satan plotted to kill Jesus; rather, His death was by God's foreordained plan (cf. Acts 2:22-23), which Satan wanted to thwart. Once it became apparent that he could not prevent the Lord's death, Satan did all he could to make that death permanent. And when he failed at that, and Jesus arose, he inspired a conspiracy to deny His resurrection (see Matt. 28:11-15).

It is therefore hardly surprising that Jesus told Peter, James, and John, **"My soul is deeply grieved, to the point of death."** *Perilupos* (**deeply grieved**) is related to the term from which we get *periphery* and carries the idea of being surrounded by sorrow. It is possible to die from sorrow just as from other strong emotions, such as fright and anger. Jesus' anguish was enough to kill Him and doubtlessly would have done so had He not been divinely preserved for another kind of death.

The agony of this temptation was unequaled. It was Jesus' most intense struggle with Satan, more agonizing even than the encounter in the wilderness. The magnitude of His grief apparently caused Jesus' subcutaneous capillaries to dilate and burst. As the capillaries burst under the pressure of deep distress and blood escaped through the pores of His skin, it mingled with His sweat, "falling down upon the ground" (Luke 22:44). It was to this experience, no doubt, that the writer of Hebrews referred in saying that Jesus "offered up both prayers and supplications with loud crying and tears to the One able to save Him from death" (Heb. 5:7).

Jesus was not grieved because of fear He would succumb to Satan's temptations. As mentioned above, He had already declared that Satan "has nothing in Me," meaning that there was no sin or evil in Him in which temptation could take root. Nor was He grieved over a possibility of not conquering sin or surviving death. He had repeatedly spoken of His coming resurrection and even of His ascension. There was no doubt in our Lord's mind about the outcome of the cross, by which He would become victor over sin, death, and the devil. Jesus was **deeply grieved, to the point of death** because of His having to *become* sin. That was the unbearably excruciating prospect that made Him sweat great drops of blood. Holiness is totally repulsed by sin. The prophet Habakkuk revealed this when he wrote, "Thine eyes are too pure to approve evil, and Thou canst not look on wickedness with favor" (Hab. 1:13).

In that deep sorrow Jesus knew His only solace was with His heavenly Father, and with each wave of temptation and anguish He retreated to a place of seclusion some distance away (see vv. 36, 39, 42). Luke reports that "He withdrew from them about a stone's throw" (Luke 22:41), which amounted to thirty to fifty yards. The intensity of temptation and of Jesus' prayer response increased with each of the three sessions and is reflected in the positions the Lord took. At first He knelt (Luke 22:41), but as the intensity escalated He fell prostrate on His face (Matt. 26:39).

While He went to be alone with His Father, Jesus asked His three dear friends to **keep watch with** Him, leaving them not only to **watch** but also to pray in view of temptation (see v. 41), just as He would be doing.

SUPPLICATION

And He went a little beyond them, and fell on His face and prayed, saying, "My Father, if it is possible, let this cup pass from Me; yet not as I will, but as Thou wilt." And He came to the disciples and found them sleeping, and said to Peter, "So, you men could not keep watch with Me for one hour? Keep watching and praying, that you may not enter into temptation; the spirit is willing, but the flesh is weak." He went away again a second time and prayed, saying, "My Father, if this cannot pass away unless I drink it, Thy will be done." And again He came and found them sleeping, for their eyes were heavy. And He left them again, and went away and prayed a third time, saying the same thing once more. Then He came to the disciples, and said to them, "Are you still sleeping and taking your rest?" (26:39-45a)

These verses focus alternately on Jesus' supplication to His heavenly Father and on the three disciples' falling asleep. On the one hand is Jesus' intense, self-giving desire to do His Father's will, even to the point of becoming sin to save sinners and by prayer to deal with temptation cast at Him. On the other hand is the disciples' indifferent, self-centered inability to watch and to confront the conflict and danger with intercession on their Lord's behalf. While Jesus, understanding the power of the enemy, retreated to prayer, they retreated into sleep.

Again going **a little beyond** the three disciples, Jesus **fell on His face and prayed** to His **Father.** Except at the time when He quoted Psalm 22:1 as He cried out from the cross, "My God, My God, why hast Thou forsaken Me?" (Matt. 27:46), Jesus always addressed God as **Father.** In so doing He expressed an intimacy with God that was foreign to the Judaism of His day and that was anathema to the religious leaders. They thought of God as Father in the sense of His being the progenitor of Israel, but not in the sense of His being a personal Father to any individual. For Jesus to address God as His Father was blasphemy to them, and "for this cause therefore the Jews were seeking all the more to kill Him, because He not only was breaking the Sabbath, but also was calling God His own Father, making Himself equal with God" (John 5:18).

Although Jesus consistently called God His Father, only on this occasion did He call Him **My Father** (cf. v. 42), intensifying the intimacy. The more Satan tried to divert Jesus from His Father's will and purpose, the more closely Jesus drew into His Father's presence. Mark adds that Jesus also addressed Him as "Abba! Father!" (Mark 14:36), Abba being an Aramaic word of endearment roughly equivalent to "Daddy." Such an address would have been unthinkably presumptuous and blasphemous to Jews.

Jesus implored the Father, **"If it is possible, let this cup pass from Me."** By asking, **"If it is possible,"** Jesus did not wonder if escaping the cross was within the realm of possibility. He knew He could have walked away from death at any time He chose. "I lay down My life that I may take it again," He explained to the unbelieving Pharisees. "No one has taken it away from Me, but I lay it down on My own initiative. I have authority to lay it down, and I have authority to take it up again" (John 10:17-18). The Father *sent* the Son to the cross, but He did not *force* Him to go. Jesus was here asking if avoiding the cross were **possible** within the Father's redemptive plan and purpose. The agony of becoming sin was becoming unendurable for the sinless Son of God, and He wondered aloud before His Father if there could be another way to deliver men from sin.

God's wrath and judgment are often pictured in the Old Testament as a cup to be drunk (see, e.g., Ps. 75:8; Isa. 51:17; Jer. 49:12). **This cup** symbolized the suffering Jesus would endure on the cross, the **cup** of God's fury vented against all the sins of mankind, which the Son would take upon Himself as the sacrificial Lamb of God.

As always with Jesus, the determining consideration was God's will. "I did not speak on My own initiative," He declared, "but the Father Himself who sent Me has given Me commandment, what to say, and what to speak" (John 12:49; cf. 14:31; 17:8). He therefore said submissively, **"Yet not as I will, but as Thou wilt."** This conflict between what **I will** and what **Thou wilt** reveals the reality of the amazing fact that Jesus was truly being tempted. Though sinless and unable to sin, He clearly could be brought into the real conflict of temptation (see Heb. 4:15).

But when the Lord returned to the three disciples, He **found them sleeping.** That discovery, though not unexpected, must have added greatly to His grief and distress. No one can disappoint and hurt us so deeply as those we love. Jesus was not surprised, because in His omniscience He was perfectly aware of their weakness and had predicted that it would, that very night, be manifested even in desertion (see v. 31). But that knowledge did not alleviate the pain caused by their not being sensitive enough or caring enough to watch and pray with Him in the last hours of His life.

Just as these same three disciples had slept when Jesus was transfigured (Luke 9:28, 32), they were sleeping at the moment of the greatest spiritual conflict in the history of the world. They were oblivious to the agony and need of their Lord. Despite His warnings of their abandonment and of Peter's denial, they felt no need to be alert, much less to seek God's strength and protection. (How we can thank the Lord for the gift of the Holy Spirit, who continually prays for us! See Rom. 8:26-27.)

It was probably after midnight, and the need for sleep at that hour was natural. Jesus and the disciples had had a long and eventful day, and they had just finished a large meal and walked perhaps a mile or so from the upper room to the Mount of Olives. But even the disciples' limited and confused perception of His imminent ordeal and of their desertion of Him that He had predicted should have motivated and energized them enough to stay awake with Him at this obviously grave time.

In fairness, it should be noted that sleep is often a means of escape, and the disciples may have slept more out of frustration, confusion, and depression than apathy. They could not bring themselves to face the truth that their dear friend and Lord, the promised Messiah of Israel, not only would suffer mockery and pain at the hands of wicked men but would even be put to death by them. As a physician, Luke perhaps was especially diagnostic in viewing their emotional state, and he reports that, as we might expect, they were "sleeping from sorrow" (22:45).

But even that reason did not excuse their lack of vigilance. They did not fully believe Jesus' predictions of His death and of their desertion primarily because they did not want to believe them. Had they accepted Jesus' word at face value, their minds and emotions would have been far too exercised to allow sleep.

The startling events and controversies of the last few days—the institution of the Lord's Supper, Jesus' repeated predictions of His suffering and death, the prediction of their fleeing in the time of trial, and the obvious anguish He now experienced—should have provided more than sufficient motivation and energy to keep them awake. But it did not. Had they sought the Father's help in prayer as Jesus did and as He exhorted them to do, they not only would have stayed awake but would have been given the spiritual strength and courage they so desperately needed.

The disciples' predicted desertion of Jesus began here, as they left Him alone in His great time of need. His heart must have broken when He **said to Peter,** but also for the benefit of James and John, **"So, you men could not keep watch with Me for one hour?"**

Considering the circumstances, the rebuke was especially mild. It was not Jesus' purpose to shame the disciples but to strengthen them and teach them their need for divine help. **"Keep watching and praying,"** He implored, **that you may not enter into temptation."**

The Greek verbs behind **keep watching and praying** are present imperatives and carry the idea of continuous action, indicated in the NASB by **keep.** The need for spiritual vigilance is not occasional but constant. Jesus was warning His disciples to be discerning enough to know they were in spiritual warfare and to be prepared by God to resist the adversary. He was warning them of the danger of self-confidence, which produces spiritual drowsiness.

The only way to keep from being engulfed in temptation is to be aware of Satan's craftiness and not only to go immediately to our heavenly Father in prayer when we are already under attack but to pray even in anticipation of coming temptation. Peter perhaps first began to learn that lesson on this night in the garden. And after serving faithfully as an apostle for many years, he admonished Christians: "Be of sober spirit, be on the alert. Your adversary, the devil, prowls about like a roaring lion, seeking someone to devour" (1 Pet. 5:8). He also gave the assurance, however, that "the Lord knows how to rescue the godly from temptation" (2 Pet. 2:9).

We cannot overcome Satan or the flesh by our own power, and we risk serious spiritual tragedy when we think we can. When a military observer spots the enemy, he does not single-handedly engage him in battle. He simply reports what he saw and leaves the matter in the commanding officer's hands. In the same way, believers dare not attempt to fight the devil but should immediately flee from him into the presence of their heavenly Father. As our Lord taught, we are to pray for God not to "lead us into temptation, but deliver us from evil" (Matt. 6:13).

As Jesus here acknowledges, doing what is right is often difficult, because although **the spirit is willing, . . . the flesh is** still **weak.** Regenerated people who truly love God have a desire for righteousness, and they can claim with Paul that they genuinely want to do good. But they also confess with Paul that they often do not practice in the unredeemed flesh what their regenerated spirits want them to do. And, on the other hand, they sometimes find themselves *doing* things that, in the inner redeemed person, they do *not* want to do (Rom 7:15-20). Like Paul, they discover that "the principle of evil is present in [them]," that there is a law of sin within their fleshly humanness that wages war against the law of righteousness in their redeemed minds (vv. 21-23).

In light of that troublesome and continuing conflict, Paul then lamented, "Wretched man that I am! Who will set me free from the body of this death?" Answering his own question, he exulted, "Thanks be to God through Jesus Christ our Lord! So then, on the one hand I myself with my mind am serving the law of God, but on the other, with my flesh the law of sin" (vv. 24-25). The only source of victory is the power of Jesus Christ.

The fact that Jesus **again . . . came and found them sleeping** indicates that the disciples fell asleep even after He had awakened and admonished them. **Their eyes were heavy,** and because they would not seek the Father's help they found themselves powerless even to stay awake, much less to offer intercession for or consolation to their Master.

After He found the disciples sleeping the second time, Jesus **left them again, and went away and prayed a third time.** Although the gospels do not indicate it specifically, it would seem possible that, as already mentioned, Jesus had three sessions of prayer in response to three specific waves of Satanic attack, just as in the wilderness. It took three attempts for Satan to exhaust his malevolent strategy against the Son of God. Each time Jesus suffered more extreme torment of soul, but each time He responded with absolute resolution to do the Father's will. After the third siege, our Lord said **the same thing once more** to His heavenly Father, that is, "Thy will be done" (see v. 42).

In these prayers, as in all His others, Jesus gives His followers a perfect example. Not only do we learn to confront temptation with prayer but we learn that prayer is not a means of bending God's will to our own but of submitting our wills to His. If Jesus submitted His perfect will to the Father's, how much more should we submit our imperfect wills to His? True prayer is yielding to what God wants for and of us, regardless of the cost — even if the cost is death. The nature or character of our praying in the face of temptation should be to cry out to the Lord for His strength to resist the impulse to rebel against God's will, which is what all sin is.

We can be sure that the more sincerely we seek to do God's will, the more severely Satan will attempt to lure us from it, just as he did with Christ. And like our Lord, our response should be prayerful, single-minded determination to draw near to God.

After the third time of supplication Jesus was the victor and Satan was the vanquished. The enemy of His soul was defeated, and Christ remained unscathed in perfect harmony with the will of His Father, calmly and submissively ready to suffer and to die. And in that death He was prepared to take upon Himself the sins of the world. If the very Son of God needed to cry out to His heavenly Father in time of temptation and grief, how much more do we? That was the lesson He wanted the eleven, and all His other disciples after them, to learn.

After the third session of prayer, Jesus **came to the disciples, and said to them, "Are you still sleeping and taking your rest?"** Even after the two rebukes and heartfelt admonitions from the Lord, the three men were **still sleeping.** Their eyes were still heavy (cf. v. 43) because they were controlled by the natural rather than by the spiritual. They were so totally subject to the flesh and its needs that they were indifferent to the needs of Christ. They were even indifferent to their own deepest needs, because, just as Jesus had warned a short while before, they were about to be overwhelmed by fear for their own lives and by shame of Christ. Yet instead of following their Master's example through agonizing in prayer, they blissfully rested in sleep.

Jesus was teaching the disciples that spiritual victory goes to those who are alert in prayer and who depend on their heavenly Father. The other side of that lesson, and the one the disciples would learn first, was that self-confidence and unpreparedness are the way to certain spiritual defeat.

STRENGTH

"Behold, the hour is at hand and the Son of Man is being betrayed into the hands of sinners. Arise, let us be going; behold, the one who betrays Me is at hand!" (26:45b-46)

The word **behold** is used to call attention to something. As Jesus walked back to the three disciples, the men coming to arrest Him were already within sight. In fact, they arrived "while He was still speaking" (v. 47). As they approached, Jesus could make out the Roman soldiers from Fort Antonia and the chief priests and elders. Most clearly of all, He could see Judas, who led the motley contingent.

With great sadness, Jesus said, **"The hour is at hand."** He was not sad because He was unwilling to face the cross but because He was about to become sin. And His sadness was made the more bitter because His beloved disciples would not stand with Him as He gave His all for them. With a strength made even more magnificent by its contrast with their weakness, **the Son of Man** graciously submitted to **being betrayed into the hands of sinners.**

There was nothing more that Jesus needed to do and nothing more the disciples were willing to do. **"Arise,"** Jesus therefore said, **"let us be going; behold, the one who betrays Me is at hand!"** Rather than being weakened and deterred by the temptations, Jesus became stronger and more resolved; and instead of waiting for His enemies to come to Him, He went out to meet them.

With the courage of invincibility, Jesus had made the ultimate and final act of commitment to His heavenly Father, who He knew would raise Him from the dead on the third day. As He moved toward the crowd who came to arrest Him, He also resolutely moved toward the cross. "For the joy set before Him [He] endured the cross, despising the shame" (Heb. 12:2).

Because Jesus resisted every ploy and temptation of Satan, the adversary fled from Him that night, and he will likewise flee from every believer who resists him in God's power (James 4:7). "Walk by the Spirit," Paul declared, "and you will not carry out the desire of the flesh" (Gal. 5:16).

Matthew 26:36-46 gives the pattern and sequence of spiritual tragedy, which may be summarized in the words: confidence, sleep, temptation, sin, and disaster.

Self-confidence always opens the door to temptation. The first step of a believer's falling into sin is false confidence that he is able to be faithful to the Lord in his own power. Like the disciples on the Mount of Olives, he is certain he would never forsake Christ or compromise His Word.

Following self-confidence comes sleep, representing indifference to evil and lack of moral and spiritual vigilance. The sleeping believer has little concern for what he reads or listens to, even when it is clearly unchristian and debasing.

The third step is temptation, which Satan's system is constantly ready to place in the way of God's people. As with Jesus, the temptation appeals to one's personal rights and calls for rebellion against God.

The fourth step is sin, because a believer who is spiritually self-confident, who is indifferent to sin, and who does not turn to the Lord for help will inevitably fall into sin. No person, not even a Christian, has the capacity within himself to withstand Satan and avoid sin.

The fifth and final stage in the sequence is disaster. Just as temptation that is not resisted in God's power always leads to sin, sin that is not confessed and cleansed leads to spiritual tragedy.

That is the pattern the disciples followed that last night of Jesus' earthly life and that every believer follows when he does not depend wholly on the Lord.

But this passage also contains the pattern for spiritual victory, manifested and exemplified by Jesus. The way of victory rather than tragic defeat is confidence in God rather than self, moral and spiritual vigilance rather than indifference, resisting temptation in God's power rather than in our own, and holding to obedience rather than to the rebellion of sin.

The Traitor's Kiss
(26:47-56)

15

And while He was still speaking, behold, Judas, one of the twelve, came up, accompanied by a great multitude with swords and clubs, from the chief priests and elders of the people. Now he who was betraying Him gave them a sign, saying, "Whomever I shall kiss, He is the one; seize Him." And immediately he went to Jesus and said, "Hail, Rabbi!" and kissed Him. And Jesus said to him, "Friend, do what you have come for." Then they came and laid hands on Jesus and seized Him. And behold, one of those who were with Jesus reached and drew out his sword, and struck the slave of the high priest, and cut off his ear. Then Jesus said to him, "Put your sword back into its place; for all those who take up the sword shall perish by the sword. Or do you think that I cannot appeal to My Father, and He will at once put at My disposal more than twelve legions of angels? How then shall the Scriptures be fulfilled, that it must happen this way?" At that time Jesus said to the multitudes, "Have you come out with swords and clubs to arrest Me as against a robber? Every day I used to sit in the temple teaching and you did not seize Me. But all this has taken place that the Scriptures of the prophets may be fulfilled." Then all the disciples left Him and fled. (26:47-56)

Besides Jesus, the participants in this narrative are the mixed crowd that came to arrest Him, the traitor Judas, and the eleven disciples. The crowd attacked Jesus, Judas betrayed Him with a kiss, Peter presumptuously tried to defend Him with a sword, and the disciples defected from Him in terror. But amidst those tragic activities, all of which appeared to work toward Jesus' disgrace and defeat, the undaunted majesty and triumph of the Savior continued to manifest themselves as God's prophetic Word was unerringly fulfilled.

THE ATTACK OF THE CROWD

And while He was still speaking, behold, Judas, one of the twelve, came up, accompanied by a great multitude with swords and clubs, from the chief priests and elders of the people. (26:47)

While Jesus was still speaking to the eleven disciples in the garden, admonishing them to be spiritually vigilant and announcing to them His imminent betrayal (vv. 45-46), **behold, Judas, one of the twelve, came up.**

It seems strange and inappropriate that **Judas** would still be called **one of the twelve** while he was in the very act of betrayal. One would think Matthew would have been loath to refer to him in such a way. By the time the gospels were written, Judas's name had long been a byword among Christians, a synonym for treachery and infamy. Why, we might wonder, was he not referred to as the false disciple or the one who counted himself among the twelve?

But, in fact, all four gospel writers specifically speak of Judas as "one of the twelve" (Matt. 26:14, 47; Mark 14:10, 20, 43; Luke 22:47; John 6:71), whereas no other disciple is individually designated in that way. The writers clearly identify Judas as the betrayer of Jesus, but they do not speak of him with overt disdain or hatred. They are remarkably restrained in their descriptions and assessments of him, never using derogatory epithets or fanciful episodes, as did many extrabiblical writers.

The apocryphal writing *The Story of Joseph of Arimathea* taught that Judas was the son of the brother of the high priest Caiaphas and that he was sent by Caiaphas to infiltrate the disciples and discover a way to destroy Jesus.

According to another apocryphal writing, *The Acts of Pilate,* Judas went home after the betrayal and found his wife roasting a chicken. When he told her he was planning to kill himself because he was afraid Jesus would rise from the dead and take vengeance on him, she replied that Jesus would no more rise from the dead than the chicken she was cooking would jump out of the fire and crow—at which instant the chicken was said to have done just that.

An ancient manuscript called *Coptic Narratives of the Ministry and*

Passion maintained that Judas's wife was exceedingly greedy and that he was nothing more than the pawn of a manipulative wife. In the ancient Near East, to accuse a man of being subjugated to a dominating wife was considered highly slanderous.

A twelfth-century writing called *The Legendary Aura* claimed that Judas's parents threw him into the sea when he was an infant, because even at that early age they supposedly sensed he was diabolical and deserved to be destroyed. Somehow he managed to survive and grow to adulthood, and, according to the legend, soon after marrying a beautiful older woman, he discovered she was his mother.

Such bizarre accounts are common in extrabiblical literature. They are concocted to demonstrate the vileness of Judas and to reveal the contempt with which he was viewed. The gospel writers, by contrast, simply call him **one of the twelve.** Rather than minimizing the heinousness of Judas' treachery, this heightens the insidiousness of his crime more than any list of epithets could do.

When the traitor came to the garden, he was **accompanied by a great multitude with swords and clubs, from the chief priests and elders of the people.** This **great multitude** was not the typical spontaneous crowd of admirers that often sought Him out. It was rather a carefully-selected group brought together for the sole purpose of arresting Him and putting Him to death.

The **multitude** included officers of the Temple (Luke 22:52), who were granted limited police powers by the Romans in matters concerning Jewish religion and society. This group was probably armed with **clubs.** The multitude also included a cohort of Roman soldiers (John 18:3), which, at full strength, comprised 600 men. Because they had to have Roman permission to exercise the death penalty, the Jewish leaders had requested Roman soldiers to join in the arrest. These soldiers from Fort Antonia in Jerusalem, and perhaps some of the Temple police as well, were armed with **swords.** The soldiers probably were also included because on a previous occasion when the Temple police were sent to arrest Jesus, they came back empty handed (John 7:32, 44-46).

Apparently the Jewish leaders had intended for some time to accuse Jesus of rebellion against Rome. In that way His death could be blamed on the Roman government, and they themselves would be safe from reprisal by the many Jews who as yet still admired Him. In order to take advantage of the opportunity, **the chief priests and elders** must have hurried to Pilate to request the immediate use of his troops. Or perhaps they previously had arranged with the governor to have the soldiers available on short notice. Under intimidation because he did not want to risk another insurrection, especially in the midst of an important Jewish feast (see Mark 15:6-7), the Roman governor granted the request.

When he left the upper room, Judas must have rushed to meet with the Jewish leaders and inform them that the propitious time they had been waiting for was at hand. Although Judas's original arrangement had been only with the chief priests and other Temple officials (Luke 22:4), the Pharisees also became involved in the plot (John 18:3), as did the Sadducees and the entire Sanhedrin (Mark 15:1; Acts 23:6). And because the multitude not only included representatives **from the chief priests and elders** but the chief priests and elders themselves (Luke 22:52), those leaders obviously wanted to make sure Jesus did not overpower them or slip through their fingers again. When all four gospel accounts are compared, it becomes evident that the total number of men who came with Judas to the garden may have been as high as a thousand.

That mixed multitude was a prophetic portrait of the world's treatment of Christ, a vivid illustration of its wickedness, mindlessness, and cowardice. Instead of humbly welcoming the Son of God, embracing their long-awaited Messiah, and falling at His feet in adoration and worship, they arrogantly came to put Him to death.

Their wicked intent was manifest first of all in the gross injustice of their accusations and actions, which had no relation to truth or justice. Jesus had broken neither Mosaic nor Roman law. He had committed no immoral or illegal act. His only offense was in not recognizing or obeying the man-made, legalistic rabbinical traditions. Pilate had no love or respect for Jesus, but he acknowledged He was not guilty of breaking any Roman law, much less of inciting a rebellion (John 19:4). Yet to protect his own position with Rome and to keep from arousing the discontent of the Jewish leaders, he was perfectly willing to allow an innocent man to be executed.

Second, the multitude not only was unjust but mindless. The majority of them probably had little idea of what they were doing or of the reasons for it. The Roman soldiers, of course, were simply obeying orders as they were trained to do, without questioning the purpose or propriety. Most of those in the multitude had no personal grudge against Jesus, and some of them probably had never heard of Him before. Yet they had no compunction about participating in His arrest. In their spiritual darkness they had no ability to recognize Jesus as the very source and incarnation of truth and righteousness. In any case, they cared little for truth, righteousness, or anything else of spiritual value, but only for their personal welfare. Most of them were hirelings who were indifferent to the justice of what they did as long as they were paid and did not get into trouble with their superiors.

That multitude has had counterparts in every age of church history. Countless millions have been incited against the cause of Christ without having the least notion of who He is or of what He taught. They become willing victims of someone else's ungodly prejudice and join in causes that are patently unjust.

A third characteristic of the multitude in the garden was cowardice.

Not only the leaders, but probably the soldiers and Temple police as well, preferred to arrest Jesus in this dark, isolated place rather than in the streets of Jerusalem in broad daylight. A riotous mob can be intimidating even to armed men. And despite the advantages of darkness and isolation, the cowardly, apprehensive leaders felt it necessary to bring a thousand men, including several hundred armed soldiers, to arrest a dozen men who were known to be peaceful.

A guilty conscience always produces cowardice. The wicked fear they may receive justice for their injustice and therefore seek protection in numbers and in darkness. They are afraid of exposure and opposition, and they take no public stand or action unless the odds are overwhelmingly in their favor.

The multitude was also profane. What an unbelievable sacrilege was committed that night by the murderous, sinful men who dared to lay hands on the sinless Son of God!

The unbelieving world has always disdained the name of God, the Word of God, and the things of God. No pagan deity is so openly blasphemed by mankind as is the Lord Jesus Christ. Few evidences testify more boldly that the world is now in the hands of Satan than the fact that it is the true God who is most often blasphemed and mocked.

THE KISS OF THE TRAITOR

Now he who was betraying Him gave them a sign, saying, "Whomever I shall kiss, He is the one; seize Him." And immediately he went to Jesus and said, "Hail, Rabbi!" and kissed Him. And Jesus said to him, "Friend, do what you have come for." (26:48-50a)

Judas had left the upper room after dark (John 13:30) and gone directly to the chief priests, with whom he had already consummated the agreement to betray Jesus for thirty pieces of silver (Matt. 26:14-16). He had been looking for "a good opportunity to betray Him to them apart from the multitude" (Luke 22:6), and now was the ideal time. Judas rightly surmised that Jesus would later go to the Garden of Gethsemane (see John 18:2), which was well away from the crowds of Jerusalem. Pilgrims thronged the streets throughout most of the night during this high time of Passover week, when the two days of sacrifice overlapped (see chap. 12 of this volume). Only in darkness and in such a remote place as this could they take Jesus captive without arousing attention.

Judas was severely disappointed that Jesus did not turn out to be the kind of Messiah he expected. Jesus did not overthrow Rome or even the powerful Jewish religious leaders, and consequently He had acquired no positions of prestige and power with which to reward His disciples. Instead of teaching them how to conquer and control, Jesus taught them how to submit and serve. Instead of Judas's being richer than when he began to follow Jesus, it is quite likely he was poorer—except for the money he stole from the group's treasury (John 12:6).

Judas was already possessed by Satan (Luke 22:3), and therefore what he did was no longer under his control. Yet it was under the compulsion of his own unbelief, greed, and ambition that he had opened himself to Satan's presence.

Delivering up Jesus was in the mind of Satan, the mind of Judas, the minds of the Jewish religious leaders, and in the mind of Rome. But it was in the "predetermined plan and foreknowledge of God" ages before it entered the mind of Satan or the minds of those godless men (Acts 2:23). Even while doing Satan's business, Judas and his co-conspirators were being used to fulfill a divinely ordained plan that would result in the salvation of sinners like the very ones set on killing Him.

Because it was dark and because many in the multitude probably did not know Jesus by sight, Judas, **the one who was betraying Him,** had prearranged **a sign, saying, "Whomever I shall kiss, He is the one; seize Him."**

Kiss is from *phileō,* a verb referring to an act of special respect and affection, much as is still displayed today in many Arab cultures and even among some Europeans. In the ancient Near East such a **kiss** was a sign of homage.

Because of his lowly status, a slave would kiss the feet of his master or other notable person, as would an enemy seeking mercy from a monarch. Ordinary servants would perhaps kiss the back of the hand of the one they greeted, and those above the level of servant would sometimes kiss the palm of the hand. To kiss the hem of a person's garment was a sign of reverence and devotion. But an embrace and a kiss on the cheek was the sign of close affection and love, reserved only for those with whom one had a close, intimate relationship. A kiss and embrace were an accepted mark of affection of a pupil for his teacher, for example, but only if the teacher offered them first.

Therefore, of all the signs Judas could have selected, he chose the one that would turn out to be the most despicable, not because of the act itself but because he perverted it so hypocritically and treacherously. He could have pointed out Jesus in countless other ways that would have been just as effective. For whatever debauched reason he may have had, Judas chose to feign his innocence and affection before Jesus and the disciples to the very end. It is hard to imagine that even so wicked a person as Judas could have flagrantly displayed his treachery in the very face of the one who had graciously taught and befriended him for three years. But Satan, who filled him, knows no embarrassment and has no restraint on his wretchedness.

The raucous cries of the crowd to crucify Him must have been painful to Jesus' ears. He had taught them, healed them, and offered them the very bread of life, and yet they had turned against Him in contempt and derision. Even the hatred of the chief priests, elders, Pharisees, and Sadducees was painful to Him, because He loved and would have redeemed even those wicked men. The brutality of the soldiers who would beat Him, spit on Him, and place a crown of thorns on His head was painful to Jesus' spirit as well as His body. Even the cowardly indifference of Pilate would wound Jesus' heart, because He came to forgive and to save even that pagan Gentile.

But Judas must have wounded Jesus more grievously than all the others together, because he had been a disciple and friend, an intimate with whom Jesus unreservedly had shared His love, His companionship, and His truth. It is impossible to imagine what our Lord must have felt when Judas brashly approached Him **and said, "Hail, Rabbi!" and kissed Him.** Yet His grief was not for Himself but for this man who was so engulfed by greed and self-will that he would stoop to betray the dearest Friend he ever had or could have.

Kissed translates an intensified form of the verb used in verse 48 and carries the idea of fervent, continuous expression of affection. It was the word used by Luke of the woman who came into the Pharisee's house and kissed Jesus' feet, wiping them with her hair and anointing them with perfume (Luke 7:38, 45). It was also used by Luke to describe the father's reception of the repentant son in the parable of the prodigal (15:20) and of the grieving Ephesian elders on the beach near Miletus as they bade farewell to their beloved Paul (Acts 20:37). It was just such intense affection that Judas feigned for Christ.

Judas was so caught up in his deceitful display that even Jesus' sobering words, "Judas, are you betraying the Son of Man with a kiss?" (Luke 22:48) did not deter him. It is probable that Judas was now so much under Satan's domination that his actions were no longer voluntary.

In deep sadness, but with perfect composure in the face of Judas's perfidy, Jesus said simply, **"Friend, do what you have come for."** The Lord did not use the usual word (*philos*) for **friend,** which He used of the Twelve in John 15:14. Instead He addressed Judas merely as *hetairos,* which is better translated "fellow," "comrade," or "companion." Jesus had offered Himself to be Judas's friend, and more than that, to be his Savior. But the opportunity for salvation had passed, and in light of Judas's unspeakable treachery, even *fellow* was a gracious form of address.

Do what you have come for was Jesus' farewell statement to the son of perdition. For Judas those were the last words of Christ, and one can imagine that the words will ring as a torment in his ears throughout all eternity in hell. Judas exposed himself outwardly as the enemy of Christ he had always been inwardly, and until the end of history his name will be synonymous with treachery.

Judas's betrayal not only reflected the wickedness of the sinful world but the wretchedness of the false disciple. He is the epitome of a sham believer, the quintessence of a spurious Christian.

A false Christian is first of all motivated by self-interest, which for Judas was exhibited most obviously in his greed, because he was a thief (John 12:6). But it is likely that he also craved prestige, glory, and power, which he expected to share with Jesus when He overthrew Rome and established His earthly kingdom. He sought to use Jesus for his own sinful ends, and when he discovered that the Lord would not be so used, he turned on Him in open rejection and betrayal. He was like the seeds planted in rocky soil that spring up for a little while but wither when exposed to the heat of the sun (Matt. 13:5-6). When disappointment and testing came, he fell away (see vv. 20-21). He is the fruitless branch that is cut off and burned (John 15:6).

Second, a false disciple is also marked by deceit and hypocrisy. He masquerades in the guise of devotion to Christ, His Word, and His church. He is like a tare planted among wheat; only God can with certainty distinguish him from the real thing. He pays homage to Christ on the outside but hates Him on the inside. Like Judas, his outward signs of affection for the Lord cover a heart that despises Him.

But when a false believer is confronted with a price to pay for his association with Christ, his superficial interest in the church and the things of God invariably withers, and he is exposed as the impostor he has always been.

Judas's particular act of betrayal and its direct consequences were unique, but his basic attitude toward Jesus is characteristic of every false believer. Every age has found Judases in the church, those who outwardly feign allegiance to Christ but who at heart are His enemies. They identify themselves with the church for many different reasons, but all of the reasons are self-serving. Whether it is to get ahead in business by appearing respectable, to gain social acceptance by being religious, to salve a guilty conscience by means of pretended righteousness, or to accomplish any other purpose, the underlying motive always is to serve and please self, not God.

Judas is the archetype of Christ rejecters and the supreme example of wasted privilege and opportunity. He is the picture of those who love money, having forsaken the priceless Son of God for thirty pieces of silver (cf. Matt 13:22). He is the classic hypocrite, who feigned love and loyalty for Christ even as he delivered Him up for execution. He is the supreme false disciple, the son of Satan who masquerades as a son of God.

THE PRESUMPTION OF PETER

Then they came and laid hands on Jesus and seized Him. And behold, one of those who were with Jesus reached and drew out his sword, and struck the slave of the high priest, and cut off his ear. Then Jesus said to him, "Put your sword back into its place;

for all those who take up the sword shall perish by the sword. Or do you think that I cannot appeal to My Father, and He will at once put at My disposal more than twelve legions of angels?" (26:50b-53)

As soon as He was identified by Judas, the soldiers **came and laid hands on Jesus and seized Him.** When they saw their Master being arrested, the disciples asked, "Lord, shall we strike with the sword?" (Luke 22:49). But **one of those who were with Jesus** did not wait for a reply but **reached and drew out his sword, and struck the slave of the high priest, and cut off his ear.**

As we might guess, this act was performed by the impulsive and volatile Peter (John 18:10), who obviously was one of the two disciples who had armed themselves (Luke 22:38). It may have been that the synoptic writers did not identify Peter because their gospels were written earlier than John's, when Peter could have been in danger of reprisal from the Jewish authorities.

John also informs us that the man Peter struck was named Malchus (John 18:10), who, because he was in the forefront of the multitude, was probably a high-ranking **slave of the high priest.** Peter doubtlessly had aimed for Malchus's head but **cut off** only **his ear** when the man ducked. Peter probably was emboldened by the fact that a few moments earlier when Jesus told the multitude who He was, "they drew back, and fell to the ground" (John 18:6). Seizing that time of vulnerability, Peter perhaps thought he would kill as many as he could before he himself was slain. Or perhaps he assumed he was invincible, thinking that Jesus would not allow Himself or His disciples to be harmed.

As was often the case, however, Peter reacted in the wrong way. When the Lord had told the disciples, "Let him who has no sword sell his robe and buy one" (Luke 22:36), He was speaking of spiritual, not physical, preparedness. As Jesus had made clear many times, and as Paul later declared to the Corinthian church, "The weapons of our warfare are not of the flesh, but divinely powerful for the destruction of fortresses" (2 Cor. 10:4).

The church has never made advances by physical warfare, and every time it has tried, the cause of Christ has been severely harmed. There are no holy wars. Every war fought in the name of Christ has been utterly unholy, contradicting and undermining everything His Word teaches. The kingdom of God does not advance with fleshly weapons or by fleshly strategy. The battleground is spiritual, and it makes no sense to fight with physical weapons.

Jesus told Pilate, "My kingdom is not of this world. If My kingdom were of this world, then My servants would be fighting, that I might not be delivered up to the Jews; but as it is, My kingdom is not of this realm" (John 18:36). Wars such as the Crusades that are fought in the name of

Christ are an affront to Christ. In reality, they are crusades against the very One who is claimed to be served.

Jesus gave Peter two important reasons that explain why the use of physical weapons cannot be used to defend, much less extend, His kingdom. First of all, to do so is fatal. **"Put your sword back into its place,"** Jesus told Peter; **"for all those who take up the sword shall perish by the sword."** Jesus was not philosophizing by declaring that everyone who takes up arms will himself be killed by arms or that a person who uses violence will be killed violently. His point was that those who commit acts of violence to achieve personal ends will face punishment by civil authorities, **the sword** representing a common means of execution in the ancient world. He was simply reiterating the divine standard set forth in Genesis: "Whoever sheds man's blood, by man his blood shall be shed, for in the image of God He made man" (9:6). To protect the sanctity of human life, God declares that the one who wantonly takes the life of another person is subject to capital punishment.

God has given human government the right to execute murderers. "It does not bear the sword for nothing," Paul said; "for it is a minister of God, an avenger who brings wrath upon the one who practices evil" (Rom. 13:4). The apostle willingly applied that law to himself. In his defense before Festus he said, "If then I am a wrongdoer, and have committed anything worthy of death, I do not refuse to die" (Acts 25:11).

In telling Peter to put his **sword back into its place** Jesus was saying, in effect, "No matter how wicked and unjust my arrest is, you have no right to take vigilante action. If you take a life while doing that, your own life will justly be forfeited as punishment."

Jesus' arrest and subsequent trials were clearly unjust, but they were nevertheless carried out within the framework of the legal systems of that day. Although it exercised its power only by the permission of Rome, the Sanhedrin was a civil as well as religious governing body in Israel. Pilate was the duly appointed Roman governor. Jesus' point was that personal violent action against even an unjust governing body is wrong. God has the sovereign right to overrule human governments, as He has done frequently throughout history, but no individual has such a right.

Jesus was not speaking about self-defense or the defense of loved ones or friends from an attacker. Nor was he talking about fighting in the armed forces of one's country. He was referring to violently taking justice into one's own hands. Under no circumstances does a Christian or anyone else have the right to dispense personal justice, even to defend Christ's name or Word.

Second, trying to defend Christ and His kingdom by physical force is foolish. **"Do you not think that I cannot appeal to My Father,"**

Jesus said, **"and He will at once put at My disposal more than twelve legions of angels?"** Trying to defend Christ with a sword not only is morally wrong according to God's law but is also pointless. After having seen Jesus' divine power demonstrated hundreds of times, why did Peter think his Lord needed the puny help of one sword, or even a thousand swords?

A full Roman legion was composed of 6,000 soldiers. **More than twelve legions of angels** therefore would be in excess of 72,000. If a single angel of God could slay 185,000 men in one night, as with the Assyrian troops of Sennacherib (2 Kings 19:35), the power of 72,000 angels is unimaginable. Jesus explained to his impetuous disciple that He had immediate access to supernatural forces that easily could destroy the entire Roman army, not to mention the mere cohort of 600 soldiers (John 18:3) they now faced. Peter's demonstration of self-willed bravery was therefore unnecessary and absurd. The Lord's battles are won in His power alone, and any human efforts on His behalf that are not made in submission to His divine will and strength are presumptuous and futile.

THE FULFILLMENT OF PROPHECY

"How then shall the Scriptures be fulfilled, that it must happen this way?" (26:54)

For Peter to violently oppose Jesus' arrest was also to oppose the fulfillment of God's prophesied plan of redemption. According to God's own **Scriptures**, He reminded Peter again that **"it must happen this way."** On at least three other occasions (see Matt. 16:21; 17:22-23; 20:18-19; cf. 12:40; 17:9, 12) He had told the disciples that it was necessary that He suffer, die, and be raised from the dead.

As David predicted, a close and trusted friend would betray the Messiah (Pss. 41:9; 55:12-14). Isaiah foretold that He would be "despised and forsaken of men, a man of sorrows, and acquainted with grief; . . . smitten of God, and afflicted. . . . pierced through for our transgressions, . . . crushed for our iniquities; . . . [chastened] for our well-being . . . [that] by His scourging we are healed." He would be oppressed, afflicted, and slaughtered like a lamb that does not cry out. "The Lord was pleased to crush Him, putting Him to grief; if He would render Himself as a guilt offering." He "will justify the many, as He will bear their iniquities" (Isa. 53:3-5, 7, 10-11).

Because Peter boasted too loudly, prayed too little, slept too much, and acted too fast, he seemed invariably to miss the point of what Jesus was saying and doing. The Lord therefore had to explain to him again that what was happening was in God's perfect plan. "Put the sword into the sheath," He said; "the cup which the Father has given Me, shall I not drink it?" (John 18:11). Then, in the only instance recorded in Scripture of Jesus' healing a fresh wound, "He touched [Malchus's] ear and healed him" (Luke 22:51). In a sovereign act of miraculous grace, Jesus undid Peter's damage.

THE DEFECTION OF THE DISCIPLES

At that time Jesus said to the multitudes, "Have you come out with swords and clubs to arrest Me as against a robber? Every day I used to sit in the temple teaching and you did not seize Me. But all this has taken place that the Scriptures of the prophets may be fulfilled." Then all the disciples left Him and fled. (26:55-56)

With an overtone of sarcasm **Jesus** pointed up the subterfuge and cowardice of **the multitudes** who now confronted Him in the garden. "Am I so dangerous," He said to them, "that you had to come out in such great numbers and **with swords and clubs to arrest Me as against a robber?** Am I so elusive that you had to capture me by stealth in the dead of night? You know very well that **every day I used to sit in the temple teaching.** Why did you **not seize Me** then?"

Jesus knew that no amount of truth or logic would dissuade His enemies from executing their plot against Him. They knew their charges were spurious and unjust and that they had had countless opportunities to arrest Him publicly. But when evil men are determined to have their way, they will not be deterred by such considerations as truth, justice, legality, or righteousness.

Jesus then told the crowd what He had just reminded Peter of: **All this has taken place that the Scriptures of the prophets may be fulfilled.** "Whatever your personal reasons and motivations may be," He was saying, "you are unwittingly accomplishing what your own **Scriptures** have said through **the prophets** that you would do to your Messiah. Completely apart from your own evil intentions, God is sovereignly using you to accomplish His righteous and gracious purposes. And in doing so, He will demonstrate that His infallible Word through **the prophets** will **be fulfilled.**"

Those words obviously gave little comfort or courage to the disciples. At last it dawned on them that their Lord was finally a captive of His enemies and that He would neither do anything Himself nor allow them to do anything to interfere. Although the leaders of the multitude had said they sought only Jesus (John 18:5), the disciples were fearful they would be arrested as accomplices, and therefore **all the disciples left Him and fled.**

The "little faith" disciples did not trust Jesus to save them and were afraid to risk suffering and perhaps even dying with Him. Just as He had predicted earlier that evening, when the Shepherd was struck the sheep scattered (Matt. 26:31).

It is easy to criticize the disciples for their faithlessness and cowardice. But every honest believer knows that at times he has run from possible embarrassment, ridicule, or mockery because of his association with Christ. We have to confess that we, too, have left our Lord and fled when the cost of discipleship has seemed too high.

Just as there are common marks of false disciples there are common characteristics of defective disciples, as the eleven proved to be on this occasion. First of all, they were unprepared. All of them, including the three Jesus chose to accompany Him into the garden, had fallen asleep at this time of Jesus' great struggle. Because they confused good intentions with spiritual strength, they were powerless when testing came. They were overconfident and felt no need of prayer. Had they taken to heart the Lord's marvelous promises in the Upper Room discourse (John 13–17), they would have had the divinely provided wisdom and strength to meet the crisis.

But because they had paid little attention to Jesus' teaching and had neglected prayer, the disciples discovered they were unprepared and inadequate. It is an absolute spiritual law that a believer who neglects the study of God's Word and neglects fellowship with Him in prayer will be unprepared (cf. Matt. 26:41). When testing comes he will be weak, afraid, unfaithful, and ineffective.

A second mark of a defective disciple is impulsiveness. The eleven disciples, and Peter in particular, reacted on the basis of emotion rather than revelation. They did not look at the situation from the perfect perspective of God's truth but from the imperfect and distorted perspective of their own understanding. Therefore, instead of acting on the basis of God's Word and in the promised power of His Spirit, they reacted on the basis of their emotions and in the weakness of their own resources.

The believer who fails to saturate himself in God's Word and to have fellowship in God's presence becomes a captive of circumstances. His thinking is based on the emotions of the moment, and his actions are based on the impulses of the moment.

A third mark of a defective disciple is impatience. Because the disciples refused to take Jesus' truth and promises to heart, they became anxious and impatient when things did not go as they thought they should. They could not wait for the Lord's deliverance and so devised their own.

Many Christians take the easy route of fleeing from trouble rather than trusting God to see them through it. Instead of trusting the Savior to deliver them, and in so doing to demonstrate His grace and power, they try to avoid trouble at any cost and thereby bring reproach upon Him.

A fourth mark of a defective disciple is carnality. The disciples, typified by Peter, depended wholly on their own fleshly power to protect them. Because he refused to trust His Lord's way and power, Peter had nothing to rely on but his sword, which was pathetically inadequate even from a human perspective.

When believers lose their fleshly weapons or discover those weapons are ineffective, they sometimes simply flee in desperation.

The major participant in this garden scene was Jesus Himself, and in Matthew's account we see His triumph even while His enemies were taking Him captive. Through their evil plot to put Him to death He would accomplish the divine plan for giving men eternal life.

All of His disciples deserted Him, and one betrayed Him, yet the divine work of redemption continued to be fulfilled on schedule, precisely according to God's sovereign and prophesied plan. As the disciples' faithfulness decreased, Jesus' demonstration of power and glory increased. As the plans of His enemies seemed to prosper, the plan of God prospered still more in spite of them.

It is not clear exactly when it happened, but perhaps right after Judas's kiss, Jesus took the initiative and confronted the multitude. To assure His enemies that He was not trying to hide or escape, and perhaps to strip Judas of any credit for identifying Him, He said, "Whom do you seek?" When they replied, "Jesus the Nazarene," He said, "I am He," and at that those words "they drew back, and fell to the ground" (John 18: 4-6). "I am He" translates *egō eimi,* which literally means "I am," the covenant name of God (see Ex. 3:14).

The exact reason for the multitude's temporary immobility is not revealed, but doubtless it was caused by the overwhelming power of Christ. Although the Jews in the group would have associated Jesus' words with the name of God, on a previous occasion when He claimed that name for Himself they were enraged rather than fearful and tried to stone Him to death (John 8:58-59). And that name would have had no significance at all to the 600 Roman soldiers. In addition, it seems almost certain that many of the men in that huge crowd could not hear what Jesus was saying. Therefore their instantly and involuntarily falling to the ground as one man was not caused so much by fear as by a direct, miraculous burst of the power of God. It was as if the Father were declaring in action what He had previously declared in words: "This is My beloved Son" (Matt. 3:17; 17:5). The multitude was able to rise only when God's restraining hand was lifted.

Perhaps while they were still lying dazed and perplexed on the ground, Jesus again "asked them, 'Whom do you seek?'" and they again replied, "Jesus the Nazarene" (John 18:7). He then said, "I told you that I am He; if therefore you seek Me, let these go their way" (v. 8), referring to the disciples.

The multitude that night reacted to being cast to the ground much as the homosexuals of Sodom reacted to being struck blind. Those wicked men were so consumed by their sexual perversion that even in blindness they persisted to the point of exhaustion, futilely trying to satisfy their lust (Gen. 19:11). In a similar way the men who came to arrest Jesus were so bent on their ungodly mission that they crawled up out of the dirt as if nothing had happened, determined at all costs to carry out their wicked scheme. Though not to the degree of being indwelt by Satan as was Judas, the entire multitude was subservient to the prince of this world.

Jesus had already unmasked the duplicity and cowardice of the leaders of the multitude when He asked why they had not arrested Him earlier in the week. He not only had been in Jerusalem every day but had been the focus of public attention on several occasions, most notably when He entered the city triumphantly and when He cleansed the Temple of the money changers and sacrifice merchants.

In His confrontation with Judas, the Lord also demonstrated His majesty and His sovereignty. He not only had predicted Judas's betrayal but had declared that even that vile act would fulfill God's prophecy (Matt. 26:21, 24). When the moment of arrest came, He faced it without resistance, anger, or anxiety. He was as perfectly confident of following His Father's plan and of being under His Father's care at that moment as when He performed His greatest miracles or was transfigured on the mountaintop.

In His confrontation with Peter and the other disciples, Jesus demonstrated His perfect faithfulness in face of their utter faithlessness. While they demonstrated their absence of trust in the Son, the Son demonstrated His absolute trust in His Father.

The Illegal, Unjust Trial of Christ

16

(26:57-68)

And those who had seized Jesus led Him away to Caiaphas, the high priest, where the scribes and the elders were gathered together. But Peter also was following Him at a distance as far as the courtyard of the high priest, and entered in, and sat down with the officers to see the outcome. Now the chief priests and the whole Council kept trying to obtain false testimony against Jesus, in order that they might put Him to death; and they did not find any, even though many false witnesses came forward. But later on two came forward, and said, "this man stated, 'I am able to destroy the temple of God and to rebuild it in three days.'" And the high priest stood up and said to Him, "Do you make no answer? What is it that these men are testifying against You?" But Jesus kept silent. And the high priest said to Him, "I adjure You by the living God, that You tell us whether You are the Christ, the Son of God." Jesus said to him, "You have said it yourself; nevertheless I tell you, hereafter you shall see the Son of Man sitting at the right hand of Power, and coming on the clouds of heaven." Then the high priest tore his robes, saying, "He has blasphemed! What further need do we have of witnesses? Behold, you have now heard the blasphemy; what do you think?" They answered and said, "He is deserving of death!" Then they spat in His face and

beat Him with their fists; and others slapped Him, and said, "Prophecy to us, You Christ; who is the one who hit You?" (26:57-68)

The Jews had always prided themselves on their sense of fairness and justice, and rightly so. The judicial systems in the modern Western world have their foundations in the legal system of ancient Israel, which itself was founded on the standards set forth in their Scriptures, the Old Testament.

The essence of the Old Testament system of jurisprudence is found in Deuteronomy:

> You shall appoint for yourself judges and officers in all your towns which the Lord your God is giving you, according to your tribes, and they shall judge the people with righteous judgment. You shall not distort justice; you shall not be partial, and you shall not take a bribe, for a bribe blinds the eyes of the wise and perverts the words of the righteous. Justice, and only justice, you shall pursue, that you may live and possess the land which the Lord your God is giving you. (16:18-20)

As the Hebrews worked out specific judicial procedures following those general principles, they determined that any community that had at least 120 men who were heads of families could form a local council. In later years, after the Babylonian exile, that council often was composed of the synagogue leadership. The council came to be known as a sanhedrin, from a Greek term (*sunedrion*) that had been transliterated into Hebrew and Aramaic, as it now is into English. It literally means "sitting together." A local sanhedrin was composed of up to 23 members, and the Great Sanhedrin in Jerusalem was composed of 70 chief priests, elders, and scribes, with the high priest making a total of 71. In both the local and Great sanhedrins an odd number of members was maintained in order to eliminate the possibility of a tie vote.

When referring to the national body in Jerusalem, *sunedrion* is usually translated "Council" in the *New American Standard Bible* (see, e.g., Matt. 26:59; Mark 14:55) and when referring to a local body is translated "court" (see Matt. 5:22; 10:17; Mark 13:9). As we learn from Luke, the Great Sanhedrin in Jerusalem was also sometimes referred to as "the Senate of the sons of Israel" (Acts 5:21) or "the Council of the elders" (Luke 22:66; Acts 22:5).

Members of local sanhedrins were to be chosen because of their maturity and wisdom, and the Great Sanhedrin was to be composed of those who had distinguished themselves in a local council and had served a form of apprenticeship in the national council. But long before Jesus' day, membership in the Great Sanhedrin had degenerated largely into appointments based on religious or political favoritism and influence. The Herods, especially Herod the Great, exercised considerable control over the Great Sanhedrin, and even the pagan Romans sometimes became involved in the appointment or removal of a high priest.

The general requirements of fairness and impartiality prescribed in Deuteronomy 16:18-20 and elsewhere in the Mosaic law were reflected in the rabbinical requirements that guaranteed an accused criminal the right to a public trial, to defense counsel, and conviction only on the testimony of at least two reliable witnesses. Trials were therefore always open to public scrutiny, and the defendant had the right to bring forth evidence and witnesses in his own behalf, no matter how damning the evidence and testimony against him might be.

To guard against false witnessing, whether given out of revenge or for a bribe, the Mosaic law prescribed that a person who knowingly gave false testimony would suffer the punishment the accused would suffer if found guilty (Deut. 19:16-19). A person who gave false testimony in a trial that involved capital punishment, for example, would himself be put to death. For obvious reasons, that penalty was a strong deterrent to perjury and an effective protection of justice. An additional deterrent was the requirement that accusing witnesses in a capital case were to initiate the execution, making them stand behind their testimony by action as well as words (Deut. 17:7). It was that law to which Jesus made indirect reference when He told the accusers of the woman taken in adultery, "He who is without sin among you, let him be the first to throw a stone at her" (John 8:7).

Rabbinical law required that a sentence of death could not be carried out until the third day after it was rendered and that during the intervening day the members of the court were to fast. That provision had the effect of preventing a trial during a feast, when fasting was prohibited. The delay of execution also provided additional time for evidence or testimony to be discovered in the defendant's behalf.

Simon Greenleaf was a famous professor of law at Harvard University in the last century. In his book *The Testimony of the Evangelists* ([Jersey City, NJ: Frederick P. Linn, 1881], pp. 581-84) a section written by lawyer Joseph Salvador gives fascinating and significant information about proper Sanhedrin trial procedure. Because a defendant was protected against self-incrimination, his confession, no matter how convincing, was not sufficient in itself for conviction.

On the day of the trial, according to Salvador, the court officers would require all evidence against the accused person to be read in the full hearing of open court. Each witness against him would be required to affirm that his testimony was true to the best of his knowledge and was based on his own direct experience and not on hearsay or presumption. Witnesses also had to identify the precise month, day, hour, and location of the event about which they testified. A council itself could not initiate charges against a person but could only consider charges brought before it by an outside party.

A woman was not allowed to testify because she was considered to lack the courage to give the first blow if the accused were convicted and sentenced to death. Children could not testify because of their immaturity, nor could a slave, a person of bad character, or a person who was considered mentally incompetent.

There was always to be presumption of innocence, and great latitude was given the accused in presenting his defense. In a local council, eleven votes out of the total of twenty-three were required for acquittal, but thirteen were required for conviction. If the accused was found innocent, he was freed immediately. But if he was found guilty, the sentence was not pronounced until two days later and, as mentioned above, the council members were required to fast during the intervening day. On the morning of the third day the council was reconvened, and each judge, in turn, was asked if he had changed his decision. A vote for condemnation could be changed to acquittal, but not the reverse.

If a guilty verdict was reaffirmed, an officer with a flag remained near the council while another officer, often mounted on horseback, escorted the prisoner to the place of execution. A herald went before the slow-moving procession declaring in a loud voice, "This man [stating his name] is led to punishment for such a crime; the witnesses who have sworn against him are such and such persons; if any one has evidence to give in his favor, let him come forth quickly." If, at any time before the sentence was carried out, additional information pertaining to innocence came to light, including the prisoner's recollection of something he had forgotten, one officer would signal the other, and the prisoner would be brought back to the council for reconsideration of the verdict. Before the place of execution was reached, the condemned person was urged to confess his crime, if he had not already done so, and was given a stupefying drink to dull his senses and thereby make his death less painful.

The governing principle in capital cases was: "The Sanhedrin is to save, not destroy, life." In addition to the above provisions, the president of the council was required to remind prospective witnesses of the preciousness of human life and to admonish them to be certain their testimony was both true and complete. No criminal trial could be begun during or continued into the night, the property of an executed criminal could not be confiscated but was passed to his heirs, and voting was done from the youngest member to the oldest in order that the former would not be influenced by the latter. And if a council voted unanimously for conviction, the accused was set free, because the necessary element of mercy was presumed to be lacking.

It is obvious that, when properly administered, the Jewish system of justice was not only eminently fair but merciful. It is just as obvious that the system did not operate either fairly or mercifully in Jesus' trial, because the Sanhedrin violated virtually every principle of its own system of jurisprudence. Jesus was illegally tried without first having been charged with a crime. He was tried at night and in private, no defense was permitted Him, and the witnesses against Him had been bribed to falsify their testimony. He was executed on the same day He was sentenced, and, consequently, the judges could not have fasted on the intervening day that should have transpired and had no opportunity to reconsider their verdict. The only procedure that was properly followed was the offering of the stupefying drink, but that was done by Roman soldiers, not by representatives of the Sanhedrin (Mark 15:23).

As is clear from the gospel accounts, Jesus had two major trials, one Jewish and religious and the other Roman and secular. Because Rome reserved the right of execution to its own courts and administrators, the Sanhedrin was not allowed to dispense capital punishment (John 18:31). The fact that it did so on several occasions, as with the stoning of Stephen (Acts 6:12-14; 7:54-60), does not prove the legality of it. It is likely, however, that many illegal executions by the Sanhedrin were simply overlooked by Roman authorities for the sake of political expediency. For them, the loss of a single life was a small price to pay to keep order and peace. The only blanket exception that Rome granted was for the summary execution of a Gentile who trespassed a restricted area of the Temple.

It is also significant that both the Jewish religious and Roman secular trials of Jesus had three phases, meaning that, within about twelve hours, Jesus faced legal proceedings on six separate occasions before His crucifixion. The Jewish trial began with His being taken before the former high priest Annas in the middle of the night. Annas then sent Him to the presiding high priest, Caiaphas, who had quickly convened the Sanhedrin at his own house. Caiaphas and the Sanhedrin met a second time after daylight on Friday morning.

After the Jewish religious leaders had concluded their sham hearings, they took Jesus to the Roman procurator, Pilate, first of all because they could not carry out a death sentence without his permission. But they also went to him because a Roman crucifixion would help obscure their own nefarious involvement in what they knew were totally unjust proceedings and condemnation.

When Pilate discovered Jesus was a Galilean, he sent Him to Herod Antipas, the tetrarch of Galilee and Perea, who was in Jerusalem for the Passover. After being questioned and treated with contempt by Herod and his soldiers, Jesus was sent back to Pilate, who reluctantly consented to His crucifixion.

Matthew 26:57-68 reveals at least five aspects of that illegal and unjust treatment of our Lord: the convening of the Sanhedrin (vv. 57-58), the conspiracy to convict Jesus without evidence (vv. 59-61), the confrontation to induce His self-incrimination (vv. 62-64), the condemnation based on false charges and testimony (vv. 65-66), and the conduct of the court in the physical and verbal abuse of Jesus (vv. 67-68).

THE ILLEGAL AND UNJUST CONVENING OF THE SANHEDRIN

And those who had seized Jesus led Him away to Caiaphas, the high priest, where the scribes and the elders were gathered together. But Peter also was following Him at a distance as far as the courtyard of the high priest, and entered in, and sat down with the officers to see the outcome. (26:57-58)

After the disciples fled in fear, the Temple police, Roman soldiers, and the others **who had seized Jesus** then **led Him away.** But we learn from John that, before they took Him to **Caiaphas,** they "led Him to Annas first; for he was father-in-law of Caiaphas, who was high priest that year" (John 18:13).

Some twenty years earlier, Annas had served as high priest for a period of four or five years. But although he had been replaced as ruling high priest, he not only continued to carry the title but also continued to wield great influence in Temple affairs, largely through the five sons who succeeded him and now through Caiaphas, his son-in-law.

It was God's design for high priests to serve for life. But the position had become so politicized that some of them served only a few years or even months, because they came into disfavor with a king or a Roman official. Some scholars believe that Annas had been removed from office by Rome because they feared too much power was being amassed by one man.

Annas controlled the Temple money changers and sacrifice sellers to such an extent that their operations were sometimes referred to as the Bazaars of Annas. It is likely that no Temple merchant could operate without being approved by Annas and agreeing to give him a large percentage of the profits.

A Jew never came to the Temple empty-handed. He always brought either a gift of money or a sacrifice to offer the Lord. But he could not offer Gentile coins, because they often carried the likeness of a ruler, which was considered a form of idolatry. Since the vast majority of coins used during New Testament times were either Roman or from a Gentile country under Roman control, Jews had to exchange such coins for Jewish ones before they could place their offerings in the bell-shaped receptacles in the Temple. And because the money changers in the Temple held a monopoly, they were able to charge exorbitant exchange fees.

A Jew who came to offer a sacrifice to God had to use an unblemished animal that had been certified by the priests. And although he could legitimately bring one of his own animals, the corrupt priests who were in charge of certification would seldom accept an animal not bought from a Temple merchant. Like those who needed to exchange their money, Jews who wanted to sacrifice were at the mercy of Annas's Temple establishment. It was for that reason that Jesus had twice cleansed the Temple of the money changers and sacrifice sellers, declaring in anger that they had profaned His Father's house of prayer by making it a den of robbers (John 2:13-17; Mark 11:15-17). It was immediately after the second cleansing that the infuriated Temple authorities "began seeking how to destroy Him" (Mark. 11:18).

Jesus was a persistent threat to Annas's power, prestige, security, and prosperity, for which He was bitterly despised by the high priest. In addition to that, Annas resented Jesus for His holiness, truth, and righteousness, because those virtues were a judgment on his own vile character. Everything Jesus said and did angered Annas, because, like Judas, his absolute rejection of Christ had placed him utterly in the hands of Satan, the great choreographer who was staging this heinous travesty against God's Son. Annas was one of a large cast of characters who were now manipulated by hell.

Annas may have instructed the arresting officials to bring Jesus to him first, or the officials may have reasoned that a charge against Jesus by such a powerful dignitary would not be contested when He was brought before the Sanhedrin for trial. In any case, taking Him first to Annas allowed Caiaphas time to assemble the Sanhedrin at his own house (see v. 59).

Although Annas had many personal reasons for hating Jesus and wanting Him dead, his first comments to the Lord indicate that he was still searching for a capital charge that would appear legal. In questioning Jesus "about His disciples, and about His teaching," (John 18:19), Annas violated two major procedural requirements. First, he had Jesus arraigned before an indictment was brought against Him, and, second, he tried to induce Jesus to incriminate Himself.

Jesus did not answer the question directly, but His response was a stinging exposure and indictment of Annas's duplicity and chicanery. "I have spoken openly to the world," He said; "I always taught in synagogues, and in the temple, where all the Jews come together; and I spoke nothing in secret. Why do you question Me? Question those who have heard what I spoke to them; behold, these know what I said" (John 18:20-21). Jesus merely pointed out the obvious. Countless thousands had heard Him teach and preach and could testify first-hand about who His disciples were and about what He taught. Jesus also, in effect, challenged Annas's illegal attempt to make Him testify against Himself.

Annas was embarrassed, infuriated, and frustrated. Because of their complicity, the entire assemblage was also angered, and "one of the officers," perhaps to help his superior save face, "gave Jesus a blow, saying, 'Is that the way You answer the high priest?' " (John 18:22).

Some years later, the apostle Paul was brought before the Sanhedrin and, like His Lord, was struck simply for telling the truth. But unlike His Lord, he became angry and vehemently rebuked the presiding officer for his illegal treatment. Only when he learned that he was addressing the high priest did he apologize (Acts 23:1-5).

Jesus, however, never lost His composure, accepting His abuse with perfect calmness. He simply said to the officer who struck Him, "If I have spoken wrongly, bear witness of the wrong; but if rightly, why do you strike Me?" (John 18:23).

In complete exasperation and having no other recourse, "Annas therefore sent Him bound to Caiaphas the high priest" (v. 24). It was the middle of the night, perhaps shortly after midnight, because cock crowing, which normally began about 3:00 A.M., had not yet started (see Matt. 26:74).

Jesus was then brought before **Caiaphas, the high priest,** at whose house **the scribes and the elders were** illegally **gathered together** as the supreme Jewish Council (see v. 59). Contrary to expectations, however, no charge had yet been brought against Him. The high court of Judaism had been illegally convened at night to illegally try a man who had not even been indicted.

Though not as clever as his father-in-law, **Caiaphas** was equally devious and corrupt. He, too, was greedy, unprincipled, materialistic, and power hungry. He, too, despised Jesus' truthfulness and righteousness because they were a judgment on his own wretched ungodliness.

During this time, **Peter also was following** Jesus **at a distance,** first to the house of Annas and then **as far as the courtyard of the high priest** Caiaphas. Out of a conflicting mixture of cowardice and commitment, **Peter** tried to be as near His Lord as prudence permitted without being discovered, and he **sat down with the officers to see the outcome.**

The fact that Peter and others were sitting in **the courtyard of the high priest** reveals still another infraction of Jewish legal protocol. As previously noted, the Sanhedrin was permitted to hold a trial involving capital punishment only in the Temple and only in public. The private meeting at Caiaphas's house clearly violated both stipulations.

THE ILLEGAL AND UNJUST CONSPIRACY TO CONVICT JESUS

Now the chief priests and the whole Council kept trying to obtain false testimony against Jesus, in order that they might put Him to death; and they did not find any, even though many false witnesses came forward. But later on two came forward, and said, "this man

stated, 'I am able to destroy the temple of God and to rebuild it in three days.'" (26:59-61)

The **chief priests** are mentioned separately probably because they were the primary instigators of Jesus' arrest (see v. 47). But as Matthew makes clear, **the whole Council,** or Sanhedrin, was present.

The **Council** was empowered to act only as judge and jury in a legal proceeding. They could not instigate charges but could only adjudicate cases that were brought before them. But because they as yet had no formal charge against Jesus, they were forced to illegally act also as prosecutor in order to carry out their predetermined plan to convict and execute Him. Consequently, they **kept trying to obtain false testimony against Jesus, in order that they might put Him to death.**

Because Jesus was innocent of any wrongdoing, the only possible way to convict Him would be on the basis of **false testimony.** His accusers would have to be liars. Because the Council was so controlled by satanic hatred of Jesus, they now were willing to do whatever was necessary to condemn Him, even if that meant violating every biblical and rabbinical rule of justice. To accomplish their wicked conspiracy they found themselves perverting the very heart of the Sanhedrin's purpose, stated earlier in this chapter: "to save, not destroy, life." Their purpose now, however, was not to discover the truth about Jesus and certainly not to save His life. Their single, compelling desire was to **put Him to death.**

But try as they would, **they did not find any** legitimate charges against Him, **even though many false witnesses came forward.** During that first attempt to manufacture a charge, **even** the **many false witnesses** who were willing to perjure themselves could not devise a story that would stand scrutiny even in that corrupt and biased proceeding! Their testimonies not only were spurious but grossly inconsistent with each other (Mark 14:56), as is typically the case with liars.

The frustration of the assembly continued to mount until **later on two witnesses** finally **came forward** with a charge that seemed usable. They asserted that Jesus **stated, "I am able to destroy the temple of God and to rebuild it in three days."** Mark's more detailed account reports that they claimed Jesus said, "I will destroy this temple made with hands, and in three days I will build another made without hands" (Mark 14:58). Or perhaps Matthew reported one of the witness's words and Mark the other's, in which case the testimony even of those two men was not consistent.

Jesus' actual words were, "Destroy this temple, and in three days I will raise it up" (John 2:19), and His hearers concluded that He was referring to the Jerusalem Temple building He had just cleansed (v. 20). The two false witnesses not only shared that false assumption but accused Jesus of saying, on the one hand, that He Himself was **able to destroy the temple of God,** and on the other, "*I will* destroy this temple" (Mark

14:58, emphasis added). Mark notes that "not even in this respect was their testimony consistent" (v. 59).

In addition to the inconsistency of their statements, which itself made the testimonies inadmissable in a legitimate hearing, the two men did not relate the year, month, day, and location of the incident they claimed to have witnessed, as they were required to do by law.

The fact that not a single witness could be found to convict Jesus of wrongdoing is one of the strongest apologetics in all of Scripture for His moral and spiritual perfection. If any fault could have been found in Him it would have come to light. Even if demons had to provide the information, it would certainly have been presented. Demons are not omniscient, but they would have known of any sin Jesus committed had He been guilty of it, and they would have rushed to produce such evidence against Him through their wicked minions in the Sanhedrin. But neither Jesus' human nor demonic enemies could find in Him the least transgression of God's moral or spiritual law. His only transgressions had been against the man-made, legalistic, and unscriptural rabbinic traditions.

The ones who were ultimately on trial that day were those who stood in judgment of the perfect, sinless Son of God. That tribunal of sinful, unjust, and hate-filled men will one day stand before God's heavenly tribunal and themselves be eternally condemned to the lake of fire.

THE ILLEGAL AND UNJUST CONFRONTATION TO INDUCE SELF-INCRIMINATION

And the high priest stood up and said to Him, "Do you make no answer? What is it that these men are testifying against You?" But Jesus kept silent. And the high priest said to Him, "I adjure You by the living God, that You tell us whether You are the Christ, the Son of God." Jesus said to him, "You have said it yourself; nevertheless I tell you, hereafter you shall see the Son of Man sitting at the right hand of Power, and coming on the clouds of heaven." (26:62-64)

The frustration of the Council members became unbearable as they desperately tried to get the trial concluded before dawn, when people would start milling about the city and their illegal venture would risk being discovered. They also, no doubt, wanted to conclude the affair quickly so they could make preparations for their own Passover sacrifices and duties that afternoon.

Trying again to steer Jesus into self-incrimination, **the high priest** and presiding officer therefore **said to** Him, **"Do you make no answer? What is it that these men are testifying against You?"** Probably gazing squarely into Caiaphas's eyes, **Jesus kept silent**, adding still more to the high priest's consternation. Since the testimonies of the two **men** were inconsistent, they should have been rejected by the court. A rebuttal by Jesus not only would have been futile but would have given the false testimony and the entire illegal proceedings the appearance of legitimacy.

Jesus stood majestically **silent.** It was the silence of innocence, the silence of dignity, the silence of integrity, the silence of infinite trust in His heavenly Father. It was a silence in which the lying words against Him reverberated in the ears of the guilty judges and of the false witnesses they had bribed. Goaded by that silence, which accentuated the travesty of justice over which he presided, the enraged **high priest** continued to badger Jesus, saying, **"I adjure You by the living God, that You tell us whether You are the Christ, the Son of God."**

Appealing to the most sacred oath a Jew could utter, Caiaphas demanded that Jesus either affirm or deny His messiahship and deity. He was saying, in effect, "Answer my question truthfully, on the basis that You are standing before the living God, who knows all things."

Although none of the Council, except Joseph of Arimathea, if he was still present, believed in Jesus' deity, they were strongly hoping He would openly make that claim for Himself so that they could charge Him with blasphemy. The Mosaic law provided that "the one who blasphemes the name of the Lord shall surely be put to death" (Lev. 24:16).

But a claim to deity would be blasphemous only if it were false, which it would be for any human being ever born—except Jesus. Although He had never flaunted or made public issue of His messiahship and deity, He had given numerous attestations to both, beginning early in His ministry. In the synagogue at His hometown of Nazareth, He read a well-known messianic passage from Isaiah and then declared, "Today this Scripture has been fulfilled in your hearing" (Luke 4:18-21). His first specific claim to messiahship was made to the Samaritan woman at Jacob's well. In response to her statement that "Messiah is coming (He who is called Christ)," Jesus said, "I who speak to you am He" (John 4:25-26). He had readily accepted the messianic epithets shouted to Him as He entered Jerusalem the previous Monday (Matt. 21:9). He continually referred to God as His heavenly Father, which the Jewish leaders rightly interpreted as a claim of deity (John 5:17-18), and He had declared to the unbelieving Jewish leaders in Jerusalem, "Before Abraham was born, I am" (John 8:58), taking that ancient appellation of God (see Ex. 3:14) for Himself.

Jesus finally gave the affirmation the Sanhedrin had been waiting to hear. **You have said it yourself;** He replied. Mark's account makes the acknowledgment of messiahship and deity even more explicit, as he quotes Jesus' saying directly, "I am" (Mark 14:62).

Then, referring to Psalm 110:1 and Daniel 7:13, Jesus added, **"Nevertheless I tell you, hereafter you shall see the Son of Man sitting at the right hand of Power, and coming on the clouds of**

heaven." "Not only am I the Messiah and the Son of God," He was saying, "but one day you will see Me glorified with My Father in heaven and returning to earth as your Judge" (cf. Matt. 25:31-46).

Son of Man was a commonly acknowledged title of the Messiah, the one Jesus most often used of Himself, and **Power** was a figurative designation of God. Because the ungodly members of the Sanhedrin had refused to receive Jesus as their Lord and Savior, they had sealed their doom to face Him at the end time as their Judge and Executioner. The accused would then become the accuser, and the judges would become the judged.

THE ILLEGAL AND UNJUST CONDEMNATION OF JESUS

Then the high priest tore his robes, saying, "He has blasphemed! What further need do we have of witnesses? Behold, you have now heard the blasphemy; what do you think?" They answered and said, "He is deserving of death!" (26:65-66)

Upon that unambiguous confession by Jesus, **the high priest tore his robes** in horror, **saying, "He has blasphemed!"** The unbelieving members of the Sanhedrin had long ago discounted Jesus' claims of deity. He had pleaded with them, "If I do not do the works of My Father, do not believe Me; but if I do them, though you do not believe Me, believe the works, that you may know and understand that the Father is in Me, and I in the Father" (John 10:37-38). In other words, even if they could not believe the divine source of His teaching, how could they argue against the divine power behind His countless public miracles?

They had closed their minds to the truth, and no amount of evidence would open their eyes to it. Like many people throughout the ages who have rejected Christ, it was not that they had carefully examined the evidence about Him and found it to be untrue or unconvincing but that they refused to consider the evidence at all. Even God's own Holy Spirit cannot penetrate such a willful barrier to His truth and grace. Miracles do not convince the hard-hearted.

When **the high priest** ceremoniously **tore his robes,** he did so not out of grief and indignation over the presumed dishonor of God's name but rather out of joy and relief that, at last, Jesus had placed Himself into their hands, condemning Himself out of His own mouth. Although Leviticus 21:10 strictly forbade the high priest's tearing his garments, the Talmud held that judges who witnessed blasphemy had a right to tear their robes if they later sewed them up. By his traditional and theatrical display, Caiaphas dramatically gave the appearance of defending God's name, but inwardly he gloated over the illegal, unjust, and devilish victory he imagined he had just won.

"**What further need do you have of witnesses?**" he asked the Council rhetorically. And with that he asked for an immediate verdict: "**Behold, you have now heard the blasphemy; what do you think?**" He did not bother to have the members polled individually and the results tabulated by scribes, as judicial protocol required, but simply called for verbal support of the predetermined conclusion of guilt.

With one voice **they answered and said, "He is deserving of death!"** The decision was unanimous as "they all condemned Him to be deserving of death" (Mark 14:64). The unanimous vote to convict should have given Jesus His freedom automatically, because the necessary element of mercy was lacking. But by this time the Sanhedrin had relinquished even the semblance of legality and justice. Because we know that Joseph of Arimathea was a member of the Council but did not consent to Jesus' condemnation (Luke 23:50-51), he obviously had left the proceedings before this final judicial farce transpired.

The verdict of guilty and the sentence of death were not based on careful consideration of full and impartial evidence and testimony. It was a senseless mob reaction, much like the one which, a few hours later, these same leaders would instigate and orchestrate regarding the release of Barabbas and the crucifixion of Jesus (Matt. 27:20-21).

THE ILLEGAL AND UNJUST CONDUCT OF THE COURT

Then they spat in His face and beat Him with their fists; and others slapped Him, and said, "Prophecy to us, You Christ; who is the one who hit You?" (26:67-68)

Discarding the last vestige of decorum and decency, the supreme court of Israel degenerated into a crude, mindless rabble. With total lack of inhibition, the religious aristocracy of Judaism—the high priest and chief priests, the elders, the scribes, the Pharisees, and the Sadducees—revealed their true decadence, as some of them **spat in Jesus' face and beat Him with their fists.**

To Jews, the supreme insult was to spit in another's face (see Num. 12:14; Deut. 25:9). The impressive tomb of Absalom is still standing in the Kidron Valley just outside Jerusalem. But for thousands of years that monument has been spat on by Jewish passersby to show their contempt for Absalom's treacherous rebellion against his father, David.

Others in the Council, perhaps the less rowdy older members, merely **slapped Him.** And instead of spitting on Jesus they threw verbal abuse in His face. After blindfolding Him (Luke 22:64), they demanded sarcastically, "**Prophecy to us, You Christ; who is the one who hit You?**"

Luke also reports that "they were saying many other things against Him, blaspheming" (22:65). The true blasphemers here were the accusers, not the accused. Jesus had not blasphemed because He was indeed God, but the ungodly Sanhedrin blasphemed repeatedly as they condemned, humiliated, and abused the sinless Son of God. And when these judges of Israel tired of tormenting Jesus, they turned Him over to the Temple police for further maltreatment (Mark 14:65).

As the later mob reaction before Pilate would prove conclusively, the ungodly religious leaders who rejected and profaned Jesus were a microcosm of the Jewish nation. Spiritually and morally Israel was a rotting carcass waiting to be devoured by vultures, as indeed it was devoured by Rome less than forty years later. In A.D. 70 the Temple was burned and razed, most of Jerusalem was destroyed, and hundreds of thousands of its citizens were slaughtered without mercy.

Every person who rejects Christ spits in His face, as it were, and is guilty of blasphemy against God, who sent His beloved Son to save that person and all mankind from sin. The irony is that all who misjudge Jesus will themselves be rightly judged by Him one day. Men continually misjudge Jesus, but He will never misjudge them. The tables will be turned. The criminals will no longer unjustly condemn and crush the innocent but will themselves be justly condemned and crushed.

Even in the midst of the cruel injustice against Him, our Lord's grace shined undiminished. Throughout His ordeal, "while being reviled, He did not revile in return; while suffering, He uttered no threats, but kept entrusting Himself to Him who judges righteously" (1 Pet. 2:23). This was His divinely-appointed time, and He resolutely and gladly faced hell's moment of seeming victory. He would not turn or be turned from suffering and death, because only in that way could He bear "our sins in His body on the cross, that we might die to sin and live to righteousness" (v. 24).

The Restoration of a Sinning Saint

17

(26:69-75)

Now Peter was sitting outside in the courtyard, and a certain servant-girl came to him and said, "You too were with Jesus the Galilean." But he denied it before them all, saying, "I do not know what you are talking about." And when he had gone out to the gateway, another servant-girl saw him and said to those who were there, "This man was with Jesus of Nazareth." And again he denied it with an oath, "I do not know the man." And a little later the bystanders came up and said to Peter, "Surely you too are one of them; for the way you talk gives you away." Then he began to curse and swear, "I do not know the man!" And immediately a cock crowed. And Peter remembered the word which Jesus had said, "Before a cock crows, you will deny Me three times." And he went out and wept bitterly. (26:69-75)

The single greatest gift God could conceivably give to mankind is forgiveness of sins. Without forgiveness, there could be no salvation from sin, no reconciliation with God, no spiritual life, no victory over death, no prospect of heaven.

The Lord revealed Himself to Moses as "the Lord, the Lord God, compassionate and gracious, slow to anger, and abounding in lovingkindness and truth; who keeps lovingkindness for thousands, who forgives iniquity, transgression and sin" (Ex. 34:6-7). The prophet Micah proclaimed, "Who is a God like Thee, who pardons iniquity?" (Mic. 7:18). The apostle John declared, "If we walk in the light as He Himself is in the light, we have fellowship with one another, and the blood of Jesus His Son cleanses us from all sin. . . . If we confess our sins, He is faithful and righteous to forgive us our sins and to cleanse us from all unrighteousness" (1 John 1:7, 9).

Peter's denial of the Lord is usually looked on as a great tragedy, which it obviously was. But viewed in the light of Peter's repentance and the Lord's gracious forgiveness, the story also brings great encouragement.

In all the history of redemption, few saints have fallen to the depths of sin and unfaithfulness that Peter did in denying Jesus. Yet few saints have been so powerfully used by God as Peter was after he repented and was restored. The account of his denial is a sobering testimony to the weakness of the flesh, but it is also an encouraging testimony to the power of God's grace. Even in the extremity of His children's sin, the Lord is there to forgive and to restore.

Every Christian at times comes before the Lord overwhelmed and broken by the awareness of his sinfulness. A person who never has such an experience either is very cold spiritually or is not a Christian at all. Nothing is more shattering to a believer than suddenly realizing he has denied the Lord by what he has said or not said, done or not done. And yet nothing is more exhilarating to him than knowing God's gracious forgiveness of the unfaithfulness after it is confessed.

Peter's denial was not merely a spontaneous response to unexpected danger or embarrassment. He had already laid the groundwork for defection. Or, to use another metaphor, he had taken many steps toward denying Christ before he entered the courtyard of Caiaphas.

The first step was his boasting that "even though all may fall away because of You, I will never fall away" (Matt. 26:33). In speaking those words Peter not only revealed unfounded confidence in himself but directly contradicted His Lord's prediction that all the disciples would fall away that very night (v. 31). Based on his feelings of self-confidence and devotion to Jesus, Peter considered himself incapable of disloyalty. He could imagine nothing that would cause him to waver, and not even the Lord's explicit prediction could convince him otherwise. He was certain he had come to the place of spiritual maturity, with his priorities straight, his convictions steadfast, and his faithfulness invulnerable. It was therefore inconceivable to him that he could be capable of defecting from the Lord.

Peter's second step toward denial was insubordination, manifested in his defiantly persisting to reject Jesus' assessment of him. Even when the Lord singled him out and predicted he not only would flee like the rest but would deny Him three times before the next morning dawned,

Peter blatantly contradicted Him and continued to defend his own faithfulness. Intensifying his previous assertion, he declared, "Even if I have to die with You, I will not deny You," and his unjustified but impressive-sounding verbiage prompted the other disciples to say "the same thing" (v. 35). Mark reports that Peter repeatedly insisted on his loyalty (Mark 14:31).

Peter did not take seriously the voice of the living God he confessed with his mouth, and he rejected and resented His reproof. Like many believers since, he proudly refused to submit Himself to God's Word and Spirit.

Peter's third step toward denying Christ was prayerlessness. Like his boasting and insubordination, his prayerlessness was a manifestation of sinful self-confidence.

When Jesus took Peter, James, and John farther into the garden and left them to watch and pray while He spoke intimately with His Father, all three of the disciples fell asleep. When He found them asleep, Jesus addressed Peter as leader and spokesman of the Twelve, saying, "So, you men could not keep watch with Me for one hour? Keep watching and praying, that you may not enter into temptation" (Matt. 26:40-41). The Lord went away to pray privately two more times, and each time Peter and the others fell back to sleep (vv. 43, 45). Jesus had just warned them that "the spirit is willing, but the flesh is weak" (v. 41), but they felt no weakness and saw no need to be watchful or prayerful. Because they did not take seriously the Lord's warnings about their deficiencies and frailties, they did not take seriously His admonition to be prepared and strengthened. Self-confidently trusting their own judgment above the Lord's, they were indifferent to His call to prayer.

Peter's fourth step toward denial was his independent, self-generated impulsiveness. Sensing no need to ask the Lord's advice or help, he took matters into his own hands. As soon as the officers laid hands on Jesus, Peter "reached and drew out his sword, and struck the slave of the high priest, and cut off his ear" (Matt. 26:51: cf. John 18:10). Although Jesus had repeatedly taught the disciples that it was the Father's plan for Him to suffer, die, and be raised (Matt. 16:21; 17:22-23; 20:18-19), Peter refused to believe Him. And because it was not in Peter's plan for his Master to be harmed, he was willing to defy both human and divine authority in drawing his sword against those who came to arrest Jesus.

A fifth step toward Peter's denial of Christ was his compromise in allowing himself to be in a place of spiritual danger—such as the courtyard of the high priest—where his faith might be tested above his ability to resist. The Lord's promises not to allow His children "to be tempted beyond what [they] are able" (1 Cor. 10:13) and "to rescue the godly from temptation" (2 Pet. 2:9) do not apply to willful disobedience.

Peter could not accept the word of the Lord because he was so controlled by his ego and self-sufficiency that he felt infallible. And perhaps because he had just seen the entire multitude suddenly fall at Jesus' feet (John 18:6), he also felt invincible as long as the Lord was nearby. If Jesus could miraculously save him from drowning when he tried to walk on the water (Matt. 14:31), He could protect him now.

But again Jesus had to tell Peter he was out of God's will and pointed out to him how foolishly presumptuous he was to think that He, Jesus, needed to depend on Peter for safety (Matt. 26:52-53). Well-meaning and humanly courageous as he was, Peter continually placed his self-centered human understanding above the Lord's divine revelation. His own human will was a barrier to obeying the Lord's will.

It was therefore inevitable that Peter would collapse when his bravado proved hollow and his self-sufficiency came up deficient.

PETER'S COLLAPSE

Now Peter was sitting outside in the courtyard, and a certain servant-girl came to him and said, "You too were with Jesus the Galilean." But he denied it before them all, saying, "I do not know what you are talking about." And when he had gone out to the gateway, another servant-girl saw him and said to those who were there, "This man was with Jesus of Nazareth." And again he denied it with an oath, "I do not know the man." And a little later the bystanders came up and said to Peter, "Surely you too are one of them; for the way you talk gives you away." Then he began to curse and swear, "I do not know the man!" And immediately a cock crowed. And Peter remembered the word which Jesus had said, "Before a cock crows, you will deny Me three times." (26:69-75a)

At first reading, the gospels seem to give contradictory accounts of the first phases of Jesus' trial. John reports that He was first taken to the house of Annas, the former high priest (John 18:13), whereas Matthew speaks of His being taken to the house of Caiaphas, the son-in-law of Annas and the ruling high priest at the time (Matt. 26:57).

The seeming discrepancy, however, is easily explained. In the ancient world it was common for several generations of a family to live under the same roof. It is therefore likely that the palatial mansion of the high priest had been enlarged over the years to accommodate Annas's five sons, who had successively served as high priests, and now Caiaphas and his family. Large homes of that day backed to the street, with living areas facing a private, inner courtyard. With such a layout, Annas and Caiaphas would have had separate "houses," or wings, of the manor while sharing a common courtyard. Consequently, the courtyard of Annas, of which

John speaks (18:15-16), and the courtyard of Caiaphas, which Matthew mentions (26:57-58), were the same place. When Jesus was transferred from Annas's house to Caiaphas's, He was simply taken through the common courtyard or perhaps through a connecting passageway.

Peter had followed Jesus and His captors as far as the gate of the high priests' mansion, but he was not allowed to enter the courtyard until another "disciple, who was known to the high priest, went out and spoke to the doorkeeper, and brought in Peter" (John 18:16). It seems most likely that the other disciple was John, since he liked to refer to himself anonymously, but there is no indication from the New Testament or from other sources as to how he had come to know the high priest. Nor is there any indication as to how long John was in the courtyard or what he did while there. He was used of the Lord to gain Peter's entrance, and after that he disappeared from the scene.

Peter wanted to see the outcome of Jesus' trial, although he should have known what it would be, because the Lord had told the disciples of it so often. He was afraid, yet he could not keep from following the Lord at a distance, even into the very lair of His enemies. His love for Christ was weak, but it was real. As he kept vigil, he hoped to go unnoticed in the large crowd of minor officials, soldiers, servants, and other onlookers who had assembled in the large courtyard.

By the time Jesus appeared before Caiaphas, it was probably about 1:00 A.M. While **Peter was sitting outside in the courtyard,** "with the officers, and warming himself at the fire" (Mark 14:54), **a certain servant-girl came to him and said, "You too were with Jesus the Galilean."** The term **Galilean** was frequently used as an epithet of derision by citizens of Jerusalem, who felt themselves superior to their less sophisticated neighbors to the north. To refer to someone as a **Galilean** was to suggest he was backward and unprogressive.

The words of the **servant-girl** are slightly different in the various gospels, which suggests she made the same basic statement several times, and the fact that Peter **denied it before them all** indicates that many people in the crowd had heard her accusation. The order of the denials also seems to vary among the four gospels, which could be explained by the writers' reporting different aspects of the three incidents of denial, each of which may have lasted several minutes or longer and involved considerably more dialogue than is recorded in Scripture.

Apparently Peter first said to the girl, "Woman, I do not know Him" (Luke 22:57), and then to the others (**them all**) who had been listening, **"I do not know what you are talking about."** Peter had been called by Christ, lived with Him, learned from Him, and witnessed thousands of miracles performed by Him. He was not a young or new convert but the veteran of three years of intensive discipleship and the leader of the Twelve. Yet this intimate friend who only a few hours earlier had vowed to die before he would forsake Christ now denied even knowing Him.

Had Jesus commanded Peter to physically stand beside Him and defend Him whatever the cost, perhaps Peter could have mustered the courage for such a heroic display. He had, after all, drawn his sword and started to take on the entire retinue of soldiers and Temple police singlehandedly. But he stumbled when a much less dangerous demand was made of him. He may have planned how he would defend himself if confronted by soldiers in the courtyard, but he was totally unprepared when caught off guard by the much less threatening challenge that now faced him. He was prepared to do battle on his own terms but not on Satan's and much less on Christ's. Because of his self-assurance, he had neglected the Lord's admonition to be on guard and to pray. Consequently he was vulnerable to a blind-side attack from a source he never expected.

In much the same way, Christians can plan detailed strategy for evangelism or for the defense of a cherished doctrine or moral standard, only to be confronted by an issue or circumstance they had never considered and for which they are totally unprepared. Like Peter, we often carefully prepare on the basis of our own wisdom and resources while neglecting the guidance of God's Word and the empowering and leading of His Spirit which He provides through prayer.

Peter was like Elijah, who was brave when facing the 850 prophets of Baal and Asherah, but who, after he left the mountaintop of victory, foundered in fear over what one woman, Jezebel, might do to him. Peter was a living illustration of Paul's admonition "Let him who thinks he stands take heed lest he fall" (1 Cor. 10:12). In the courtyard his valiant protestations were no longer heard, and the arrogant hero shriveled into a cringing coward. His self-preserving instincts prevailed, and his boldness evaporated.

A person's involuntary response to the unexpected is a more reliable indicator of his character than his planned reaction to a situation he anticipates. It is when we are caught off guard that our true character is most likely to show itself. Peter's proud self-confidence was his Achilles' heel, and that, of course, was precisely where Satan aimed his arrow of temptation. Peter's stubborn trust in himself and his unwillingness to fully trust in the Lord made him vulnerable to the simple taunt of a young servant girl.

To escape embarrassment, Peter inconspicuously "went out onto the porch" (Mark 14:68), which apparently was near **the gateway.** He probably walked away slowly so as not to attract attention or give the impression he was running away after being caught in a lie. The porch, or vestibule, was the second warmest place in the courtyard, protected by a wall in back and a roof overhead. Perhaps Peter wanted to be nearer the exit in case a Temple officer tried to arrest him. It was also darker there, and he would less likely be recognized than by the fire. But despite his precautions, "a little later" (Luke 22:58), **another servant-girl saw him.**

Obviously seeking to humiliate Peter, this **servant-girl** did not address him directly but rather **said to** the other bystanders **who were there, "This man was with Jesus of Nazareth."** An unidentified man also joined in the accusation, saying, "You are one of them too!" (Luke 22:58a). To the girl, Peter **denied . . . with an oath, "I do not know the man,"** and to the other person he said with growing irritation, "Man, I am not!" (Luke 22:58b). This time he not only lied but did so **with an oath,** hoping to reinforce the deceit. A Jewish **oath** was always assumed to be made in God's presence, whether or not His name was invoked. In effect, therefore, Peter called God as a witness to his lie. Angry, frustrated, embarrassed, trapped, and frightened, Peter desperately tried to hide his identity and especially his association with Jesus.

Going against the very grain of his nature as a child of God, Peter vehemently refused to acknowledge his relationship to his Savior and Lord. Because he was relying on his own wisdom and resources, he did not have the courage to confess Christ publicly. Although he was perplexed and weak, he continued to resist the Lord's truth and the Lord's help. Even when his exposure was obvious, Peter persisted in arrogant self-reliance.

Like many Christians who know the Bible well, are experienced in the things of God, and are active in the church, Peter felt himself to be spiritually complete. As Peter would soon discover, however, that is when a believer is most vulnerable of all.

Determined to stay near his Lord despite the embarrassment and danger, Peter perhaps drifted across the courtyard toward Caiaphas's wing of the mansion, hoping perhaps to discover how the proceedings were going. By this time Jesus had been declared a blasphemer and was being beaten, spat upon, and taunted (see Mark 14:64-65). Because at one point Jesus was able to look at Peter (Luke 22:61), it is possible that much of Jesus' abuse was witnessed by Peter and the others in the courtyard.

Probably incited by the events they saw transpiring in Caiaphas's chambers, the crowd intensified its dogging of Peter. **A little while later,** which Luke specifies as being "after about an hour" (22:59), **the bystanders came up and said to Peter, "Surely you too are one of them; for the way you talk gives you away."** Peter's Galilean accent was readily recognized, and he was cornered again.

We learn from John that Peter was also recognized by sight. One member of the crowd was a slave of the high priest and a relative of

217

Malchus, the man "whose ear Peter cut off." Having been among the multitude who came to arrest Jesus, he said to Peter, "Did I not see you in the garden with Him?" (John 18:26).

At this point Peter hit rock bottom. Still refusing either to claim or to rely on Jesus, he dug himself still deeper into the denial as **he began to curse and swear, "I do not know the man!"** *Katanathematizō* (**to curse**) is a very strong term that involved pronouncing death upon oneself at the hand of God if one were lying. In perhaps the most serious taking of the Lord's name in vain that is conceivable, Peter said, in essence, "May God kill and damn me if I am not speaking the truth." *Omnumi* (to **swear**) was a less extreme pledge of truthfulness but was nevertheless a strong affirmation.

Peter had lost all sense of reality and seemingly all awareness of God. Comparison of the gospel accounts reveals that there were three periods or incidents of accusation and denial and that each incident involved repeated accusations by members of the crowd and repeated denials by Peter. As the accusations became more specific and incriminating, Peter's denials became more intense and extreme.

Even "while [Peter] was still speaking" (Luke 22:60), **immediately a cock crowed** "a second time" (Mark 14:72). At this time also "the Lord turned and looked at Peter" (Luke 22:61), apparently through a window overlooking the courtyard. The look must have penetrated the disciple's very soul, burning deep into his heart and conscience the evil of his sin. Seeing his Lord standing there with His hands bound and His face covered with spit and bruises was more than Peter could bear.

As if that visual indictment were not enough, while he stood transfixed, suffering the most excruciating pain of his life as he looked into his Lord's eyes, **Peter** also **remembered the word which Jesus had said, "Before a cock crows, you will deny Me three times."** As Jesus' remembered words augmented His gaze, Peter's already unbearable anguish was made still more unbearable.

PETER'S REPENTANCE

And he went out and wept bitterly. (26:75b)

The true Peter is not seen in his denial but in his repentance, the first stage of which was deep remorse. Finally realizing the grievousness of his sin, he turned from it in revulsion. Like Judas, he fled into the night; but unlike Judas, he returned to the Lord in faith. His faith had slipped and weakened, but it was genuine faith, and Jesus Himself had prayed that it would not fail (Luke 22:32).

When the magnitude of what he had done finally dawned on Judas, he experienced great regret and a kind of remorse. He probably wished he could live the last three years, and especially the last few hours, of his life over again. But he had no change of heart. He had never repented of his sins and received Jesus as Lord and Savior, and therefore, contrary to Peter, Judas had no faith to weaken. Jesus could not hold Judas because Judas never belonged to Him.

Overwhelmed by His Savior's love and grace and by his own sin and unfaithfulness, Peter **went out and wept bitterly.** We are not told where he went or how long he stayed there. He may have returned to the Garden of Gethsemane, where earlier he had felt no need to pray. Wherever it was, it became a private place of confessing sin and seeking forgiveness.

Peter's tragic experience in the garden teaches a profound lesson about self-trust and unpreparedness and about God's forgiveness and restoration of a sinning saint. Although the awareness probably did not come to the disciple until his anguish subsided, he had learned never to distrust Jesus' word again. It finally dawned on him that what the Lord said would happen would happen.

It was not until Peter saw the Lord's face and remembered the Lord's words that he came to his senses, acknowledged his sin and helplessness, and repented. His sin did not make him repent. Many people are very much conscious of sin in their lives, readily admitting its reality and its consequences. But until it is surrendered to Christ for forgiveness and cleansing, the mere acknowledgement of it will only drive a person deeper into despair and hopelessness and even deeper into sin. Forgiveness and restoration come only from turning from sin to God. That is why true preaching and teaching of the gospel is not simply calling people to turn from their sin. It is lifting up the Lord Jesus Christ so that, in His righteousness and grace, sinful men not only will discover the heinousness of their sin but also the only hope for its removal.

The Lord made good His promise that Peter's faith would not fail. After appearing to the disciples several times after His resurrection, Jesus three times questioned Peter about his love for Him, just as Peter had three times denied that love. And just as he had thrice denied his love for Christ, Peter then thrice affirmed it (John 21:15-17).

Many years later, near the end of his life, Peter no doubt still remembered vividly that experience in the courtyard. The tragic event was probably in his mind as he admonished fellow believers: "Beloved, knowing this beforehand, be on your guard lest . . . you fall from your own steadfastness, but grow in the grace and knowledge of our Lord and Savior Jesus Christ" (2 Pet. 3:17-18).

The Traitor's Suicide
(27:1-10)

18

Now when morning had come, all the chief priests and the elders of the people took counsel against Jesus to put Him to death; and they bound Him, and led Him away, and delivered Him up to Pilate the governor.

Then when Judas, who had betrayed Him, saw that He had been condemned, he felt remorse and returned the thirty pieces of silver to the chief priests and elders, saying, "I have sinned by betraying innocent blood." But they said, "What is that to us? See to that yourself!" And he threw the pieces of silver into the sanctuary and departed; and he went away and hanged himself. And the chief priests took the pieces of silver and said, "It is not lawful to put them into the temple treasury, since it is the price of blood." And they counseled together and with the money bought the Potter's Field as a burial place for strangers. For this reason that field has been called the Field of Blood to this day. Then that which was spoken through Jeremiah the prophet was fulfilled, saying, "And they took the thirty pieces of silver, the price of the one whose price had been set by the sons of Israel; and they gave them for the Potter's Field, as the Lord directed me." (27:1-10)

In recent years in the United States, twice as many people have killed themselves as have killed others. Because experts believe that many seemingly natural deaths are actually self-inflicted, the incidence is probably much higher than what is reported. Suicide ranks among the top ten killers in the United States, and many other countries have rates that are even higher.

Researchers who analyze human behavior list five primary reasons for committing suicide. I believe most people kill themselves for retaliation. Because they are angry over an offense or mistreatment, they take their own lives as a means of hurting those who have hurt them. Whether their abuse was real or imagined, they invariably succeed in inflicting deep pain on those they seek to hurt. This is almost always the case when young people kill themselves. And usually it is their parents they want to hurt irremediably.

Some people take their own lives for the sake of reunion with loved ones who have already died. Older spouses who were particularly dependent on their mates sometimes decide to join them in death rather than endure the loneliness and frustration of life without them.

Some people take their lives out of a desire for rebirth. With the increased influence of Eastern religions, many Westerners have been persuaded of the reality of reincarnation, and by committing suicide they hope to be reborn into a better form or circumstance.

A particularly distorted reason for suicide is referred to as retroflex, the killing of oneself in place of someone else who is unreachable. Some years ago a man killed himself because a brutal Nazi war criminal could not be found and brought to justice.

For some people, suicide is an extreme form of self-retribution. Considering their guilt to be unforgivable and unremediable, some people, in effect, sentence themselves to capital punishment and carry out the sentence by their own hand.

Because every human being is made in the image of God and belongs to Him, no one has the right to murder anyone, even himself. Suicide is self-murder and is rebellion against God's sovereign right over life and death. It is an act of sin and unbelief, a clear violation of the sixth commandment, "You shall not murder" (Ex. 20:13).

According to the common definition of suicide, Scripture reports only two instances. Although Saul and his armor bearer took their own lives, they did so only because they faced a much more brutal and humiliating death at the hands of the enemy. But in the usual sense, only the deaths of Ahithophel (see 2 Sam. 17) and Judas were suicide.

Because Judas's sin was so monstrous, it is not difficult to understand how unrelieved guilt drove him to take his own life. He committed the most heinous crime any man has ever committed or could commit, betraying the only truly innocent and perfect man who has ever lived. Because he could not live with his guilt, Judas had only two choices. He could have gone to Jesus for forgiveness and salvation, which the Lord had so often offered. But because he would not do that, his only recourse was self-destruction.

For the account of Judas's suicide, Matthew briefly interrupts his portrayal of Jesus' trial. His purpose in presenting the story of Judas's final hours of life was not simply to show the dreadful fate of Christ's betrayer but also to show, by several contrasts, the beauty, purity, and majesty of the one betrayed. Jesus is exalted even against the backdrop of sordid sin and death.

THE CONTRAST BETWEEN THE WICKED LEADERS AND THE SINLESS CHRIST

Now when morning had come, all the chief priests and the elders of the people took counsel against Jesus to put Him to death; and they bound Him, and led Him away, and delivered Him up to Pilate the governor. (27:1-2)

Contrary to rabbinical law, the first two phases of Jesus' religious trial were carried out during the night and away from the Temple. He had first been brought before the former high priest Annas, probably in the hope that this wicked conniver could concoct a charge against Jesus that would justify the death penalty. When that failed, Christ was brought before the acting high priest, Caiaphas, and the hastily-assembled Sanhedrin. Even with willing false witnesses that group was also unable to indict Jesus. Only when He confessed to being the Christ and God's Son did they discover a way to destroy Him. Although He spoke the truth, they convicted Him of blasphemy and being worthy of death (Matt. 26:63-66). He was sentenced to death for the truth, for being who He indeed is.

Now when morning had come, Matthew recounts, **all the chief priests and the elders of the people took counsel against Jesus to put Him to death.** Although they had already reached a verdict about His guilt and punishment, they still had two hurdles. First, they had to devise a way to make their decision appear legal under rabbinical law. Mark mentions that in addition to **all the chief priests and the elders,** "scribes, and the whole Council" were present (15:1). Second, because the people knew that all trials involving the death penalty had to be conducted in the daytime and in the Temple court, they had to wait until **morning** of that Passover Friday to reconvene the Sanhedrin in its legitimate council chamber (Luke 22:66). The **counsel** they took among themselves amounted to reasserting the charges **against Jesus** and reaffirming the verdict **to put Him to death** (see Luke 22:67-71).

223

After that point, however, the Jewish leaders dropped all pretense of legality. As explained in chapter 16 of this volume, rabbinical law required that a sentence of death could not be carried out until the third day after it was rendered and that during the intervening day the members of the court were to fast. The delay of execution provided additional time for evidence or testimony to be discovered in the defendant's behalf. Because Friday was a holy day for Judean Jews, which included virtually all the religious leaders, and the next day was the Sabbath, the earliest legitimate execution of Jesus could not have been until Sunday—assuming the trial itself had been legitimate. On this occasion, however, the Sanhedrin did not bother to give even the semblance of compliance with that requirement. Now that Jesus was finally in their custody, they determined to destroy Him as quickly as possible.

But because they were not allowed to administer the death penalty themselves (John 18:31), the Jewish leaders now had to convince the Roman governor to give immediately the required permission for Jesus' execution. Therefore **they bound Him, and led Him away, and delivered Him up to Pilate the governor.** With that hearing, the first phase of Jesus' secular, Roman trial would begin.

Pontius **Pilate** had been the Roman **governor** of Judea since A.D. 26, when Tiberius Caesar was emperor, and continued to govern until the year 36. Jesus was taken to the Praetorium, the official provincial residence of the governor, and to keep from being ceremonially defiled and thereby prevented from celebrating the Passover later that day, the Jewish leaders waited outside (John 18:28).

THE CONTRAST BETWEEN GUILTY JUDAS AND INNOCENT JESUS

Then when Judas, who had betrayed Him, saw that He had been condemned, he felt remorse and returned the thirty pieces of silver to the chief priests and elders, saying, "I have sinned by betraying innocent blood." But they said, "What is that to us? See to that yourself!" And he threw the pieces of silver into the sanctuary and departed; and he went away and hanged himself. (27:3-5)

We are not told where Judas was during the Jewish mock trials. He doubtless had followed the multitude from the Mount of Olives to Annas's house and was waiting nearby, perhaps in the courtyard where Peter was. It is possible that he was called as one of the witnesses against Jesus, but that seems unlikely. Judas still had the onus of being a disciple of Jesus, and, in any case, the very fact he was a traitor would have made his testimony suspect. Because Judas had fulfilled his usefulness to them, the chief priests and elders wanted nothing more to do with him. He was now a rejected outcast—to them, to the disciples, and to Jewish society in general.

Then when could be translated "at that time," which seems to fit the context. Even before dawn it had became obvious to Judas and the others in the courtyard that the foregone verdict of the Jewish leaders had been confirmed. Now **Judas, who had betrayed Him, saw** with his own eyes **that He had been condemned.** Although *horaō* (**saw**) was sometimes used in the figurative sense of being aware of or perceiving, its use here suggests literal, physical sight. If Peter was able to see Jesus during at least part of the trial (Luke 22:61), then others in the courtyard could have seen Him as well. Judas had seen Jesus maligned, spat upon, beaten, and mocked. Now he watched in bewilderment as his **condemned** Teacher was taken to Pilate.

As Judas watched Jesus being carried away to Pilate, the full enormity of his treachery finally began to dawn on him as he realized the Jewish leaders did indeed intend to put Jesus to death. The one last obstacle was the permission of Pilate, which Judas had no reason to believe would be denied. Once Pilate consented, Jesus' death would be inevitable.

The sight was devastating to Judas, more than even his money-hungry mind, his sordid soul, and his seared conscience could deal with. **He felt remorse** as he began to experience the intense, excruciating pain that is unique to profound guilt.

No man could be more evil than Judas Iscariot. Only eleven other men in all of history have had the intimate, personal relationship he had with the incarnate Son of God. No man has ever been more exposed to God's perfect truth, both in precept and example. No man has been more exposed firsthand to God's love, compassion, power, kindness, forgiveness, and grace. No man has had more evidence of Jesus' divinity or more firsthand knowledge of the way of salvation. Yet in all of those three indescribably blessed years with Jesus, Judas did not take so much as the first step of faith.

In a way that defies comprehension, Judas persistently resisted and rejected God's truth, God's grace, and even God's own Son. Also in a way that defies understanding, he managed to completely conceal his wicked rebellion from everyone but Jesus. His hypocrisy was so complete and deceptive that even when Jesus predicted that one of the disciples would betray Him, Judas was not suspected.

Judas was so totally trapped in the darkness and corruption of sin that he became a willing instrument of Satan. Because this false disciple had totally renounced Christ, "Satan entered into Judas who was called Iscariot" (Luke 22:3), and it was then a simple matter to persuade him to betray Jesus (John 13:2). Judas's heart was so utterly hardened to the things of God that long before he consciously considered betraying Him, Jesus called him a devil (John 6:70).

Even so, Judas could not escape the divinely designed signal of guilt that reminds men of their sin and warns them of its consequences. Just as pain is an intrinsic and automatic warning of physical danger, guilt is an intrinsic and automatic warning of spiritual danger. It was not that Judas suddenly became afraid of God, else he would have turned in desperation to the One he knew could forgive him. Nor was he afraid of men. Although he was now discarded and despised by the Jewish leaders, they had no reason to harm him. It was rather that Judas suddenly realized the horrible wrongness of what he had done. An innate awareness of right and wrong is divinely built into every human being and cannot be totally erased, no matter how deep a person may fall into depravity or how consciously and rebelliously he may turn against God. This is intensified by the convicting pressure of the Spirit of God.

Judas's **remorse** was not repentance of sin, as the King James Version suggests. Matthew did not use *metanoeō*, which means a genuine change of mind and will, but *metamelomai,* which merely connotes regret or sorrow. He did not experience spiritual penitence but only emotional **remorse.** Although he would not repent of his sin, he could not escape the reality of his guilt. Genuine sorrow for sin (*metamelomai*) can be prompted by God in order to produce repentance (*metanoeō*), as Paul declares in 2 Corinthians 7:10. But Judas's **remorse** was not prompted by God to lead to repentance but only to guilt and despair.

Because he was a kind of witness against Jesus, perhaps Judas thought that by admitting the wickedness of what he had done he would be punished as a false witness, as Deuteronomy 19:16-19 prescribed. Under that provision, he would have been crucified himself, suffering the penalty imposed on the one he caused to be falsely convicted. Instead of looking to Jesus' for forgiveness and trusting in His atoning death, Judas's perverted mind may have led him to believe that by dying he somehow could atone for his own sin.

Proof that Judas's sorrow was ungodly and selfish is seen in the fact that he made no effort to defend or rescue Jesus. He had no desire to vindicate or save Jesus but only to salve his own conscience, which he attempted to do by returning **the thirty pieces of silver to the chief priests and elders.**

While some of the Jewish religious leaders were escorting Jesus to Pilate, others remained in the Temple. It was there that Judas confronted them (see v. 5) and confessed that he had **sinned by betraying innocent blood.** Had he been concerned about forgiveness for his sin and had he really believed on the Lord, he would have approached Jesus, not the chief priests and elders. He hoped somehow to assuage his guilt simply by returning the blood money. Like Pilate, who recognized Jesus' innocence but nevertheless permitted His death, Judas knew he had betrayed **innocent blood,** but he did not come to Christ's defense or seek His forgiveness.

Had Judas been able to remember one fault in Jesus, one deficiency or sin, he may have been able to rationalize his treachery. But even Jesus' arch enemy in the human realm could not escape confessing His innocence. Like the Jewish religious leaders, the Roman political leaders, the false witnesses, and even the demons, Judas could find no fault in Jesus. In His sovereign power, God caused even His enemies to testify to the Son's sinless purity.

Yet despite his confession, Judas had not changed his mind about who Jesus was or about his own need for salvation. He had simply become aware of the wickedness of what he had done and wanted relief from the overwhelming guilt that now tormented every part of his being. The money he had wanted so badly now burned in his hands like a live coal.

Sin never brings the satisfaction it promises. Instead of happiness it brings sorrow, and instead of pleasure it produces pain. It poisons with a pang that cannot be relieved apart from God's forgiving grace.

In reply to Judas's agonized appeal, the chief priests and elders callously replied, **"What is that to us? See to that yourself!"** True to the characterization Jesus had given of them a few days earlier, the religious leaders of Israel were adept at laying heavy religious burdens on men's shoulders, while not lifting a finger themselves to help relieve those burdens (Matt. 23:4). They had no more concern for Judas than for Jesus and were as cold-heartedly indifferent to his remorse as they were to Jesus' innocence, which, in effect, they had already acknowledged.

Judas likely realized he was cursed, because the Mosaic law made clear that "cursed is he who accepts a bribe to strike down an innocent person" (Deut. 27:25). But because the Sanhedrin had paid the betrayal bribe, they were hardly in a position to indict and punish Judas for taking it. If they cared nothing for justice regarding Jesus, they certainly cared nothing for it regarding Judas, especially if it would bring their own indictment as well.

In utter desperation and frustration Judas defiantly **threw the pieces of silver into the sanctuary and departed.** Some interpreters assert that the money was cast into the Temple treasury, suggesting that Judas's final public act was a gesture of charity. But *naos* (**sanctuary**) refers specifically to the inner holy place of the Temple, where only priests were allowed to enter. Judas intentionally threw the money into a place where only the priests could retrieve it. He did not throw it there out of charity but out of spite, wanting them to feel guilty and forcing the chief priests to handle the blood money again themselves.

Following that, **he went away and hanged himself.** Considering himself already cursed because of his treachery and having unrelieved pain from having committed the greatest crime in human history, he may have reasoned that hanging was the only escape and a fitting death, knowing that "he who is hanged is accursed of God" (Deut. 21:23). We cannot know Judas's mind, but self-retribution seems a credible explanation for what he did. If so, he took his own life as an act of ultimate self-punishment, in a way that was certain to be cursed by God, thereby inflicting upon himself what his overpowering sense of guilt caused him to believe he justly deserved.

But death does not relieve guilt; it makes it permanent and intensified beyond comprehension. As Jesus repeatedly declared, hell is a place of eternal torment, of "weeping and gnashing of teeth" (Matt. 8:12; 13:42, 50; 22:13; 24:51; 25:30). It is a place of "unquenchable fire, where their worm does not die, and the fire is not quenched" (Mark 9:43-44). Judas today cries out in the eternal pain of his undiminished guilt.

According to Acts 1:18, when Judas committed suicide he fell headlong and "burst open in the middle and all his bowels gushed out." Although this account and the one in Matthew report different aspects of his death, they are compatible. He must have hanged himself from a weak limb of a tree on a hillside, and when the limb broke under his weight he fell down the slope and was crushed on the rocks below.

THE CONTRAST BETWEEN THE HYPOCRISY OF MEN AND THE PROPHECY OF GOD

And the chief priests took the pieces of silver and said, "It is not lawful to put them into the temple treasury, since it is the price of blood." And they counseled together and with the money bought the Potter's Field as a burial place for strangers. For this reason that field has been called the Field of Blood to this day. Then that which was spoken through Jeremiah the prophet was fulfilled, saying, "And they took the thirty pieces of silver, the price of the one whose price had been set by the sons of Israel; and they gave them for the Potter's Field, as the Lord directed them." (27:6-10)

Because **the chief priests** were forced to take back **the pieces of silver,** they had to devise a way to dispose of it. After their unjust and despicable treatment of Jesus, one wonders why they suddenly became concerned about legal propriety. They knew it was **not lawful to put** the money **into the temple treasury, since it** was **the price of blood,** and for some hypocritical reason they decided to honor that particular restriction. But by admitting it was **blood** money they condemned themselves out of their own mouths. By definition, **the price of blood** referred to money illegitimately paid and received to falsely convict a man of a crime that led to his execution. Strangely and perversely, the chief priests and elders had no compunction about taking the money out of the Temple treasury to pay Judas for the betrayal, but now they had qualms about putting it back. In doing so, they testified before the world to their guilt and hypocrisy. It is interesting to note how callous and unfeeling they were about their crime, in contrast to the overwhelming agony of Judas that drove him to kill himself in a vain attempt to relieve his guilt.

They counseled together and decided to use **the money** to buy **the Potter's Field as a burial place for strangers.** As a good will gesture to the public and also to salve their own consciences, they hit upon the idea of buying a field where potters had collected clay to use in their trade. Perhaps the clay was depleted and the field was available for a cheap price. The religious leaders may have reasoned that they would use the defiled money to buy a defiled and useless field in which to bury defiled **strangers,** a term often used by Jews as a euphemism for Gentiles. Or the field may have been used to bury any traveler who died while visiting Jerusalem, especially those who were indigent.

For that reason, Matthew explains, **that field has been called the Field of Blood to this day,** referring to the time, some thirty years later, when his gospel was written. The Potter's Field had come to be called **the Field of Blood,** because it was common knowledge that it had been purchased with blood money. And by that name, the entire city testified to Jesus' innocence, acknowledging that He had been falsely accused, falsely condemned, and falsely executed.

In the naming of that field, **that which was spoken through Jeremiah the prophet was fulfilled,** saying, **"And they took the thirty pieces of silver, the price of the one whose price had been set by the sons of Israel; and they gave them for the Potter's Field, as the Lord directed me."**

The fact that this quotation comes from Zechariah 13:11-12 and not from the book of **Jeremiah** has caused some interpreters to accuse Matthew of error. Others have tried to relate the quotation to sections of Jeremiah 18 or 19, although it clearly does not fit. The explanation is found in the Jewish division of the Old Testament into three sections— the Law, the Writings, and the Prophets. In the rabbinical order of the prophetic books, Jeremiah was always listed first. For that reason the entire prophetic category was sometimes referred to as **Jeremiah,** just as the entire section of the Writings was sometimes referred to as the Psalms, its opening book. **Spoken through Jeremiah the prophet** was therefore the equivalent of saying, "recorded in the prophetic books."

Like every other incident in the life of our Lord, that one did not catch God by surprise but was a precise fulfillment of specific prophecy in His omniscient plan. Even in Judas's death, God's Word was honored and the Lord Jesus Christ was glorified.

What Shall I Do with Jesus?

19

(27:11-26)

Now Jesus stood before the governor, and the governor questioned Him saying, "Are You the King of the Jews?" And Jesus said to him, "It is as you say." And while He was being accused by the chief priests and elders, He made no answer. Then Pilate said to Him, "Do you not hear how many things they testify against You?" And He did not answer him with regard to even a single charge, so that the governor was quite amazed. Now at the feast the governor was accustomed to release for the multitude any one prisoner whom they wanted. And they were holding at that time a notorious prisoner, called Barabbas. When therefore they were gathered together, Pilate said to them, "Whom do you want me to release for you? Barabbas, or Jesus who is called Christ?" For he knew that because of envy they had delivered Him up. And while he was sitting on the judgment seat, his wife sent to him saying, "Have nothing to do with that righteous Man; for last night I suffered greatly in a dream because of Him." But the chief priests and the elders persuaded the multitude to ask for Barabbas, and to put Jesus to death. But the governor answered and said to them, "Which of the two do you want me to release for you?" And they said, "Barabbas." Pilate said to them, "Then what shall I do with

Jesus who is called Christ?" They all said, "Let Him be crucified!"
And he said, "Why, what evil has He done?" But they kept shouting
all the more, saying, "Let Him be crucified!" And when Pilate saw
that he was accomplishing nothing, but rather that a riot was
starting, he took water and washed his hands in front of the
multitude, saying, "I am innocent of this Man's blood; see to that
yourselves." And all the people answered and said, "His blood be
on us and on our children!" Then he released Barabbas for them;
but after having Jesus scourged, he delivered Him to be crucified.
(27:11-26)

Jesus Christ makes a claim on every human heart, and every heart
must decide what to do with Him. The most important and inescapable
question every human being faces is the one that Pilate asked in this
passage: "What shall I do with Jesus who is called Christ?"
Scripture clearly proclaims Jesus as being fully God. Long before
His birth it was divinely predicted that He would be called Immanuel,
which means "God with us" (Matt. 1:23; cf. Isa. 7:14). He was called by
divine names, such as "the Holy and Righteous One" (Acts 3:14). It
declares that to know Jesus is to know God the Father (John 8:19; 14:7
), to hate Him is to hate the Father (15:23), and to believe in Him is to
believe in the Father (Matt. 10:40; John 12:44; 14:1). It affirms that to
see Him is to see the Father (John 14:9), to honor Him is to honor the
Father (5:23), and to receive Him is to receive the Father (Mark 9:37). It
proclaims that Jesus is omnipotent (Matt. 28:18), omnipresent (Matt.
28:20), changeless (Heb. 13:8), creator of the world (John 1:3), able to
forgive sin (Mark 2:5-10), and is to be worshiped as God (Phil. 2:9-11;
cf. Matt. 28:9; Heb. 1:6).
Yet Scripture also declares that Jesus was fully human. He was
born into the world just as every other infant, He was circumcised, He
grew in body and mind, and He experienced hunger, thirst, pain,
weariness, temptation, and death.
The Old Testament gave precise details about the coming of the
Savior-King. Among many other things, it predicted that in His human
life He would be supernaturally conceived (Isa. 7:14), born in Bethlehem
(Mic. 5:2), be Semitic in the line of Abraham and of David (Gen. 9:26;
22:18; 2 Sam. 7:13), be of the tribe of Judah (Gen. 49:10), and would
perform miracles (Isa. 35:5-6). In His death He would be executed by
rulers (Ps. 2:1-2), forsaken by God (Ps. 22:1), betrayed by a friend for
thirty pieces of silver (Ps. 41:9; Zech. 11:12), and have His beard plucked
out and be spit upon (Isa. 50:6). In His resurrection He would rise in
three days (Hos. 6:2), would not experience decay of His flesh (Ps. 16:10),
and would conquer death (Isa. 25:8).
Scripture declares that Jesus Christ is perfectly holy, perfectly

loving of His heavenly Father and of the world He came to redeem, perfectly forgiving of sins and merciful to those who come to Him, perfectly compassionate, perfectly faithful, and perfectly prayerful. He is the central theme of Scripture, both in the Old and New Testaments. And, whether men recognize it or not, He is the dominant figure in all human history and the determiner of the destiny of every human being.

It is on that incalculably crucial issue that Matthew 27:11-26 focuses.

After reporting Judas's suicide, Matthew resumes the account of Jesus' trial, which began its secular, Roman phase when the Jewish leaders bound Jesus "and led Him away, and delivered Him up to Pilate the governor" (27:2).

Having failed to find a legitimate charge against Jesus, the Sanhedrin had falsely accused Him of blasphemy and being worthy of death when He truthfully acknowledged He was "the Christ, the Son of God" (26:63-66; cf. Luke 22:70). But because they did not have the authority to exact the death penalty themselves (John 18:31), the Jewish leaders were forced to ask permission of the Roman governor, Pontius Pilate.

Most of Palestine was under the nominal monarchial dominion of three sons of Herod the Great. Herod Antipas ruled Galilee and Perea, Philip ruled the sparsely populated northeast area, and Archelaus ruled Judea, Samaria, and Idumea. But the supreme Roman official over Judea was the procurator, or governor, who also had command of the Roman troops.

In reporting Jesus' Roman trial, Matthew continues to exalt Christ as the sinless, pure, sovereign, and glorious King. Like the Jewish religious leaders, the Roman political leaders could find no fault in Him. Even with all their efforts, the courts of men failed to produce a legitimate indictment against the perfect Son of God. The record stands in Scripture for men and women of all ages to discover that Jesus Christ was put to death for no crime or sin of His own but by the hatred of sinful men.

In 27:11-26 Matthew presents four elements in Jesus' trial before Pilate that demonstrate His innocence and His perfection.

THE ACCUSATION OF THE JEWS

Now Jesus stood before the governor, and the governor questioned Him saying, "Are You the King of the Jews?" And Jesus said to him, "It is as you say." And while He was being accused by the chief priests and elders, (27:11-12a)

The first element demonstrating Jesus' perfection and innocence is the negative accusation of the Jewish religious leaders. When the chief priests and elders first brought Jesus to Pilate (Matt. 27:1-2), it was still very early on Friday morning, probably around five o'clock. John reports that "they led Jesus therefore from Caiaphas into the Praetorium, and it was early; and they themselves did not enter into the Praetorium in order that they might not be defiled, but might eat the Passover" (John 18:28). The Praetorium was the governor's residence in Jerusalem and was probably located in the Fortress of Antonia, which was just north of the Temple. The Praetorium also served as a judgment hall, where the governor adjudicated matters brought before him.

As mentioned in previous chapters, although northern Jews, including those from Galilee such as Jesus and the disciples, had celebrated the Passover on the previous day, the southern Jews, which included the vast majority of the religious leaders, celebrated it a day later, which in that year was Friday. The members of the Sanhedrin therefore had not yet offered their sacrifices or eaten the Passover meal, and because rabbinical tradition taught that entering a Gentile home or building was ceremonially defiling, they refused to enter the Praetorium.

The extreme of their wicked hypocrisy is seen in their knowingly making false accusations against Jesus while in the very process of transgressing both scriptural law and their own standards regarding judicial process. They were meticulous about observing man-made restrictions regarding supposed ceremonial contamination but were totally insensitive to the demands of simple justice. They maintained fastidious commitment to a foolish, arrogant superstition while resolutely seeking the execution of the Son of the living God (cf. Matt. 23:23).

We can be sure that Pilate was more than a little perturbed at being roused at such an early hour, but he was even more concerned about raising the ire of the Jewish leaders, especially in the midst of their great religious festival, when Jerusalem was swelled to bursting with pilgrims. And because they would not come in to him, the governor "therefore went out to them," probably on a porch or balcony, "and said, 'What accusation do you bring against this Man?'" (John 18:29). That question was perhaps the first and only legal act in the trial of Jesus. Before the governor would hear the case, he insisted that a formal indictment be presented.

Doubtlessly taking full advantage of the leverage they had over Pilate because of his fear of political trouble, the Jewish leaders responded with arrogance and sarcasm. They self-righteously asserted, "If this Man were not an evil-doer, we would not have delivered Him up to you" (John 18:30). In effect, they rebuked the governor for indirectly impugning their integrity. But it was not their intent for Pilate to give Jesus a fair hearing but simply to approve and administer the death sentence they had already decreed.

Pilate was already aware of who Jesus was and of the animosity the Jewish leaders had for Him. Because their concerns were purely religious, the governor had no desire to become involved and therefore told them, "Take Him yourselves, and judge Him according to your law" (v. 31). In saying that, Pilate gave tacit, if not explicit, permission for Jesus' execution, because he knew that, according to their laws, the most serious religious offenses were punishable by death.

The Sanhedrin made no effort to secure Roman permission for execution when they stoned Stephen (Acts 6:12-15; 7:54-60) or when, some years later, they plotted Paul's death (23:12-15). Their telling Pilate, "We are not permitted to put anyone to death" (John 18:31b) was duplicitous. Their design was not simply to have Jesus put to death but to avoid responsibility for it, and possible reprisal from their own people, by having the Romans execute Him for a supposed political offense.

But overshadowing that satanic plan was the divine plan of God, who used the adversary's destructive scheme to fulfil His own redemptive purpose. By demanding a Roman execution, the Jewish leaders unwittingly made certain that "the word of Jesus might be fulfilled, which He spoke, signifying by what kind of death He was about to die" (John 18:32).

In order to satisfy Pilate's demand for a specific charge and to secure Jesus' conviction under Roman law, the chief priests and other leaders fabricated the allegation of sedition. That charge, of course, had nothing to do with the supposed blasphemy for which they had just sentenced Jesus to death. "We found this man misleading our nation and forbidding to pay taxes to Caesar," they lied, "and saying that He Himself is Christ, a King" (Luke 23:2). They charged Jesus with being an insurrectionist, of undermining Roman taxation, and even of claiming to be a competing political ruler.

Had Jesus been guilty of any one of those allegations, Pilate would have known of it and would long since have arrested and executed Him. As virtually every Jew and many Gentiles in Palestine well knew, however, Jesus was a man of peace and was in total submission to Roman political authority. He willingly paid taxes and taught His followers to do likewise. He even taught that if a soldier commanded a person to carry his gear for a mile, which by Roman law he was permitted to do, the person should carry it two miles (Matt. 5:41). Jesus not only did not rebel against the emperor but had publicly declared that citizens should "render to Caesar the things that are Caesar's" (Matt. 22:21). And when His admirers had wanted to make Him king by force He had disappeared from their midst (John 6:15). The accusations against Jesus were such obvious lies that one wonders what sort of fool the Jewish leaders thought Pilate to be.

In response to the indictments, as **Jesus stood before the governor, . . . the governor questioned Him saying, "Are You the King of the Jews?"** Pilate knew full well that the charges were spurious, and his question to Jesus was merely procedural. In light of Rome's absolute intolerance of insurrection, Pilate's indifferent reaction served to dramatically underscore his awareness of the preposterousness of the Sanhedrin's allegations.

Jesus' first response to Pilate was a counter question: "Are you saying this on your own initiative, or did others tell you about Me?" (John 18:34). Surprised and taken aback, the governor retorted, "I am not a Jew, am I? Your own nation and the chief priests delivered You up to me; what have You done?" (v. 35). To which Jesus replied, "My kingdom is not of this world. If My kingdom were of this world, then My servants would be fighting, that I might not be delivered to the Jews; but as it is, My kingdom is not of this realm" (v. 36).

It was perhaps at this point that Jesus said, **"It is as you say."** Commenting further about the true nature of His kingship, He said, "You say correctly that I am a king. For this I have been born, and for this I have come into the world, to bear witness to the truth. Everyone who is of the truth hears My voice" (John 18:37). Although he admitted to having no comprehension of what Jesus meant by "truth," Pilate "went out again to the Jews, and said to them, 'I find no guilt in Him.'" (v. 38).

In this context, "find" represented a judicial verdict. Pilate acquitted Jesus of any civil or criminal wrongdoing. In modern parlance, He threw the case out of court for lack of evidence. He exercised "summary judgment."

Not only were the charges patently false, but Pilate knew that the Jewish leaders themselves hated Rome passionately. Had Jesus actually been an insurrectionist, they would have supported Him and sought to protect Him, not brought Him before a Roman court and demanded His execution. He knew quite well that "it was for envy" of Jesus, not loyalty to Rome, that "they had delivered Him up" (Matt. 27:18).

The high priests, chief priests, elders, scribes, Pharisees, and Sadducees all hated Jesus because He undermined their religious influence with and stature before the people. He exposed their sinfulness, hypocrisy, and doctrinal error. He was popular, whereas they were not. He could heal, whereas they could not. He taught truth, whereas they did not. Their true motivation was transparent even to a pagan politician. The governor probably suspected something of what they were up to when they requested the escort of Roman soldiers in arresting Jesus. But he already knew that Jesus was no danger to Rome and probably thought that, after condemning and flogging Jesus in their own court, the Jewish leaders would be satisfied and that His threat to them would end.

But the Council leaders would not be put off by Pilate's verdict of innocent. As he stood before them again on the balcony of the Praetorium, Jesus continued to be **accused by the chief priests and elders.** Luke reports that "they kept on insisting, saying, 'He stirs up the people, teaching all over Judea, starting from Galilee, even as far as this place'"

(23:5). They increased the pressure on the governor as they desperately grasped for a charge that would arouse his concern. All this failing effort emphasizes the perfect virtue of the Savior.

THE ATTITUDE OF THE LORD

He made no answer. Then Pilate said to Him, "Do you not hear how many things they testify against You?" And He did not answer him with regard to even a single charge, so that the governor was quite amazed. (27:12b-14)

The second element in this account that demonstrates the perfection and innocence of Christ was His own attitude. To Pilate's consternation, Jesus **made no answer** to the intensified accusations of the chief priests and elders.

The Jewish leaders had already rendered their predetermined verdict of guilty, and the governor his verdict of not guilty, declaring, "I find no guilt in Him" (John 18:38). He knew that the original charges against Jesus not only were religious rather than political but were spurious and made out of envy. He also knew that the charges they had just made regarding insurrection, not paying taxes, and claiming to be a king were manufactured solely for his benefit, in order to give a political basis for judgment against Him.

Pilate knew the truth, and the Jews were opposing the truth. The Jews had unjustly convicted Him, and Pilate had justly exonerated Him. Jesus therefore refused to say anything else because there was nothing more to say.

Hoping that Jesus would come to His own defense and help expose the duplicitous Jewish leaders, **Pilate said to Him, "Do you not hear how many things they testify against You?"** But again Jesus **did not answer him with regard to even a single charge.** Understandably, **the governor was quite amazed.** Pilate had confronted hundreds of accused men, most of whom loudly protested their innocence and were willing to say or do anything to save themselves. Many of them doubtlessly made countercharges against their accusers or else passionately pled for mercy. A person who said nothing in his own defense was unheard of and astounding. But Jesus' innocence was so obvious that it demanded no defense on His part.

"Where is the revolutionary who opposes Rome, the tax-dodging protester, and the rival to Caesar's throne?" Pilate must have mused. The Man who stood before him was calm, serene, undefensive, and completely at peace. As Isaiah had predicted some seven centuries earlier, although "He was oppressed and He was afflicted, yet He did not open His mouth; like a lamb that is led to slaughter, and like a sheep that is silent before its shearers, so He did not open His mouth" (Isa. 53:7).

Pilate not only was amazed but in a quandary. He was convinced of Jesus' innocence and was repulsed by the chicanery of the chief priests and elders. Yet he did not dare offend them, because his own position with Rome was now precarious due to the contemptuous miscalculations he had previously made regarding Jewish religious convictions.

He had governed Judea for some four or five years, but his rule had been marked by several serious misjudgments that threatened his office and even his life. First, he had deliberately offended the Jews by having his soldiers carry ensigns into Jerusalem that carried the likeness of Caesar. Because the Jews considered such images to be idolatrous, previous governors had carefully avoided displaying the emblems in public, especially in the holy city of Jerusalem. When a delegation of Jews persistently asked Pilate to remove the ensigns, he herded them into an amphitheater and threatened to have his soldiers cut off their heads if they did not desist. When the group bared their necks and threw themselves to the ground, defiantly asserting their willingness to die, Pilate withdrew both his threat and the ensigns. He had been sent to Palestine to keep the peace, not foment a revolution, which a massacre of those men would surely have precipitated.

A short while later, Pilate forcefully took money from the Temple treasury to erect an aqueduct. When the Jews again openly rioted, Pilate sent soldiers disguised as civilians among them to brutally slaughter many of the unsuspecting and unarmed protesters. Luke's reference to "the Galileans, whose blood Pilate had mingled with their sacrifices" (13:1) may relate to an additional cruel facet of that massacre.

Pilate's third public offense against the Jews was almost his undoing. He had special shields made for his guard at Fort Antonia and, no doubt intending to gain favor with the emperor, ordered likenesses of Tiberius engraved on the shields. This time the Jewish leaders appealed directly to Caesar, and Pilate's scheme backfired. Tiberius was more concerned about the genuine prospect of rebellion than the insincere flattery of Pilate, and he demanded that the shields be removed immediately.

Pilate was now justifiably afraid that another riot by the Jews would cost him his procuratorship. His brutal and senseless ambush of some Samaritan worshipers a few years later brought exactly that result. When the Samaritans appealed to the governor's immediate superior, the legate of Syria, that official ordered Pilate to Rome to explain his actions. His political career was ended, and tradition holds that he eventually committed suicide in Gaul, to which he had been banished.

We learn from Luke that when Pilate heard the Jewish leaders say Jesus was stirring up the people, "starting from Galilee, even as far as this place," he asked if Jesus were a Galilean. When told that Jesus was

What Shall I Do with Jesus? (27:11-26)

27:12b-14

indeed from that region, he felt certain he had found a solution to his dilemma. He immediately sent Jesus to Herod Antipas, who ruled Galilee but was visiting in Jerusalem at the time (Luke 23:5-7). With His appearance before Herod, the second phase of Jesus' political trial began.

For his own perverse reasons, "Herod was very glad when he saw Jesus; for he had wanted to see Him for a long time, because he had been hearing about Him and was hoping to see some sign performed by Him" (Luke 23:8). Because Antipas had beheaded John the Baptist, Jesus had never visited the tetrarch's capital city of Tiberias in Galilee, and the ruler had never seen Him. Herod desired to meet Jesus purely out of curiosity, hoping to see this famous miracle-worker perform for his private benefit.

Although Herod "questioned Him at some length," Jesus "answered him nothing. And the chief priests and the scribes were standing there, accusing Him vehemently" (Luke 23:9-10). Luke does not mention what Herod asked Jesus about, but based on what is known of that ruler, his questions were utterly superficial. Jesus therefore had even less to say to him than to Pilate. He owed the tetrarch no explanation of His teaching or His activities, about which Herod was probably well informed or easily could have been.

Whatever else Herod may have known or believed about Jesus, he knew He was no political threat to himself or to Caesar. By this time Jesus had already been beaten by the Sanhedrin, and His face was bruised, bleeding, and covered with spittle. The accused, silent prisoner appeared anything but regal or dangerous.

But resentful of Jesus' silence and probably hoping to mollify the howling, infuriated Jews, "Herod with his soldiers, after treating Him with contempt and mocking Him, dressed Him in a gorgeous robe and sent Him back to Pilate" (Luke 23:11). The word rendered "gorgeous" literally means bright and resplendent, suggesting the royal apparel that had often been worn by Jewish kings at their coronations.

Although Herod did not declare Jesus not guilty, as Pilate had done, he acknowledged no charge against Him, and once again Christ's innocence was manifested. The tetrarch mocked and mistreated Christ, but he could find no fault in Him.

THE ANIMOSITY OF THE CROWD

Now at the feast the governor was accustomed to release for the multitude any one prisoner whom they wanted. And they were holding at that time a notorious prisoner, called Barabbas. When therefore they were gathered together, Pilate said to them, "Whom do you want me to release for you? Barabbas, or Jesus who is called Christ?" For he knew that because of envy they had delivered Him up. And while he was sitting on the judgment seat, his wife sent

to him saying, "Have nothing to do with that righteous Man; for last night I suffered greatly in a dream because of Him." But the chief priests and the elders persuaded the multitude to ask for Barabbas, and to put Jesus to death. But the governor answered and said to them, "Which of the two do you want me to release for you?" And they said, "Barabbas." Pilate said to them, "Then what shall I do with Jesus who is called Christ?" They all said, "Let Him be crucified!" And he said, "Why, what evil has He done?" But they kept shouting all the more, saying, "Let Him be crucified!" (27:15-23)

The third element in this narrative that demonstrates Jesus' perfection and innocence was also the third phase of His political trial. The first two ended in acquittal, one by specific declaration and the other by default.

Had he had the courage to do it, Pilate could have ended the trial after Jesus' first appearance before him, and he could have ended it now. But with his own career and perhaps his life in jeopardy, he could not directly defy the Jewish establishment without risking a riot during the most tumultuous week of the year in Jerusalem.

Christ therefore stood once again before the governor, who at this time "summoned the chief priests and the rulers and the people, and said to them, 'You brought this man to me as one who incites the people to rebellion, and behold, having examined Him before you, I have found no guilt in this man regarding the charges which you make against Him. No, nor has Herod, for he sent Him back to us; and behold, nothing deserving death has been done by Him'" (Luke 23:13-15).

Having failed in passing off responsibility to Herod and in convincing the Jewish leaders of Jesus' innocence, Pilate discovered another possible way to avoid executing this obviously guiltless man. When "the multitude went up and began asking [Pilate] to do as he had been accustomed to do for them" (Mark 15:8), he remembered that **at the feast** of the Passover **the governor was accustomed to release for the multitude any one prisoner whom they wanted.**

As an act of diplomacy and to help reduce tension and bitterness in the subjected nation of Israel, a custom had begun, probably before Pilate took office, of releasing **any one prisoner** during the Passover celebration. Because **they were holding at that time a notorious prisoner, called Barabbas,** the governor probably expected the common people, who were known to have acclaimed and admired Jesus, to choose His release above that of **Barabbas.** If the multitude demanded Jesus' release, the Jewish leaders could not blame Pilate.

Little is known about **Barabbas** except that he was a robber, murderer, and insurrectionist (Luke 23:25; John 18:40). He was probably not a Zealot but an independent rogue who fought Rome more for personal gain than patriotism. This arch-criminal was as great a threat to his fellow countrymen as to their oppressors. Because of the severity of his crimes, he was doubtlessly scheduled for execution, and Jesus probably was crucified on the cross originally constructed for Barabbas.

It was now "about the sixth hour" (John 19:14), which by Roman reckoning would be 6:00 A.M. By this time a throng of Jews had assembled in front of the Praetorium, attracted by the large gathering of religious leaders as well as by the specific summons of Pilate (Luke 23:13). **When therefore they were gathered together, Pilate said to them, "Whom do you want me to release for you? Barabbas, or Jesus who is called Christ?"** Although he despised the Jews, the governor had learned enough about their practices and beliefs to know that they looked forward to a promised deliverer, whom they **called Christ,** or Messiah. He also knew that many Jews had ascribed that title to **Jesus.** And he could hardly have failed to know of Jesus' triumphal entry into Jerusalem a few days earlier and His boisterous acclamation by the multitudes.

Pilate **knew that because of** their **envy** of Jesus, the religious leaders **had delivered Him up,** and by pitting the people against those leaders, he hoped to safely release Him.

While he was sitting on the judgment seat, Pilate's deliberation was interrupted when his **wife sent to him saying, "Have nothing to do with that righteous Man; for last night I suffered greatly in a dream because of Him."** It was surely not her practice to interrupt her husband when he was in the midst of a trial, especially one so sensitive as this. To be **sitting on the judgment seat** was to be acting in the official capacity of judge, and not even a governor's wife would have dared intrude on such proceedings except in a serious crisis. She knew what Pilate's original verdict had been but was afraid that the Jewish leaders would coerce him into changing his mind.

It is possible that Pilate and his wife already had discussed Jesus many times that week. His triumphal entry was common knowledge, as were His healing miracles, including the recent raising of Lazarus just outside Jerusalem. They knew of His daring and dramatic cleansing of the Temple and probably laughed over the consternation He caused the chief priests and the Temple merchants by that act.

Whatever the wife's personal understanding of **righteous** may have been, she was correct in her assessment of this **Man,** and she **suffered greatly** because of that awareness. Matthew does not explain the source of her **dream,** and there is no justification in insisting it was given directly by God. Everything that happened here was according to "the predetermined plan and foreknowledge of God" (Acts 2:23). But although God worked supernaturally through the dream, Pilate's wife may simply have been convinced of Jesus' innocence in her own mind and had the dream as a result of that concern. In any case, she was frightened for her husband and insisted that he have no part in Jesus' condemnation or punishment. In doing so, she added her attestation to Jesus' perfection and innocence.

Pilate's problem was now compounded. Pressures both to release and to condemn Jesus were increasing, and he was caught in the middle. While the messenger was relaying the message of caution from Pilate's wife, **the chief priests and the elders** took advantage of the opportunity and **persuaded the multitudes to ask for Barabbas, and to put Jesus to death.** The governor realized that he had again underestimated the craftiness of the Jewish leaders and overestimated the convictions of the fickle **multitudes.**

Unaware of what the leaders had managed to accomplish among the crowd while his attention was turned to his wife's warning, the still-hopeful **governor answered and said to them, "Which of the two do you want me to release for you?"** Without hesitation and seemingly with one voice, **they said, "Barabbas."**

Because Jesus had been declared not guilty under Roman law, Pilate was now legally free to release Him as well as Barabbas. He realized, however, that the sole purpose of the crowd in asking for Barabbas's release was to compel him to condemn Jesus. Nevertheless, in a final effort to render justice, the bewildered **Pilate said to them, "Then what shall I do with Jesus who is called Christ?"** Again without hesitation and with one voice, **they all said, "Let Him be crucified!"**

The multitude clearly wanted blood, not justice, and even to the hardened, pagan mind of Pilate their vicious response must have been blood chilling. **"Why, what evil has He done?"** he rebutted, again proclaiming the Lord's innocence before the world. As he should have known, that question only inflamed the mob to greater frenzy, causing them to keep **shouting all the more, saying, "Let Him be crucified!"** Just as they had done before Herod, but with even greater vehemence, they demanded nothing less than Jesus' death.

THE ACQUIESCENCE OF THE GOVERNOR

And when Pilate saw that he was accomplishing nothing, but rather that a riot was starting, he took water and washed his hands in front of the multitude, saying, "I am innocent of this Man's blood; see to that yourselves." And all the people answered and said, "His blood be on us and on our children!" Then he released Barabbas for them; but after having Jesus scourged, he delivered Him to be crucified. (27:24-26)

The fourth element in this account that demonstrates Jesus'

What Shall I Do with Jesus? (27:11-26)

27:24-26

perfection and innocence was the acquiescence of the Roman governor to the will of the multitude, which had been incited against Christ by the Satan-led religious leaders. It did not matter to them that not a single accusation against Him had stood before Annas, before Caiaphas, before the entire Sanhedrin, before Herod, or before Pilate. In their willful spiritual blindness they had no concern for truth, for justice, or for righteousness. They rather pursued unfounded and irrational vengeance on an innocent man who not only had never done them harm but who had healed their diseases and offered them eternal life.

Therefore, **when Pilate saw that he was accomplishing nothing, but rather that a riot was starting, he took water and washed his hands in front of the multitude, saying, "I am innocent of this Man's blood; see to that yourselves."** Finally realizing that no amount of reasoning or evidence would prevail with the obsessed mob, the governor made public testimony that he did not concur with their decision and that he disavowed any complicity in it.

Pilate could not afford another Jewish **riot.** As noted above, the last riot had brought severe censure by Caesar himself. Another uprising would end his career and quite possibly his life. The mob was totally out of control, and it was clear that their only pacification would be Jesus' crucifixion.

Pilate had never been known for mercy or diplomacy. Herod Agrippa I is reported to have said that Pilate was "naturally inflexible—a blend of self-will and relentlessness" (Philo of Alexandria in the *Legatio ad Gaium* [38]). It was his previous cruel indifference to the people under his jurisdiction that had gotten him into so much trouble.

Yet he did have a sense of justice. Had he been able to discover the least evidence that Jesus was guilty of a capital crime, he would have been greatly relieved and more than willing to grant His execution. That would have been by far the easier route. He had condemned many men to death and had no compunction about executing one more. But the fact that he unwaveringly maintained Jesus' innocence, rendering at least five public verdicts of not guilty, testifies to his inability to find any guilt in Him. He therefore repeatedly appealed to the Jewish leaders and to the multitudes to relinquish their demand for Jesus' death. But he was not courageous enough to risk his own welfare to protect Christ's life.

It was ironic, and doubtlessly intentional, that the governor chose a Jewish ritual to depict his renunciation of responsibility for Jesus' fate. If the ruling elders of a city were not able to determine the identity of a murderer, the Mosaic law provided that they could publicly wash their hands, pray to God, and thereby absolve themselves of any guilt regarding their inability to render justice. Using a modified form of that Jewish ceremony which he had heard of, Pilate proclaimed he was **innocent of this** innocent **Man's blood.**

Doubtlessly with a tone of both dismay and disgust, the governor then said, **"See to that yourselves."** And when he gave them what they wanted, **the people** gave him what he wanted. If he would permit Jesus' death, they would assume all blame. **"His blood be on us and on our children!"** they shouted. That declaration did not, of course, absolve Pilate of guilt, but it did proclaim for all time the people's acknowledgment of their own guilt. They soon forgot that assumption of guilt, however, and not many months later the Sanhedrin self-righteously rebuked the apostles for holding them accountable for Christ's blood (Acts 5:28).

The multitude of perhaps several thousand Jews who stood outside the Praetorium made their verdict in behalf of all Israel. It was that verdict, acknowledged by all the other unbelieving Jews through their silence, that caused the branch of Israel to be broken off the tree of God's redemptive blessing (Rom. 11:17). It is no wonder that since that fearful day, as a nation and as individuals, unredeemed Jews have been under the chastening hand of God.

At the end of Jesus' second hearing before Pilate, the governor's intent had been to "punish Him and release Him" (Luke 23:16). But the Jews would not settle for mere punishment, no matter how severe. They insisted on death. Therefore, after **he released Barabbas** according to the wishes of the crowd, Pilate had **Jesus scourged** and **delivered . . . to be crucified.**

The whip used for scourging had a short wooden handle, to the end of which were attached several leather thongs. Each thong was tipped with very sharp pieces of metal or bone. The man to be scourged was tied to a post by the wrists high over his head, with his feet dangling and his body taut. Often there were two scourgers, one on either side of the victim, who took turns lashing him across the back. Muscles were lacerated, veins and arteries were torn open, and it was not uncommon for the kidneys, spleen, or other organs to be exposed and slashed. As would be expected, many men died of scourging before they could be taken out for execution. We do not know the full extent of Jesus' wounds, but He was so weakened by them that He was not able to carry His own cross (Mark 15:21).

Despite the accusatory verbiage of that tragic night, it was not really Jesus who was on trial, but the rest of the world. The Jewish religionists condemned themselves as they viciously demanded His crucifixion. The fickle multitudes condemned themselves as they mindlessly went along with their leaders. Herod condemned himself as he mocked the King of kings. Pilate condemned himself as he willingly allowed an innocent man to be put to death, choosing the world above the Son of God.

And through that ridicule, scorn, and blood, the sinless Son of God was still further exalted.

The Wickedness of the Crucifixion
(27:27-44)

20

Then the soldiers of the governor took Jesus into the Praetorium and gathered the whole Roman cohort around Him. And they stripped Him, and put a scarlet robe on Him. And after weaving a crown of thorns, they put it on His head, and a reed in His right hand; and they kneeled down before Him and mocked Him, saying, "Hail, King of the Jews!" And they spat on Him, and took the reed and began to beat Him on the head. And after they had mocked Him, they took His robe off and put His garments on Him, and led Him away to crucify Him.

And as they were coming out, they found a man of Cyrene named Simon, whom they pressed into service to bear His cross.

And when they had come to a place called Golgotha, which means Place of a Skull, they gave Him wine to drink mingled with gall; and after tasting it, He was unwilling to drink. And when they had crucified Him, they divided up His garments among themselves, casting lots; and sitting down, they began to keep watch over Him there. And they put up above His head the charge against Him which read, "THIS IS JESUS THE KING OF THE JEWS." At that time two robbers were crucified with Him, one on the right and one on the left. And those passing by were hurling

abuse at Him, wagging their heads, and saying, "You who are going to destroy the temple and rebuild it in three days, save Yourself! If You are the Son of God, come down from the cross." In the same way the chief priests also, along with the scribes and elders, were mocking Him, and saying, "He saved others; He cannot save Himself. He is the King of Israel; let Him now come down from the cross, and we shall believe in Him. He trusts in God; let Him deliver Him now, if He takes pleasure in Him; for He said, 'I am the Son of God.'" And the robbers also who had been crucified with Him were casting the same insult at Him. (27:27-44)

The crucifixion of Jesus Christ was the climax of redemptive history, the focal point of God's plan of salvation. God's redeeming work culminated in the cross, where the Lord Jesus bore the sins of the world. But also in the crucifixion of Christ the wickedness of man reached its apex. The execution of the Savior was the vilest expression of evil in human history, the utter depth of man's depravity. The death of Jesus Christ was therefore the supreme revelation of the gracious love of God while also being the ultimate expression of the sinfulness of man.

And whereas John's gospel focuses on the crucifixion primarily from the perspective of God's redemptive love and grace, Matthew's focus is primarily from the perspective of man's wickedness. Man's wickedness attempted to kill Jesus shortly after His birth, tried to discredit His teaching, and made every effort to mislead and corrupt His disciples. Man's wickedness had betrayed Him, denied Him, arrested, maligned, and battered Him. But the incomparable manifestation of man's wickedness was in His crucifixion.

David Thomas wrote:

> [For thousands of] years wickedness had been growing. It had wrought deeds of impiety and crime that had wrung the ages with agony, and often roused the justice of the universe to roll her fiery thunderbolts of retribution through the world. But now it had grown to full maturity; it stands around this cross in such gigantic proportions as had never been seen before; it works an enormity before which the mightiest of its past exploits dwindle into insignificance, and pale into dimness. It crucifies the Lord of life and glory. (*The Gospel of Matthew* [Grand Rapids: Kregel, 1979 (reprint of 1873 edition)], p. 536)

Jesus' enemies so hated Him that even His death seemed to be a disappointment, because it ended their opportunity to spew venom on Him even as He suffered the agony of crucifixion. The heartless intensity of the evil words and deeds of those who participated in His death beggar description.

Matthew 27:27-44 portrays four groups of evil people at the crucifixion who derided and abused Christ: the ignorant wicked (vv. 27-37), the knowing wicked (v. 38), the fickle wicked (vv. 39-40), and the religious wicked (vv. 41-44).

THE IGNORANT WICKED

Then the soldiers of the governor took Jesus into the Praetorium and gathered the whole Roman cohort around Him. And they stripped Him, and put a scarlet robe on Him. And after weaving a crown of thorns, they put it on His head, and a reed in His right hand; and they kneeled down before Him and mocked Him, saying , "Hail, King of the Jews!" And they spat on Him, and took the reed and began to beat Him on the head. And after they had mocked Him, they took His robe off and put His garments on Him, and led Him away to crucify Him.

And as they were coming out, they found a man of Cyrene named Simon, whom they pressed into service to bear His cross.

And when they had come to a place called Golgotha, which means Place of a Skull, they gave Him wine to drink mingled with gall; and after tasting it, He was unwilling to drink. And when they had crucified Him, they divided up His garments among themselves, casting lots; and sitting down, they began to keep watch over Him there. And they put up above His head the charge against Him which read, "THIS IS JESUS THE KING OF THE JEWS."(27:27-37)

The ignorant wicked were the callous Roman soldiers who actually performed the crucifixion under orders from Pilate, who finally had succumbed to the intimidation of the Jewish religious leaders. The Roman governor had publicly declared Jesus' innocence several times, but for fear of a riot that almost certainly would have cost his career and possibly his life, he capitulated to the execution. He had perverted Roman justice by agreeing to convict a man whom no one was able to legitimately charge with a crime against the state. He had sinned against his own convictions, integrity, and conscience, and against the truth. He bargained his eternal soul for temporary security.

In an even worse way, the Jewish leaders had perverted not only scriptural principles of justice but their own rabbinical traditions. Although they had been unable to properly charge Jesus with sin against God, they were determined to destroy Him, whatever the cost to Scripture, justice, truth, or righteousness.

Although **the soldiers of the governor** were under his orders to scourge and crucify Jesus (v. 26), they exhibited their own wickedness by far exceeding what basic duty required. As they **took Jesus into the**

Praetorium, they decided to make public sport of their prisoner **and gathered the whole Roman cohort around Him** to watch.

A full **Roman cohort** amounted to 600 soldiers, and because this particular cohort served the Roman governor at his **Praetorium** at Fort Antonia in Jerusalem, it was probably composed of elite legionnaires. They were not necessarily all, or even mostly, Italian, because Rome typically conscripted soldiers from among its occupied countries. Because most men would be reluctant to fight against their own countrymen, they were frequently sent to neighboring regions that spoke the same or similar language. We can be sure that none of this cohort was Jewish, because Rome had granted a special exemption of Jews from Roman military service. It is likely that the contingent in Jerusalem was composed largely of Syrians, who spoke Aramaic, the most common conversational and trade language of Palestine.

Because Pilate's primary headquarters were in Caesarea, this **cohort** may have been stationed there, traveling from place to place with the governor as his military escort. If so, they would have been even less familiar with Judaism than the average Roman soldier in Jerusalem and probably had never heard of Jesus. To them, He was simply another condemned prisoner, whom they were free to abuse as much as they pleased, as long as he was not killed before the designated execution. If they considered Jesus to be in any way unique, it was only in that He had apparently claimed to be some sort of king. What they did to Him was therefore unrelated to religious or personal animosity. Their torment of Jesus was wicked and inexcusable, but it was done out of spiritual ignorance.

Jesus' face was swollen from the slaps and beatings He received from the Temple police and was covered with spittle from His Jewish tormentors. He was bleeding profusely from the scourging, with terrible lacerations from His shoulders down, exposing muscles, ligaments, blood vessels, and perhaps even internal organs. Because He had not spoken for the past hour or so, the soldiers may have considered Him mentally deranged and worthy only of ridicule. They played Him as the fool, making sport of the comments they had overheard about His claim to kingship.

It did not matter to them that Jesus had never personally harmed them or that technically He was innocent according to Roman law. They had been trained to obey orders, which frequently required killing and torture. Jesus had been officially condemned, and no sense of justice or propriety, much less of mercy or compassion, tempered their cold-hearted entertainment at Jesus' expense. Although in an extreme way, they expressed the natural wickedness of every human heart that is ignorant of God.

Pilate did not initiate the mockery, but neither did he oppose it.

Despite his half-hearted efforts to acquit Jesus, Pilate was noted for cruelty and mercilessness. Having ordered Jesus' scourging and crucifixion, he would hardly have had qualms about the relatively mild abuse of mockery. It is possible that the soldiers performed their derisive actions under the governor's amused eye. The soldiers probably shared their commander's hatred of Jews and took this opportunity to vent their malice on a Jew condemned by fellow Jews. With every nerve in agony and His body quivering in pain, Jesus became the object of a fiendish game.

Jesus was either naked or nearly naked for the scourging, after which He was probably clothed with His seamless inner garment. First, the soldiers **stripped Him** of that garment **and put a scarlet robe on Him,** still further irritating His exposed, bleeding flesh. The **scarlet robe** probably belonged to one of the soldiers, who used it to keep warm while standing guard on cold nights. Mark and John report that the robe was purple (Mark 15:17; John 19:2), suggesting that the actual **scarlet** color was the closest the soldiers could come to purple, the traditional color of royalty.

Although it was far from the soldiers' intent, the use of scarlet was reminiscent of Isaiah's declaration that "though your sins are as scarlet, they will be as white as snow; though they are red like crimson, they will be like wool" (Isa. 1:18). Just as the soldiers clothed Jesus in the scarlet robe, He willingly clothed Himself in the scarlet sins of the world in order that those who believe in Him might be freed from that sin.

To add to the pain as well as to the ridicule, **after weaving a crown of thorns,** the soldiers **put it on His head.** Many kinds of **thorns** were prevalent in Palestine at that time, and the particular variety used is unknown. The purpose was to mimic the wreath that Caesar wore on official occasions and that could be seen on Roman coins that bore his image. As the mock **crown** was pressed **on His head,** blood ran down from the new wounds to mingle with the blood that already covered the rest of His body. Like the scarlet robe, the crown of thorns became an unintended symbol of the sins that Jesus was about to take upon Himself. After the Fall, thorns and thistles became painful reminders of the curse that sin had brought to the world (Gen. 3:18), the curse from which the world ever since has longed to be freed (Rom. 8:22).

Jesus' face was now even more unrecognizable and His pain more intense. But still not content, the soldiers next placed **a reed in His right hand.** Like the robe and the crown of thorns, the **reed** was meant to represent royalty, mimicking a monarch's scepter, the symbol of his authority and power. Such a scepter could also be seen in Caesar's hand on Roman coins.

To complete the sarcastic taunt, the soldiers even **kneeled down before Him and mocked Him saying, "Hail, King of the Jews!"** The Jewish religious leaders had mocked Jesus as a prophet (Matt. 26:68), and now the Roman soldiers mocked Him as a king. Then, just as the Jews had done, **they spat on Him,** casting on Him what was considered the ultimate indignity.

Next in their brutal amusement they **took the reed** from His hand and, to further ridicule His supposed authority, **began to beat Him on the head,** which was already swollen, lacerated, and bleeding. It was as if to say, "Your kingliness is a joke. Look how easily we strip you of your dignity and your authority. We beat you with your own scepter. Where is your power? Where is your royal army to defend you from your enemies?" From John we learn that they struck Jesus with their fists as well as with the reed (John 19:3).

One day Christ will wield a true scepter, a rod of iron with which He will rule the world, including His subdued enemies (Rev. 19:15). Then the tables will be turned, and the mocking and derision will be by God of the ungodly. Then He who sits in the heavens will laugh, and the Lord will scoff at them (Ps. 2:4).

But in His incarnation, Jesus' humiliation was essential to God's plan for the Son, "who emptied Himself, taking the form of a bond-servant, and being made in the likeness of men. And being found in appearance as a man, He humbled Himself by becoming obedient to the point of death, even death on a cross" (Phil. 2:7-8).

Through all of that torment and pain Jesus said nothing either in defense or in reproach. He had predicted His mocking, His suffering, and His crucifixion long before Pilate or his soldiers knew who He was (Matt. 16:21; 20:18-19). That was God's plan countless ages before it was the plan of wicked men, and it was for that very purpose that He had come to earth. As men fulfilled their evil and destructive design, God fulfilled His gracious and redemptive design. Christ was on the divine schedule, which even His enemies were unwittingly fulfilling in minute detail.

We learn from John that during this time Pilate brought Jesus out before the Jews, asserting again that he found no fault in Him. Jesus stood again on the porch of the Praetorium, "wearing the crown of thorns and the purple robe. And Pilate said to them 'Behold, the Man!'" (John 19:4-5). Although he had agreed to the crucifixion and had permitted Jesus to be brutally beaten and mocked, the governor obviously still hoped, perhaps due to his wife's warning, that Jesus' life could be spared. But "when the chief priests and the officers saw Him, they cried out, saying, 'Crucify, crucify!'" As if to wash his hands of the whole unjust affair again, "Pilate said to them, 'Take Him yourselves, and crucify Him, for I find no guilt in Him.' The Jews answered him, 'We have a law, and by that law He ought to die because He made Himself out to be the Son of God.' When Pilate therefore heard this statement, he was the more afraid" (vv. 6-8). Although they repeated only the religious charges against Jesus, the clear implication is that the Jewish leaders were insisting on

Rome's complicity in His execution. In effect, they refused to crucify Jesus by themselves, even with Pilate's permission.

Taking Jesus back into the Praetorium, Pilate asked Him where He was from but received no answer. When he then told Jesus that he had power of life and death over Him, the Lord responded, "You would have no authority over Me, unless it had been given you from above; for this reason he who delivered Me up to you has the greater sin" (John 19:10-11). Although he had little comprehension of what Jesus meant, Pilate was convinced all the more of His innocence of any civil crime and once again "made efforts to release Him, but the Jews cried out, saying, 'If you release this Man, you are no friend of Caesar'" (v. 12).

Still holding out against them, Pilate brought Jesus to "the judgment seat at a place called The Pavement, but in Hebrew, Gabbatha," and mockingly said, "Behold your King!" Infuriated by Pilate's continued defiance of them, the Jewish leaders "cried out, 'Away with Him, away with Him, crucify Him!'" In one last taunt, Pilate asked, "Shall I crucify your King?" to which the chief priests hypocritically replied, "We have no king but Caesar." Frustrated and exhausted, Pilate resigned himself to the injustice and "delivered Him to them to be crucified" (John 19:13-16).

As representatives of the people, the chief priests here pronounced the culminating apostasy of Israel. Rejecting God's Son, they publicly, although insincerely, declared allegiance to the pagan emperor.

Picking up the account at this point, Matthew reports that **after they had mocked Him** further, **they took His robe off and put His garments on Him, and led Him away to crucify Him.**

Some interpreters suggest that only the cross-beam or the upright post was carried, but in all probability it was the entire cross, weighing in excess of 200 pounds, that the victim carried. He would normally be surrounded by a quaternion, four soldiers who would escort the prisoner through the crowds to the place of execution. A placard bearing the prisoner's indictment was often placed around his neck, giving notice to others of the high price to be paid for the crime.

It was during the grueling procession through the streets of Jerusalem that Jesus gave His last, and very brief, public message. "There were following Him a great multitude of the people, and of women who were mourning and lamenting Him," Luke reports. Turning to them Jesus said, "Daughters of Jerusalem, stop weeping for Me, but weep for yourselves and for your children. For behold, the days are coming when they will say, 'Blessed are the barren, and the wombs that never bore, and the breasts that never nursed.' Then they will begin to say to the mountains, 'Fall on us,' and to the hills, 'Cover us.' For if they do these things in the green tree, what will happen in the dry?" (Luke 23:27-31).

Having children was considered the greatest blessing a Jewish woman could have, and only a tragedy of awesome dimensions could cause her to wish otherwise. Jesus' reference to the green and dry tree related to a popular proverb that meant if something bad occurred under good circumstances, it would be much worse under bad. His point was that if the Romans did such a terrible thing as to crucify one innocent Jewish man, what could they be expected to do to the guilty nation of Israel? If they executed a man who had committed no offense against them, what would they do to a people who rebelled?

The Lord was, of course, referring to A.D. 70, when the Temple would be utterly destroyed and the majority of its inhabitants slaughtered by the Roman legions of Titus. From that holocaust the nation of Israel has not yet fully recovered even in modern times, because there is still no temple in Jerusalem, no sacrifices, no priesthood to offer them, and no priestly records to verify lineage. That was the horror of which Israel should have been fearful, Jesus said.

Because He was sinless and completely undefiled in body as well as in mind and spirit, Jesus was physically all that Adam was before the Fall and more. But Jesus' severe beatings and the scourging had made even Him too weak to carry the heavy cross. Not only was He suffering excruciating physical pain, but He had had no sleep the previous night and was suffering the added agonies of betrayal, defection, and denial. In addition to that, He was still suffering the accumulated pain of having been tempted by and being in continual spiritual battle with Satan. There were now no angels sent to minister to Him as they had after the wilderness temptations, and His body was all but depleted of strength. More even than all of that, He knew perfectly that He faced the indescribably painful prospect of taking upon Himself the sin of all mankind, of becoming sin for their sakes. And for that He would suffer the wrath of His heavenly Father which that sin deserved.

All of those agonies—physical, emotional, and spiritual—combined to utterly weaken His perfect but now emaciated body. Consequently, **as they were coming out** from the Praetorium, the soldiers **found a man of Cyrene named Simon, whom they pressed into service to bear His cross.**

Cyrene was a Greek settlement located west of Alexandria on the North African coast of the Mediterranean, directly south of Greece in what is modern Libya. It was a prosperous trade center and had a large population of Jews. **Simon** was a common Jewish name, and in all probability this man was a pilgrim who had come to Jerusalem to celebrate the Passover.

Simon was "a passer-by coming from the country" (Mark 15:21) as Jesus was being taken out of the city. Perhaps because he looked strong he was conscripted by the Roman soldiers to carry Jesus' cross. Mark also identifies Simon as "the father of Alexander and Rufus" (v. 21), indicating that those two men were Christians known to Mark and to many other believers at the time he wrote his gospel. Because Mark probably wrote from Rome, Alexander and Rufus may have been active in the church there. This Rufus may have been the man Paul greeted in his letter to Rome, and, if so, "his mother and mine" would refer to Simon's wife (see Rom. 16:13).

It may have been the carrying of Jesus' cross that led Simon to faith in Him. What began as a forced and probably resented act of physical servitude became the opportunity for spiritual life. Not only Simon himself but his entire family came to salvation, and his wife became like a mother to the apostle Paul.

Because the Mosaic law required that executions be performed outside the city (Num. 15:35) and also because hanging on a tree was considered a curse (Deut. 21:23; cf. Gal. 3:13), Jesus was taken outside Jerusalem to be crucified. And because crucifixion was a vivid means of showing the populace the price for opposing Rome, crosses were generally erected beside a well-traveled road, if possible on a hill, bluff, or other promontory where they would be visible to all.

The place chosen for Jesus' crucifixion was a hill on the outskirts of Jerusalem **called Golgotha, which means Place of a Skull.** As an outcast both of Israel and of Rome, Jesus "suffered outside the gate" (Heb. 13:12).

Luke refers to the hill of crucifixion as "the place called The Skull" (23:33), and as several gospels explain, **Skull** translates a Greek term (*kranion*) equivalent to the Hebrew/Aramaic **Golgotha** (see John 19:17). The name Calvary is derived from the Latin word (*calvaria*) for skull, or cranium.

Contrary to what some scholars have suggested, the **Place of a Skull** was not a burial ground where skulls were commonly found. Jews would not allow dead bodies to be exposed, and no part of a human skeleton was to be seen in Israel. Rather the name referred to a particular site that had the appearance of a skull. Such a hill, commonly called Gordon's Calvary, is the traditional site and can still be viewed today a short distance from Jerusalem's northern wall.

Before the soldiers nailed Jesus to the cross and it was placed upright in the ground, **they gave Him wine to drink mingled with gall.** The word translated **gall** simply referred to something bitter, which Mark identifies as myrrh (15:23), a narcotic that also was used as a perfume (see Ps. 45:8; Prov. 7:17), as an ingredient of anointing oil for priests (Ex. 30:23), and for embalming (John 19:39). It was quite expensive and was one of the gifts presented to the infant Jesus by the magi (Matt. 2:11).

Because crucifixion was designed to inflict maximum pain, the **gall,** or myrrh, was not offered as an act of mercy on the part of the soldiers. It was simply used to stupefy a victim to keep him from struggling violently as the nails were driven into his hands and feet.

From extrabiblical sources it is known that wealthy Jewish women would often provide wine mixed with myrrh to those about to be executed, especially by crucifixion. Contrary to the soldiers, their purpose was to ease the pain of "him who is perishing," following the admonition of Proverbs 31:6. It may have been that such a group of women also offered Jesus the stupefying drink.

But Jesus did not want His senses dulled, **and after tasting** the mixture, **He was unwilling to drink.** As He had already declared in the garden, first in prayer to His heavenly Father (Matt. 26:39) and then to Peter as He was being arrested (John 18:11), He was determined to drink the cup the Father had given Him. He would endure the full measure of pain—physical, emotional, and spiritual.

When they had crucified Him does not refer to the finished execution but to raising Him upright and placing the vertical beam into the hole prepared for it. It was at that point that the actual crucifixion began.

Crucifixion originated in Persia, where a deity named Ormazd was believed to consider the earth sacred. Because a criminal who was executed had to be raised above the earth in order not to defile it, he was suspended on a large pole and left there to die. The practice was picked up by the Carthaginians and then by the Greeks and especially the Romans, whose extensive use caused it to become identified with them. It is estimated that by the time of Christ the Romans had crucified some 30,000 men in Israel alone, primarily for insurrection. The crucifixion of only three men outside Jerusalem was therefore virtually insignificant in the eyes of Rome.

None of the gospel writers describes the procedure for securing Jesus to the cross. The literal Greek text is even less revealing than most English renderings, saying simply, "The having crucified Him ones parted His garments." It is only from Thomas's comments several days after the resurrection that we learn about Jesus' being nailed by His hands and feet (John 20:25), rather than being tied with cords or thongs as was often the case.

Judging from nonbiblical descriptions of crucifixion in New Testament times, Jesus was placed on the cross as it lay flat on the ground. First His feet were nailed to the upright beam and then His arms stretched across the horizontal beam and nailed through the wrists just above the hand, allowing a slight bend at the knees when the body was extended. The cross was then picked up and dropped into the hole, causing excruciating pain as the weight of His body pulled at the already torn flesh around the nails.

In his book *The Life of Christ,* Frederick Farrar describes crucifixion as follows:

A death by crucifixion seems to include all that pain and death can have of the horrible and ghastly—dizziness, cramp, thirst, starvation, sleeplessness, traumatic fever, shame, publicity of shame, long continuance of torment, horror of anticipation, mortification of intended wounds—all intensified just up to the point at which they can be endured at all, but all stopping just short of the point which would give to the sufferer the relief of unconsciousness.

The unnatural position made every movement painful; the lacerated veins and crushed tendons throbbed with incessant anguish; the wounds, inflamed by exposure, gradually gangrened [when a victim took several days to die]; the arteries—especially at the head and stomach—became swollen and oppressed with surcharged blood, and while each variety of misery went on gradually increasing, there was added to them the intolerable pang of a burning and raging thirst, and all these physical complications caused an internal excitement and anxiety, which made the prospect of death itself—of death, the unknown enemy, at whose approach man usually shudders most—bear the aspect of a delicious and exquisite release.

One thing is clear. The first century executions were not like the modern ones, for they did not seek a quick, painless death nor the preservation of any measure of dignity for the criminal. On the contrary, they sought an agonizing torture which completely humiliated him. And it is important that we understand this, for it helps us realize the agony of Christ's death. (Vol. 2 [New York: E. P. Dutton, 1877], pp. 403-4)

Dr. Truman Davis gives an additional description of Jesus' crucifixion:

At this point another phenomenon occurs. As the arms fatigue, great waves of cramps sweep over the muscles knotting them in deep, relentless, throbbing pain. With these cramps comes the inability to push Himself upward. Hanging by His arms, the pectoral muscles are paralyzed and the intercostal muscles are unable to act. Air can be drawn into the lungs but cannot be exhaled. Jesus fights to raise Himself in order to get even one short breath. Finally, carbon dioxide builds up in the lungs and in the blood stream and the cramps partially subside. Spasmodically He is able to push Himself upward to exhale and bring in the life-giving oxygen. . . .

Hours of this limitless pain, cycles of twisting, joint-rending cramps, intermittent partial asphyxiation, searing pain as tissue is torn from His lacerated back as He moves up and down against the rough timber; then another agony begins. A deep crushing pain in the chest as the pericardium slowly fills with serum and begins to compress the heart.

It is now almost over . . . the compressed heart is struggling to pump heavy, thick, sluggish blood into the tissues. The tortured lungs are making a frantic effort to gasp in small gulps of air. ("The Crucifixion of Jesus; The Passion of Christ from a Medical Point of View," *Arizona Medicine,* vol. 22, Mar. 1965, pp. 183-87)

It was not Matthew's purpose, however, to focus on the physical particulars of the crucifixion that led to Christ's yielding up His life, but rather on the character of the crucifiers.

Through all of that torment the callous soldiers sat impassively, as they had done many times before. They had no idea who Jesus was, except for what was written on the sign above His head as a sarcastic taunt by Pilate. They doubtlessly were aware that Pilate, governor of the region and their military commander, had repeatedly declared Jesus innocent of any crime against Rome. But Jesus was probably not the first innocent man they had seen executed. They had no religious concern about Jesus' identity and no moral concern about His innocence. Out of their wicked ignorance they, too, eventually joined in mocking Jesus, saying, "If You are the King of the Jews, save Yourself!" (Luke 23:36-37).

Jesus had repeatedly told the disciples of His coming suffering, scorn, and death, and it had been predicted by Isaiah and other prophets hundreds of years before that. The Messiah would be "despised and forsaken of men, a man of sorrows, and acquainted with grief; and like one from whom men hide their face, He was despised, and we did not esteem Him" (Isa. 53:3). Not only was He to suffer unjustly at the hands of wicked men but He endured that affliction for the very sake of those responsible for it—which, in the fullest sense, includes every fallen, sinful human being who has ever lived and who will ever live. "He was pierced through for our transgressions," Isaiah goes on to say, "He was crushed for our iniquities; the chastening for our well-being fell upon Him, and by His scourging we are healed. . . . The Lord has caused the iniquity of us all to fall on Him" (vv. 5-6).

Christians in the early church are reported to have begged God's forgiveness for the unknown sufferings they caused Jesus, realizing they could not conceive of the full extent of the pain He endured at men's hands, a pain to which they knew their own sins had contributed.

The King James Version of verse 35 contains the additional words: "that it might be fulfilled which was spoken by the prophet, They parted my garments among them, and upon my vesture did they cast lots." The oldest known manuscripts of Matthew, however, do not include those words, suggesting that some well-intentioned scribe added to Matthew's gospel the prediction from Psalm 22:18 that is quoted in John 19:24.

Jewish men normally wore five pieces of clothing: sandals, an inner cloak, a headpiece, a belt, and an outer cloak, or tunic. The four soldiers **divided up** the first four pieces of Jesus' **garments among themselves** by **casting lots.** Because "the tunic was seamless, woven in one piece," they decided not to cut it into four pieces but to "cast lots for it, to decide whose it shall be" (John 19:23-24). Having done that, they sat down near the cross and **began to keep watch over Him there.** The quaternion was required to remain with the victim until his death was certain, making sure that friends or family members did not rescue him or seek to reduce his suffering by putting him to death by a swifter means.

As a final mockery of Jesus and affront to the Jewish leaders, Pilate had instructed the soldiers (see John 19:19a) to **put up above His head the charge against Him which read, "THIS IS JESUS THE KING OF THE JEWS."** Matthew recorded an abbreviated version of the full inscription, which read, "JESUS THE NAZARENE, THE KING OF THE JEWS," and was "written in Hebrew, Latin, and in Greek" (John 19:19b-20). Greek was the most nearly universal language in the empire at that time, Aramaic (closely related to Hebrew) was the language of Palestine, and Latin was the official language of Rome. By those three languages the governor made certain that virtually every person who passed by could read the inscription.

The chief priests insisted that the wording of the inscription be changed to "He said, 'I am King of the Jews.'" But Pilate refused to concede to them again, declaring with finality, "What I have written I have written" (John 19:21-22).

THE KNOWING WICKED

At that time two robbers were crucified with Him, one on the right and one on the left. (27:38)

The second group present at the crucifixion was simply composed of the **two robbers,** who might be described as the knowing wicked. **Robbers** translates *lēstēs,* which denotes a brigand who plunders as he steals. These men were not petty thieves or even common robbers, but cruel bandits who took pleasure in tormenting, abusing, and often killing their victims. It is possible they were associates of Barabbas, who had probably been destined for the middle cross between them before he was released and Jesus took his place. They were not patriots who plundered the Romans to help secure the freedom of their country but hardened criminals whose only loyalty was to themselves. They were as great a threat to their own countrymen as to the Romans.

In all likelihood the **two robbers** were Jewish or at least lived in the Jewish society of Palestine. Consequently, they would have had some knowledge of Judaism and the Jewish Messiah. They likely would have known something about Jesus of Nazareth and the fact that He and His followers claimed He was the predicted Messiah. Therefore their rejection of Jesus was more serious than that of the soldiers.

Like the soldiers, they must have known about the groundless charges of the Jewish religious leaders and the numerous exonerations by Pilate. Yet they were not content to ignore Jesus but rather, as Matthew mentions later in his account (v. 44), cast insults at Him.

The specific, conscious reason for their hatred of Jesus is not clear. They apparently were not driven by religious concerns, and Jesus had certainly done them no harm. But their naturally wicked hearts somehow recognized His life as a righteous judgment on their sinfulness, and they joined the jeering crowds and the religious leaders in the mocking.

Like those of many people today, the lives of the two robbers revolved around material possessions and fleshly satisfaction. They had as little concern for religion, common morality, and justice as did the pagan Roman soldiers. Having a greater love for the things of the world than the things of God, they used their dying breath to vent their pent-up anger on the only one who could give them hope.

THE FICKLE WICKED

And those passing by were hurling abuse at Him, wagging their heads, and saying, "You who are going to destroy the temple and rebuild it in three days, save Yourself! If You are the Son of God, come down from the cross." (27:39-40)

Another group present at the crucifixion might be called the fickle wicked. Referred to by Matthew simply as **those passing by,** this crowd was probably composed largely of Jewish pilgrims who had come to celebrate the Passover. Because Jerusalem could not house all the visitors, the majority of them had to camp outside the city or stay in nearby towns and villages. Consequently, there was much heavier traffic in and out of Jerusalem than usual.

This particular crowd of passers-by almost certainly included inhabitants of Judea and Galilee who had previously admired Christ and perhaps even followed Him for a while. They had heard Him preach and seen Him perform miracles and expose the malicious hypocrisy of the scribes, Pharisees, and other religious leaders. Some of them no doubt had participated in His triumphal entry a few days earlier and had joined in shouting hosannas to His name. They had seen Him cleanse the Temple of the money changers and sacrifice sellers and probably cheered Him for that while listening to His teaching.

It is also almost certain that these former admirers had earlier in the day called for Jesus' crucifixion and had followed the soldiers and Jesus to the Place of the Skull to witness the execution they had demanded. These were the fickle wicked who had a place for Jesus only when He satisfied their wants. They were fascinated by Him, knew who He claimed to be, and had witnessed countless demonstrations of power that verified that claim.

But although they were grateful for His miracles and awed by His preaching, they had no desire for Him to cleanse them of cherished sins or to give Him control of their lives. They had expected Him to be their kind of Messiah, a Messiah who would overthrow Rome and establish Israel as sovereign over the Gentile world. The fact that He had allowed Himself to be arrested, mocked, beaten, scourged, and tried before the pagan Pilate while offering no verbal, much less miraculous, defense was proof enough in their minds that He was not the Messiah whom they, and most of Israel, wanted and expected.

As they passed by beneath the cross they **were hurling abuse at Him, wagging their heads.** The verb behind **hurling abuse** is in the imperfect tense, indicating repeated, continuous defamation. To emphasize their disdain, they were also **wagging their heads** in mockery, **and saying, "You who are going to destroy the temple and rebuild it in three days, save Yourself!"** Just as David had predicted some thousand years earlier, those who looked on the Messiah sneered at Him, mocked Him, and wagged their heads, saying, in essence, "Commit yourself to the Lord; let Him deliver him; let Him rescue him, because He delights in him" (Ps. 22:7-8).

You who are going to destroy the temple and rebuild it in three days referred to the testimony of the false witnesses during the hearing before Caiaphas. Misusing a statement Jesus had made almost three years earlier referring to His death and resurrection (see John 2:19-21), those witnesses accused Him of claiming power to rebuild the Jerusalem Temple in three days (Matt. 26:61). "If you could really do such a miraculous thing as that," His tormentors were saying, "surely You can **save yourself** from death now. **If You are the Son of God, come down from the cross."**

While Pilate was listening to the warning sent by his wife, the chief priests and elders had been inciting the multitude to demand the release of Barabbas and the crucifixion of Jesus, perhaps telling them of His claims to rebuild the Temple and to be the Son of God (see Matt. 27:19-20). Some of those people were now throwing the accusations in Jesus' face as He was suspended on the cross. It was not enough that He was dying in agony. The wicked, mindless, heartless, and fickle crowd had changed in a few days from acclaiming Jesus as the Messiah to condemning Him as a blasphemer.

Many people today are like them. They may have been raised in the church, heard the truths of the gospel many times, and know that Jesus Christ claimed to be the Son of God. They may have been baptized, made a profession of faith, and attended church regularly for a while. But because Jesus does not fulfill their worldly, selfish expectations they lose interest in the things of God. They may be quite willing to have the church attack evils in society but are quite unwilling to be confronted with their own sin and need for repentance and forgiveness. In effect, they mock and sneer at Jesus as they turn their backs on His truth, His righteousness, and His lordship. The world is full of passers-by who once praised Jesus but now ridicule Him.

THE RELIGIOUS WICKED

In the same way the chief priests also, along with the scribes and elders, were mocking Him, and saying, "He saved others; He cannot save Himself. He is the King of Israel; let Him now come down from the cross, and we shall believe in Him. He trusts in God; let Him deliver Him now, if He takes pleasure in Him; for He said, 'I am the Son of God.'" And the robbers also who had been crucified with Him were casting the same insult at Him. (27:41-44)

By far the most wicked of those who harassed Jesus at the cross were the religious leaders, in particular **the chief priests** and **the scribes and elders.** They were the primary instigators of the crucifixion, just as Jesus had predicted (Mark 8:31; Matt. 20:18; cf. Mark 14:43). The Pharisees had been Christ's earliest and most persistent critics, and they had begun to plot His death many years before (Matt. 12:14) and were involved in His arrest (John 18:3). But apparently they played a somewhat secondary role in His trials and condemnation, not being mentioned again until the day following the crucifixion, when, with the chief priests, they asked Pilate to order the tomb sealed (Matt. 27:62-64).

The chief priests and **the scribes and elders** represented the entire religious leadership of Israel, including the reigning and the retired high priests and the Pharisees and Sadducees, all of whom resolutely opposed Jesus and sought His destruction. Although its hearings and condemnation of Jesus were illegal by its own standards as well as by Mosaic law, the supreme ruling council of Israel, the Sanhedrin, fully approved the ultimate and irreversible decision to put Jesus to death (26:59; Mark 15:1).

Those men were the religious authorities and the supposed spiritual leaders of Judaism. Many of them, such as the scribes, had devoted their lives to the study of God's Word and the rabbinical traditions. Because Judaism was rightly seen as the only true religion, these men were held to be the most revered religious men not only in Israel but in the world. If any group of people should have known God's truth and recognized and received the Messiah, it was those men. Yet they not only opposed and condemned Jesus themselves but enticed the people to support them in their wicked rejection of Him.

Perhaps because they felt above addressing Jesus directly as He hung like a criminal on the cross, the leaders spoke to the crowds as they **were mocking Him, and saying, "He saved others; He cannot save Himself."** In saying that Jesus **saved others,** those men again acknowledged the reality of His miracles, which they had never been able to deny. They criticized Him for healing on the Sabbath (Mark 3:2) and accused Him of receiving His miraculous power from Satan (Matt. 12:24), but the reality of His miracle-working power was far too obvious and extensive to repudiate. But because He attacked their apostasy and they were convinced that God was on their side, the religious leaders were also convinced that Jesus was *not* of God and therefore could not now **save Himself.**

If **He is the King of Israel,** as He claims, they continued, **let Him now come down from the cross, and we shall believe Him.** That declaration, of course, was knowingly false and meant only as a taunt. They had not believed Jesus either for the truths He taught or for the miracles He performed. If He came **down from the cross,** they would not **believe Him,** any more than they believed in Him when He rose from the dead, just as Abraham had declared in Jesus' story about Lazarus (Luke 16:30-31). One more miracle, or a dozen more, would not have persuaded them to **believe Him.**

The only kind of power, natural or supernatural, with which those religious leaders were concerned was that which would serve their own expectations and interests. It would seem certain that, if Jesus had used His power to conquer Rome and establish Israel as the supreme nation on earth as most Jews expected, those leaders and most other Jews would have followed Him enthusiastically. But they would not have believed in Him as Lord and Savior but only given Him the superficial loyalty necessary to achieve their own ends—just as His nominal followers have done throughout history and continue to do today.

Jesus was not their kind of Messiah, and they had no desire to follow Him in the way He demanded. They did not want to be made righteous but successful. They did not want to be cleansed but selfishly satisfied. They did not want to give up anything for God but wanted from Him only the worldly, material advantages they cherished. When they realized Jesus offered no such favors, they had no more use for Him.

"He trusts in God," they continued hypocritically; **"let Him deliver Him now, if He takes pleasure in Him."** They did not believe Jesus truly trusted in God but that He was an ungodly fraud. And they obviously did not think God would **deliver Him** or that God took **pleasure in Him,** because they considered Jesus a blasphemer. Nor does it seem likely that they intentionally quoted Psalm 22:8, derisively applying it to Jesus. Even to their perverse minds that would have been an irreverent treatment of Scripture. It was rather that they unwittingly fulfilled Scripture as they mocked Jesus, just as Judas, Caiaphas, Pilate, and many others had unwittingly fulfilled it.

Next they mocked Jesus' person, throwing in His face the many claims He had made, but which they had never believed, to being **the Son of God.** To their unbelieving and ungodly minds, the fact that Jesus either could not or would not save Himself was ultimate proof that He was not the Messiah and God's Son. It was inconceivable to them that the Messiah would permit such mistreatment of Himself or that God would permit such mistreatment of His Son. They were utterly blind to what Scripture taught about the Messiah's suffering and atoning death, and they took Jesus' crucifixion to be final and irrefutable proof that His claims were spurious.

Those men had much to do with religion but nothing to do with God. But because they professed great knowledge of Him and presumed to be pleasing to Him, they were the guiltiest of those who participated in Jesus' death (cf. John 19:11). Although they claimed to stand in Moses' seat, they contradicted what Moses taught, and although they claimed to speak for God, they were in fact His enemies and children of Satan (John 8:44).

One day the Lord "will pour out on the house of David and on the inhabitants of Jerusalem, the Spirit of grace and of supplication, so that they will look on Me whom they have pierced; and they will mourn for Him" (Zech. 12:10). In the crucifixion the religious leaders represented all Israelites who at that time rejected their Messiah and "pierced" Him. Everyone who rejects Christ shares in the guilt of His crucifixion and of putting Him to open shame, even more so if, like those religious leaders, a person has had special privileges from God and exposure to His truth (Heb. 6:4-6).

Matthew again mentions (see v. 38) the two **robbers . . . who had been crucified with Him.** As already noted, they took the lead of the chief priests, scribes, and elders in vilifying Jesus, **casting the same insult at Him.**

However, one of them would have a change of heart and come to saving faith. Through the Holy Spirit he came to see Jesus for who He really is and pleaded in his dying moments: "Jesus, remember me when You come in Your kingdom," to which the Savior graciously replied, "Truly I say to you, today you shall be with Me in Paradise" (Luke 23:42-43).

Many others who had mocked Christ at the cross later came to trust Him as Savior and Lord. After Peter's Spirit-empowered message at Pentecost, the hearers "were pierced to the heart, and said to Peter and the rest of the apostles, 'Brethren, what shall we do?' And Peter said to them, 'Repent, and let each of you be baptized in the name of Jesus Christ for the forgiveness of your sins; and you shall receive the gift of the Holy Spirit.' . . . So then, those who had received his word were baptized;

and there were added that day about three thousand souls" (Acts 2:37-38, 41).

By the working of God's sovereign grace, even some of the scoffing, condemning religious leaders came to salvation during the early days of the church, including "a great many of the priests" (Acts 6:7).

God's Miraculous Commentary on the Cross

(27:45-53)

21

Now from the sixth hour darkness fell upon all the land until the ninth hour. And about the ninth hour Jesus cried out with a loud voice, saying "Eli, Eli, lama sabachthani?" that is, "My God, My God, why hast Thou forsaken Me?" And some of those who were standing there, when they heard it, began saying, "This man is calling for Elijah." And immediately one of them ran, and taking a sponge, he filled it with sour wine, and put it on a reed, and gave Him a drink. But the rest of them said, "Let us see whether Elijah will come to save Him." And Jesus cried out again with a loud voice, and yielded up His spirit. And behold, the veil of the temple was torn in two from top to bottom, and the earth shook; and the rocks were split, and the tombs were opened; and many bodies of the saints who had fallen asleep were raised; and coming out of the tombs after His resurrection they entered the holy city and appeared to many. (27:45-53)

Some years ago as I was driving to a meeting on Good Friday morning, I heard a radio program on which the speaker was making an attempt to acknowledge it as a very special day. It was a day, he said, when a certain man was prosecuted for crimes he did not commit and, although innocent, was sentenced to death. The speaker was of course talking about the crucifixion of Christ. He commented on the inspiration of that special Person and of all others like Him who stand unflinchingly for what they believe in, disregarding the consequences.

But as well-meaning as that speaker may have been, he utterly missed the true significance of Jesus' death. Like most people in Western society, he knew many of the bare facts of the crucifixion but had no grasp of its meaning apart from the obvious travesty of human justice. And from what was said on that program, Jesus' resurrection was considered to be more myth and legend than history. No divine purpose, activity, or accomplishment were so much as hinted at.

As noted in a previous chapter, by the time of Christ the Romans had crucified some 30,000 men in Palestine alone. It seems probable that some of whose men were also innocent of the charges against them. The majority of them were executed for insurrection and doubtlessly were sincere patriots who hoped to free their people from oppression. They died nobly for a cause they believed in. Why, then, we may ask, does history remember the name of only one of those men?

The answer is clear almost from the opening words of Scripture. The sin of Adam and Eve not only caused their own fall and that of all their descendants but also brought corruption of the entire earth. It was for that reason Paul declared that the physical world groans like a woman in childbirth, longing to be restored to its God-designed perfection (Rom. 8:19-22).

Immediately after the Fall, God gave the first veiled promise of deliverance from the sin that had cursed mankind and the rest of the world. He told Satan, "I will put enmity between you and the woman, and between your seed and her seed; he shall bruise you on the head, and you shall bruise him on the heel" (Gen. 3:15). Because men, not women, carry the seed of procreation, the seed of Eve was a prediction of the virgin birth of Christ, who would have no human father and who would be bruised temporarily "on the heel" by Satan but would bruise Satan permanently "on the head."

When God provided the ram as a substitute for Isaac, whom He had ordered his father, Abraham, to sacrifice (Gen. 22:1-14), He provided a beautiful picture of the sacrificial offering of His own Son, Jesus Christ— except that for Him no substitute was or could be provided. And through the animal sacrifices prescribed in the law of Moses, God portrayed to His people the necessity of shedding blood for the remission of sin. But the blood of those animals had no power to remove the slightest sin, and the sacrifices had to be repeated continuously throughout the history of Israel. Yet imperfect as they were, they nevertheless pictured the true, sufficient, and once-for-all sacrifice for sins that Christ's blood shed on the cross would provide. Only one of the 30,000 crucified died for the sins of the world!

Isaiah graphically predicted that the coming Messiah would be "pierced through for our transgressions, . . . crushed for our iniquities," carrying in His own body the sins of all fallen mankind (Isa. 53:5). Zechariah predicted that one day God's chosen people will turn as a nation to the One whom they had pierced, "and they will mourn for Him, as one mourns for an only son" (Zech. 12:10).

In the New Testament Paul explains that on the cross Christ was made a curse for us who deserve to be cursed (Gal. 3:13). Peter declares that He "died for sins once for all, the just for the unjust, in order that He might bring us to God, having been put to death in the flesh, but made alive in the spirit" (1 Pet. 3:18; cf. Heb. 9:28), and John speaks of Christ as the supreme sacrificial "Lamb who has been slain" (Rev. 13:8).

But nowhere in Scripture is the meaning of the cross delineated more powerfully than in Matthew 27:45-53, which records six miracles that form Almighty God's own commentary on the meaning of the cross.

SUPERNATURAL DARKNESS

Now from the sixth hour darkness fell upon all the land until the ninth hour. (27:45)

When Jesus was born, the night sky around Bethlehem was filled with supernatural light as "the glory of the Lord shone around" the shepherds in the field (Luke 2:9). John spoke of Jesus as "the light of men" and "the true light which, coming into the world, enlightens every man" (John 1:4, 9). Jesus spoke of Himself as "the light of the world" (John 8:12; cf. 12:35-36).

But the first miraculous sign that accompanied Jesus' death was not glorious light but dread darkness. **From the sixth hour** (noon), when the sun is at its zenith, supernatural **darkness fell upon all the land until the ninth hour** (3:00 p.m.). Jesus' crucifixion had begun at the third hour, or 9:00 A.M. (Mark 15:25), and when the darkness began He had been on the cross for three hours.

During those first three hours, the silence was broken by Jesus only three times. The first was by His saying, "Father, forgive them; for they do not know what they are doing" (Luke 23:34), and a short while later He said to the penitent thief beside Him, "Truly I say to you, today you shall be with Me in Paradise" (23:43). Shortly after that He said to His mother, "Woman, behold, your son!" and to John, "Behold your mother!" (John 19:26-27).

At the beginning of the second three hours the great **darkness**

fell upon all the land. The Greek *gē* (**land**) can also be translated *earth*, indicating the entire world. It is therefore not possible from the text to determine how widespread the darkness was. God was equally able, of course, to make the darkness local or universal. Shortly before the Exodus, He caused a great darkness to cover the land of Egypt (Ex. 10:14-15), and some forty years later He caused the sun to "stand still," probably by temporarily stopping the rotation of the earth (Josh. 10:12-13; cf. 2 Kings 20:9-11).

Several interesting reports in extrabiblical literature suggest that the darkness at Jesus' crucifixion was worldwide. The early church Father Origen (*Against Celsus,* 2.33) reported a statement by a Roman historian who mentioned such a darkness. Another church Father, Tertullian, wrote to some pagan acquaintances about an unusual darkness on that day, "which wonder is related in your own annals and preserved in your own archives to this day." There was also a supposed report from Pilate to Emperor Tiberius that assumed the emperor's knowledge of a certain widespread darkness, even mentioning that it was from twelve to three in the afternoon.

To describe this darkness Luke used the word *ekleipō,* which has the literal meaning of failing, or ceasing to exist, and is the term from which *eclipse* is derived. But a normal astronomical eclipse would have been impossible during the crucifixion, because the sun and moon were far apart on that day. Regardless of its extent, therefore, the darkening of the sun was by the supernatural intervention of God. During that three-hour period, Luke explains, the sun was obscured (23:45).

The purpose for the darkness is not explained in the gospels or elsewhere in Scripture, but according to the *Babylonian Talmud* many rabbis had long taught that darkening of the sun was a judgment of God on the world for an unusually heinous sin. If, indeed, that was God's intention at the crucifixion, He presented a gigantic object lesson to the world regarding the greatest sin ever committed by fallen mankind.

Some interpreters have suggested the darkness was a means of God's casting a great veil over the sufferings of Christ, and others that it was an act of divine fatherly sympathy given to cover the nakedness and dishonoring of His Son.

But in light of many scriptural teachings and events, it would seem that the crucifixion darkness was indeed a mark of divine judgment. In speaking of Assyria's being used by God to punish Israel, Isaiah spoke of "darkness and distress" that would cover the land, when "even the light is darkened by its clouds" (Isa. 5:30). In describing the day of the Lord, the same prophet declared that "the stars of heaven and their constellations will not flash forth their light" and that "the sun will be dark when it rises, and the moon will not shed its light. Thus I will punish the world for its evil," God said, "and the wicked for their iniquity" (13:10-11).

Also speaking of the day of the Lord, the prophet Joel wrote of "a day of darkness and gloom, a day of clouds and thick darkness" (Joel 2:2). Amos asked rhetorically, "Will not the day of the Lord be darkness instead of light, even gloom with no brightness in it?" (Amos 5:20). Zephaniah wrote, "Listen, the day of the Lord! In it the warrior cries out bitterly. A day of wrath is that day, a day of trouble and distress, a day of destruction and desolation, a day of darkness and gloom, a day of clouds and thick darkness" (Zeph. 1:14-15).

In those Old Testament passages and many others the judgment of God is directly associated with darkness, and similar association is found in the New Testament. Peter declares that God cast the rebellious angels "into hell and committed them to pits of darkness, reserved for judgment" (2 Pet. 2:4). In much the same words, Jude speaks of those angels being "kept in eternal bonds under darkness for the judgment of the great day" (Jude 6). Jesus Himself frequently spoke of divine judgment in terms of "outer darkness," where "there shall be weeping and gnashing of teeth" (Matt. 8:12; 22:13; 25:30).

The cross was a place of immense divine judgment, where the sins of the world were poured out vicariously on the sinless, perfect Son. It was therefore appropriate that great supernatural darkness express God's reaction to sin in that act of judgment.

SOVEREIGN DEPARTURE

And about the ninth hour Jesus cried out with a loud voice, saying "Eli, Eli, lama sabachthani?" that is, "My God, My God, why hast Thou forsaken Me?" And some of those who were standing there, when they heard it, began saying, "This man is calling for Elijah." And immediately one of them ran, and taking a sponge, he filled it with sour wine, and put it on a reed, and gave Him a drink. But the rest of them said, "Let us see whether Elijah will come to save Him." (27:46-49)

A second miracle occurred at **about the ninth hour,** or three o'clock in the afternoon, through an inexplicable event that might be called sovereign departure, as somehow God was separated from God.

At that time **Jesus cried out with a loud voice, saying, "Eli, Eli, lama sabachthani?"** As Matthew explains, the Hebrew **Eli** (Mark uses the Aramaic form, "Eloi," 15:34) means, **My God,** and **lama sabachthani** means, **Why hast Thou forsaken Me?**

Because Jesus was quoting the well-known Psalm 22, there could have been little doubt in the minds **of those who were standing there** as to what Jesus was saying. They had been taunting Him with His claim to be God's Son (v. 43), and an appeal for divine help would have been expected. Their saying, **"This man is calling for Elijah,"** was not conjecture about what He said but was simply an extension of their cruel, cynical mockery.

In this unique and strange miracle, Jesus was crying out in anguish because of the separation He now experienced from His heavenly Father for the first and only time in all of eternity. It is the only time of which we have record that Jesus did not address God as Father. Because the Son had taken sin upon Himself, the Father turned His back. That mystery is so great and imponderable that it is not surprising that Martin Luther is said to have gone into seclusion for a long time trying to understand it and came away as confused as when he began. In some way and by some means, in the secrets of divine sovereignty and omnipotence, the God-Man was separated from God for a brief time at Calvary, as the furious wrath of the Father was poured out on the sinless Son, who in matchless grace became sin for those who believe in Him.

Habakkuk declared of God, "Thine eyes are too pure to approve evil, and Thou canst not look on wickedness with favor" (Hab. 1:13). God turned His back when Jesus was on the cross because He could not look upon sin, even—or perhaps especially—in His own Son. Just as Jesus loudly lamented, **God** the Father had indeed **forsaken** Him.

Jesus did not die as a martyr to a righteous cause or simply as an innocent man wrongly accused and condemned. Nor, as some suggest, did He die as a heroic gesture against man's inhumanity to man. The Father could have looked favorably on such selfless deaths as those. But because Jesus died as a substitute sacrifice for the sins of the world, the righteous heavenly Father had to judge Him fully according to that sin.

The Father forsook the Son because the Son took upon Himself "our transgressions, . . . our iniquities" (Isa. 53:5). Jesus "was delivered up because of our transgression" (Rom. 4:25) and "died for our sins according to the Scriptures" (1 Cor. 15:3). He "who knew no sin [became] sin on our behalf" (2 Cor. 5:21) and became "a curse for us" (Gal. 3:13). "He Himself bore our sins in His body on the cross" (1 Pet. 2:24), "died for sins once for all, the just for the unjust" (1 Pet. 3:18), and became "the propitiation for our sins" (1 John 4:10).

Jesus Christ not only bore man's sin but actually *became* sin on man's behalf, in order that those who believe in Him might be saved from the penalty of their sin. Jesus came to teach men perfectly about God and to be a perfect example of God's holiness and righteousness. But, as He Himself declared, the supreme reason for His coming to earth was not to teach or to be an example but "to give His life a ransom for many" (Matt. 20:28).

When Christ was **forsaken** by the Father, their separation was not one of nature, essence, or substance. Christ did not in any sense or degree cease to exist as God or as a member of the Trinity. He did not cease to be the Son, any more than a child who sins severely against his human father ceases to be his child. But Jesus did for a while cease to know the intimacy of fellowship with His heavenly Father, just as a disobedient child ceases for a while to have intimate, normal, loving fellowship with his human father.

By the incarnation itself there already had been a partial separation. Because Jesus had been separated from His divine glory and from face-to-face communication with the Father, refusing to hold on to those divine privileges for His own sake (Phil 2:6), He prayed to the Father in the presence of His disciples, "Glorify Thou Me together with Thyself, Father, with the glory which I had with Thee before the world was" (John 17:5). At the cross His separation from the Father became immeasurably more profound than the humbling incarnation during the thirty-three years of His earthly life.

As already mentioned, the mystery of that separation is far too deep even for the most mature believer to fathom. But God has revealed the basic truth of it for us to accept and to understand to the limit of our ability under the illumination of His Spirit. And nowhere in Scripture can we behold the reality of Jesus' sacrificial death and the anguish of His separation from His Father more clearly and penetratingly than in His suffering on the cross because of sin. In the midst of being willingly engulfed in our sins and the sins of all men of all time, He writhed in anguish not from the lacerations on His back or the thorns that still pierced His head or the nails that held Him to the cross but from the incomparably painful loss of fellowship with His heavenly Father that His becoming sin for us had brought.

Soon after He cried out to God about being forsaken, "Jesus, knowing that all things had already been accomplished, in order that the Scriptures might be fulfilled, said, 'I am thirsty'" (John 19:28). As John then makes clear (v. 29), it was at that time that **immediately one of them ran, and taking a sponge, he filled it with sour wine, and put it on a reed, and gave Him a drink.**

The **one** who **ran** to help Jesus was probably one of the Roman military guards, and by **taking a sponge** and filling **it with sour wine**, he hoped temporarily to slake Jesus' thirst. The **sour wine** was a cheap wine highly diluted with water that was a common drink for laborers and soldiers. Because it had a high water and low alcohol content, it was especially helpful in quenching thirst. John gives the added detail that the **reed** was a hyssop branch (John 19:29), which would not have been longer than eighteen inches. In order for such a short branch to reach Jesus' lips, the horizontal beam of the cross would have had to be rather low to the ground.

Offering the **drink** to Jesus was perhaps an act of mercy, but it was minimal in its effect and served only to prolong the torture before death brought relief. **But the rest** of those standing near the cross used that gesture of kindness as another opportunity to carry their mockery of the Lord still further, saying, **"Let us see whether Elijah will come to save Him."**

It seems incredible that even the pitch darkness of midday did not alarm the wicked crowd. They were so bent on scorning Jesus that even such a momentous phenomenon as the blocking out of the sun did not deter them. Being aware of the many Old Testament associations of unnatural darkness with judgment, it would seem they would at least briefly have considered the possibility that divine judgment was occurring at that very moment. But the single thought now on their minds was to make Jesus' death painful and humiliating. They had no comprehension of the amazing alienation of the Son from the Father.

SELF-GIVING DEATH

And Jesus cried out again with a loud voice, and yielded up His spirit. (27:50)

A third miracle of the cross was Christ's self-giving death, the Son's willing sacrifice of Himself for the sins of the world in obedience to His Father's will.

The fact that **Jesus cried out again with a loud voice** (cf. v. 46; Mark 15:37; Luke 23:46) demonstrated considerable physical strength, even after the beatings, scourging, crown of thorns, nail wounds, and hanging in agony for several hours. Jesus did not gradually fade away, His life ebbing little by little until gone. Even now He made it evident that He was not at the point of utter exhaustion and that He had the resources to stay alive if He so desired.

The last words the Lord **cried out** from the cross were first, "It is finished" (John 19:30), indicating that the work His Father had sent Him to accomplish was complete. Then, once again addressing God as His Father, He said, "Father, into Thy hands I commit My spirit" (Luke 23:46).

Aphiēmi (**yielded up**) has the basic meaning of letting go or sending away, indicating an act of volition. Jesus' life was not taken from Him by men, but rather He surrendered **His spirit** by the conscious act of His own sovereign will. As He had explained to the Twelve, no one could or would take His life from Him. "I lay it down on My own initiative," He said. "I have authority to lay it down, and I have authority to take it up again" (John 10:18).

As just noted, Jesus' ability to speak from the cross in a loud voice indicated a reserve of energy unheard of for a person in His physical condition. Nevertheless, even in light of His severe bodily condition, Jesus died much sooner than normal. Therefore when Joseph of Arimathea informed Pilate of Jesus' death and asked for His body, the governor was surprised and asked a centurion to give verification (Mark 15:43-45).

Both of those facts attest to Jesus' voluntary surrendering of **His spirit.** He did not take His own life, but He willingly gave it up to those who sought to take it and who otherwise could not have succeeded.

On the cross the Father judged the sin of the world that the Son took upon Himself, and the Son, who divinely controls living and dying, willingly surrendered His life as penalty for that sin.

SANCTUARY DEVASTATION

And behold, the veil of the temple was torn in two from top to bottom, (27:51a)

The fourth miracle that occurred during the crucifixion was the divine devastation of the sanctuary, as **the veil of the temple was torn in two.**

Naos (**temple**) does not refer to the Temple as a whole but to the inner sanctuary, the Holy of Holies, where God dwelt in His symbolic presence. A huge woven **veil** separated the Holy of Holies from the rest of the Temple, and Josephus reports that this massive curtain was predominantly blue and was ornately decorated.

Once a year the high priest was allowed to pass through the veil on the Day of Atonement to sprinkle blood on the altar for the sins of the people, and that only for a brief period of time. Because, like God's presence in the Holy of Holies, even that special sacrifice was only symbolic. The ritual had to be repeated every year, anticipating the one, true sacrifice for sins that the Son of God Himself one day would offer.

When Christ gave up His spirit, that once-for-all sacrifice was completed and the need for a **veil** no longer existed. By coming to the Son, any man could now come to God directly, without need of priest, sacrifice, or ritual. Consequently, **the veil was torn in two from top to bottom** by God's miraculous act, because the barrier of sin was forever removed for those who put their trust in the Son as Lord and Savior.

By rending the Temple veil, God was saying, in effect, "In the death of My Son, Jesus Christ, there is total access into My holy presence. He has paid the full price of sin for everyone who trusts in Him, and I now throw open My holy presence to all who will come in His name." The writer of Hebrews admonished, "Let us therefore draw near with confidence to the throne of grace, that we may receive mercy and may find grace to help in time of need" (Heb. 4:16).

The Father's dramatic tearing of the veil was made while the Temple was filled with worshipers, which included not only countless priests but also many thousands of pilgrims who were at that very moment celebrating the Passover sacrifice. Although the Temple was not destroyed until some forty years later, in A.D. 70, the sacrificial system of Israel and its attendant priesthood ceased to have even symbolic value when the veil was torn in two and the Holy of Holies was exposed. The ceremonies and priestly functions continued until the Temple was destroyed, but their divine significance ended when Christ died, as the Old Covenant was abrogated and the New inaugurated.

SOIL DISTURBANCE

and the earth shook; and the rocks were split, (51a)

A fifth miracle that occurred during the crucifixion was a supernaturally caused earthquake. Immediately after Jesus died and the Temple veil was torn in two, **the earth shook; and the rocks were split.** Making still another statement about His Son to the world, and especially to His chosen people, the Father brought a devastating earthquake to Jerusalem and the surrounding area.

Again the Old Testament gives insight into the significance of the occurrence. When God appeared to Moses on Mt. Sinai, "the whole mountain quaked violently" (Ex. 19:18), and when He appeared to Elijah on a mountain, "a great and strong wind was rending the mountains and breaking in pieces the rocks before the Lord, . . . and after the wind an earthquake" (1 Kings 19:11). David sang of the earth's shaking and trembling when the Lord became angry (2 Sam. 22:8; Ps. 18:7; cf. 77:18). Isaiah spoke of the Lord's punishing His people through "thunder and earthquake and loud noise" (Isa. 29:6), and Jeremiah of His venting His wrath on the nations of the earth by causing it to quake (Jer. 10:10; cf. Nah. 1:5). The book of Revelation tells of God's causing the stars to fall to earth and of mountains and islands being "moved out of their places" during the final judgment (6:13-14).

In the original creation there were no earthquakes, because the earth, like all else that God made, was perfect. Before the Fall, Adam and Eve lived in a perfect environment on earth in the very presence of God. But when they sinned, not only were they cursed and separated from God but the earth they inhabited was cursed as well. Since that time, both literally and figuratively, the earth has been reeling under the destructive forces both of Satan's evil corruption and of God's divine judgment. One day there will be a new heaven and a new earth, but until that time when the usurper will be forever banished to the lake of fire and the true Sovereign, Jesus Christ, reigns in His kingdom, the earth will continue to suffer corruption and destruction.

Speaking of God's judgment on unbelievers, the writer of Hebrews declares, "His voice shook the earth then, but now He has promised, saying, 'Yet once more I will shake not only the earth, but also the heaven.' And this expression, 'Yet once more,' denotes the removing of those things which can be shaken, as of created things, in order that those things which cannot be shaken may remain" (Heb. 12:26-27).

At the cross Jesus earned the right to take the title deed to the earth from the hand of His Father (Rev. 5:9-10). Therefore when God shook the earth at the death of His Son, He gave the world a foretaste of what He will do when one day He shakes the earth in judgment at the coming of the King of kings. Because Jesus became "obedient to the point of death, even death on a cross," His heavenly Father "highly exalted Him, and bestowed on Him the name which is above every name, that at the name of Jesus every knee should bow, of those who are in heaven, and on earth, and under the earth, and that every tongue should confess that Jesus Christ is Lord, to the glory of God the Father" (Phil. 2:8-11).

SUBDUING DEATH

and the tombs were opened; and many bodies of the saints who had fallen asleep were raised; and coming out of the tombs after His resurrection they entered the holy city and appeared to many. (27:52-53)

The sixth miracle at the crucifixion was closely related to the previous one, as the supernatural earthquake not only gave the world a foretaste of divine judgment but also caused many **tombs** to be **opened.**

The significant miracle of that event, however, was not the mere opening of tombs, as could occur during any earthquake. The great miracle was that **many bodies of the saints who had fallen asleep were raised.** After the veil of the Temple was torn in two and the earth around Jerusalem was violently shaken, the Lord selectively **raised** the **bodies** of certain believers who had died.

Matthew points out that **many,** but not all, **bodies of the saints** who had died **were resurrected,** making clear that this **resurrection** was divinely restricted to a limited number of believers. They had trusted in God during the time before and under the Old Covenant, and some of those bodies may have been in their graves many hundreds of years. When Jesus died, their spirits came from the abode of righteous spirits and were joined with their glorified bodies that came out of the graves. This was full and final resurrection and glorification, making this miracle another foretaste of God's sovereign work during the end times, when "all the dead in Christ shall rise" (1 Thess. 4:16).

It is important to note that the phrase **and coming out of the tombs** should be followed by a period, indicating the close of the sentence. **After His resurrection** begins a new sentence and introduces a distinct truth, namely, that those select resurrected saints then **entered the holy city and appeared to many.**

Those saints did not appear in Jerusalem until after the Lord's own resurrection, because He was divinely appointed to be "the first fruits of those who are asleep" (1 Cor. 15:20). And just as Christ Himself appeared after His resurrection only to those who already believed in Him, it would also seem that the **many** to whom the resurrected saints appeared were all believers. We are not told what they said to their brethren in **the holy city,** but their appearance in bodily form not only testified to Christ's resurrection but also to God's promise to raise all those who put their trust in Christ (1 Cor. 15:22, 51-53).

Through those six miracles the Father was saying that the cross is the only hope for eternal life. When one's sin is carried away by Christ's atoning death, the wrath of God is appeased for that believer, and he is delivered from the death and condemnation that the Lord endured on his behalf. For those who believe in the Son, access to God is open wide, and they are assured of living in His eternal and indestructible kingdom in eternal and indestructible bodies.

Responses to the Death of Christ
(27:54-56)

22

Now the centurion, and those who were with him keeping guard over Jesus, when they saw the earthquake and the things that were happening, became very frightened and said, "Truly this was the Son of God!" And many women were there looking on from a distance, who had followed Jesus from Galilee, ministering to Him, among whom was Mary Magdalene, along with Mary the mother of James and Joseph, and the mother of the sons of Zebedee. (27:54-56)

This brief passage presents two responses to the death of Christ, both of them positive. The first was by the centurion and his fellow soldiers who stood at the foot of cross, and the second was by the women standing some distance away. Another response at this same time (by the unbelieving crowd) is recorded by Luke, and a fourth (by the fearful disciples) is implied in all four gospels.

Those responses are representative of the responses men have made to God throughout history, and they have a powerful and practical application even for our own time.

SAVING FAITH

Now the centurion, and those who were with him keeping guard

over Jesus, when they saw the earthquake and the things that were happening, became very frightened and said, "Truly this was the Son of God!" (27:54)

As the title might suggest, a **centurion** (from the Latin word for 100) was a military officer in charge of 100 men and was therefore of significant rank. This particular officer had been given the responsibility of supervising the three crucifixions. It is likely that he and the other soldiers **who were with him keeping guard over Jesus** had been in the Praetorium when He was first brought there by the Jewish leaders. They may have been with the cohort of Roman soldiers who accompanied the chief priests and elders to the Garden of Gethsemane to arrest Jesus. They doubtlessly had heard the charges brought against Him by those leaders and had also heard Pilate's repeated declaration of Jesus' innocence of any crime against Rome. They may even have overheard the conversation between Pilate and Jesus about His being King of the Jews (John 18:33-37).

Those soldiers probably participated in Jesus' scourging, in placing the crown of thorns on His head, in taunting Him, and in beating Him with the mock scepter. On Golgotha they had nailed Him to the cross, indifferently gambled for His garments, and jeered at Him while He hung there in agony.

If those men were religious at all, they were idolaters. And if they were from the garrison at Pilate's headquarters in Caesarea they probably had little knowledge of Judaism and perhaps no previous knowledge at all about Jesus. If they knew anything of Jesus' teachings or activities it was by hearsay. They were at the cross simply because it was their duty to make certain the execution was carried out properly and without interference.

Because Pilate had pronounced Jesus innocent, they knew He was no threat to Rome. But because the governor finally consented to His crucifixion, they had no choice but to carry out the command. To those men Jesus was no more than a bizarre figure who apparently made a foolish and utterly harmless claim to be some sort of religious king. It was obvious when they first saw Jesus that He posed no military or political threat to Rome, and it must have seemed strange to them that the Jewish leaders took Him so seriously. When He was brought before Pilate, He had already been beaten and spit upon, and He looked anything but regal or dangerous. He neither looked nor talked like the many insurrectionists the soldiers had seen and probably helped execute. He not only had no band of fighting men to come to His defense but had no visible followers at all. And because He did not even offer any self-defense, the guards may have thought Him mentally deranged. When He eventually spoke to Pilate, He claimed to rule a kingdom that was not of this world, sounding to them like He was completely out of touch with reality.

The hatred of Jesus by the Jewish leaders and the multitude was obvious enough to the soldiers, but the reason for it was anything but obvious. They had heard the screams of "Crucify, crucify," but could hardly have had any idea what was behind the intense bitterness. His supposed claim to be the Son of God seemed just as ludicrous and harmless as His claim to be a king.

But as the fourth hour of His crucifixion began, several things happened to change the soldiers' attitude, and **when they saw the earthquake and the things that were happening,** the soldiers **became very frightened.**

The first thing to unnerve them would have been the sudden darkness. They would not have been aware of the tearing of the Temple veil and probably not the opening of the graves. But they could not escape noticing the earthquake with its violent splitting of rocks, and that was a terrifying experience even for hardened legionnaires. *Phobeō* (**very frightened**) is the term from which we get *phobia* and refers to sheer terror, the absolute panic that causes rapid heartbeat, profuse sweating, and extreme anxiety. It is the verb form of the word used by Matthew to describe the disciples' response to seeing Jesus walk on the water, thinking He was a ghost (14:26). It is also the word used to describe the reaction of Peter, James, and John when they glimpsed Jesus' divine glory and heard the Father speak directly to them on the Mount of Transfiguration (17:6).

The context and circumstances of the passage clearly indicate, however, that the centurion and his men were **frightened** of much more than the darkness and earthquake. They sensed that those awesome natural phenomena had a supernatural origin, and their primary fear was not of those events themselves but of the divine power behind them. Their emotional fright soon turned to spiritual, reverential awe, as testified by the fact that they did not run for their lives or try to find a place of safety but rather declared, **"Truly this was the Son of God!"**

Mark (15:39) tells us that it was the centurion who actually spoke the words, but Matthew makes clear that he spoke for his men as well. All of them suddenly realized that Jesus was not deluded or deranged but was indeed who the Jews had accused Him of claiming to be. As already noted, they had heard their own commander repeatedly affirm Jesus' innocence, and they may have heard of the warning by Pilate's wife, who declared Jesus not only to be innocent but righteous (Matt. 27:19). More than that, the few words Jesus spoke during His appearances before Pilate and from the cross must have penetrated their pagan, hardened minds. They now knew they stood in the presence of One somehow related to deity.

The soldiers' fear gives witness to their awareness of sin, and their reverential awe gives witness to their being confronted by God's holiness and righteousness. And just as Isaiah in his Temple vision (Isa. 6), they suddenly realized they stood under God's judgment and condemnation.

And I believe the soldiers' confession of Jesus' deity gives witness to the possibility of their salvation. Both their fear and their confession were spiritual responses to Christ. From Luke we learn that the centurion, and presumably the other soldiers as well, not only confessed Jesus' divinity but "began praising God" (23:47).

The deep conviction of the men is seen in their introducing the confession with **truly.** They proclaimed without reservation or qualification that the Man at whose feet they now stood was indeed **the Son of God.**

Some scholars maintain that, because of the Greek construction of the text and because of the soldiers' pagan background, their statement should be rendered, "Truly this was *a* son of God," as seen in some modern versions. The linguistic argument is based on what is called an anarthrous construction, meaning the Greek noun does not have a definite article ("the"). Such is the case in the text of Matthew 27:54, where there is no Greek article (**the**) before **Son.** Ordinarily in such constructions the indefinite article ("a") is understood. But it is clear from secular Greek literature, as well as from many other passages in the New Testament, that the anarthrous construction does not always demand the indefinite article.

When Caiaphas commanded Jesus, "I adjure You by the living God, that You tell us whether You are the Christ, the Son of God" (Matt. 26:63), he used the definite article (Greek *ho*) before "Son." By saying, "I adjure You by the living God," the high priest had already made obvious that he was talking about the true, biblical God of the Jews, and it goes without saying that their Messiah could only be *that* God's Son, not the son of any other god. He was accusing Jesus of claiming to be the Son of Yahweh, the creator, covenant God of Israel revealed in the Old Testament.

The same accusation was made by the Jews before Pilate, except without the definite article. "We have a law," they said, "and by that law He ought to die because He made Himself out to be the Son of God" (John 19:7). If Jesus had been claiming to be the Son of any but the true God, the Jews would have considered Him a heretic but not a blasphemer. Not only that, but the Jews believed their God had but one divine Son. It is completely untenable, therefore, to take the Greek phrase *huion theou* in John 19:7 to mean anything but "*the* Son of God," despite the fact that it does not contain the definite article.

The same Greek phrase (without the definite article) was used by the angel who announced to Mary that the child born to her would "be called the Son of God" (Luke 1:35). And after Jesus walked on the water, a similar phrase (*theou huios*), also without the definite article, was used by the disciples when they confessed before Jesus, "You are certainly God's Son" (Matt. 14:33). In both of those anarthrous constructions the idea of *the* Son, rather than *a* Son, is indisputable.

It was doubtlessly the very words that the Jewish leaders used to accuse Jesus before Pilate ("He made Himself out to be *the Son of God*") that the centurion picked up and used himself. The great difference was that he and his fellow soldiers now believed those words to be true. The declaration **"Truly this was the Son of God!"** became for them a profession of faith in Christ. I firmly believe with the noted commentator R. C. H. Lenski that "this Gentile, called Longinusin tradition, came to faith beneath the dead Savior's cross" (*The Interpretation of St. Matthew's Gospel* [Minneapolis: Augsburg, 1961], p. 1133).

The gracious and profound words of Jesus that they heard, His humble, self-giving demeanor, and His complete lack of anger or vindictiveness all worked in the hearts of the soldiers. But the only way they could have known with such certainty that Jesus was **truly** God's **Son** was through the illumination and conviction of the Holy Spirit.

Even after Peter had spent several years under Jesus' instruction and had witnessed hundreds and perhaps thousands of divinity-affirming miracles, Jesus made clear to him that it was God the Father, not Peter's human wisdom and understanding, that inspired his confession that Jesus was the Messiah and the Son of God (Matt. 16:16-17). Paul assured the Corinthians that "no one can say, 'Jesus is Lord,' except by the Holy Spirit" (1 Cor. 12:3).

Only God's Spirit could have inspired the confession of the centurion and his men, and only His Spirit could have inspired them to praise God (Luke 23:47). The gospel writers, not to mention the Holy Spirit who inspired them, would not have left the soldiers' meaning open to question. Had the soldiers had in mind *a* son of some unnamed pagan deity, Matthew and the other writers would have made that clear. When Scripture speaks of God in the singular it always refers to the true God, unless the context specifically indicates otherwise. Luke did not speak of the soldiers' praising their own god or gods, that is, some pagan deity, but rather "praising God," which could mean only the true God. However limited their theological understanding may have been at that time, those men **truly** confessed the true **Son** of the true **God.**

The faith of the soldiers is of great significance, and was especially so in the early church. Their testimony was, as it were, Jesus' own final testimony from the cross. Although given after He had died, that testimony dramatically proclaimed that His grace extends to every sinner, even to those who put him to death. During the very process of His crucifixion, Jesus Christ became the object of the faith of His crucifiers!

His prayer "Father, forgive them" (Luke 23:34) did not go unanswered. First, one of the thieves who had been jeering Christ turned to faith in Him. Now, after He had breathed His last, the men who had beaten, taunted, and crucified Christ turned to Him and were forgiven and saved. Jesus had declared, "And I, if I be lifted up from the earth, will draw all men to Myself" (John 12:32). The very men who in unbelief and derision had literally lifted Him from the earth had indeed been drawn to Him in repentance and faith.

A contrasting response to that of the soldiers is seen in that of the crowd of observers around the cross. "And all the multitudes who came together for this spectacle, when they observed what had happened, began to return, beating their breasts" (Luke 23:48).

Like the soldiers, those people were alarmed about the darkness and the earthquake. And also like the soldiers, they realized that those terrifying phenomena were not caused naturally. Many of them doubtlessly had heard Jesus preach and seen Him perform miracles. Perhaps some of them had themselves been healed by Him. These people knew much better than the soldiers what Jesus stood for and who He claimed to be. They knew how He had all but banished disease from Palestine and had even raised people from the dead. They remembered that, with the rest of the multitude a few days earlier, they had hailed Jesus as the Messiah. They had heard Jesus' gracious words from the cross and could not have helped suspecting that God's hand was in the awesome events they were now observing.

But as they "began to return, beating their breasts" in fear and remorse, they showed no sign of repentance. They were perhaps over-whelmed by a sense of guilt and foreboding about their participation in the execution of an innocent man. Like Judas, they may have wished sincerely that they could somehow undo the terrible wrong they had done. They probably realized that God was expressing disfavor through the darkness and earthquake and that they were the objects of that disfavor. But they made no confession, either of their sin or of Christ's lordship. They felt sorry for Him, but they did not try to help Him. They knew they were under His judgment, but they did not seek His mercy. They neither gave Christ help nor sought help from Him, and instead of turning to Him like the soldiers, they turned away.

It is probable that many people in this crowd eventually returned to Him in faith. A few weeks later, upon hearing Peter's indictment that "God has made Him both Lord and Christ—this Jesus whom you crucified," many of his hearers "were pierced to the heart, and said to Peter and the rest of the apostles, 'Brethren, what shall we do?'" After he explained the way of salvation, many who had been in the crowd beneath the cross became numbered among the 3,000 souls converted at Pentecost (Acts 2:36-41).

But the convictions of most of those who turned away from Jesus at the cross remained shallow, and the seed of the gospel was never able to take root and grow into saving faith. Unlike those whom Paul commended in Corinth, most of those who beat their breasts at Golgotha did not have the sorrow "that is according to the will of God [and that] produces a repentance without regret, leading to salvation." They evidently had only "the sorrow of the world [that] produces death" (2 Cor. 7:10).

SYMPATHETIC LOYALTY

And many women were there looking on from a distance, who had followed Jesus from Galilee, ministering to Him, among whom was Mary Magdalene, along with Mary the mother of James and Joseph, and the mother of the sons of Zebedee. (27:55-56)

The reaction of the second group Matthew mentions was especially beautiful. Unlike the soldiers, who went from unbelief to belief, the **many women** who **were there** were already believers. Their response to the crucifixion could be described as sympathetic loyalty.

From John's account we know that some of the **women,** as well as John, had earlier been at the foot of the cross (John 19:25-27). But perhaps because they could not bear to observe the suffering of their Lord so closely, those women were now **looking on from a distance.** They were not afraid of the soldiers or the Jewish leaders and had no concern for their own safety or welfare. They were not ashamed of being identified with Jesus. They withdrew because they were devastated at the suffering and death of the one they had loved so dearly. Their grief was deep and their hopes seemed shattered, but their courage was undaunted.

Sympathetic loyalty is one of most beautiful and distinguishing characteristics of godly women, generally being more evident in them than in godly men. A spiritual woman has the capacity for incredible loyalty in the face of ridicule and danger. Except for John, the rest of the disciples had fled in fear. Even Peter, who mustered enough courage to follow Jesus as far as the house of Caiaphas, was not to be found at the cross.

The great Bible expositor G. Campbell Morgan described those women as "hopeless, disappointed, bereaved, heartbroken; but the love He had created in those hearts for Himself could not be quenched, even by His dying; could not be overcome, even though they were disappointed; could not be extinguished, even though the light of hope had gone out, and over the sea of their sorrow there was no sighing wind that told of the dawn" (*The Gospel According to Matthew* [Old Tappan, N.J.: Revell, 1929], p. 318).

We do not know the number of women who were there, but Matthew's speaking of them as **many** perhaps would suggest up to a dozen. However many they were, these women were among those **who**

had followed Jesus from Galilee, ministering to Him.

Devoted women had traveled with and served Jesus for a long while. Among the earliest of them were "Mary who was called Magdalene, from whom seven demons had gone out, and Joanna the wife of Chuza, Herod's steward, and Susanna, and many others who were contributing to their [Jesus' and the disciples'] support out of their private means" (Luke 8:2-3). Throughout His ministry, such women ministered generously and lovingly to Jesus and the Twelve with their financial resources, their talents, and their hospitality. It is probable that many, if not most, of the meals they ate were prepared by those faithful women.

Ministering translates *diakoneō,* which has the basic meaning of serving and is the verb form of the noun from which *deacon* is derived. Although the feminine form of the term was not used to describe a specific type of ministry until many years later in the early church, if at all (see Rom. 16:1, where "servant" could be translated "deaconess"), those **ministering** women were, in effect, the first deaconesses.

Throughout the Old Testament, godly women are acclaimed. The psalmist extolled the Lord by declaring that "He makes the barren woman abide in the house as a joyful mother of children. Praise the Lord!" (Ps. 113:9). And even apart from the possible office of deaconess, the role of women in the early church centered in their faithfulness as wives and mothers and in their practical care for fellow believers. The kind of elderly widow Paul declared was worthy of support by the church was one who has "a reputation for good works, . . . has brought up children, . . . has shown hospitality to strangers, . . . washed the saints' feet, . . . assisted those in distress, and . . . devoted herself to every good work" (1 Tim. 5:10; cf. Luke 4:39; 10:40).

Far from being spiritually demeaning, such self-giving acts of practical helpfulness are a mark of womanly excellence and spiritual maturity—a truth Jesus had a very difficult time teaching the disciples (see John 13:3-16).

The ministry of godly women has always been of great significance in the church. Those women by the cross were the primary believing eyewitnesses to Jesus' crucifixion, and a woman was the first person to see the Lord after His resurrection. Those faithful women certainly would have had a special place of respect and affection in the early church. When the apostles were first preaching the gospel and testifying of their experiences with Jesus, it is hard to imagine that they did not frequently acknowledge the courage and devotion of those women—who remained with the Lord during His time of agony and death, while they, His specially chosen and trained men, had fled and were hiding out in some obscure part of Jerusalem.

Through His direction of Matthew's pen, the Holy Spirit identifies some of those godly women by name. The first is **Mary Magdalene,** the one from whom Jesus had cast out seven demons (Luke 8:2). **Magdalene** was not part of her family name but simply indicated she was from the town of Magdala, on the western shore of the Sea of Galilee, just south of Capernaum. She probably was identified in that way because she was unmarried and could not be identified by her husband or sons, as was the common practice in that day.

The second woman mentioned is **Mary the mother of James and Joseph.** This **James** was one of the apostles and was commonly referred to as James the Less (Mark 15:40) or James the son of Alphaeus (Matt. 10:3; Acts 1:13) to distinguish him from the other James, who, with Peter and his brother John, constituted the inner circle of the Twelve. John identifies this Mary as "the wife of Clopas" (John 19:25), apparently a variant of Alphaeus.

The third woman is identified as Salome by Mark (15:40) but is referred to by Matthew simply as **the mother of the sons of Zebedee,** in other words, Zebedee's wife. The **sons of Zebedee** were James and John (Matt. 4:21) and were nicknamed by Jesus "Sons of Thunder" (Mark 3:17). From John's gospel we learn that Mary the mother of Jesus was also at the cross (19:26), although she may not have been with the other women at this time.

The first of the three women Matthew mentions was not married, the second was identified by her children, and the third by her husband. The implication seems to be that divine dignity is bestowed on all categories of womanhood. God has a marvelous and blessed role for women He has gifted with singleness, for women who are faithful mothers, and for women who are faithful wives. And perhaps in order not to suggest a secondary rank for the single woman or for the formerly wicked woman, Mary Magdalene is here named first.

Conspicuously absent from the scene at the cross were the Twelve, except for John. Judas had committed suicide, and the other ten were hiding for fear of their lives. During their Lord's greatest time of need, they had temporarily violated the basic principle of discipleship. "He who does not take his cross and follow after Me," Jesus said, "is not worthy of Me" (Matt. 10:38). At this time the disciples not only did not have the courage to risk bearing their own crosses but did not even have the courage to stand with their Lord as He bore His.

The Amazing Burial of Jesus

(27:57-66)

And when it was evening, there came a rich man from Arimathea, named Joseph, who himself had also become a disciple of Jesus. This man went to Pilate and asked for the body of Jesus. Then Pilate ordered it to be given over to him. And Joseph took the body and wrapped it in a clean linen cloth, and laid it in his own new tomb, which he had hewn out in the rock; and he rolled a large stone against the entrance of the tomb and went away. And Mary Magdalene was there, and the other Mary, sitting opposite the grave.

Now on the next day, which is the one after the preparation, the chief priests and the Pharisees gathered together with Pilate, and said, "Sir, we remember that when He was still alive that deceiver said, 'After three days I am to rise again.' Therefore, give orders for the grave to be made secure until the third day, lest the disciples come and steal Him away and say to the people, 'He has risen from the dead,' and the last deception will be worse than the first." Pilate said to them, "You have a guard; go, make it as secure as you know how." And they went and made the grave secure, and along with the guard they set a seal on the stone. (27:57-66)

One of the majestic attributes of God is His absolute sovereignty, His supreme rulership and ultimate control over all things in the universe. He has created and He sustains all things that exist, and He ordains and brings to pass all things that happen.

The chronicler wrote, "Thine, O Lord, is the greatness and the power and the glory and the victory and the majesty, indeed everything that is in the heavens and the earth; Thine is the dominion, O Lord, and Thou dost exalt Thyself as head over all. Both riches and honor come from Thee, and Thou dost rule over all, and in Thy hand is power and might; and it lies in Thy hand to make great, and to strengthen everyone" (1 Chron. 29:11-12). Again he declared, "O Lord, the God of our fathers, art Thou not God in the heavens? And art Thou not ruler over all the kingdoms of the nations? Power and might are in Thy hand so that no one can stand against Thee" (2 Chron. 20:6).

Job said of the Lord, "He is unique and who can turn Him? And what His soul desires, that He does" (Job 23:13). The psalmist wrote, "Our God is in the heavens; He does whatever He pleases" (Ps. 115:3), and, "Whatever the Lord pleases, He does, in heaven and in earth, in the seas and in all deeps" (Ps. 135:6). The writer of Proverbs said, "There is no wisdom and no understanding and no counsel against the Lord" (Prov. 21:30). Through Isaiah, the Lord Himself proclaimed, "I am God, and there is no other; I am God, and there is no one like Me, declaring the end from the beginning and from ancient times things which have not been done, saying, 'My purpose will be established, and I will accomplish all My good pleasure'" (Isa. 46:9-10).

After a period of divinely-inflicted madness because of his arrogant pride, even the pagan Nebuchadnezzar confessed that God's "dominion is an everlasting dominion, and His kingdom endures from generation to generation. And all the inhabitants of the earth are accounted as nothing. But He does according to His will in the host of heaven and among the inhabitants of earth; and no one can ward off His hand or say to Him, 'What hast Thou done?'" (Dan. 4:34-35).

The apostle Paul summarized all those truths in the simple statement that God "works all things after the counsel of His will" (Eph. 1:11).

It is, of course, far beyond human ability to fathom *how* the infinite, eternal mind of God is able to execute the greatest as easily as the least thing He devises. In order to have even a small grasp of that great truth it is necessary to understand that God rules this world through two interrelated means: miracles and providence.

In order to accomplish His purposes, God sometimes supernaturally interrupts the natural processes that He Himself has ordained and ordered. In doing so, He overrules what we commonly call natural law, thereby accomplishing what is scientifically inexplicable. Such divine interruption is called *miracle*.

Creation itself was the first great interruption of the natural status quo, when in six days God created the universe from nothing, ex nihilo. The flood of Noah's day was a worldwide, supernatural disruption of virtually every natural process. The plagues in Egypt and the death of the firstborn were a local, but no less supernatural, intervention in the course of nature, as were the parting of the Red Sea and the provision of manna in the wilderness. The Lord supernaturally caused the sun to stand still for Joshua and caused the walls of Jericho to fall without any mechanical means. He caused the ground to swallow Korah and his rebellious followers and miraculously provided Samson with extraordinary physical strength, by which, among other things, he singlehandedly killed 1,000 men (Judg. 15:15-16).

God made an ax head float, a donkey speak, a chariot of fire carry Elijah to heaven without dying, the mouths of hungry lions to be shut, and a great fish to swallow Jonah and carry him in his belly for three days without harm to the prophet.

The second supernatural way in which God executes His will is through divine providence. Like *Trinity*, the term *providence* is not found in Scripture, although the reality of it is explicit or implicit on every page. Providence refers to God's independent superintendency of the universe through the operation of normal and natural processes and happenings. Through His sovereign providence, God is able to take the virtually infinite number of events and circumstances, as well as the innumerable personal attitudes, ambitions, and abilities that exist in the natural and demonic worlds and cause them all to work together in meticulous precision to perfectly fulfill His divine will.

Through miracle, God interrupts and overrules the operation of normal and natural processes and events, whereas through providence He takes them as they are and orchestrates them to accomplish His predetermined will. From a human perspective, therefore, providence seems even more astounding than miracle. In miracle, God "simply" replaces natural events and circumstances with those of His own special making, usually within a short period of time and often instantaneously. Providence, however, involves the infinitely more complex task of taking natural events and circumstances, as well as the limited but real freedoms of human and demonic minds and wills and, often over vast periods of time, superintending all of those elements in the flawless fulfillment of His own foreordained plans. Multiplied myriads of individual and seemingly random plans, choices, actions, and events continually work together in a divinely-synchronized strategy to perform God's predestined plan.

Throughout Scripture, God is shown to control the thunder and the lightning, the rain and the snow, the rivers and the mountains, the heat and the cold, the animals and the birds, the cities and the nations, the newborn and the dying, the healthy and the sick, the poor and the rich, the weak and the strong, the simple and the complex, the ruler and the ruled, the human and the demonic, and the natural and the supernatural in sovereign freedom.

Joseph was one of twelve brothers born to Jacob in fulfillment of God's covenant promise to Abraham. Because of the jealous hatred of his brothers, Joseph was sold into slavery, taken to Egypt, falsely accused of seducing his employer's wife, thrown into prison, and divinely enabled to interpret dreams for a fellow prisoner and then for the pharaoh. Joseph was eventually elevated to rulership second only to Pharaoh himself and because of that high position was able to rescue his own family from famine and was marvelously reunited with them. Without the use of a single miracle, God sovereignly, by providence, directed every moment of Joseph's life and the lives of those around him. Realizing that profound truth, Joseph was able to say to his repentant brothers, "As for you, you meant evil against me, but God meant it for good in order to bring about this present result, to preserve many people alive" (Gen. 50:20; cf. 45:5).

In another beautiful picture of providence, God directed the lives of the godly Naomi, her Moabite daughter-in-law Ruth, and her future son-in-law, Boaz. Through the faithful witness of Naomi, Ruth was brought to faith in the true God, and through the unselfish love of Boaz, Ruth was brought into the lineage of the Messiah, becoming the great-grandmother of David.

Although the book of Esther does not contain the name of God, it relates one of the most profound testimonies in Scripture to His power in providence. There are no miracles recorded in the book, yet God is shown to be at work in a way that goes beyond the miraculous. The Jewish exile Esther found favor with King Ahasuerus, ruler of the great Medo-Persian empire, and became his highly favored queen. When a plan by a wicked official named Haman to annihilate all the Jews in the empire became known to her and her foster-father Mordecai, Esther interceded for her people at great personal risk. Even as queen, she not only could have been put to death for coming before the king uninvited but also for revealing herself as being Jewish. But by the king's subsequent edicts given on Esther's behalf, the evil Haman was hanged on the gallows he had prepared for Mordecai, and the Jewish people were spared extermination.

In his divinely inspired wisdom, the ancient writer could declare, "The mind of man plans his way, but the Lord directs his steps" (Prov. 16:9), and, "Many are the plans in a man's heart, but the counsel of the Lord, it will stand" (Prov. 19:21). Jeremiah confessed, "I know, O Lord, that a man's way is not in himself; nor is it in a man who walks to direct his steps" (Jer. 10:23). Paul reminds believers that their lives are uniquely directed by their heavenly Father. "For it is God who is at work in you," he says, "both to will and to work for His good pleasure" (Phil. 2:13). Jesus declared, "My Father is working until now, and I Myself am working" (John 5:17). Even during the incarnation, the Father and the Son were functioning in perfect harmony to carry out Their sovereign, divine will.

Nowhere in Scripture is God's incredible and amazing providence more evident than in Jesus' burial. His burial is often passed over quickly in commentaries, sermons, and Bible studies as being simply a necessary event between His death and resurrection. There is a strong tendency to rush immediately from His death to His resurrection, mentioning His burial only in passing. Yet Matthew's account of His burial conveys several astounding truths that give remarkable testimony to the superintendency of God.

Although a touching and interesting story, the burial of Jesus seems somewhat mundane and ordinary compared to His dramatic and substantive death and resurrection. Yet even His burial provides its own demonstrations of God's sovereign control. There were no miracles in the trial of Christ, in His crucifixion, or in His burial, but the providence of God controlled every detail.

Especially in Matthew's account, every detail of Jesus' burial, including the scheming of His enemies, is a testimony to His Sonship, messiahship, and kingship. There is no human explanation for these events. He is again shown to be none other than the promised Son of God and the sovereign Ruler of God's kingdom.

JOSEPH OF ARIMATHEA

And when it was evening, there came a rich man from Arimathea, named Joseph, who himself had also become a disciple of Jesus. This man went to Pilate and asked for the body of Jesus. Then Pilate ordered it to be given over to him. And Joseph took the body and wrapped it in a clean linen cloth, and laid it in his own new tomb, which he had hewn out in the rock; and he rolled a large stone against the entrance of the tomb and went away. (27:57-60)

The first focal point in Matthew's account relates to the fulfillment of two key prophecies, one by Isaiah and the other by Jesus Himself.

Isaiah 53 is the Old Testament's most beautiful and detailed prediction of the Messiah's suffering and death. Included in that prediction is the statement that "His grave was assigned with wicked men, yet He was with a rich man in His death" (v. 9). That obscure prophecy would have been impossible to comprehend fully until the Messiah's burial actually took place. We now understand that the Holy Spirit was revealing that, although Christ's enemies intended to bury Him with common criminals, God's plan was that He be buried not with the wicked but in the tomb of a wealthy man, who, by inference, was godly.

The second prophecy fulfilled in Jesus' burial was His own declaration that "just as Jonah was three days and three nights in the belly of the sea monster, so shall the Son of Man be three days and three nights in the heart of the earth" (Matt. 12:40; cf. 16:21; 26:61).

When it was evening refers to the period from 3:00 P.M. until 6:00 P.M., which period the Jews considered to be the end of the day and the beginning of the **evening.** It was "about the ninth hour," or 3:00 P.M., that Jesus spoke His last words from the cross and "yielded up His spirit" (Matt. 27:46-50).

For two reasons it was imperative that Jesus die several hours before the end of the day. First, because the Sabbath began at six o'clock that day, He had to be taken down from the cross before then and prepared for burial in order not to profane the Sabbath. Second, as explained in detail below, He had to be buried before the end of that day, Friday, in order to be in the earth at least a part of three separate days before His resurrection, as He Himself declared He would be.

John explains that "the Jews therefore, because it was the day of preparation, so that the bodies should not remain on the cross on the Sabbath (for that Sabbath was a high day), asked Pilate that their legs might be broken, and that they might be taken away" (John 19:31). The fact that it was the day before the Sabbath proves conclusively that Jesus was crucified on Friday, commonly referred to by Jews as "the day of preparation."

Although rabbinical tradition had added many extreme and foolish restrictions to Sabbath observance, God Himself had commanded His people to "remember the sabbath day, to keep it holy" (Ex. 20:8). Among other things, even food preparation had to be done the day before in order not to work on the Sabbath. When the Lord provided manna for the children of Israel in the wilderness, He gave a double portion on Friday in order that no collection of it would have to be made on the Sabbath.

The Mosaic law also required that the corpse of an executed criminal not be left hanging "all night on the tree, but you shall surely bury him on the same day (for he who is hanged is accursed of God), so that you do not defile your land which the Lord your God gives you as an inheritance" (Deut. 21:23). If such a thing was defiling on an ordinary day of the week, it would be more defiling on the Sabbath. And, as John points out in the passage above, the particular Sabbath that was about to begin was especially holy because it was also the high day of the Passover feast. It would therefore have been extraordinarily defiling for dead bodies to be hanging on crosses just outside the north wall of Jerusalem, possibly in sight of the Temple, on such a high holy day.

Nowhere is the ungodly hypocrisy of the Jewish leaders more evident than in their insistence that Jesus' body be taken down before the Sabbath. They had no compunction about murdering the Lord of the Sabbath, yet they were meticulous in not wanting to defile the Sabbath by having His body hanging on the cross after that day began.

Because the Romans would not permit a crucified man to be taken down before he was dead, the Jewish leaders requested of Pilate that the legs of the three men be broken to insure quick death. In such cases a large wooden mallet was used to shatter the legs of a victim, making it impossible for him to raise himself in order to breathe. Although the added pain would be excruciating, it was short-lived, because death resulted quickly from suffocation.

According to the eminent Bible scholar Alfred Edersheim, the soldiers would then administer what was called the death stroke, which consisted of jabbing a spear into the heart (*The Life and Times of Jesus the Messiah* [Grand Rapids: Eerdmans, 1953], 2:612). The reason for adding the death stroke to the crushing of the legs seems to have been to remove all doubt as to death having occurred.

Because Pilate did not dare to offend the Jewish leaders any further, he gave orders for the men's legs to be broken. After breaking the legs of the two men on either side of Jesus, however, the soldiers saw that He was already dead. Consequently, "one of the soldiers pierced His side with a spear, and immediately there came out blood and water" (John 19:34). Once more Scripture was fulfilled. As John went on to explain (v. 36), the psalmist had declared of the Messiah centuries earlier that "He keeps all his bones; not one them is broken" (Ps. 34:20). The Romans would not have known of that psalm and, in any case, would not have fulfilled it purposely. They fulfilled the prediction because they were divinely directed to do so, whatever their human reasons may have been.

Again as John explains, prophecy was also fulfilled by the spear wound, because "another Scripture [Zech. 12:10] says, 'They shall look on Him whom they pierced'" (John 19:37). Because the soldier already acknowledged that Jesus was dead, he had no human reason to administer the death stroke with the spear. But he unwittingly did so in fulfillment of God's Word, and the resulting wound was so deep that Jesus could tell Thomas to place his hand into it (John 20:27). Precisely as prophesied, no bone in Jesus' body was broken, and His side was pierced.

In what many Bible students take to be a messianic psalm, David wrote, "Reproach has broken my heart" (Ps. 69:20). Some medical experts believe that, under extreme circumstances, it is possible for the human heart literally to burst from emotional strain, causing blood to spill into the pericardium surrounding the heart and mix there with the lymphatic fluid. If that were the case with Jesus, His death fulfilled yet another prophecy.

As soon as a victim was declared dead, his body was taken down from the cross and ordinarily was thrown into a common grave for criminals, as Isaiah had prophesied the Messiah's enemies had planned for Him (Isa. 53:9). The Romans had absolutely no respect for the corpses, which often were thrown into a grave left open to scavenger animals and birds. Sometimes the bodies were simply cast onto a burning garbage dump, such as the one that continually smoldered in the Hinnom Valley (Gehenna) just south of Jerusalem.

By the time Jesus died, even John apparently had left Golgotha and only the few faithful women remained. They were not able to care for the body by themselves, especially in the short time remaining before the end of the day, and, in any case, they had no burial place for Jesus.

But at the exact moment necessary, God moved in the heart of a godly man. Therefore, **when it was evening, there came a rich man from Arimathea, named Joseph, who himself had also become a disciple of Jesus.** As explained above, the **evening** hours were from 3:00 to 6:00 P.M., at which time the next day, in this case the Sabbath, was considered to begin. Had Joseph asked for the body any earlier, Jesus would not have been dead, and had he come any later, he could not have prepared the body for burial before the Sabbath began.

Joseph not only was **a rich man,** fulfilling Isaiah's prophecy (Isa. 53:9), but was "a prominent member of the Council," the Sanhedrin, and "was waiting for the kingdom of God" (Mark 15:43). Contrary to the other members, however, he was "a good and righteous man" who "had not consented to their plan and action" to condemn and execute Jesus (Luke 23:50-51).

The only thing known with certainty about **Arimathea** is that it was "a city of the Jews" (Luke 23:51), that is, in Judea. Although Galilee was in the heartland of ancient Israel, it had become populated with many Gentiles and often was associated with the region to the east frequently referred to as Galilee of the Gentiles (see Matt. 4:15; cf. Isa. 9:1). Judea, however, was by far the most distinctly Jewish area of Palestine and was considered the land of the Jews. Because Joseph presumably would have had his burial site close to where he lived, it is generally assumed that **Arimathea** was near Jerusalem. Many scholars believe Arimathea was a form of the ancient Ramah, the city a few miles north of Jerusalem from which Samuel came.

At some point during the past three years, Joseph had **become a**

disciple of Jesus, although "a secret one, for fear of the Jews" (John 19:38). The Greek text uses the verb form of **disciple** and could be translated, "was discipled to (or by) Jesus." Joseph was a follower of and learner from **Jesus,** suggesting that he must have heard our Lord preach and teach and that he probably witnessed many of His miracles.

Because, as already noted, he was a secret disciple, Joseph had followed and learned from Jesus at a distance. It is possible he had first heard Jesus in the company of other Sanhedrin members as they came to criticize and condemn Him and, while listening to Him preach, was convinced of Jesus' messiahship. But to have made his allegiance to Christ public not only would have cost him his place in the Sanhedrin but would have jeopardized his economic, social, and family welfare as well.

But now Joseph "gathered up courage" (Mark 15:43) and **went to Pilate and asked for the body of Jesus.** We learn from Mark that "Pilate wondered if He was dead by this time, and summoning the centurion, he questioned him as to whether He was already dead. And ascertaining this from the centurion, he granted the body to Joseph" (Mark 15:44-45).

The body of a victim normally would be given only to a family member. Often, however, even that humane consideration was not permitted, because public desecration of the body by throwing it into an open grave or onto a garbage heap was sometimes used as an additional warning about the serious consequences of opposing Rome.

But having already granted the Jewish leaders' request to make sure the crucified men were dead and removed from their crosses before the Sabbath, and not wanting to anger those leaders any further, **Pilate** may have been glad to grant **the body of Jesus** to Joseph and have the matter ended. Because of their humiliation and intimidation of him, Pilate had no inclination to do the Sanhedrin a favor. But he could ill afford offending them again. He would not have known Joseph's motive and perhaps assumed he was acting in behalf of his colleagues. Without asking for an explanation, Pilate immediately ordered Jesus' body **be given over to** Joseph.

Joseph probably came to Pilate with little hope of receiving the body, and there are many reasons why his request might not have been granted. He certainly did not expect Jesus to rise from the dead or else he would not have given such careful attention to the body's preparation and permanent interment. Yet his great love for Jesus led him to face the wrath of his fellow Council members and friends as well as the wrath of Pilate in order to offer this last gesture of respect to Christ.

The Lord had sovereignly caused the Jewish leaders to do their part in demanding that the bodies be taken down from the crosses before the end of the day. He had caused Pilate to grant that permission, caused

Joseph's request for the body, and caused Pilate's permission once again. Now the Lord caused Joseph to secure, prepare, and inter Jesus' body before Friday evening ended. None of those people realized they were fulfilling prophecy. As far as his own motives and understanding were concerned, even the godly Joseph did what he did for personal reasons. It seemed only right that this innocent Man in whom he had placed his faith have a respectable burial. There is no indication Joseph was even aware he was doing God's will, much less fulfilling God's Word.

Joseph did not hurry because he was afraid of violating the Sabbath. He had already defiled himself for Sabbath observance by going into the Praetorium to see Pilate and was about to defile himself further by handling the dead body of Jesus. He operated with haste because, like every other participant in this great drama, he was being moved under God's divinely ordained and scripturally predicted power and according to His timetable.

The more God's Word is studied honestly and objectively, the more convincingly its inerrancy is demonstrated. Over and over it proves itself accurate in every detail.

After removing it from the cross, **Joseph took the body and wrapped it in a clean linen cloth, and laid it in his own new tomb, which he had hewn out in the rock.** Because of his devotion to Christ and because the tomb was very near Golgotha (John 19:42), it seems probable that, although he was a wealthy man and had many servants, Joseph carried **the body** himself.

John reports that Nicodemus, a prominent Pharisee and almost certainly a member of the Sanhedrin (see John 3:1), joined Joseph at the tomb, "bringing a mixture of myrrh and aloes, about a hundred pounds weight." Together, "they took the body of Jesus, and bound it in linen wrappings with the spices, as is the burial custom of the Jews" (19:39-40). Unlike the Egyptians, the Jews did not attempt to embalm bodies but simply encased them in strongly perfumed burial cloths to help mask the stench of decay.

As pointed out in *The Harmony of the Gospels* (Robert L. Thomas and Stanley N. Gundry, eds. [Chicago: Moody, 1978], p. 250), "The disciples who had openly followed Jesus during His lifetime ran away at the end, but the two who had kept their faith secret while He was alive . . . came forward publicly to give Him an appropriate burial."

Although the gospels mention only that Mary Magdalene and Mary the mother of James and Joses were watching the burial (Matt. 27:61; Mark 15:47), it is possible that they assisted Joseph and Nicodemus. Later, they prepared their own spices and came to the tomb early Sunday morning, planning to further anoint Jesus' body (Luke 23:56-24:1).

After the body was wrapped, Joseph **rolled a large stone against the entrance of the tomb and went away.** Graves were commonly secured in some way, often with **a large stone** placed over **the entrance,** in order to prevent desecration of the body by animals or birds and to prevent grave robbers from stealing the valuables that were often buried with the deceased.

TWO MARYS

And Mary Magdalene was there, and the other Mary, sitting opposite the grave. (27:61)

A second group of people at Jesus' burial were used to give evidence of the deity of Christ in an unusual and wonderful way.

Of the "many women" who had observed the crucifixion from a distance and who had faithfully served Jesus during His Galilean ministry (vv. 55-56), only **Mary Magdalene . . . and the other Mary,** the mother of James the Less and Joseph (Mark 15:47), had followed Joseph of Arimathea to the tomb. After they perhaps helped Joseph and Nicodemus wrap Jesus' body in the spices and after the great stone was rolled into place to secure it, the two Marys were **sitting opposite the grave.** Apparently the two men had left, and these women were now alone at the tomb, engulfed by deep sorrow.

The special contribution of those two women is not evident until early on Sunday morning, when they returned to the sepulcher to finish anointing Jesus' body. At that time they became the first witnesses to Jesus' resurrection. When they arrived, the stone had already been rolled away from the entrance by an angel, and the women entered the tomb (Mark 16:45a). While the guards stood frozen with fear (Matt. 28:4), the angel, "sitting at the right, wearing a white robe, . . . said to them, 'Do not be amazed; you are looking for Jesus the Nazarene, who has been crucified. He has risen; He is not here; behold, here is the place where they laid Him. But go, tell His disciples and Peter, "He is going before you into Galilee; there you will see Him, just as He said to you"'" (Mark 16:5b-7).

God did not choose any of the disciples but rather two women to be the priority witnesses to the resurrection of Christ. Mary Magdalene not only was one of the first two persons to know of Jesus' resurrection but was the first person to whom He appeared (John 20:11-17).

CHIEF PRIESTS AND PHARISEES

Now on the next day, which is the one after the preparation, the chief priests and the Pharisees gathered together with Pilate, and said, "Sir, we remember that when He was still alive that deceiver said, 'After three days I am to rise again.' Therefore, give orders for the grave to be made secure until the third day, lest the

disciples come and steal Him away and say to the people, 'He has risen from the dead,' and the last deception will be worse than the first." Pilate said to them, "You have a guard; go, make it as secure as you know how." And they went and made the grave secure, and along with the guard they set a seal on the stone. (27:62-66)

The third group God providentially directed in relation to Jesus' burial was **the chief priests and the Pharisees.** Unwittingly, and certainly unintentionally, they provided still further testimony to Jesus' deity.

As already noted, **the next day** after the crucifixion was the Sabbath, for which the previous day was the day of **preparation.** Also as noted, it was not an ordinary Sabbath but was Passover Sabbath and therefore a high holy day (see John 19:31).

Two very unusual things occurred in this event. First of all, it was highly unusual for Jewish religious leaders to meet with a pagan, secular ruler on any Sabbath, and even more unusual for them to do so on a high Sabbath. More amazing still, the wording and context suggest that, contrary to their normal practice, they actually entered Pilate's council chambers in the Praetorium. On the previous day they had been careful not to go into the Praetorium at all but rather sent Jesus inside to see Pilate. In order to speak with the leaders themselves, the governor had to come out on the porch. Perhaps because it was a high Sabbath, the priests and Pharisees thought there would be no one around to see them enter. Or they may simply have been willing to risk being seen in order to accomplish their purpose. If they so flagrantly violated Mosaic law and rabbinic tradition by falsely condemning Jesus to death, they would surely not have winced at such a relatively minor infraction as Sabbath defilement if it became necessary for their wicked purposes.

The second unusual detail was that **the chief priests** were largely Sadducees and therefore were strong theological opponents of **the Pharisees.** The gospels record only one other instance of those two groups being together (Matt. 21:45), and in both instances their only common motivation was hatred of Jesus.

Although Jesus was now dead, these men were still concerned about His continuing influence. They therefore said to Pilate, **"Sir, we remember that when He was still alive that deceiver said, 'After three days I am to rise again.' Therefore, give orders for the grave to be made secure until the third day."** Even in His death, Christ's enemies despised Him so vehemently that they would not utter His name, referring to Him only as **that deceiver.**

At some point during or just after the crucifixion, the Pharisees remembered that several years earlier, when they had demanded a sign from Jesus, He told them, "An evil and adulterous generation craves for a sign; and yet no sign shall be given to it but the sign of Jonah the prophet; for just as Jonah was three days and three nights in the belly of the sea monster, so shall the Son of Man be three days and three nights in the heart of the earth" (Matt. 12:38-40). Because Jonah came out alive after the three days and nights, the Pharisees rightly understood that Jesus was claiming He would be buried in the earth and arise alive after that same period of time.

The disciples had not taken Jesus literally then or when, on numerous other occasions, He had told them privately about His suffering, death, and resurrection (Matt. 16:21; 17:23; 20:19). The religious leaders did not believe Jesus either, but they took His prediction seriously, thinking He would try to pull off a hoax to make the people think He actually died and was resurrected. Now that He was dead, they were afraid His disciples would try to perpetrate a similar hoax.

The expression "three days and three nights" that Jesus had used in the prediction of His burial (Matt. 12:40) did not refer necessarily to three full twenty-four hour days. "A day and a night" was a Jewish colloquialism that could refer to any part of a day.

When Queen Esther instructed Mordecai to tell the Jews to fast "for three days" (Esth. 4:16), it becomes obvious that she did not have in mind three full days. It was "on the third day," at the end of the fast, that she "put on her royal robes and stood in the inner court of the king's palace" to intercede for her people (5:1).

The Talmud, the major Jewish commentary on Scripture and tradition, specifies that "a day and a night makes one *onah*, and a part of an *onah* is as the whole."

In the same way, people today speak of visiting a certain place for three days, without necessarily meaning three full twenty-hour periods. To arrive on a Monday morning, for example, and leave on the following Wednesday afternoon is generally considered a three-day visit.

That Jesus had in mind only a part of the first and third days is made clear by the numerous references to His rising *on* the third day (Matt. 16:21; 17:23; 20:19). It is also clear that the Jewish religious leaders themselves took Jesus to mean *on* the third day. Although they used the phrase **after three days** in giving Pilate the reason for their request, they asked Him to post a guard over the tomb **until the third day**, indicating that they used those two phrases synonymously.

To insist on a full three-day burial not only precludes Jesus' rising on the third day but also requires pushing the day of crucifixion back to Wednesday, in order for Him to have been in the ground all of Thursday, Friday, and Saturday. In that case, parts of five consecutive days would have been involved—from Wednesday morning, when the crucifixion would have begun, until daybreak on Sunday, which would have been some twelve hours after that day had begun at 6:00 P.M. the previous evening. But such an extended chronology cannot be squared with the gospel accounts.

The crucifixion is specifically said to have been on Friday, "the day before the Sabbath" (Mark 15:42), and the resurrection to have been sometime before dawn on Sunday, "the first day of the week" (Mark 16:2; Luke 24:1; John 20:1). To argue for a full three-day burial is to presume serious, and very obvious, scriptural error.

Their telling Pilate to **give orders for the grave to be made secure** reflects the religious leaders' continued control over the governor because of his fear they would report him to Caesar and cause his downfall. Ironically, their fear was that **the disciples** might **come and steal Him away and say to the people, "He has risen from the dead."** That fear was totally unfounded, because, despite Jesus' repeated teaching about it, the disciples still did not believe that He would literally rise from the dead.

After the transfiguration, Peter, James, and John were puzzled about what Jesus had just told them about His rising from the dead (Mark 9:10). It was not that they did not understand the meaning of resurrection, because that was a commonly held doctrine among most Jews of the day. But because they could not conceive of the Messiah's dying, they obviously could not conceive of His rising from the dead (cf. 9:32). Even when Peter and John came to Jesus' tomb and found it empty, "as yet they did not understand the Scripture, that He must rise again from the dead" (John 20:9).

But whether the chief priests and Pharisees knew of that disbelief or not, they assumed the disciples would make the claim in Jesus' behalf in order to perpetuate His memory and perhaps keep some of His following for themselves.

If such a thing were to happen, they assured Pilate, **the last deception will be worse than the first.** The implication was that Jesus' claim to kingship would then be verified in the eyes of the gullible people and, though dead, He would become an even **worse** threat to Rome than before. They were saying, in effect, "If the multitudes hailed Him as their Messiah and King on His entry into Jerusalem a few days ago, think how much more they will acclaim Him as their King if they are led to believe He has conquered death and risen from the dead. Even though the idea is preposterous, if they really believe He is alive, they will also believe Rome has no power over Him and that He is invincible. Then you will really have an uprising on your hands."

Wanting to take no risks, either of offending the Jewish leaders or of facing another insurrection, **Pilate said to them, "You have a guard; go, make it as secure as you know how."** No doubt pleased with themselves for once again making the powerful Roman governor bow to their demands, **they went and made the grave secure, and along**

with the guard they set a seal on the stone. The **seal** was probably furnished by Pilate and gave warning that the tomb was under Roman protection.

The purpose of the Jewish leaders and of Pilate was to prevent a hoax. But the Lord's purpose was to take even their unbelieving antagonism and use it to prove the reality of Christ's resurrection and deity. Even Jesus' enemies helped assure that, in order for His resurrection to be genuine, He would have to be supernaturally raised. Despite their later efforts to spread the rumor that the disciples did indeed steal Jesus' body (Matt. 28:11-14), they knew that they themselves had made that impossible.

Those remarkable truths about the burial of our Lord should deepen every Christian's appreciation of Paul's declaration that "God causes all things to work together for good to those who love God, to those who are called according to His purpose" (Rom. 8:28). When we cannot see why we are going through trouble and conflicts, we need to hold on to the certainty that God's sovereign, providential power enlists every circumstance and happening in the universe for His glory and for our good.

The Resurrection
of Christ
(28:1-10)

24

Now after the Sabbath, as it began to dawn toward the first day of the week, Mary Magdalene and the other Mary came to look at the grave. And behold, a severe earthquake had occurred, for an angel of the Lord descended from heaven and came and rolled away the stone and sat upon it. And his appearance was like lightning, and his garment as white as snow; and the guards shook for fear of him, and became like dead men. And the angel answered and said to the women, "Do not be afraid; for I know that you are looking for Jesus who has been crucified. He is not here, for He has risen, just as He said. Come, see the place where He was lying. And go quickly and tell His disciples that He has risen from the dead; and behold, He is going before you into Galilee, there you will see Him; behold, I have told you." And they departed quickly from the tomb with fear and great joy and ran to report it to His disciples. And behold, Jesus met them and greeted them. And they came up and took hold of His feet and worshiped Him. Then Jesus said to them, "Do not be afraid; go and take word to My brethren to leave for Galilee, and there they shall see Me." (28:1-10)

Like every piece of good literature, Matthew's gospel is not a random collection of facts or ideas or stories but has a specific plan and purpose. Chapter 28 is not simply a closing group of anecdotes about the life of Christ but is the powerful climax of everything else he has written under the guidance of the Holy Spirit.

The central event of that climax, the resurrection of Jesus Christ, is also the central event of God's redemptive history. The resurrection is the cornerstone of the Christian faith, and everything that we are and have and hope to be is predicated on its reality. There would be no Christianity if there were no resurrection.

The message of Scripture has always been a message of resurrection hope, a message that death is not the end for those who belong to God. For the believer, death has never been an end but rather a doorway that leads to eternity with God. Abraham willingly obeyed God's command to sacrifice his only son, Isaac, because, in faith, "he considered that God is able to raise men even from the dead" (Heb. 11:19). The psalmists declared, "God will redeem my soul from the power of Sheol; for He will receive me" (Ps. 49:15) and that "with Thy counsel Thou wilt guide me, and afterward receive me to glory" (Ps. 73:24). Isaiah proclaimed, "Your dead will live; their corpses will rise" (Isa. 26:19). Through Daniel the Lord assures His people that, although they die, one day they "will awake . . . to everlasting life" (Dan. 12:2). Hosea assures believers that the Lord will raise up all believers to live before Him (Hos. 6:2). Job asked rhetorically, "If a man dies, will he live again?" and then declared, "All the days of my struggle I will wait, until my change comes" (Job 14:14). That ancient man of God even foresaw the reality of resurrection, proclaiming to his three friends, Bildad in particular: "I know that my Redeemer lives, and at the last He will take His stand on the earth. Even after my skin is destroyed, yet from my flesh I shall see God" (Job 19:25-26).

Such has been the promised hope of God's people throughout history, a hope predicated on the resurrection of Jesus Christ. It is His resurrection that guarantees ours. "Now Christ has been raised from the dead," Paul declares, "the first fruits of those who are asleep. For since by a man came death, by a man also came the resurrection of the dead. For as in Adam all die, so also in Christ all shall be made alive" (1 Cor. 15:20-22).

It is also tragically true, however, that throughout history many have denied, despised, and mocked the truth of resurrection, especially Christ's. But only a fool tries to explain away resurrection, because the death and resurrection of Jesus Christ are man's only hope of salvation and eternal life.

An early Protestant missionary to the Ryukyu Islands in the western Pacific discovered a strange mass grave. The grave marker revealed that more than 11,000 heads taken from bodies of Christians were buried there. On further investigation he learned that in 1637 the Japanese government, which then controlled the Ryukyus, ordered all Christians in the empire exterminated. Because they knew Christians believed in the resurrection, the heads of martyred believers were buried a great distance from the bodies, in the belief that their resurrection would thereby be prevented.

The resurrection of Jesus Christ is the single greatest event in the history of the world. It is so foundational to Christianity that no one who denies it can be a true Christian. Without resurrection there is no Christian faith, no salvation, and no hope. "If there is no resurrection of the dead," Paul explains, "not even Christ has been raised; and if Christ has not been raised, then our preaching is vain, your faith also is vain" (1 Cor. 15:13-14). A person who believes in a Christ who was not raised believes in a powerless Christ, a dead Christ. If Christ did not rise from the dead, then no redemption was accomplished at the cross and "your faith is worthless," Paul goes on to say; "you are still in your sins" (v. 17).

It is hardly surprising, therefore, that the first sermon on the day the church was born focused on the resurrection of Christ. After charging his hearers with Jesus' death, Peter declared, "And God raised Him up again, putting an end to the agony of death, since it was impossible for Him to be held in its power" (Acts 2:23-24). Peter continued to preach the resurrection to his fellow Jews (Acts 4:10) as well as to Gentiles (10:40).

Paul preached the resurrection continually. In the synagogue at Antioch of Pisidia he declared that "God raised [Jesus] from the dead" and "He whom God raised did not undergo decay" (Acts 13:30, 37). He proclaimed the resurrection before the Sanhedrin in Jerusalem (23:6), before the governor, Felix (24:15, 21), and before King Agrippa (26:8). The resurrection is a central and strongly emphasized theme of Paul's epistles. He declared that Christ "was buried, and that He was raised on the third day according to the Scriptures" (1 Cor. 15:4), that "He who raised the Lord Jesus will raise us also with Jesus and will present us with you" (2 Cor. 4:14; cf. Gal. 1:1), and that the Father "raised Him from the dead, and seated Him at His right hand in the heavenly places" (Eph. 1:20; Col. 2:12). Paul longed to know Christ "and the power of His resurrection and the fellowship of His sufferings" (Phil. 3:10).

Peter spoke of our "living hope through the resurrection of Jesus Christ from the dead, to obtain an inheritance which is imperishable and undefiled and will not fade away, reserved in heaven" (1 Pet. 1:3-4). In his vision on Patmos, John beheld the Lord Jesus Christ, who declared, "I am the first and the last, and the living One; and I was dead, and behold, I am alive forevermore" (Rev. 1:17-18).

The foundation of all our hope is expressed in Jesus' own words:

"I am the resurrection and the life; he who believes in Me shall live even if he dies" (John 11:25), and, "Because I live, you shall live also" (14:19).

Even the most irreligious person who knows anything about Christian history and doctrine knows that Christians believe Jesus Christ rose from the dead. But the unbelieving world has many reactions to that belief, most of them negative and all of them wrong.

One of the most common modern reactions is that of rationalism, which rejects the idea of resurrection and all other supernatural elements of Scripture because such things cannot be explained by scientific observation and human reason. This humanistic philosophy considers man's mind to be the ultimate reality, and only that which his own mind can perceive and comprehend is recognized as true or significant.

Many people are simply indifferent to the resurrection, not caring whether it is true or not. Religion in general, and Christianity in particular, are of no concern to them. Other people do not believe in resurrection because of ignorance about its nature and meaning. They may never have heard of such a thing or never have heard it explained accurately and clearly.

Some people are intentionally hostile. They do not reject the resurrection because it seems unprovable to human reason or because they have honest doubt or lack proof. They denounce it simply because they hate the things of God. Some people even seem to consider it their role in life and history to try to discredit the resurrection.

The gospel writers, however, and every other leader in the early church realized that their supreme role in life and history was to proclaim the reality of the resurrection and the many other truths about Jesus Christ. Although the disciples, and most of Jesus' other followers, were slow to believe their Lord actually rose from the dead, they soon became so overwhelmed by its reality that they could think or talk of little else.

Although they reveal the same divine truths in perfect harmony with one another, each of the gospel writers presents the resurrection from a distinctive perspective. Matthew does not approach the resurrection from a scholarly, historical, analytical, or evidential perspective but focuses rather on the emotional reaction of a group of women who loved Jesus deeply.

COMPASSION

Now after the Sabbath, as it began to dawn toward the first day of the week, Mary Magdalene and the other Mary came to look at the grave. (28:1)

After the Sabbath translates an unusual construction in the Greek, *opse de sabbatōn*. The phrase could also be rendered, "well after the Sabbath," indicating that a considerable amount of time had elapsed since the Sabbath ended. The actual time was from sundown the previous evening, when **the Sabbath** had ended, until **it began to dawn** the following day, which was Sunday, **the first day of the week,** totaling perhaps ten hours. John states specifically that when the women came "it was still dark" (20:1).

The first day of the week also translates an interesting Greek phrase, which literally means, "day one with reference to the Sabbath." The Jews did not have names for days of the week, such as Monday, Tuesday, and so on, but simply numbered them in relation to the Sabbath. **Sabbath** means "seventh," and, although it was at the end of the week, because it was the central and holy day, all other days were reckoned by it—as the first, second, third, and so forth, day after the Sabbath.

As explained in the previous chapter of this volume, because Jews considered reference to "a day" as meaning any part of that day, Sunday was the third day of Jesus' interment, the day which He had repeatedly predicted would be the day of His resurrection (see Matt. 16:21; 17:23; 27:64; Mark 10:34; Luke 18:33).

The phrase "after the Sabbath" could also refer figuratively to the new day of rest for God's people. As a commemoration of God's resting after creation, the Sabbath was to be a day of rest and worship for Israel (Ex. 20:8-11). But the day before Jesus arose from the grave was the last divinely ordained Sabbath for His people, because on the following day the New Covenant in Jesus Christ was ushered in. That Sunday was the dawning not only of a new day but of a new era in redemptive history.

It is because of the resurrection that Christians worship on Sunday rather than on the Sabbath.

At that predawn hour on Sunday morning **Mary Magdalene and the other Mary came to look at the grave.** Although they had witnessed Joseph's and Nicodemus's wrapping Jesus' body in the linen cloths and spices (Matt. 27:61), the women had secured and prepared their own spices (probably a small amount in comparison to that brought by Nicodemus) with which they would personally anoint the Lord (Luke 24:1). Although Salome, the mother of James and John and the wife of Zebedee (Mark 16:1; cf. Matt. 27:56), and Joanna (Luke 24:10) were also there, Matthew focuses only on the two Marys.

The other Mary was the mother of James and Joseph and the wife of Clopas (see Matt. 27:56; John 19:25). The women obviously thought Jesus would still be in the grave and would remain there, or else they would not have brought the anointing spices. They had not come to see Jesus risen but **to look at the grave** where they expected His body to still be lying. They had been among the women who ministered to Jesus in Galilee and who had stood with Him at the cross (Matt. 27:55-56). Now they came to the garden hoping that somehow the great stone could be removed so they could minister to Him one last time (Mark 16:3). But despite their lack of faith in Jesus' promises to rise on the third day, they came to the tomb out of deep affection for their Lord.

Jewish tradition wrongly held that the spirit of a dead person left the body four days after death because by that time the body had become so disfigured by decay that the spirit could no longer recognize it. That tradition may be reflected in Martha's comment to Jesus about her brother, Lazarus: "Lord, by this time there will be a stench, for he has been dead four days" (John 11:39). Perhaps the two Marys and the other women came to Jesus' grave with the intent of anointing His body one more time before His spirit departed from it.

The women did not have confidence in Jesus' resurrection, but they had great love and great devotion for Him. What they lacked in faith they compensated for in loving compassion, and what they lacked in understanding they made up for in courageous devotion.

TERROR

And behold, a severe earthquake had occurred, for an angel of the Lord descended from heaven and came and rolled away the stone and sat upon it. And his appearance was like lightning, and his garment as white as snow; and the guards shook for fear of him, and became like dead men. And the angel answered and said to the women, "Do not be afraid; for I know that you are looking for Jesus who has been crucified. He is not here, for He has risen, just as He said. Come, see the place where He was lying. And go quickly and tell His disciples that He has risen from the dead; and behold, He is going before you into Galilee, there you will see Him; behold, I have told you." (28:2-7)

No sooner had the women reached the tomb than they found the stone had been moved aside by a **severe earthquake.** This was the second supernaturally caused earthquake in connection with Jesus' death and burial, the first one having occurred at the moment of His death (Matt. 27:51).

God caused an earthquake on Mount Sinai just before He revealed the law to Moses (Ex. 19:18) and on Mount Horeb when He revealed Himself to Elijah (1 Kings 19:11). In the end times He will also send numerous earthquakes (Joel 2:10; Matt. 24:7; Rev. 6:12; 8:5; 11:13-19). Now, within three days, He caused two earthquakes just outside Jerusalem.

This **earthquake had occurred** when **an angel of the Lord descended from heaven,** causing the earth around the grave to tremble violently. The angel had come to open the secured and sealed grave, and when he arrived he **rolled away the stone and sat upon it.** Although it had probably taken several strong men some time to put the stone in place, the angel removed it in an instant.

The angel did not move the stone in order to let Jesus out of the tomb, as many Easter stories and paintings suggest. If Jesus had the power to raise Himself from the dead, which He did (John 10:18), He certainly had the relatively minor power required to escape a sealed grave. As He demonstrated during several postresurrection appearances, just as He was no longer bound by death, He was no longer bound by the limitations of the physical world or of time (see Luke 24:31; John 20:26). In His glorified form He could escape a closed grave just as easily as He could enter a closed room. In comparing the gospel accounts, it becomes clear that Jesus had already left the tomb when the stone was rolled away. The angel moved the stone not to let Jesus out but to let the women and the apostles in.

From John's gospel it seems that Mary Magdalene apparently left the garden as soon as she "saw the stone already taken away from the tomb" (20:1). Before the angel appeared, "she ran and came to Simon Peter, and to the other disciple whom Jesus loved, and said to them, 'They have taken away the Lord out of the tomb, and we do not know where they have laid Him'" (v. 2). Obviously she had missed the angel's announcement of Jesus' resurrection. She was so overwrought at discovering the tomb empty that she ran frantically to the two most prominent disciples, Peter and John, to tell them what she thought was terrible news. It did not occur to her that Jesus might be risen as He had predicted, and she assumed that someone had stolen the body and hidden it. It is obvious that Peter and John did not consider the possibility of resurrection either, and they immediately ran to the tomb to find out what they could (John 20:3-4).

Meanwhile the angel had manifested himself to those who were near the tomb, and **his appearance was like lightning.** The description suggests that God transmitted some of His own Shekinah glory to the angel, just as He had transmitted a measure of it to Moses on Sinai when the covenant was renewed (Ex. 34:29). In a similar way, the angel's glistening **garment** that was **as white as snow** suggests God's purity and holiness. The angel bore the very imprimatur of the character of God in order to make clear to the observers not only that he was a supernatural messenger but that he was an agent of God and not Satan.

The **guards** were so awestruck that at first they **shook for fear of him. Shook** translates a Greek term that has the same root as "earthquake" in verse 2, indicating that the soldiers experienced personal earthquakes of both mind and body. But after a brief moment of shaking, they then **became like dead men,** paralyzed with fear. The idea seems to be that they not only became rigid but unconscious, completely traumatized by what they saw.

The women were also frightened, but, unlike the soldiers, they received comfort from God's messenger. Aware of their fright, **the angel answered and said to the women, "Do not be afraid."** Perhaps a better translation than **answered** would be "explained," because **the women,** too terrified to speak, had not asked a question.

The soldiers had good reason to be afraid. Not only was the angel's appearance terrifying in itself but, because they had been charged with protecting the grave, an empty tomb could spell their death. The women, however, had no reason to fear, and the angel's first words were meant to give them comfort and assurance.

They had not come expecting to find Jesus raised, but in His gracious mercy God overlooked their weak faith and their lack of understanding. Acknowledging their great love, God responded with great love. **"I know that you are looking for Jesus who has been crucified,"** the angel said to them; **"He is not here, for He has risen, just as He said."**

Has risen translates a Greek aorist passive and can also be rendered, "has been raised." Jesus Himself had power to give up His life and to take it up again (John 10:18). But Scripture makes clear that He also was raised by the power of the Father (Rom. 6:4; Gal. 1:1; 1 Pet. 1:3) and of the Holy Spirit (Rom. 8:11). The entire Trinity participated in the resurrection of Jesus.

The angel gently reminded the women that Jesus' resurrection should not surprise them, because it happened **just as He said.** Luke reports that they then "remembered His words" (24:8).

Next the angel invited the women to **come, see the place where He was lying.** At this point the women went into the tomb and observed that it was indeed empty. The angel joined them in the tomb and reiterated the same basic message, saying, "Do not be amazed; you are looking for Jesus the Nazarene, who has been crucified. He has risen; He is not here; behold, here is the place where they laid Him" (Mark 16:6). Perhaps the message was repeated because the women found it so hard to believe, despite the fact that they now remembered Jesus' predictions that He would rise on the third day.

When Peter and John entered the tomb a short while later, they "beheld the linen wrappings lying there, and the face-cloth, which had been on His head, not lying with the linen wrappings, but rolled up in a place by itself" (John 20:6-7). The burial clothes were just as they were when Joseph and Nicodemus laid the body to rest, except for the face-cloth, which was set to one side. Jesus did not have to be unwrapped any more than He had to have the stone removed. At one moment He was encased in the linen, and the next He was free, leaving the wrappings unchanged.

While the women were in the tomb, another angel joined the first, "one at the head, and one at the feet, where the body of Jesus had been lying" (John 20:12). Their positions are reminiscent of the two golden cherubim who were on either side of the Mercy Seat on the Ark of the Covenant (Ex. 25:18). The two angels in the garden were posted at either end of the tomb of Jesus, who, by the sacrifice He had just made of His own life, became the true and eternal Mercy Seat for sinful mankind.

The two angels gave still another reminder to the women. "Why do you seek the living One among the dead?" they asked. "He is not here, but He has risen. Remember how He spoke to you while He was still in Galilee, saying that the Son of Man must be delivered into the hands of the sinful men, and be crucified, and the third day rise again" (Luke 24:5-7). For a third time the women were told the glorious truth of Jesus' resurrection, a truth whose fulfillment they should have been eagerly expecting.

One of the angels then said, **"Go quickly and tell His disciples that He has risen from the dead."** The women's fascination must quickly turn to proclamation. They did not have time to revel in the marvelous reality of the good news but were to go immediately and announce it to the cowering disciples, who were still hiding in Jerusalem.

It would seem more than justified for the Lord to have allowed the disciples to suffer in fear, despair, and agony for a week or so before telling them the good news. They had stubbornly refused to believe that Jesus would die and be raised, although He had told them of His death and resurrection many times. But in His gracious mercy God sent the women to tell the disciples as soon as possible, so they would not have to experience another moment of misery and grief. He did not rebuke them for their lack of faith and for their cowardice but rather sent them messengers with a gracious word of hope and comfort.

One wonders why God chose to reveal the truth of the resurrection first to those women rather than to the disciples. One commentator suggests that it was because God chooses the weak to confound the strong. Another suggests the women were rewarded for their faithful service to the Lord in Galilee. Another holds that, because death came by a woman in a garden, so new life was first announced to a woman in a garden. Others propose that it was because the deepest sorrow deserves the deepest joy or that supreme love deserves supreme privilege.

But Scripture offers no such explanations. It seems obvious that the women were the first to hear the angelic announcement of the resurrection simply because they were there. Had the disciples been there, they, too, would have heard the good news directly from the angel rather than indirectly from the women.

This is analogous to the reality that the closer a believer stays to the Lord and to His work, the more he is going to witness and experience the Lord's power. Those who are there when the Lord's people gather for worship and prayer, who are there when His Word is being taught, who are there when the lost are being won to Christ, who are there when others are being served in His name, who are regular in their times of private prayer—those are the ones who will most often experience first-hand the work of God.

The angel's further instruction to the women was to tell Jesus' disciples that "**He is going before you into Galilee, there you will see Him; behold, I have told you.**" Earlier in the week Jesus had told the eleven remaining disciples, "After I have been raised, I will go before you to Galilee" (Matt. 26:32). Being both Jewish and Gentile, Galilee represented the world at large. It was there that Jesus began His ministry, in "Galilee of the Gentiles, " where "the people who were sitting in darkness saw a great light" (Matt. 4:15-16). It would also be in Galilee that the disciples would receive the Great Commission from the Lord to "go therefore and make disciples of all the nations" (Matt. 28:19).

It was not that Jesus would first appear to the disciples in Galilee, because He manifested Himself to them several times before that. He appeared to Peter (Luke 24:34), to the two disciples on the road to Emmaus (Luke 24:15; cf. Mark 16:12), to ten of the disciples as they were assembled on resurrection evening (John 20:19), to all eleven disciples eight days later (John 20:26), and to seven of the disciples as they were fishing in the Sea of Galilee (John 21:1).

But Jesus' supreme appearance to the disciples was to be in **Galilee**, where He "appeared to more than five hundred brethren at one time" (1 Cor. 15:6) and where He would commission the eleven to apostolic ministry.

JOY

And they departed quickly from the tomb with fear and great joy and ran to report it to His disciples. (28:8)

Obediently responding to the angel's command, the women **departed quickly** from the tomb. And although they had the angel's comforting assurance, the women understandably had a remnant of **fear.** But their fear was now tempered by **great joy** at learning the good news of Jesus' resurrection.

Mary Magdalene had left the tomb before the angels appeared and on her own initiative reported her findings to Peter and John, saying, "They have taken away the Lord out of the tomb, and we do not know where they have laid Him" (John 20:2). She then followed those two disciples back to the tomb, where they, too, found only the linen wrappings. The other women and the angels had left the garden, and, disappointed and confused, the two men "went away again to their own homes" (vv. 5-10). While Mary remained outside the tomb weeping, the two angels appeared to her and then the Lord Himself. It was not until Jesus called her by name, however, that she recognized Him and shouted, "Rabboni!" (vv. 11-16). She then reported her wonderful experience to the disciples in Jerusalem (v. 18).

When she told the other apostles about her encounter with the resurrected Christ, they did not believe her (Mark 16:11). Their disbelief (see also Mark 16:13; Luke 24:10-11) clearly proves that they had no intention of stealing Jesus' body in order to propagate a counterfeit resurrection, as the chief priests and Pharisees feared they would do (Matt. 27:62-64; 28:13).

WORSHIP

And behold, Jesus met them and greeted them. And they came up and took hold of His feet and worshiped Him. (28:9)

Meanwhile, as the other women were on their way to report the angel's message to the disciples, **Jesus met them and greeted them. Greeted** translates *chairete,* a common greeting that loosely rendered means something like "hello" or "good morning." It was the ordinary salutation of the marketplace and of travelers who passed each other on the road. In other words the greeting was casual and ordinary, seemingly too mundane to be appropriate for such a momentous occasion. Yet the glorified Christ, who had just finished conquering sin and death, deigned to greet those faithful women with warm, informal tenderness. As the writer of Hebrews assures us, "We do not have a high priest who cannot sympathize with our weaknesses" (Heb. 4:15).

Immediately recognizing their Lord, the women **came up and took hold of His feet and worshiped Him.** They now knew with certainty that He was the risen Messiah, the divine Son of God, and that adoration and praise were the only proper responses to His presence. They did what every person, unbeliever as well as believer, will do one day. When He comes again, "every knee [will] bow . . . and . . . every tongue [will] confess that Jesus Christ is Lord, to the glory of God the Father" (Phil. 2:10-11).

At last the full reality of the resurrection was solidifying in the minds and hearts of those women. They had heard the angel's proclamation of the resurrection, had seen the empty tomb, had beheld the risen Lord, and had even touched His glorified body. They could now do nothing but adore and worship Him.

Sir Edward Clarke wrote:

As a lawyer I have made a prolonged study of the evidences for the events of the first Easter Day. To me the evidence is conclusive, and over and over again in the High Court I have secured the verdict on evidence not nearly so compelling. Inference follows on evidence, and a truthful witness is always artless and disdains effect. The Gospel evidence for the resurrection is of this class, and as a lawyer I accept it unreservedly as the testimony of truthful men to facts they were able to substantiate. (Cited in J. R. W. Stott, *Basic Christianity* [Downers Grove, IL: InterVarsity, 1971], p. 47)

In a similar statement, the noted historian and Oxford professor Thomas Arnold wrote:

The evidence for our Lord's life and death and resurrection may be, and often has been, shown to be satisfactory; it is good according to the common rules for distinguishing good evidence from bad. Thousands and tens of thousands of persons have gone through it piece by piece as carefully as every judge summing upon a most important case. I have myself done it many times over, not to persuade others but to satisfy myself. I have been used for many years to study the histories of other times and to examine and weigh the evidence of those who have written about them, and I know of no one fact in the history of mankind which is proved by better and fuller evidence of every sort, to the understanding of a fair inquirer, than the great sign which God hath given us that Christ died and rose again from the dead. (Wilbur M. Smith, *Therefore Stand: Christian Apologetics* [Grand Rapids: Baker, 1965], pp 425-26)

HOPE

Then Jesus said to them, "Do not be afraid; go and take word to My brethren to leave for Galilee, and there they shall see Me." (28:10)

Jesus repeated the angel's message, saying, **"Do not be afraid; go take word to My brethren to leave for Galilee."** Despite the disciples' lack of faith, their cowardice, and their defection, the Lord graciously spoke of them as His **brethren.** When they arrived in **Galilee,** they would **see** Him again, and there they would experience a great convocation and commissioning by the Lord.

Matthew's brief glimpse of the resurrection is artless and un-adorned, completely lacking pretense or exaggeration. He does not argue or beg the issues but simply places the truths before the reader to be accepted for what they are.

The basic truth of the resurrection undergirds a number of other truths. First, it gives evidence that the Word of God is totally true and reliable. Jesus rose from the dead precisely when and in the way He had predicted (see Matt. 12:40; 16:21; 17:9, 23).

Second, the resurrection means that Jesus Christ is the Son of God, as He claimed to be, and that He has power over life and death. Third, the resurrection proves that salvation is complete, that on the cross Christ conquered sin, death, and hell and rose victorious. Fourth, the resurrection proves that the church has been established. Jesus had declared, "I will build My church; and the gates of Hades shall not overpower it" (Matt. 16:18). "The gates of Hades" was a Jewish colloquialism that represented death. His resurrection proved that death itself could not prevent Christ from establishing His church.

Fifth, the resurrection proves that judgment is coming. Jesus declared that the heavenly Father "has given all judgment to the Son" (John 5:22), and since the Son was now risen and alive, His judgment is certain. Sixth, the resurrection of Christ proves that heaven is waiting. Jesus promised, "In My house are many dwelling places; if it were not so, I would have told you; for I go to prepare a place for you" (John 14:2). Because Christ is alive by the resurrection, believers have the assurance that He is now preparing a heavenly dwelling for them.

The Lie That Proves the Resurrection
(28:11-15)

Now while they were on their way, behold, some of the guard came into the city and reported to the chief priests all that had happened. And when they had assembled with the elders and counseled together, they gave a large sum of money to the soldiers, and said, "You are to say, 'His disciples came by night and stole Him away while we were asleep.' And if this should come to the governor's ears, we will win him over and keep you out of trouble." And they took the money and did as they had been instructed; and this story was widely spread among the Jews, and is to this day. (28:11-15)

Some years ago the Canadian author G. B. Hardy wrote a book about life, philosophy, and destiny entitled *Countdown: A Time to Choose* (Chicago: Moody, 1971). He noted that there are really only two questions to ask with regard to destiny: (1) Has anyone ever defeated death? and (2) If so, did he make a way for us to do it also? Hardy then explains that he found the answer to both questions in the resurrection of Jesus Christ and that with that answer he also found salvation and eternal life (pp. 31-32).

But despite the fact that the resurrection is man's only hope for eternal life, the majority of people, including many who have studied it thoroughly, have rejected it. In doing so, they not only forfeit the future life but are left without true meaning or significance in the present life. Rejecting the resurrection is spiritual suicide.

Furthermore, denying the resurrection goes against the very grain of the human heart and soul. Solomon wrote that God "has also set eternity in their heart" (Eccles. 3:11). Something within man is not satisfied with present earthly living. He instinctively reaches out for immortality, for a life that transcends his present life and that will continue after he dies. Throughout history countless religions and philosophies have proposed means for man to achieve immortality, to find a better life beyond the grave.

Yet, strangely, there seems always to have been more religious than irreligious people who consciously deny the only hope for immortality. And through the years many theories have been propounded for the explicit purpose of explaining away the resurrection, especially the resurrection of Jesus Christ.

The "swoon theory" proposes that Jesus did not actually die but went into a deep coma, or swoon, from the severe pain and trauma of the crucifixion. While in the cool atmosphere of the tomb and with the stimulating aroma of the burial spices, He revived and was somehow able to unwrap Himself and escape after the grave was opened. When He showed Himself to the disciples, they erroneously assumed He had been raised from the dead.

That theory was not dreamed up until around 1600, by a man named Venturini. But the idea flies in the face of many eyewitness reports, not only by Jesus' followers but also by His enemies. The Roman soldiers standing guard over Jesus at the cross were the first to report His death. They were experts at execution and would stand to forfeit their own lives if they allowed a condemned man to escape death. They were so certain He was dead that they did not bother to break His legs, and when the spear thrust brought forth blood and water, they had final proof of His death. Joseph of Arimathea and Nicodemus, with many women as witnesses and perhaps as helpers, worked with Jesus' body for an hour or so as they wrapped it in the linen and spices. They would easily have sensed any spark of life still remaining.

For that theory to be true, Jesus would have had to survive the massive loss of blood from the scourging, the nail wounds, and the spear thrust. He would also have had to survive being wrapped tightly in the linen cloths that were filled with a hundred pounds of spices. Besides all of that, in His extremely weakened condition He would have had to endure more than forty hours without food or drink, manage to unwrap Himself, singlehandedly roll the stone away from the inside of the tomb, walk out unchallenged by the guards, and then convince His followers He had actually been dead and miraculously raised. He would have had to have developed the strength to travel countless miles in that condition to make the many appearances to His disciples over a period of forty days. Finally, He would have had to delude the apostles into thinking He entered a closed room without opening the door and ascended to heaven before their eyes. The absurdity of that theory is too obvious to be accepted by any clear-thinking person, believer or not.

The "no-burial theory" contends that there was actually no interment, that Jesus was never placed in the tomb and therefore would not have been in it on Sunday morning. His body was instead thrown into a mass grave for criminals, according to Roman custom. But neither the Jewish leaders nor the Roman guards would have bothered to secure and seal the tomb if they knew Jesus' body was not inside. Not only that, but to disprove Jesus' resurrection they would only have had to retrieve His body and put it on display.

The "hallucination theory" maintains that everyone who claimed to have seen the risen Jesus simply experienced a hallucination, induced by an ardent expectation of His resurrection. But Thomas was not the only believer who was slow to believe the Lord was alive again. Every gospel account makes clear that most of His followers, including the apostles, did *not* believe, either before or after the crucifixion, that He would be raised. Besides that, how could more than 500 people hallucinate in exactly the same way?

The "telepathy theory" proposes that there was no physical resurrection, but rather God sent divine telepathic messages to Christians that caused them to believe Jesus was alive. But that theory, among other things, makes the God of truth a deceiver and the apostles and gospel writers liars. And if such mental images did come from God, they were defective and slow to produce the intended result, because in a number of instances Jesus was not recognized when He first appeared to individuals and groups who knew Him intimately.

The "seance theory" suggests that a powerful spiritualist, or medium, conjured up the image of Jesus by means of occult power and that His followers were thereby deluded into thinking they saw Him. But if that were so, how did they hold onto His feet, put a hand in His wounded side, and eat a meal with Him? Seances deal strictly in the noncorporeal and ephemeral and are not made of such physical and tangible things as those.

The "mistaken identity theory" is based on the assumption that someone impersonated Jesus and was able to dupe His closest friends and companions into thinking he was really their Lord come back to life. But the imposter would have had to have himself scourged, crowned with thorns, pierced in his hands and feet, and wounded in the side to make such an impersonation even close to convincing. He would also have had to mimic Jesus' voice, mannerisms, and other traits to an unimaginable degree of perfection. He would have had to steal Jesus' body from the tomb and hide it. He would also have had to be an insider among Jesus' followers in order to identify and talk convincingly with the many people he met during the appearances. He would also have had to know exactly where to find the people on every occasion and been able to perform such illusions as materializing through walls and appearing and vanishing at will. And he would have had to be prepared in advance even of the crucifixion to do all of those amazing things, because the first appearance was early on resurrection morning.

The noted French philosopher Renan debunked the resurrection by foolishly claiming the whole idea was based on the hysterical delusions of Mary Magdalene (*The Life of Jesus* [New York: Carleton, 1886], pp. 356-57). But Mary was but one among more than 500 witnesses, all of whom testified to the same reality. In his book *Risen Indeed,* G. D. Yarnold advances the idea that the "material of which [Christ's] earthly body had been composed ceased to exist, or was annihilated" ([New York: Oxford, 1959], p. 22).

Besides their own unique shortcomings, all of those theories fail to explain how the apostles could be transformed from cowards to heroes and how such a dynamic entity as the church could come into existence, produce thousands of followers willing to die for their beliefs, and manage to turn the world upside down if their faith was built on illusions and falsehoods.

Such unbelieving critics also fail to explain what happened to Jesus' body. If the resurrection were falsified, in whatever way, the deceit could have easily and quickly been exposed by producing the dead body. But neither the Jewish leaders nor the Romans even attempted to make such a disclosure.

The "theft theory," which contends that someone managed to steal the body and hide it, is the only one that attempts to explain the missing body. But the only ones who might have had a motive for stealing it were the disciples, in order to try to fulfill Jesus' prediction that He would rise from the dead on the third day. That, as Matthew explains in the present passage, was the explanation promulgated by the Jewish leaders.

Yet Matthew's narrative of this strange episode reveals that even that deceitful scheme became a rich and compelling apologetic not against but for the resurrection. He first describes the plot itself and then briefly tells how the proposed lie was propagated.

THE PLOT

Now while they were on their way, behold, some of the guard came into the city and reported to the chief priests all that had happened. And when they had assembled with the elders and counseled together, they gave a large sum of money to the soldiers,

and said, "You are to say, 'His disciples came by night and stole Him away while we were asleep.' And if this should come to the governor's ears, we will win him over and keep you out of trouble." (28:11-14)

They refers to the women to whom Jesus had just spoken and who **were** obediently **on their way** to give the disciples His message to meet Him in Galilee (vv. 5-10).

At this same time, **behold, some of the guard came into the city and reported to the chief priests all that had happened.** Only **some of the guard** went **into the city** of Jerusalem **and reported to the chief priests,** probably as representatives of the whole contingent, which may have numbered as many as a dozen. For all of them to have gone together would have attracted considerable attention, and word of their mission would surely have reached Pilate's ear. Because it was still early on the third day after Jesus' crucifixion, Pilate would immediately have had them arrested and probably executed, both for leaving their post while on duty and for failing to fulfill their assignment to protect Jesus' body from theft (see 27:62-66). Presumably the rest of **the guard** remained at the tomb.

Because they were in the temporary service of the Jewish religious leaders, the soldiers wisely **reported to the chief priests all that had happened** at the tomb. They had much less to fear from the **chief priests** than from Pilate, and they probably hoped those leaders could somehow protect them from the governor.

Included in **all** the things **that had happened** were the earthquake, the rolling away of the stone, the blazing angel sitting on the stone, and the empty tomb. The soldiers knew those happenings had a supernatural origin, and it was that knowledge that caused them first to shake violently and then freeze in catatonic fear. They did not try to explain what they saw but simply reported it as best they could. It is possible that, because of the guards' report, the chief priests learned of Jesus' resurrection even before the disciples did.

But despite that firsthand, unprejudiced testimony and their own awareness that Jesus claimed He would rise from the dead on the third day, the chief priests showed no interest in verifying the guards' story. It did not really matter to them whether or not Jesus was raised, just as it did not matter that Jesus had performed marvelous miracles before their own eyes. Some of the chief priests had stood beneath the cross, taunting Jesus and saying, "Let Him come down from the cross, and we shall believe Him" (27:42). But their duplicity was now exposed, because the resurrection was a greater miracle than coming down from the cross would have been, and yet they did not believe. As Abraham told the rich man in Jesus' parable, "If they do not listen to Moses and the Prophets, neither will they be persuaded if someone rises from the dead" (Luke 16:26). The heart that is hardened to God will not be persuaded by any miracle or by any amount of evidence, no matter how compelling. The **chief priests** were so evil, self-willed, and spiritually blind that they shut their eyes to every confirmation of Jesus' claims. The god of this world had totally blinded their eyes (2 Cor. 4:4).

The Jewish leaders had been trying to get rid of Jesus since the time He was an infant. Herod tried to eliminate Christ by slaughtering all the male babies in his province in order to remove Him as a supposed threat to his throne. The religious leaders had accused Him of working miracles in the power of Satan, of being an associate of sinners, of breaking God's law by healing on the Sabbath, and of blasphemy for claiming to be the Messiah and God's Son. They perverted both biblical and rabbinical justice in order to convict Him, employed blackmail to get Him crucified, used armed force to try to keep His body in the grave, and now engaged in bribery to hide the truth of His resurrection.

The soldiers' news brought alarm, fear, and confusion to the religious leaders, but it did not bring repentance or faith. They were without excuse. They were informed about the resurrection and did not try to deny it. Their only concern was to keep that news from their fellow Jews, fearing that many would accept Him as the Messiah and that their own influence, power, and wealth would be severely diminished.

The first reaction was to quickly convene the Sanhedrin, **and when they had assembled with the elders,** they **counseled together** as to how they might best obstruct the spreading of the news the soldiers had brought. **Counseled together** was a formal phrase used of official decisions (see also Matt. 12:14; 22:15; 27:1, 7), and at this meeting the Sanhedrin decided on a three-point resolution: to bribe the soldiers, to spread a lie about the body, and to protect the soldiers from possible reprisal by Pilate.

The amount of the **large sum of money** is not specified, but because there were possibly a dozen guards to be bribed and the Sanhedrin was desperate, it probably was a considerable **sum.** *Argurion* (**money**) literally means silver, and is the same word used in Matthew 26:15 for the bribe given to Judas to betray Jesus. Because they had so much at stake, the Sanhedrin did not hesitate to pay a high price for the lie to be spread.

The second part of the resolution was a plan to disseminate the falsehood as widely as possible. Because the soldiers were at the tomb and had their own reasons for spreading the lie, they were the obvious candidates for the job. The soldiers were therefore instructed **to say, "His disciples came by night and stole Him away while we were asleep."** Both the guards and the Sanhedrin knew full well that was not true, otherwise they would not have had to devise such a false and preposterous story. The purpose of the lie was to hide the truth.

Those soldiers became the first persons to preach that antigospel falsehood. They were pagan, materialistic, self-indulgent, and hardened to every sort of evil. Telling what to them was a trivial and insignificant lie was a small price to gain the Sanhedrin's favor and protection.

The third part of the Sanhedrin's resolution offered protection to the soldiers. **"If this should come to the governor's ears,"** the chief priests reassured them, **"we will win him over and keep you out of trouble."** As already noted, the soldiers knew that if Pilate thought Jesus' body was stolen while they slept, their lives would be forfeit.

By threatening to make an unfavorable report to Caesar, the Jewish religious leaders had usually managed to have their way with Pilate. They knew he would not risk trouble with Caesar over the disposition of a Jewish corpse. If the Sanhedrin came to the soldiers' defense, the governor probably would give them no more than a reprimand.

By that resolution the Jewish leaders willfully rejected Christ, despite the evidence, and that spiritual obstinacy gave testimony to the apostasy of Israel's leaders.

THE PROPAGATION

And they took the money and did as they had been instructed; and this story was widely spread among the Jews, and is to this day. (28:15)

The soldiers gladly **took the money,** overjoyed that they not only would not be punished but would even be rewarded. They were therefore more than willing to do the Sanhedrin's bidding and **did as they had been instructed.**

Matthew then comments that **this story was widely spread among the Jews, and is to this day.** Matthew wrote his gospel some thirty years later, about A.D. 63, the time to which **this day** refers. The tomb guards were the first to **spread** the falsehood, but the Sanhedrin doubtlessly began spreading it **among the Jews** by many other means as well.

The Sanhedrin's lie was still common among the Jews of the second century. The church Father Justin Martyr wrote in chapter 103 of his *Dialogue with Trypho,* "You [Jewish leaders] have sent chosen and ordained men throughout all the world to proclaim that a godless and lawless heresy had sprung from one Jesus, a Galilaean deceiver, whom we crucified, but his disciples stole him by night from the tomb . . . and now deceived men by asserting that he has risen from the dead and ascended into heaven" (*The Ante-Nicene Fathers,* vol. 1 [Grand Rapids: Eerdmans, 1973], p. 253). That same falsehood can be heard even today.

But as wicked and self-serving as the Sanhedrin's plan was, it fit perfectly into God's much greater and sovereign plan. God did not want unbelievers to proclaim the true gospel, even had they wanted to. The Lord would not send out messengers to preach the resurrection who did not believe in the One who was raised. In His eternal wisdom, God permitted those guardians of the grave, who could have spread the factual, historic truth of the resurrection, to become victimized by the corrupt Jewish leaders. The resurrection of the Son of God would be proclaimed only by those whose hearts were committed to the risen Savior and Lord.

Evidence for the resurrection is supplied by the very **story** that denies it. And because it came from Jesus' enemies rather than His friends, it should be all the more convincing to skeptics. Intending to conceal the truth, the Sanhedrin and the soldiers actually reinforced it.

Although the explanation that the disciples stole Jesus' body accounts for the missing corpse, in some ways it is even more absurd than the other negative theories mentioned at the beginning of this chapter.

In the first place, if their story had been true, the Jewish leaders could surely have found the stolen body with little difficulty. They had the resources of hundreds of men, including military men, and even the power of Rome behind them in this instance. It would have been utterly impossible for eleven unlearned and unsophisticated men to have succeeded in eluding a search for any length of time. The simplest way to have disproved the resurrection was to locate the body and put it on display for all the world to see. Yet there is no evidence that the Sanhedrin even attempted to find the body they claimed the disciples had stolen. The failure of the Sanhedrin to make such a search is strong evidence that they themselves actually believed Jesus was raised.

Another obvious flaw in the Sanhedrin's lie was the basic idea itself. To suggest that the disciples stole the body was to show complete ignorance of those men's state of mind at the time. They had not believed Jesus' many predictions of His resurrection, and, now that He had been crucified, they were hopelessly dejected and afraid. If anything, they had even less belief in His resurrection after His death than they had had before.

When the women reported Jesus' resurrection to the eleven apostles and the other believers with them in Jerusalem, "these words appeared to [the apostles] as nonsense, and they would not believe them" (Luke 24:11). Their personal prejudices and human understanding, common to most Jews of that day, prevented them from accepting the idea of the Messiah's death, thereby making belief in His resurrection impossible. Those men did not have the least motive for stealing Jesus' body. Because He had been given an uncommonly fine burial by Joseph and Nicodemus—a much better burial than the disciples could have afforded—what better place for His body to remain than in the garden tomb? The apostles had no reason to counterfeit a resurrection they did not even believe in themselves. How could it be that the men who fled for their lives while Jesus was still alive would, after His death, suddenly muster the courage and ingenuity to steal the body and then boldly start preaching and teaching in the name of a Jesus they knew was dead?

When the apostles finally came to believe in the reality of Jesus' resurrection, there was no stopping their proclamation of that grand and beautiful truth. Those who had shortly before been skeptical cowards became unflinching zealots in their proclamation of the risen Christ. But they had no such zeal immediately after the resurrection, because they did not even believe it, much less have a desire to proclaim it.

It was highly implausible that all of the soldiers would have gone to sleep long enough for the disciples to have moved the stone and stolen the body, and even more implausible that the noise from moving the stone would not have awakened a single soldier.

The Roman military divided the night into four watches of between two and three hours each. A certain number of the men would keep watch while the rest slept, keeping up the rotation until dawn. Three hours was not a long period of time to stay awake, especially if one were under threat of imprisonment or death for sleeping on watch.

Perhaps the most patently absurd problem with the proposed lie was that, had the soldiers all been asleep, how could they have known who stole the body? And if some onlooker had told the soldiers what happened, why did they not immediately search for the thieves and try to retrieve the body rather than run to the chief priests to report their failure?

The testimony of Jesus' enemies was in some ways even more astounding than that of His friends would be. It was because the soldiers and the Sanhedrin could not deny that the tomb had been supernaturally opened and Jesus supernaturally released that the lie was concocted. Had the resurrection been a hoax, it would have been an easy one to expose.

Some commentators have suggested that the disciples were the first to bribe the soldiers, asking them to report the empty tomb story to the Sanhedrin. But as just mentioned, the disciples had no motive for doing such a thing. Besides that, where would they have come up with enough money to make a bribe attractive to the soldiers?

Other people have suggested that the disciples cleverly distracted the soldiers and sneaked the body out while the guards were not looking. But had they found such courage, how did they manage to draw all the soldiers far enough away to prevent their hearing the giant stone's being moved? And how did they manage to keep the grave cloths just as they had been when covering Jesus' body. Had the disciples tried such a maneuver, they would have been in the utmost hurry to get Jesus' body out as quickly as possible. They had no reason to take off the wrappings, because the body would already have started to decompose. In addition to that, the body would have been much easier to carry while wrapped.

Why, we might ask, did Matthew sound such a negative note on the climactic event in Christ's work almost at the end of his gospel account? Brief as the passage is, it is still longer than his final few words about the Great Commission.

The answer would seem to be twofold. First, the account serves to demonstrate Israel's full and final apostasy as a nation, of whom those Jewish leaders were representative. They denied Jesus' resurrection just as they had opposed everything else He said or did. Second, the efforts of those enemies is perhaps the strongest human testimony to the reality of the resurrection, causing it to have the exact opposite effect from what was intended.

Matthew's account simply but forcefully shows that any explanation but the actual bodily resurrection of Jesus contradicts the facts and offends reason. The truth of the resurrection is so absolute that even a lie against it helps prove it. Whether the testimony is from Jesus' friends or His enemies, the same conclusion is inevitable. No other historical event is so thoroughly attested by sound evidence as is the resurrection of Jesus Christ.

Simon Greenleaf, famous nineteenth-century professor of law at Harvard wrote, "All that Christianity asks of men . . . is, that they would be consistent with themselves; that they would treat its evidences as they treat the evidence of other things; and that they would try and judge its actors and witnesses, as they deal with their fellow men, when testifying to human affairs and actions, in human tribunals. . . . The result . . . will be an undoubting conviction of their integrity, ability and truth" (*Testimony of the Evangelists, Examined by the Rules of Evidence Administered in Courts of Justice* [Grand Rapids: Baker, 1965; reprint], p. 46).

Paul declared, "If you confess with your mouth Jesus as Lord, and believe in your heart that God raised Him from the dead, you shall be saved; for with the heart man believes, resulting in righteousness, and with the mouth he confesses, resulting in salvation" (Rom. 10:9-10). Salvation is equal to eternal life, to deliverance from sin, and to godly hope. Salvation determines a person's destiny in the presence of God in the glories of heaven forever. And salvation belongs only to those who believe in the resurrection of Jesus Christ and who confess Him as Lord and Savior and thereby identify themselves with Him.

The hymnist Robert Lowry wrote the following beautiful lines that are sung in the popular Easter hymn "Christ Arose":

Death cannot keep his prey,
  Jesus, My Savior!
He tore the bars away,
  Jesus, my Lord!

Up from the grave He arose,
  With a mighty triumph o'er His foes;
He arose a victor from the dark domain,
  And He lives forever with His saints to reign.
He arose! He arose!
  Hallelujah! Christ arose!

Making Disciples of All Nations
(28:16-20)

But the eleven disciples proceeded to Galilee, to the mountain which Jesus had designated. And when they saw Him, they worshiped Him; but some were doubtful. And Jesus came up and spoke to them, saying, "All authority has been given to Me in heaven and on earth. Go therefore and make disciples of all the nations, baptizing them in the name of the Father and the Son and the Holy Spirit, teaching them to observe all that I commanded you; and lo, I am with you always, even to the end of the age." (28:16-20)

If a Christian understands all the rest of the gospel of Matthew but fails to understand this closing passage, he has missed the point of the entire book. This passage is the climax and major focal point not only of this gospel but of the entire New Testament. It is not an exaggeration to say that, in its broadest sense, it is the focal point of all Scripture, Old Testament as well as New.

This central message of Scripture pertains to the central mission of the people of God, a mission that, tragically, many Christians do not understand or are unwilling to fulfill. It seems obvious that some Christians think little about their mission in this world, except in regard to their own personal needs. They attend services and meetings when it is convenient, take what they feel like taking, and have little concern for anything else. They are involved in the church only to the extent that it serves their own desires. It escapes both their understanding and their concern that the Lord has given His church a supreme mission and that He calls every believer to be an instrument in fulfilling that mission.

If the average evangelical congregation were surveyed concerning the primary purpose of the church, it is likely that many diverse answers would be given. Several purposes, however, would probably be prominent. A large number would rank fellowship first, the opportunity to associate and interact with fellow Christians who share similar beliefs and values. They highly value the fact that the church provides activities and programs for the whole family and is a place where relationships are nurtured and shared and where inspiration is provided through good preaching and beautiful music. A favorite verse for such church members is likely to be, "By this all men will know that you are My disciples, if you have love for one another" (John 13:35).

At a level perhaps a step higher, some Christians would consider sound biblical teaching to be the church's principal function, expounding Scripture and strengthening believers in knowledge of and obedience to God's revealed truth. That emphasis would include helping believers discover and minister their spiritual gifts in various forms of leadership and service. Like fellowship, that too is a basic function of the church, because God "gave some as apostles, and some as prophets, and some as evangelists, and some as pastors and teachers, for the equipping of the saints for the work of service, to the building up of the body of Christ; until we all attain to the unity of the faith, and of the knowledge of the Son of God, to a mature man, to the measure of the stature which belongs to the fulness of Christ" (Eph. 4:11-13).

Adding a more elevated level, some members would consider praise of God to be the supreme purpose of the church. They emphasize the church as a praising community that exalts the Lord in adoration, homage, and reverence. Praise is clearly a central purpose of God's people, just as it has always been and will always be a central activity of heaven, where both saints and angels will eternally sing praises to God. "Worthy art Thou, our Lord and our God," sing the twenty-four elders lying prostrate before God's throne, "to receive glory and honor and power; for Thou didst create all things, and because of Thy will they existed, and were created" (Rev. 4:10-11; cf. 5:8-14).

Paul declares that God has "predestined us to adoption as sons through Jesus Christ to Himself, according to the kind intention of His will, to the praise of the glory of His grace . . . to the end that we who were the first to hope in Christ should be to the praise of His glory" (Eph. 1:5-6, 12; cf. v. 14). Later in that same epistle he exults, "To Him be the glory in the church and in Christ Jesus to all generations forever and ever" (3:21).

Jesus came into the world to manifest God's glory, the "glory as of the only begotten from the Father" (John 1:14), as "the radiance of His glory and the exact representation of His nature" (Heb. 1:3). Just as their Lord, Jesus Christ, came into the world with the supreme purpose of glorifying His Father, so those who belong to Christ have that same purpose. We are to praise, honor, and glorify our God in every dimension of life.

All of those emphases are thoroughly biblical and should characterize every body of believers. But neither separately nor together do they represent the central purpose and mission of the church in the world. The supreme purpose and motive of every individual believer and every body of believers is to glorify God.

The mission that flows out of our loving fellowship, our spiritual growth, and our praise is that of being God's faithful and obedient instruments in His divine plan to redeem the world. That plan began in eternity past, before the foundation of the world. But it did not go into effect until Adam chose to sin, fell from fellowship with God, and was spiritually separated from Him. Since that fateful day in the Garden of Eden, fallen, natural man has been trying to hide from God, and God has been redeeming men back to Himself. From that first time of sin, it has always been God who, solely out of His own gracious love, has taken the initiative to restore men to righteousness. God has always taken the initiative for man's salvation and restoration, from His first call to Adam, "Where are you?" (Gen. 3:9), to His last call in Revelation: "The Spirit and the bride say, 'Come.' And let the one who hears say, 'Come.' And let the one who is thirsty come; let the one who wishes take the water of life without cost" (Rev. 22:17).

It was not until sinful mankind persisted in withdrawing further and further from God that He divided them into separate nations. When He needed a witnessing nation to the world, He called out Israel as His chosen people through Abraham. When Israel failed in that calling, God chose a remnant from among them to do what the nation would not. When the nation of Israel rejected her Messiah and King, Jesus Christ, God called out the church, His new chosen instrument to redeem the world.

God has been drawing, is now drawing, and, until the final judgment, will continue to draw sinful men back to Himself and to restore the world that sin has corrupted—all for the purpose of bringing glory to Himself. When sinners are saved, God is glorified, because their salvation cost Him the death of His own Son, the immeasurable price that His magnanimous grace was willing to pay.

The supreme way in which God chose to glorify Himself was

through the redemption of sinful men, and it is through participation in that redemptive plan that believers themselves most glorify God. Through Christ, God was "reconciling the world to Himself, not counting their trespasses against them," Paul declares, "and He has committed to us the word of reconciliation" (2 Cor. 5:19). That is a work of such magnitude and graciousness that even the heavenly angels long to look into it (1 Pet. 1:12).

Nothing so much glorifies God as His gracious redemption of damned, hell-bound sinners. It was for that ultimate purpose that God called Abraham, that in him "all the families of the earth shall be blessed" (Gen. 12:3). It was never the Lord's intention to isolate Israel as His sole focus of concern but rather to use that specially chosen and blessed nation to reach all other nations of the world for Himself. Israel was called to "proclaim good tidings of His salvation from day to day" and to "tell of His glory among the nations, His wonderful deeds among all the peoples" (1 Chron. 16:23-24; cf. Ps. 18:49). Like her Messiah, Israel was to be "a light to the nations so that [the Lord's] salvation may reach to the end of the earth" (Isa. 49:6; cf. 42:10-12; 66:19; Jonah 3:1-10).

It has never been God's will for any person "to perish but for all to come to repentance" (2 Pet. 3:9). He "desires all men to be saved, and to come to the knowledge of the truth" (1 Tim. 2:4). God's heart has always yearned to bring sinful, rebellious men back to Himself, to give them new, righteous, and eternal life through His Son, Jesus Christ. He so greatly "loved the world, that He gave His only begotten Son, that whoever believes in Him should not perish, but have eternal life" (John 3:16).

Paul rejoiced that God's "grace which is spreading to more and more people may cause the giving of thanks to abound to the glory of God" (2 Cor. 4:15). The apostle admonished the Corinthian believers and all Christians: "Whatever you do, do all to the glory of God" (1 Cor. 10:31). Every time an unbeliever is saved by God's grace, God is glorified, and another voice is added to the "Hallelujah Chorus," as it were.

The great mission of the church is to so love, learn, and live as to call men and women to Jesus Christ. As sinners are forgiven and are transformed from death to life and from darkness to light, God is glorified through that gracious miracle. The glory of God is manifest in His loving provision to redeem lost men. He Himself paid the ultimate price to fulfill His glory.

Therefore the believer who desires to glorify God, who wants to honor God's supreme will and purpose, must share God's love for the lost world and share in His mission to redeem the lost to Himself. Christ came into the world that He loved and sought to win sinners to Himself for the Father's glory. As Christ's representatives, we are likewise sent into the world that He loves to bring the lost to Him and thereby bring glory and honor to God. Our mission is the same mission as that of the Father and of the Son.

In His great high priestly prayer, Christ prayed, "This is eternal life, that they may know Thee, the only true God, and Jesus Christ whom Thou hast sent. I glorified Thee on the earth, having accomplished the work which Thou hast given Me to do" (John 17:3-4). In His incarnation, Jesus glorified the Father by accomplishing His mission of providing eternal life to those who trust in Him, by reconciling lost men to the God they had forsaken. Jesus' supreme purpose on earth was "to seek and to save that which was lost" (Luke 19:10).

That is therefore also the supreme mission of Christ's church. The work of the church is an extension of the work of her Lord. "As Thou didst send Me into the world," Jesus said to His Father, "I also have sent them into the world" (John 17:18).

If God's primary purpose for the saved were loving fellowship, He would take believers immediately to heaven, where spiritual fellowship is perfect, unhindered by sin, disharmony, or loneliness. If His primary purpose for the saved were the learning of His Word, He would also take believers immediately to heaven, where His Word is perfectly known and understood. And if God's primary purpose for the saved were to give Him praise, He would, again, take believers immediately to heaven, where praise is perfect and unending.

There is only one reason the Lord allows His church to remain on earth: to seek and to save the lost, just as Christ's only reason for coming to earth was to seek and to save the lost. "As the Father has sent Me," He declared, "I also send you" (John 20:21). Therefore, a believer who is not committed to winning the lost for Jesus Christ should reexamine his relationship to the Lord and certainly his divine reason for existence.

Fellowship, teaching, and praise are not the mission of the church but are rather the preparation of the church to fulfill its mission of winning the lost. And just as in athletics, training should never be confused with or substituted for actually competing in the game, which is the reason for all the training.

How tragic that so much of Christ's church is preoccupied with trivialities. Many Christians are fascinated with the process and have no thought for the goal. They are preoccupied with the spiritually insignificant and show little commitment to reaching the lost.

The resources God has provided most churches are, for the most part, barely tapped in their efforts to call men and women and boys and girls to Jesus Christ. The contemporary church is blessed with previously unheard of means of proclaiming the saving message of Christ to the world. But like the world at large, it is frequently crippled by indulgent, self-centered preoccupations. Instead of asking, for instance, how we might get by with a smaller house or car and use the saved money in the

Lord's work, we are inclined to dream about getting bigger and nicer ones.

A counselor of my acquaintance has long had the practice of asking those who come to him for spiritual advice to show him their check stubs for the past year or so. His purpose is to help them recognize their true priorities, which invariably are reflected in the way they spend their money. Another helpful revealer of priorities is one's calendar or appointment book, because where and for what we spend our time is also a reliable barometer of our true interests and concerns.

Christian fellowship, biblical preaching and teaching, and times of praise to God are good and godly, and in many ways carry their own rewards and blessings. But reaching the lost for Christ is much more difficult and demanding, and the results are often slow in coming and the rewards are sometimes long delayed. The gospel is frequently resented by those to whom we witness, and sometimes faithful witnessing is ridiculed even by fellow believers. Yet above all others, that ministry can only be accomplished while we are on earth. We will have no opportunity in heaven to call the lost to the Savior.

In his devotional book *Quiet Talks with World Winners,* S. D. Gordon recounted the story of a group of amateur climbers who planned to ascend Mont Blanc in the French Alps. On the evening before the climb, the guides stated the basic requirement for success. Because it was an exceedingly difficult climb, one could reach the top by taking only the necessary equipment for climbing, leaving all unnecessary accessories behind.

One athletic young man discounted the guides' advice, thinking it could not possibly apply to him. He showed up for the climb with a blanket, a small case of wine, a camera, a set of notebooks, and a pocketful of snacks. Although warned again by the guides, the strong-willed young man nevertheless started out ahead of the rest to prove his superior skill and endurance.

But as the other climbers proceeded up the mountainside, they began to notice various articles left by the path. First, they noticed the young's man's food and wine, a short while later the notebooks and camera, and finally the blanket. The young man managed to reach the peak, but, just as the guides had predicted, he did so only after discarding all his unnecessary paraphernalia.

Applying that illustration to the church, Mr. Gordon comments that, unlike that young climber, who eventually paid the price for success, many Christians, when they discover they cannot reach the top with their loads, simply stop climbing and settle down on the mountainside.

In the final message of Christ reported by Matthew, Jesus gives five explicit or implicit elements that are necessary for His followers to fulfill their supreme mission on earth—to reach the mountain peak of their calling, as it were. These essential elements may be summarized as availability, worship, submission, obedience, and power.

AVAILABILITY

But the eleven disciples proceeded to Galilee, to the mountain which Jesus had designated. (28:16)

The first three elements for effectively fulfilling the church's mission are attitudes, the first of which is implied in the fact that **the eleven disciples** were where the Lord had told them to be.

As someone astutely observed many years ago, as far as a believer's service to God is concerned, the greatest ability is availability. The most talented and gifted Christian is useless to God if he is not available to be used, just as God's greatest blessings are not available to those who are not present to receive them.

Faithful discipleship does not begin with knowing where you will be serving the Lord or in what capacity. It does not start with having a clear call to a certain ministry, or occupation, or place of service. It *always* begins with simply being available to God, putting all reservations and preconceptions aside.

The eleven disciples had not received the blessing of seeing the resurrected Jesus in the garden because, unlike the faithful women, they were not there. Now, however, **the eleven** were where Jesus wanted them to be, and consequently they received His Great Commission and His great promise.

Both before and after the resurrection Jesus said He would meet His disciples in Galilee (see Matt. 26:32; 28:7, 10). He had called a great conclave of His followers for the purpose of commissioning them to reach the world in His name, and now they were gathered at the appointed place.

We are not told when or how the Lord specified the exact time and place in Galilee where they were to gather, but they were now at **the** particular **mountain which Jesus had designated** on some previous occasion.

The last recorded appearance of Jesus in Jerusalem was eight days after the resurrection, when Thomas saw the resurrected Lord for the first time (John 20:26). The journey from Jerusalem to Galilee would have taken about a week, and after they arrived there some of the disciples went fishing, during which time the Lord appeared to them again, providing a catch too heavy to haul into the boat. Then, after having breakfast with them, Jesus asked Peter three times about his love for Him and gave the commission to feed His sheep (John 21:1-17). That event would have occurred at least fifteen days after the resurrection and probably closer to twenty. Because Jesus ascended from the Mount of Olives in the presence of the disciples, they had to take another week to travel back to Jerusalem. And because Jesus' postresurrection appearances covered a total of forty days (Acts 1:3), His giving of the Great Commission on the Galilean mountainside would have had to occur some time between twenty and thirty-five days after His resurrection.

We are not told who was present when Jesus gave the Great Commission, but it seems probable that it was the group of more than five hundred that Paul mentions in 1 Corinthian 15:6. That has been the view of many biblical scholars throughout church history.

The fact that Matthew specifically mentions only **the eleven disciples** does not limit the gathering to them. The angel's message for the women to give to the disciples seems to imply that the women would also see Jesus in Galilee (see Matt. 28:7). There would have been no reason for Jesus to send the eleven to Galilee, only to have them return a few days later to the Mount of Olives for His ascension. It seems more reasonable that the Lord assembled a large group of believers and that He chose Galilee for the meeting place because most of His followers were from that region.

Because the Great Commission applies to all of His church, Jesus would surely have wanted to deliver it to the largest possible group of His faithful followers. Not only were most of Jesus' followers from Galilee, but that region was secluded and was a safe distance from Jerusalem, where most of Jesus' enemies were. And because the commission extends to all the world, Galilee, often referred to as Galilee of the Gentiles, also was appropriate for that reason.

Wherever the mountain was, it became a place of great sacredness, where more than five hundred of Jesus' disciples came with their weaknesses, confusion, doubts, misgivings, and fears. They were not the most humanly capable people in the world, nor the most intelligent or powerful or influential. But they were where the Lord wanted them to be, and that obedience gave evidence of their willingness to be used in His service. Like Isaiah after his vision in the Temple, they said, in effect, "Here am I. Send me" (Isa. 6:8).

Because they were there, they met Christ. Because they were there, they were commissioned. Because they were there, they received the Lord's promise of His continual presence and power as they ministered to the world in His name. It all started with being available.

WORSHIP

And when they saw Him, they worshiped Him; but some were doubtful. And Jesus came up and spoke to them, saying, (28:17-18a)

The second element implied here for effective fulfillment of the church's mission is the attitude of genuine worship. When God is not truly worshiped, He cannot be truly served, no matter how talented, gifted, or well-intentioned His servants may be.

The moment Jesus appeared and the disciples **saw Him, they worshiped Him,** prostrating themselves in humble adoration before their divine Lord and Savior. When they saw the risen Jesus on the hillside, their confusion disappeared and their shattered dreams were restored. Their sorrow turned into unbelievable joy and their disillusionment into unwavering hope.

The believers gathered there were not giving homage to a human dignitary or mere earthly ruler but were worshiping God's own Son, the Lord of heaven and earth. Though no spoken words are recorded, in their hearts they must have been saying with Thomas after his last doubts were assuaged, "My Lord and my God!" (John 20:28).

On but one previous occasion does Scripture say that the eleven disciples actually worshiped Jesus. After He walked to them on the water, they "worshiped Him, saying, 'You are certainly God's Son!'" (Matt. 14:33). Now their awe and their certainty of His divinity were immeasurably greater, because He was risen from the dead. It is probable that the worship of Christ on that day in Galilee has been equaled few other times in all of human history.

Yet, amazingly, **some were** still **doubtful.** That simple phrase inserted by Matthew is but one of countless small and indirect testimonies to the integrity of Scripture. In transparent honesty, the gospel writer sets forth the incident as it actually happened, with no attempt to make it more dramatic or convincing than it was. As he portrayed Jesus in His divine perfection, he also portrayed Jesus' followers, including himself, in their human imperfection.

Those who attempt to write history to their own liking are inclined to magnify that which is favorable and omit that which is not. Had Matthew and the other gospel writers contrived Jesus' resurrection, they would have had made every effort to exclude any fact or incident that would have tarnished their case. Nor would they have hesitated to falsify evidence and distort the truth. A person who lies about something of major importance has no scruples about telling lesser lies to support his primary deceit. Matthew's simple honesty testifies both to his own honesty and to the integrity of God's Word.

The identity of the doubters is not given. Because the eleven disciples are the only ones specifically mentioned in this passage, some interpreters insist that those who **were doubtful** were of that group. But as already noted, it is probable that hundreds of other believers were also present.

Exactly what was doubted is also not specified. If the fact of Jesus' resurrection was in question, then the doubters could not have included any of the eleven, because all of them had already witnessed the risen Christ, some on several occasions. It seems most likely that the doubt concerned whether or not the person who appeared to them was actually the physically risen Christ or some form of imposter. Out of that large group, only the eleven disciples and some of the women who had come to the tomb had seen the risen Christ. Perhaps some of those in the back of the crowd could not see Jesus clearly and, like Thomas, were reluctant to believe such an amazing truth without firm evidence.

As if to alleviate that doubt, **Jesus** graciously **came up and spoke to them.** Whatever the doubt was and whoever the doubters were, as the Lord came nearer and as His familiar voice sounded in their ears once again, all uncertainty was erased. Now those who had doubted fell down and joined the others in worship.

Nothing else now mattered. It made no difference where they lived, what their heritage was, what their economic or social position was, or what their nationality was. They were now in the presence of the living God.

The complete focus was on Christ. That is the essence of true worship—single-minded, unhindered, and unqualified concentration on Jesus Christ as Lord and Savior. Not simply to the Corinthians, but to every person to whom he spoke and in every place he ministered, Paul "determined to know nothing among [them] except Jesus Christ, and Him crucified" (1 Cor. 2:2). In his own life the apostle was determined to "know Him, and the power of His resurrection and the fellowship of His sufferings, being conformed to His death" (Phil. 3:10). Paul's life was so totally Christ-centered that he could say with perfect sincerity, "For to me, to live is Christ, and to die is gain" (Phil. 1:21).

SUBMISSION

"All authority has been given to Me in heaven and on earth. (28:18b)

The third element for effective fulfillment of the church's mission is another attitude, the implied attitude of submission. The focus of Jesus' declaration here is on His sovereign lordship, but in context it also clearly relates to the believer's response to His rule.

Before the Lord states the Great Commission, He establishes His divine authority to command it. It is because of His sovereign power that His followers are to have the attitude of complete, humble submission to His will.

Exousia (**authority**) refers to the freedom and right to speak and act as one pleases. In relation to God, that freedom and right are absolute and unlimited. The **all** is both reinforced and delineated by the phrase **in**

heaven and earth. The sovereign authority **given to** Jesus by His heavenly Father (see Matt. 11:27; John 3:35) is absolute and universal.

During His earthly ministry, Jesus demonstrated His authority over disease and sickness (Matt. 4:23; 9:35), over demons (4:24; 8:32; 12:22), over sin (9:6), and over death (Mark 5:41-42; John 11:43-44). Except for the forgiveness of sins, Jesus even exhibited the authority to delegate such powers to certain of His followers (Matt. 10:1; Luke 10:9, 17). He has authority to bring all men before the tribunal of God and to condemn them to eternal death or bring them to eternal life (John 5:27-29; 17:2). He had the authority to lay down His own life and to take it up again (John 10:18). He has the sovereign authority to rule both heaven and earth and to subjugate Satan and his demons to eternal torment in the lake of fire (Rev. 19:20; 20:10). Satan's tempting Jesus by offering Him rulership over the world (Matt. 4:8-9) not only was wicked but foolish, because lordship of both heaven and earth was already Christ's inheritance by divine fiat.

Even the prophet Daniel foresaw sovereign authority being given to Christ. In his night vision he beheld "One like a Son of Man . . . coming, and He came up to the Ancient of Days and was presented before Him. And to Him was given dominion, glory and a kingdom, that all the peoples, nations, and men of every language might serve Him. His dominion is an everlasting dominion which will not pass away; and His kingdom is one which will not be destroyed" (Dan. 7:13-14; cf. Isa. 9:6-7).

Jesus Himself described His coming dominion. "The sign of the Son of Man will appear in the sky," He said, "and then all the tribes of the earth will mourn, and they will see the Son of Man coming on the clouds of the sky with power and great glory" (Matt. 24:30; cf. 26:64).

Jesus' sovereign authority was **given to** Him by His Father, who "has given all judgment to the Son" (John 5:22), "made Him both Lord and Christ" (Acts 2:36), and has "highly exalted Him, and bestowed on Him the name which is above every name, that at the name of Jesus every knee should bow, of those who are in heaven, and on earth, and under the earth, and that every tongue should confess that Jesus Christ is Lord" (Phil. 2:9-11). Then, finally, in an act of adoring love and submission, "when all things are subjected to Him, then the Son Himself also will be subjected to the One who subjected all things to Him, that God may be all in all" (1 Cor. 15:28).

Before giving the commission, Jesus first established His absolute, pervasive authority, because otherwise the command would have seemed hopelessly impossible for the disciples to fulfill, and they might have ignored it. Were it not for knowing they had the Lord's sovereign demand as well as His resources to guide and empower them, those five hundred nondescript, powerless disciples would have been totally overwhelmed by the inconceivable task of making disciples for their Lord from among every nation on earth.

Submission to the absolute sovereignty of Jesus Christ is not a believer's option but is his supreme obligation. It is not negotiable or adjustable to one's own particular inclinations and plans. It is rather the attitude that says with absolute sincerity, "Whatever the Lord commands, I will do."

OBEDIENCE

Go therefore and make disciples of all the nations, baptizing them in the name of the Father and the Son and the Holy Spirit, teaching them to observe all that I commanded you; (28:19-20a)

The fourth element for effective fulfillment of the church's mission is obedience to the Lord's command, made possible only when the attitudes of availability, worship, and submission characterize the believer's life.

It was in light of His absolute, sovereign authority that Jesus commanded, **"Go therefore and make disciples of all the nations."** The transitional word is **therefore.** "Because I am sovereign Lord of the universe," Jesus was saying, "I have both the authority to command you to be My witnesses and the power to enable you to obey that command."

In light of the Old Testament teaching about Israel's mission to be God's light to the Gentiles and in light of Jesus' earthly ministry, it should not be surprising that His commission was to **make disciples of all the nations.**

Mathēteuō (**make disciples**) is the main verb and the central command of verses 19-20, which form the closing sentence of Matthew's gospel. The root meaning of the term refers to believing and learning. Jesus was not referring simply to believers or simply to learners, or He would have used other words. *Mathēteuō* carries a beautiful combination of meanings. In this context it relates to those who place their trust in Jesus Christ and follow Him in lives of continual learning and obedience. "If you abide in My word," Jesus said, "then you are truly disciples of Mine" (John 8:31). It should be noted that some disciples were not true (see John 6:66).

A person who is not Christ's true disciple does not belong to Him and is not saved. When a person genuinely confesses Christ as Lord and Savior, he is immediately saved, immediately made a disciple, and immediately filled with the Holy Spirit. Not to be Christ's disciple is therefore not to be Christ's at all.

Scripture knows nothing of receiving Christ as Savior but not as Lord, as if a person could take God piecemeal as it suits him. Every convert to Christ is a disciple of Christ, and no one who is not a disciple of Christ, no matter what his profession of faith might be, is a convert of Christ.

The very point of Jesus' encounter with the rich young ruler was that this man—although highly moral, religious, generous, and admiring of Jesus—refused to give up everything for Christ and submit to Him as Lord. He sincerely wanted eternal life and had the wisdom to come to the source of that life. But he was unwilling to give up his own life and possessions and obey Jesus' command to "come, follow Me" (Luke 18:18-23). He was willing to have Jesus as Savior but not as Lord, and Christ would not receive him on those terms. Because he refused to be Christ's disciple when the cost was made clear (like those in John 6:66), he could have no part of Christ or of the eternal life that He gives.

Some popular theologies today teach that Jesus was referring to those who are already believers when He taught such things as, "Whoever does not carry his own cross and come after Me cannot be My disciple" (Luke 14:27; cf. v. 33). Such forms of easy believism maintain that the only requirement for salvation is to "accept Jesus as Savior." Then, at some later date, a saved person may or may not become a disciple by accepting Christ as Lord of his life. Taking up one's cross and following Christ (Matt. 10:38) is looked on as a secondary, ideal level of relationship to Christ that is commendable but not mandatory.

The Great Commission is a command to bring unbelievers throughout the world to a saving knowledge of Jesus Christ, and the term the Lord uses in this commissioning is **make disciples.** The true convert is a disciple, a person who has accepted and submitted himself to Jesus Christ, whatever that may mean or demand. The truly converted person is filled with the Holy Spirit and given a new nature that yearns to obey and worship the Lord who has saved him. Even when he is disobedient, he knows he is living against the grain of his new nature, which is to honor and please the Lord. He loves righteousness and hates sin, including his own.

Jesus' supreme command, therefore, is for those who *are* His disciples to become His instruments for making disciples of all nations. Jesus' own earthly ministry was to make disciples for Himself, and that is the ministry of His people. Those who truly follow Jesus Christ become "fishers of men" (Matt. 4:19). Those who become His disciples are themselves to become disciple makers. The mission of the early church was to make disciples (see Acts 2:47; 14:21), and that is still Christ's mission for His church.

Jesus' command for His followers to **make disciples** was given only once, climactically, at the very end of His earthly ministry. Some might ask, "If it was so crucial, why did Jesus mention it only once?" The reason, no doubt, is that the motivation for reaching others for Christ is innate to the redeemed life. One might as well ask why God's command for man to "be fruitful and multiply" (Gen. 1:28) was given only once. In each case, reproduction in kind is natural to life. The call to make disciples is stated only once because it is natural for the new creation to be reproductive. It would beg the issue to repeat what is so basic.

The specific requirements Jesus gives for making disciples involve three participles: going (rendered here as **go**), **baptizing**, and **teaching**.

The first requirement makes clear that the church is not to wait for the world to come to its doors but that it is to **go** to the world. The Greek participle is best translated "having gone," suggesting that this requirement is not so much a command as an assumption.

Jesus' initial instruction to the disciples was for them to go only "to the lost sheep of the house of Israel" (Matt. 10:6; cf. 15:24). God's design was to offer salvation first to the Jews and then to use them as His missionaries to the rest of the world. The gospel is the "power of salvation to everyone who believes," but "to the Jew first" (Rom. 1:16; cf. John 4:22). But when Israel as a nation rejected the Messiah-King who was sent to her in Jesus, the invitation for salvation went directly to the entire world.

Jesus compared Israel's response to God's call to a wedding feast given by a king for his son. When the favored guests refused to accept the king's invitation and maligned and even killed some of the messengers, the king had his army destroy the ungrateful and wicked guests. He then sent his servants out to the streets and highways to invite to the feast anyone who would come (Matt. 22:1-10). The picture was of an apostate Israel who refused her Messiah and thereby forfeited the kingdom that He offered to them.

At the end of His earthly ministry, Christ had only a small remnant of believers, and it was to part of that remnant that He gave His commission to evangelize the world. The first sermon of the Spirit-filled church was preached by Peter and directed to Jews and Jewish proselytes who had come to worship in Jerusalem (Acts 2:22). But God later had to dramatically convince Peter that the gospel was also for Gentiles (10:1-48).

As he traveled throughout Syria, Asia Minor, and Greece, even the apostle Paul, "the apostle to the Gentiles," normally began his ministry in a given city at the Jewish synagogue (see Acts 9:20; 13:5; 18:4). But his message was always for Gentiles as well as Jews. At his conversion on the Damascus Road, the Lord said to him,

> Arise, and stand on your feet; for this purpose I have appeared to you, to appoint you a minister and a witness, . . . delivering you from the Jewish people and from the Gentiles, to whom I am sending you, to open their eyes so that they may turn from darkness to life and from the dominion of

Satan to God, in order that they may receive forgiveness of sins and an inheritance among those who have been sanctified by faith in Me. (Acts 26:16-18)

The second requirement for making disciples is that of **baptizing them in the name of the Father and the Son and the Holy Spirit.** To baptize literally means to immerse in water, and certain forms of baptism had long been practiced by various Jewish groups as a symbol of spiritual cleansing. The baptism of John the Baptist symbolized repentance of sin and turning to God (Matt. 3:6). As instituted by Christ, however, baptism became an outward act of identification with Him through faith, a visible, public testimony that henceforth one belonged to Him.

The initial act of obedience to Christ after salvation is to submit to baptism as a testimony to union with Him in His death, burial, and resurrection. "Do you not know," Paul asked the Roman believers, "that all of us who have been baptized into Christ Jesus have been baptized into His death? Therefore we have been buried with Him through baptism into death, in order that as Christ was raised from the dead through the glory of the Father, so we too might walk in newness of life" (Rom. 6:3-4).

Immersion is the most appropriate mode of baptism, not only because the Greek word behind it connotes immersion but even more importantly because that is the only mode that symbolizes burial and resurrection.

Although the act of baptism has absolutely no saving or sacramental benefit or power, it is commanded by Christ of His followers. The only exception might be physical inability, as in the case of the repentant thief on the cross, a prisoner who is forbidden the ordinance, or a similar circumstance beyond the believer's control. The person who is unwilling to be baptized is at best a disobedient believer, and if he persists in his unwillingness there is reason to doubt the genuineness of his faith (see Matt. 10:32-33). If he is unwilling to comply with that simple act of obedience in the presence of fellow believers, he will hardly be willing to stand for Christ before the unbelieving world.

Baptism has no part in the work of salvation, but it is a God-ordained and God-commanded accompaniment of salvation. Jesus said, "He who has believed and has been baptized shall be saved; but he who has disbelieved shall be condemned" (Mark 16:16). Jesus made clear that it is disbelief, not failure to be baptized, that precludes salvation; but He could not possibly have made the divine association of salvation and baptism more obvious than He does in that statement.

The association was indisputably clear in Peter's mind as he exhorted his unbelieving hearers at Pentecost: "Repent, and let each of you be baptized in the name of Jesus Christ" (Acts 2:38). The association was just as close in Paul's mind, as witnessed in his great manifesto of Christian unity: "There is one body and one Spirit, just as also you were called in one hope of your calling; one Lord, one faith, one baptism, one God and Father of all who is over all and through all and in all" (Eph. 4:4-6).

A person is saved by God's grace alone working through his faith as a gift of God (Eph. 2:8). But by God's own declaration, the act of baptism is His divinely designated sign of the believer's identification with His Son, the Lord Jesus Christ. Baptism is a divinely commanded act of faith and obedience.

New converts need to be taught that they should be baptized as soon as possible, not to seal or confirm their salvation but to make public testimony to it in obedience to their newfound Lord. The call to Christ not only is the call to salvation but also the call to obedience, the first public act of which should be baptism in His name.

Throughout the book of Acts, baptism is shown in the closest possible association with conversion. The three thousand souls converted at Pentecost were immediately baptized (Acts 2:41). As soon as the Ethiopian believed in Christ, he stopped his chariot so that he could be baptized (8:38). As soon as Paul received back his sight after his conversion, he was baptized (9:18). When Cornelius and his household were saved, Peter "ordered them to be baptized in the name of Jesus Christ" (10:48). As unbelievers in Corinth were being won to Jesus Christ, they were also being baptized (18:8). When Paul found some disciples of John in Ephesus who had only been baptized for repentance, he told them about Jesus, the one for whom John was merely preparing the way, and when they believed "they were baptized in the name of the Lord Jesus" (19:1-5).

In the context of the Great Commission, baptism is synonymous with salvation, which is synonymous with becoming a disciple. As already emphasized, discipleship *is* Christian life, not an optional, second level of it.

Baptism is to be made **in the name of the Father and the Son and the Holy Spirit.** Jesus was not giving a ritual formula, although that beautiful phrase from the lips of our Lord has been commonly and appropriately used in baptismal services throughout the history of the church. **In the name of** is not a sacramental formula, as seen in the fact that the book of Acts reports no converts being baptized with those precise words. Those words are rather a rich and comprehensive statement of the wonderful union that believers have with the whole Godhead.

In His statement here about baptism, Jesus again clearly placed Himself on an equal level with God **the Father** and with **the Holy Spirit.** He also emphasizes the unity of the Trinity by declaring that baptism should be done in Their one **name** (singular), not in Their separate names. As it does in many parts of Scripture, the phrase **the name** here embodies the fullness of a person, encompassing all that he is, has, and represents. When he is baptized, the believer is identified with everything that God is, has, and represents.

The pronoun Jesus uses here (*eis,* **in**) can also be rendered "into" or "unto." Those who teach baptismal regeneration—the belief that water baptism is essential for salvation—insist that it must here be translated "into." But that is a completely arbitrary translation and, in any case, cannot stand up against the many other passages that prove baptism has no part in regeneration but is rather an outward act, subsequent to regeneration, that testifies to its having taken place.

Baptism does not place a believer into oneness with the Trinity but signifies that, by God's grace working through his faith in Jesus Christ, the believer already has been made one with **the Father and the Son and the Holy Spirit.**

The third requirement for making disciples of all nations is that of **teaching them to observe all that I commanded you.** The church's mission is not simply to convert but to teach. The convert is called to a life of obedience to the Lord, and in order to obey Him it is obviously necessary to know what He requires. As already noted, a disciple is by definition a learner and follower. Therefore, studying, understanding, and obeying "the whole purpose of God" (Acts 20:27) is the lifelong task of every true disciple.

In Jesus' parting discourse to the disciples in the upper room, He said,

> If anyone loves Me, he will keep My word; and My Father will love him, and We will come to him, and make Our abode with him. He who does not love Me does not keep My words; and the word which you hear is not Mine, but the Father's who sent Me. These things I have spoken to you, while abiding with you. But the Helper, the Holy Spirit, whom the Father will send in My name, He will teach you all things, and bring to your remembrance all that I said to you. (John 14:23-26)

Jesus did not spend time teaching in order to entertain the crowds or to reveal interesting but inconsequential truths about God or to set forth ideal but optional standards that God requires. His first mission was to provide salvation for those who would come to Him in faith, that is, to make disciples. His second mission was to teach God's truth to those disciples. That is the same twofold mission He gives the church.

No one is a true disciple apart from personal faith in Jesus Christ, and there is no true disciple apart from an obedient heart that desires to please the Lord in all things. The writer of Hebrews makes that attitude of obedience synonymous with saving faith, declaring that Christ "became to all those who obey Him the source of eternal salvation" (Heb. 5:9). Thanking God for the salvation of believers in Rome, Paul said to them, "Though you were slaves of sin, you became obedient from the heart to that form of teaching to which you were committed" (Rom. 6:17).

Every Christian is not gifted as a teacher, but every faithful Christian is committed to promoting the ministry of teaching God's Word both to make and to edify disciples of Christ.

POWER

"and lo, I am with you always, even to the end of the age." (28:20b)

As crucial as are the first four elements for effective fulfillment of the church's mission, they would be useless without the last, namely, the power that the Lord Jesus Christ offers through His continuing presence with those who belong to Him. Neither the attitudes of availability, worship, and submission, nor faithful obedience to God's Word would be possible apart from Christ's own power working in and through us.

Idou (**lo**) is an interjection frequently used in the New Testament to call attention to something of special importance. *Egō eimi* (**I am**) is an emphatic form that might be rendered, "I Myself am," calling special attention to the fact of Christ's own presence. Jesus was saying, in effect, "Now pay special attention to what I am about to say, because it is the most important of all. I Myself, your divine, resurrected, living, eternal Lord, **am with you always, even to the end of the age.**"

A helpful way to keep one's spiritual life and work in the right perspective and to continually rely on the Lord's power rather than one's own is to pray in ways such as these: "Lord, You care more about this matter I am facing than I do, so do what You know is best. Lord, You love this person more than I do and only You can reach into his heart and save him, so help me to witness only as You lead and empower. Lord, You are more concerned about the truth and integrity of Your holy Word than I am, so please energize my heart and mind to be true to the text I am teaching."

Always literally means "all the days." For the individual believer that means all the days of his life. But in its fullest meaning for the church at large it means **even to the end of the age,** that is, until the Lord returns bodily to judge the world and to rule His earthly kingdom. (See Matt. 13:37-50, where Christ uses the phrase "end of the age" three times to designate His second coming.)

Jesus will not visibly return to earth and display Himself before the whole world in His majestic glory and power until **the end of the**

age. But until that time, throughout this present age, He will **always** be with those who belong to Him, leading them and empowering them to fulfill His Great Commission.

Some years ago, a missionary went to a primitive, pagan society. She became especially burdened for a young wife and eventually was used to win the woman to Christ. Almost as soon as she was saved the woman told the missionary with great sorrow, "I wish you could have come sooner, so my little boy could have been saved." When the missionary asked why it was too late, the mother replied, "Because just a few weeks before you came to us, I offered him as a sacrifice to the gods of our tribe."

Bibliography

Barclay, William. *The Gospel of Matthew.* Philadelphia: Westminster, 1959.

Broadus, John A. *Commentary on the Gospel of Matthew.* Valley Forge: Judson, 1886.

Eerdman, Charles R. *The Gospel of Matthew.* Philadelphia: Westminster, 1966.

Gabelein, Arno C. *The Gospel of Matthew.* Neptune, N.J.: Loizeaux, 1961.

Hendriksen, William. *New Testament Commentary: Exposition of the Gospel According to Matthew.* Grand Rapids: Baker, 1973.

Lange, John Peter. *Commentary on the Holy Scriptures: Matthew.* Grand Rapids: Zondervan, n.d.

Lenski, R. D. H. *The Interpretation of St. Matthew's Gospel.* Minneapolis: Augsburg, 1964.

Lloyd-Jones, D. Martyn. *Studies in the Sermon on the Mount.* Grand Rapids: Eerdmans, 1977.

Lovelace, Richard. *Dynamics of Spiritual Life.* Downers Grove, Ill.: Inter-Varsity, 1979.

Morgan, G. Campbell. *The Gospel According to Matthew.* Old Tappan, N.J.: Revell, 1939.

Pentecost, J. Dwight. *The Sermon on the Mount.* Portland: Multnomah, 1980.

Pink, Arthur W. *An Exposition of the Sermon on the Mount.* Grand Rapids: Baker, 1953.

Plummer, Alfred. *An Exegetical Commentary on the Gospel According to St. Matthew.* Grand Rapids: Eerdmans, 1963.

Sanders, J. Oswald. *Bible Studies in Matthew's Gospel.* Grand Rapids: Zondervan, 1973.

Tasker, R. V. G. *The Gospel According to St. Matthew.* Grand Rapids: Eerdmans, 1977.

Indexes

Index of Greek Words

omnumi, 218
opse de sabbatōn, 306

paradidōmi, 23, 147
parousia, 10
perilupos, 172
pharmakia, 27
phileō, 186
philos, 187

phobeō, 279
phuegō, 41
proseuchomai, 168

skandalizō, 159
sunedrion, 198
sunteleia, 11

theou huios, 280

Index of Scripture

Index of Subjects

Moody Press, a ministry of the Moody Bible Institute, is designed for education, evangelization, and edification. If we may assist you in knowing more about Christ and the Christian life, please write us without obligation: Moody Press, c/o MLM, Chicago, Illinois 60610